SYNTACTIC CHANGE IN LATE MODERN ENGLISH

Late Modern English presents a *stability paradox* to linguists; despite the many social changes that took place between 1700 and 1900, the language appeared to be structurally stable during this period. This book resolves this paradox by presenting a new, idiolect-centred perspective on language change, and shows how this framework is applicable to change in any language. It then demonstrates, through the use of four original case studies, how an idiolect-centred framework can be reconciled with corpus-linguistic methodology. These case studies concern colloquialization (the process by which oral features spread to writing) and densification (the process by which meaning is condensed into shorter linguistic units), two types of change that characterize Modern English. The case studies also shed light on the role of genre and gender in language change and contribute to the discussion of how to operationalize frequency in corpus linguistics. This study will be essential reading for researchers in historical linguistics, corpus linguistics, and sociolinguistics.

Erik Smitterberg is Senior Lecturer in English Linguistics in the Department of English at Uppsala University. Recent publications include *Late Modern English* (co-edited, 2020).

STUDIES IN ENGLISH LANGUAGE

General Editor
Merja Kytö (Uppsala University)

Editorial Board
Bas Aarts (University College London)
John Algeo (University of Georgia)
Susan Fitzmaurice (University of Sheffield)
Christian Mair (University of Freiburg)
Charles F. Meyer (University of Massachusetts)

The aim of this series is to provide a framework for original studies of English, both present-day and past. All books are based securely on empirical research, and represent theoretical and descriptive contributions to our knowledge of national and international varieties of English, both written and spoken. The series covers a broad range of topics and approaches, including syntax, phonology, grammar, vocabulary, discourse, pragmatics and sociolinguistics, and is aimed at an international readership.

Already published in this series:
Haruko Momma: *From Philology to English Studies: Language and Culture in the Nineteenth Century*
Raymond Hickey (ed.): *Standards of English: Codified Varieties around the World*
Benedikt Szmrecsanyi: *Grammatical Variation in British English Dialects: A Study in Corpus-Based Dialectometry*
Daniel Schreier and Marianne Hundt (eds.): *English as a Contact Language*
Bas Aarts, Joanne Close, Geoffrey Leech and Sean Wallis (eds.): *The Verb Phrase in English: Investigating Recent Language Change with Corpora*
Martin Hilpert: *Constructional Change in English: Developments in Allomorphy, Word Formation, and Syntax*
Jakob R. E. Leimgruber: *Singapore English: Structure, Variation, and Usage*
Christoph Rühlemann: *Narrative in English Conversation: A Corpus Analysis of Storytelling*
Dagmar Deuber: *English in the Caribbean: Variation, Style and Standards in Jamaica and Trinidad*
Eva Berlage: *Noun Phrase Complexity in English*
Nicole Dehé: *Parentheticals in Spoken English: The Syntax-Prosody Relation*
Jock O. Wong: *The Culture of Singapore English*
Marianne Hundt (ed.): *Late Modern English Syntax*

Irma Taavitsainen, Merja Kytö, Claudia Claridge and Jeremy Smith (eds.): *Developments in English: Expanding Electronic Evidence*
Arne Lohmann: *English Coordinate Constructions: A Processing Perspective on Constituent Order*
Nuria Yáñez-Bouza: *Grammar, Rhetoric and Usage in English: Preposition Placement 1500–1900*
Anita Auer, Daniel Schreier and Richard J. Watts (eds.): *Letter Writing and Language Change*
John Flowerdew and Richard W. Forest: *Signalling Nouns in English: A Corpus-Based Discourse Approach*
Jeffrey P. Williams, Edgar W. Schneider, Peter Trudgill and Daniel Schreier (eds.): *Further Studies in the Lesser-Known Varieties of English*
Jack Grieve: *Regional Variation in Written American English*
Douglas Biber and Bethany Gray: *Grammatical Complexity in Academic English: Linguistics Change in Writing*
Gjertrud Flermoen Stenbrenden: *Long-Vowel Shifts in English, c. 1050–1700: Evidence from Spelling*
Zoya G. Proshina and Anna A. Eddy (eds.): *Russian English: History, Functions, and Features*
Raymond Hickey (ed.): *Listening to the Past: Audio Records of Accents of English*
Phillip Wallage: *Negation in Early English: Grammatical and Functional Change*
Marianne Hundt, Sandra Mollin and Simone E. Pfenninger (eds.): *The Changing English Language: Psycholinguistic Perspectives*
Joanna Kopaczyk and Hans Sauer (eds.): *Binomials in the History of English: Fixed and Flexible*
Alexander Haselow: *Spontaneous Spoken English: An Integrated Approach to the Emergent Grammar of Speech*
Christina Sanchez-Stockhammer: *English Compounds and Their Spelling*
David West Brown: *English and Empire: Language History, Dialect, and the Digital Archive*
Paula Rodríguez-Puente: *The English Phrasal Verb, 1650–Present: History, Stylistic Drifts, and Lexicalisation*
Erik. R. Thomas (ed.): *Mexican American English: Substrate Influence and the Birth of an Ethnolect*
Thomas Hoffmann: *English Comparative Correlatives: Diachronic and Synchronic Variation at the Lexicon-Syntax Interface*
Nuria Yáñez-Bouza, Emma Moore, Linda van Bergen and Willem B. Hollmann (eds.): *Categories, Constructions, and Change in English Syntax*
Raymond Hickey (ed.): *English in the German-Speaking World*
Axel Bohmann: *Variation in English World-Wide: Registers and Global Varieties*

Raymond Hickey (ed.): *English in Multilingual South Africa: The Linguistics of Contact and Change*
Jeremy J. Smith: *Transforming Early English: The Reinvention of Early English and Older Scots*
Tobias Bernaisch: *Gender in World Englishes*
Lorena Pérez-Hernández: *Speech Acts in English: From Research to Instruction and Textbook Development*
Elisabeth Reber: *Quoting in Parliamentary Question Time: Exploring Recent Change*

Earlier titles not listed are also available

SYNTACTIC CHANGE IN LATE MODERN ENGLISH

Studies on Colloquialization and Densification

ERIK SMITTERBERG

Uppsala University

Shaftesbury Road, Cambridge CB2 8EA, United Kingdom

One Liberty Plaza, 20th Floor, New York, NY 10006, USA

477 Williamstown Road, Port Melbourne, VIC 3207, Australia

314–321, 3rd Floor, Plot 3, Splendor Forum, Jasola District Centre, New Delhi – 110025, India

103 Penang Road, #05–06/07, Visioncrest Commercial, Singapore 238467

Cambridge University Press is part of Cambridge University Press & Assessment, a department of the University of Cambridge.

We share the University's mission to contribute to society through the pursuit of education, learning and research at the highest international levels of excellence.

www.cambridge.org
Information on this title: www.cambridge.org/9781108463973

DOI: 10.1017/9781108564984

© Erik Smitterberg 2021

This publication is in copyright. Subject to statutory exception and to the provisions of relevant collective licensing agreements, no reproduction of any part may take place without the written permission of Cambridge University Press & Assessment.

First published 2021
First paperback edition 2024

A catalogue record for this publication is available from the British Library

Library of Congress Cataloging-in-Publication data
NAMES: Smitterberg, Erik, 1973– author
TITLE: Syntactic change in late modern English : studies on colloquialization and densification / Erik Smitterberg.
DESCRIPTION: Cambridge, UK ; New York : Cambridge University Press, 2021. | Includes bibliographical references and index.
IDENTIFIERS: LCCN 2021024718 (print) | LCCN 2021024719 (ebook) | ISBN 9781108474221 (hardback) | ISBN 9781108564984 (ebook)
SUBJECTS: LCSH: English language – 18th century – Syntax. | English language – 19th century – Syntax. | English language – Grammar, Historical. | BISAC: LANGUAGE ARTS & DISCIPLINES / Linguistics / Historical & Comparative
CLASSIFICATION: LCC PE1361 .S65 2021 (print) | LCC PE1361 (ebook) | DDC 427.009/033–dc23
LC record available at https://lccn.loc.gov/2021024718
LC ebook record available at https://lccn.loc.gov/2021024719

ISBN 978-1-108-47422-1 Hardback
ISBN 978-1-108-46397-3 Paperback

Cambridge University Press & Assessment has no responsibility for the persistence or accuracy of URLs for external or third-party internet websites referred to in this publication and does not guarantee that any content on such websites is, or will remain, accurate or appropriate.

Contents

List of Figures		*page* viii
List of Tables		ix
Acknowledgements		xi
1	Introduction	1
2	Sociocultural and Linguistic Change in Late Modern English	11
3	Aspects of Language Change	42
4	Methodological Framework	77
5	Colloquialization I: *Not*-Contraction	127
6	Colloquialization II: Co-ordination by *And*	160
7	Densification I: Nouns as Premodifiers in Noun Phrases	187
8	Densification II: Participle Clauses as Postmodifiers in Noun Phrases	222
9	Concluding Discussion	257
Appendix		269
References		271
Index		299

Figures

2.1 Lexical innovation in the *OED* by twenty-year period (data from 2018) — page 24

5.1 Contraction ratios for present-tense and past-tense forms of BE, DO, HAVE, CAN, and WILL in Drama, Fiction, and Trials (*not*-negated clauses) — 136

5.2 *Not*-negation and *no*-negation in Drama, Fiction, and Trials by period (frequencies per 1,000 words in the S-coefficient subcorpus) — 144

5.3 *Not*-contraction by finiteness and period in Drama, Fiction, and Trials — 151

7.1 Common nouns in CNNE premodified by common, genitive, temporal, and proper nouns (frequencies per 1,000 words) — 195

7.2 Common nouns in the S-coefficient subcorpus premodified by common nouns by period and genre (frequencies per 1,000 words) — 200

7.3 Common nouns in the S-coefficient subcorpus premodified by proper nouns by period and genre (frequencies per 1,000 words) — 204

7.4 Common nouns in CNNE premodified by proper nouns by semantic field and period (frequencies per 1,000 words) — 217

8.1 Participle clauses in CNNE by period (frequencies per 1,000 words) — 238

8.2 Restrictive present-participle clauses by genre and period in the S-coefficient subcorpus (frequencies per 1,000 words) — 242

8.3 Restrictive past-participle clauses by genre and period in the S-coefficient subcorpus (frequencies per 1,000 words) — 243

8.4 Non-restrictive present-participle clauses by genre and period in the S-coefficient subcorpus (frequencies per 1,000 words) — 245

8.5 Non-restrictive past-participle clauses by genre and period in the S-coefficient subcorpus (frequencies per 1,000 words) — 248

Tables

4.1	Word counts for period and genre subsamples of CONCE	*page* 109
4.2	Word counts for period and genre subsamples of the S-coefficient subcorpus	110
4.3	Newspapers included in CNNE	122
5.1	*Not*-contractions, operator contractions, and uncontracted forms in Drama, Fiction, and Trials by period (*not*-negated clauses)	133
5.2	*Not*-contractions, operator contractions, and uncontracted forms in Drama, Fiction, and Trials by operator and verb (*not*-negated clauses)	135
5.3	*Not*-contracted and uncontracted forms in Drama, Fiction, and Trials by verb function	140
5.4	*Not*-negation and *no*-negation in Drama, Fiction, and Trials by period (raw frequencies in the S-coefficient subcorpus)	144
5.5	The final glm for Drama, Fiction, and Trials	149
6.1	Co-ordination by period in CNNE	169
6.2	Co-ordination by period in CONCE (periods 1 and 3)	169
6.3	Co-ordination by genre in CONCE (periods 1 and 3)	170
6.4	Co-ordination by period in Debates (periods 1 and 3)	172
6.5	Co-ordination by period in women's letters (periods 1 and 3)	173
6.6	Co-ordination by period in men's letters (periods 1 and 3)	175
6.7	Sentence-initial *and* by period and genre in CONCE (periods 1 and 3; raw frequencies and percentages of all relevant tokens in each sample)	181
7.1	Common nouns in CNNE premodified by common, genitive, temporal, and proper nouns by period (raw frequencies)	195

7.2	Common nouns in the S-coefficient subcorpus premodified by common, genitive, temporal, and proper nouns by genre and period (raw frequencies)	198
7.3	Common nouns in the Letters genre in the S-coefficient subcorpus premodified by common nouns by period and letter writer (raw frequencies, word counts, and frequencies per 1,000 words)	203
7.4	Semantic relations between premodifying common nouns and heads in CNNE by period (raw frequencies, normalized frequencies, and percentages)	209
7.5	Semantic relations between premodifying common nouns and heads in the S-coefficient subcorpus by period (raw frequencies, normalized frequencies, and percentages)	210
7.6	Common nouns in CNNE premodified by proper nouns by semantic field and period (raw frequencies and percentages)	216
8.1	Restrictive present-participle clauses and restrictive active relative clauses in CNNE by period	233
8.2	Restrictive past-participle clauses and restrictive passive relative clauses in CNNE by period	234
8.3	Restrictive present-participle clauses and active relative clauses in the S-coefficient subcorpus by period and genre	235
8.4	Restrictive past-participle clauses and passive relative clauses in the S-coefficient subcorpus by period and genre	237
8.5	Restrictive and non-restrictive participle clauses in CNNE by period	238
8.6	Restrictive and non-restrictive participle clauses in the S-coefficient subcorpus by genre and period	241
A.1	Co-ordination by period in Drama (periods 1 and 3)	269
A.2	Co-ordination by period in Fiction (periods 1 and 3)	269
A.3	Co-ordination by period in History (periods 1 and 3)	270
A.4	Co-ordination by period in Science (periods 1 and 3)	270
A.5	Co-ordination by period in Trials (periods 1 and 3)	270

Acknowledgements

This book is the result of several years of thinking about Late Modern English, analysing data, and writing chapters. Given the long time it has been in the making, I have incurred a large number of debts along the way, and it is my pleasure to acknowledge them here.

The project was begun during my five-year position as a Royal Swedish Academy of Letters, History and Antiquities Research Fellow. I want to express my sincere gratitude to the Academy for giving me a rare opportunity to focus on research for such a prolonged period of time. Further invaluable support in the form of one-term sabbaticals was given by the Faculty of Languages at Uppsala University and by Riksbankens Jubileumsfond. The Department of English at Uppsala University has provided a very pleasant working environment during and since my fellowship, and I am very grateful to my colleagues, the administrative staff, and the librarians in Uppsala. I also gratefully acknowledge funding for conference trips from Hilda Kumlins resestipendium and the Royal Society of Arts and Sciences of Uppsala, which enabled me to present my research at international conferences.

The seminar series in English Linguistics at Uppsala University, organized by Merja Kytö, has provided me with a valuable forum for discussing several chapter drafts; some findings have also been presented at Stockholm University, in the seminar series organized by the late Nils-Lennart Johannesson. I am very grateful to present and former colleagues at these universities for their feedback. I would also like to thank the organizers of the Nineteenth International Conference on English Historical Linguistics in Essen for giving me the opportunity to present my ideas there in the form of a plenary paper in 2016, and to the conference participants for their feedback. I am additionally indebted to Mats Rydén and Terry Walker for valuable comments on several chapters, to Tove Larsson for her expert help on statistical matters for Chapter 5, to Birte Bös for helping me to access relevant previous research, and to Claudia Claridge, Peter J. Grund, and

Stefan Mähl for helpful discussions of the framework of the book at an early stage. I am very grateful to several people at Cambridge University Press for all their help during my work on the book: to Merja Kytö, the series editor, for supporting the inclusion of the book in the Studies in English Language series and for her very helpful clearance reading; to an anonymous expert reader for valuable comments on the book proposal; and to Helen Barton and Isabel Collins for all their kind assistance throughout the process.

Finally, it is my pleasure to thank my family for their help and support: my parents, Ann-Christin and Gunnar, who have always supported my choices; Oscar and Henry, who have accepted their stepdad's unusual passion for Late Modern English with admirable tolerance and occasional interest; and, of course, Sarah. As a linguist, you helped me to hone my arguments and improve the manuscript in more places than I can remember; as my wife, you provided encouragement, love, and support every step of the way. I love you.

Any remaining errors are my own responsibility.

CHAPTER I

Introduction

1.1 Aims

The three aims of this book, which are accounted for in Sections 1.1.1–1.1.3, primarily concern the syntax of Late Modern English (henceforth "LModE"), that is, the English used between *c.*1700 and *c.*1900. However, the topics discussed in the book also have wider applications that are relevant to the history of English and historical linguistics in general. The aims can be roughly characterized as theoretical, methodological, and empirical, respectively, though as I hope to demonstrate, the three are intertwined. From a theoretical perspective, I aim at reconciling the oft-cited view that language change in LModE is more limited than in other periods with what social-network theory would predict by focussing on the individual speaker's idiolect as the locus of language and language change. I then demonstrate how this perspective is compatible with historical corpus linguistics as a methodology. Finally, I aim to empirically investigate two types of change – colloquialization and densification – in nineteenth-century English through corpus-linguistic case studies of four features: *not*-contraction, co-ordination by *and*, nominal premodifiers in noun phrases, and participle clauses as postmodifiers in noun phrases.

1.1.1 *Late Modern English and the Stability Paradox*

The first aim of the present study is to examine a claim that has frequently been made in scholarship on LModE, namely that the structure of LModE features little change over time when compared with previous periods. Romaine (1998b: 7), for instance, comments on the "structural stability" of LModE. This stability is typically taken to concern phonology and grammar, while the vocabulary of LModE – which is also less connected to the structure of the language – is considered to be more open to change

(Romaine 1998b: 1–2). In addition, it is sometimes argued that changes in phonology or grammar which did take place in LModE were of different types compared with those attested for previous periods, especially from the late eighteenth century on. Strang (1970: 78–9) argues that phonological change after *c.*1770 has been characterized by "the complex analogical relationship between different parts of the language" rather than by change to the system itself, and Denison (1998: 93) suggests that, after 1776, syntactic change has typically concerned statistical preferences for particular features in different styles rather than "categorical losses or innovations". I will argue that such statements are valid when considered from the perspective of the communal language that we refer to as LModE, but less applicable to the individual idiolects that made up that communal language.

As I demonstrate in Chapter 2, the claim that LModE features little change in its structure over time is seemingly at odds with what we know about the interaction between social networks and language use. The widespread technological and sociocultural transformations that Late Modern English society underwent are likely to have created a plethora of weak network ties at the expense of pre-existing strong ones. Such weak ties are in turn assumed to facilitate language change (see, for instance, Milroy and Milroy 1985). It seems that we need to revise at least one of three assumptions, since we cannot simultaneously argue that the LModE period featured weakened social-network ties, that weakened ties facilitate language change, and that little structural change took place in LModE. Romaine (1998b: 7) rightly points out that the appearance of stability in LModE "challenges any simple-minded view of the relationship between social change and language change". I refer to this conundrum as *the stability paradox*.

The suggestion that language change in LModE differed from that observed in previous periods in the history of English may seem to provide a way out of this difficulty: perhaps plenty of language change occurred, but without affecting the overall structure of LModE. However, as noted by Beal (2004: xii, 125), this suggestion constitutes a potential challenge to the uniformitarian principle, that is, the assumption that "the linguistic processes taking place around us are the same as those that have operated to produce the historical record" (Labov 1972: 101) and "that the general properties of language and of processes of change in language have been the same throughout human history and prehistory" (Matthews 2014, s.v. *uniformitarian principle*). This principle – essentially the extension of uniformitarianism from the sciences (originally geology) to linguistics –

makes it possible to assume that the same types of language change that are operative in the present occurred at some point in the past, unless it can be shown that the conditions under which English was acquired and used have changed between then and now. (By extension, the same principle holds between two points in the past, such as Middle English and LModE.) Refuting it is thus a strong claim.

While there has been a drastic increase in scholarly interest in LModE during the last twenty-five years, our new knowledge of language change between 1700 and 1900 needs to be integrated not only into our conception of how the English language has changed through time, but also into more general theories of how and why languages can, may, and do change. Not linking these fields of scholarship has negative consequences of two types. Deductively, research on LModE will suffer from being less informed by linguistic theory than are other periods in the history of the language; inductively, findings of potential theoretical significance in LModE studies may not be fully recognized outside this specialized field because they are not explicitly connected to linguistic theory. We thus need to engage explicitly with these issues, and this book is an attempt to do so. My suggestion, which is discussed in Chapter 3, is that a possible solution to the seeming mismatch between predictions based on social-network theory and attested change in LModE is to regard the idiolect as the true locus of language change – and to regard change on the idiolectal level as the actual correlate of weak network ties.

1.1.2 *Methodological Challenges for Studying the Syntax of Late Modern English (and Other Historical Language-States)*

The second aim of the present study is to reconcile the idiolectal perspective on the study of language change with historical corpus linguistics, which is the methodology applied in the case studies of nineteenth-century syntax. Historical linguistics presents researchers with a methodological challenge: scholarship is heavily dependent on empirical data, but, as Labov (1972: 100) notes, researchers "have no control over their data". In addition, with the exception of historical statements that happen to have survived, historical linguists lack access to native-speaker evidence. Even though LModE is close in time to the present day, it has to be reconstructed mainly based on surviving texts. The best-known difficulty resulting from this limitation is the necessity to rely on what Labov (1972: 100) termed "bad data", that is, data that "may be fragmentary, corrupted, or many times removed from the actual productions of native speakers". The main problems with bad data from a linguistic perspective are (i) that information may be lacking on who produced a given text and/or on their gender, socio-economic rank, and so on, and (ii) that the selection of idiolects we have access to is biased in favour of male, literate, and/or high-status speakers.

The limitations outlined above apply to a greater or lesser extent to virtually any historical-linguistic methodology. From the idiolectal perspective on language change outlined in Chapter 3, historical corpus linguistics faces an additional problem: corpora are typically compiled with the aim of sampling several idiolects in order to limit the influence of individual language users on the overall results. To resolve this seemingly paradoxical state of affairs, my discussion in Chapter 4 will emphasize the importance of considering, among other things, the representativity of the primary sources used and the granularity of the analysis, that is, the trade-off between describing linguistic behaviour at a high level of detail in one idiolect (or a small number of idiolects) and describing linguistic behaviour at a lower level of detail in a large number of idiolects.

In addition to these points, I will also discuss and problematize several other aspects of historical (corpus) linguistics, including the choice between variationist and non-variationist designs and the interpretation of numerical data. In the organization of the book, the methodological discussion forms a conceptual bridge between the theoretical discussion and the empirical case studies.

1.1.3 Studying Colloquialization and Densification

The third aim of this book is to examine the occurrence of two types of language change in nineteenth-century English: colloquialization and densification. These are of course not the only types of change that characterize LModE syntax, but colloquialization and densification are interesting processes to consider from the perspective on language adopted in this book. The linguistic features involved are rarely the result of very recent categorical innovations; instead, they can be assumed already to have been available in virtually all idiolects, but their frequency in particular (sets of) genres increases in response to changes in genre norms. Those norms are in turn dependent on, among other things, the purposes and characteristics that writers intended for texts belonging to these genres to have. (Should they be accessible to a popular audience or mainly to specialists? Was their main purpose to entertain readers or to convey information efficiently? etc.) Within the constraints set by the genre norms, language users have a great deal of freedom regarding whether and how often they wish to use a given feature, which means that idiolectal variation can be expected to occur in the data; as will become apparent especially in Chapters 7 and 8, the intended target audience – in these cases, of different newspapers – is also a relevant factor.

Several aspects of colloquialization and densification have been studied before, but we still need detailed case studies of individual linguistic features in LModE to understand the origin of these two types of change, both of which characterized twentieth-century English. In addition, a large number of genres need to be examined, as one consequence of both types of change is increased genre diversity in writing: some but not all written genres typically take part in colloquialization and densification. This type of study can contribute to our understanding of the interplay between idiolects, genres, society, and the communal language. Each type of change will be investigated mainly by means of two case studies.

Colloquialization, first discussed (to my knowledge) in Siemund (1995) and Mair and Hundt (1995), consists in a stylistic change "away from a written norm which is elaborated to maximal distance from speech and towards a written norm that is closer to spoken usage" and "away from a written norm which cultivates formality towards a norm which is tolerant of informality and even allows for anti-formality as a rhetorical strategy" (Mair 2006b: 187). It has been well documented for twentieth-century English by, for instance, Hundt and Mair (1999); studies such as Smitterberg (2008) and Biber and Gray (2012) demonstrate that it is also in evidence during the preceding century. In the present study, I juxtapose two linguistic features that share an association with orality but differ greatly in their stylistic markedness. *Not*-contraction, for example *won't* as opposed to *will not*, was stigmatized during the LModE period, and still remains an informal feature today. It can thus be expected that LModE language users would be aware of the colloquial status of *not*-contractions and that they may avoid using them in more formal contexts owing to prescriptive pressure. The other feature examined is the use of *and* to co-ordinate linguistic units above the phrase level, for example main clauses, subordinate clauses, or predicates, as in *I [went to the theatre] and [saw a comedy]*, as opposed to units on or below the phrase level, for example noun phrases in *I bought [a suit] and [three shirts]*. While the proportions of these types of unit have been shown to differ greatly between speech and writing (e.g. Biber et al. 1999: §2.4.7.3), with phrasal co-ordination being characteristic of non-speech-related writing and vice versa, there is no particular stigma attached to the use of *and* to link super-phrasal units.¹ Language users who were affected by colloquialization as a change from below may thus increasingly have used *and* to co-ordinate clausal and clause-like material in what Hundt and Mair dub "agile" genres, such as newspaper writing, even though they would have avoided *not*-contractions in the same texts. The juxtaposition of these two features thus creates a fruitful empirical basis for discussing colloquialization during the nineteenth century.

Densification is a tendency to use less linguistic material to express a given semantic content over time (Leech et al. 2009: 249). It has mostly been studied as a condensation of information in the noun phrase. As noted by Biber and Gray (2012: 316), although in many respects this can be seen as an "anti-colloquial trend" (Leech et al. 2009: 210), colloquialization and densification are not mutually exclusive; they notably co-occur in newspaper language, for instance. In the present study, I consider two features that contribute to densification of content: nouns as premodifiers in noun phrases, as in *a book room*, and participle clauses as postmodifiers in noun phrases, as in *the lady crossing the street*. Both features take up less space than their main competitors do: depending on the noun + noun combination, noun premodifiers may be in variation with, for instance, prepositional phrases (e.g. *a room for books*); the most obvious alternative to a participle clause is a finite relative clause (e.g. *the lady who was crossing the street*).

Both colloquialization and densification potentially raise important questions about methodology, which link the second and third aims of the present study. First, a great deal of valuable research has focussed on overall trends in large amounts of primary material where we can largely disregard the influence of individual users on the overall results. However, an alternative perspective, where smaller amounts of material are examined and differences due to individual people, newspapers, and so on are identified and analysed, is also of considerable value, especially if advanced and conservative users can tell us something about the propagation of changes. Secondly, several analyses in the book necessitate a choice between the two most frequent ways of measuring the frequency of syntactic features in texts, namely a variationist approach, where the incidence of each variant is measured against the frequency of the other variant(s), and what, following Biber et al. (2016), I shall call

---

¹ The main exception in this regard concerns sentence-initial *and*, which was widely proscribed in the nineteenth century; as I show in Section 6.3.2, this use of *and* also displays different genre distributions compared with super-phrasal *and* in general.

a *text-linguistic* approach, in which raw frequencies are normalized in relation to a coefficient, typically a set number of words, to make them independent of text length. The relative merits of these two perspectives are discussed in Section 4.4 and examined empirically in three of the case studies.

1.2 Limitations in Scope

As I suggest in Chapters 2 and 3, connections between societal and linguistic developments cannot be overlooked if we wish to answer the question of why some periods in the history of a language appear to feature less change – or different kinds of change – than others. This connection between linguistic and social developments necessitated focussing on one particular LModE society for which we have ample linguistic as well as extralinguistic data; England seemed a promising choice. The discussion of linguistic and societal change, and the case studies, will thus centre on English society between 1700 and 1900, to the exclusion of other parts of the English-speaking world. LModE displayed an immense increase in both the number of varieties of English outside England and the number of speakers of those varieties. On the British Isles, English spread at the expense of Celtic languages; for instance, the majority of the native population of Ireland switched to English during the nineteenth century (Hickey 2010d: 267). Outside Britain, while the establishment of an English-speaking community in North America predates 1700, the North American population grew rapidly during the LModE period: Bailey (2010: 185) suggests a growth from *c.*210,000 to over 5.2 million between 1700 and 1800.[2] In addition, many of the regions where inner-circle and outer-circle varieties of English are used today were first settled by speakers of English during the eighteenth and nineteenth centuries (see Hickey 2004b). To some extent, the increased interest in these varieties can be viewed as a linguistic reflection of "trends in colonial and (especially) postcolonial studies" (Smith 2015: 197). As World Englishes became an integral part of English linguistics, the origin and development of extra-territorial varieties also came to be regarded as an important area of historical research. A few examples of recent explorations of different aspects of such varieties, including syntax, are Hickey (2004a), Fritz

---

[2] This growth includes migrants from non-Anglophone regions and enslaved people who did not speak English on arrival in America. Conversely, there was a massive decline in the population of Native Americans, many of whom did not speak English.

(2007), Dollinger (2008), and Reuter (2017). Although there are good reasons for restricting the scope of the present study to England, any LModE variety deserves equally full treatment.

The bulk of this book is concerned with syntactic change. The theoretical discussion in Chapters 2 and 3 also includes lexis and phonology, as considering data from different areas enriches the account of connections between language and society. In contrast, much of the methodological discussion in Chapter 4, as well as all case studies in Chapters 5–8, focusses on syntactic features.

The case studies all concern nineteenth-century English. Several macro-level studies of a large number of features, such as Biber and Gray (2012), have examined developments between centuries; the complementary aim of the present study was to consider change within a narrower time frame by sampling several periods from the same century. It follows that it was necessary to limit the period covered by case studies to one century in order to make the amount of data manageable, and the 1800s was the natural choice for three reasons. First, colloquialization and/or densification have been described by scholars such as Hundt and Mair (1999), Mair (2006b), and Leech et al. (2009), as they took place in the 1900s. It is then a natural research question whether the time-depth of these changes can be extended to the preceding century. Secondly, Biber and Gray (2012: 326) associate the growing pressure towards popularization as well as "the rise of highly educated populations in specialized fields" with the "development of near-universal education", which is a feature of the nineteenth century. The nineteenth century is also the first century when all the standard *not*-contractions were used in print (Brainerd 1989 [1993]: 177), which makes the 1800s a suitable period for analyses. Thirdly, newspaper language is of special importance to the case studies, because it has been affected by both colloquialization and densification (Biber and Gray 2012: 316). This makes the nineteenth century particularly relevant to the discussion, as it was a pivotal phase in the development of the newspaper; Brown (1985: 1) even claims that "'[t]he news' as we understand it is a nineteenth-century creation". Taken together, these circumstances presented compelling arguments for focussing the empirical section of the volume on the 1800s.

Finally, the case studies are mainly based on corpora that may be thought fairly small by today's standards. Owing to a combination of factors, including the recency of the period and the number of literate speakers, the textual evidence for LModE is more copious than for any preceding period. More importantly, owing to recent advances in digitization, optical character recognition, and so on, the early twenty-first century has witnessed an increased interest in – and availability of – very large corpora and other text collections,[3] which are based on electronically available material and provide previously unavailable windows onto linguistic variation in LModE. As Davies (2012: 163) notes, corpora like COHA (the Corpus of Historical American English) allow researchers to examine both features with lower frequencies and earlier states of change compared with smaller text collections. Results based on very large corpora can also shed light on more fine-grained linguistic environments. As I discuss in Chapter 4, however, there are several reasons why the availability of these corpus giants does not invalidate the use of smaller corpora such as those used in the present study, and the two main corpora used provided sufficient data for most analyses (see Section 4.5).

1.3 The Structure of This Book

The remainder of the book is structured as follows. In Chapters 2 and 3, I address the main theoretical aim of the study. Chapter 2 begins with an account of the role of social networks and language change; I then introduce the stability paradox by examining both the social structure of English society and the linguistic structure of English between 1700 and 1900. Chapter 3 is devoted to showing how an idiolect-centred perspective on language and language change can help to resolve the stability paradox. I also demonstrate why some of the most important changes that occurred during the LModE period have left surprisingly small traces in surviving texts, and discuss the role of linguistic and extralinguistic factors in language change.

Chapter 4 focusses on various aspects of methodology. I first discuss historical corpus linguistics and show how this methodology can be reconciled with an essentially idiolect-based view of language. I then address colloquialization and densification – and their connection to the case studies – in detail. The choice between a variationist and a text-linguistic approach to frequency is discussed in a separate subsection, since that choice has important consequences for several of the case studies. Finally, I describe a crucial aspect of any corpus-linguistic endeavour, namely, the corpora used for the case studies: a Corpus of Nineteenth-Century English (henceforth CONCE) and the Corpus of Nineteenth-Century Newspaper English (henceforth CNNE).

---

[3] Such collections include the extensive database of quotations in the *OED* (*Oxford English Dictionary*), which has been used as a makeshift corpus in some studies (see Hoffmann 2004 for critical discussion).

The four case studies are accounted for in separate chapters, the two chapters on colloquialization (Chapters 5 and 6) preceding the two that treat densification (Chapters 7 and 8). I begin by considering *not*-contraction in Chapter 5. A multifactorial analysis of the choice between contracted and uncontracted forms enables me to show which of the factors analysed have an independent effect on the proportion of contraction; I also consider a number of additional parameters, including *no*-negation and word order. The different units co-ordinated by *and* are the subject of Chapter 6, where the results are divided into two main parts: a quantitative analysis of the proportions of three main types of conjoins, followed by a smaller, partly qualitative study of sentence-initial *and*, a stigmatized feature of LModE writing.

Chapter 7 addresses one of the most conspicuous features of LModE and Present-Day English noun phrases compared with earlier periods: the prevalence of nouns in the premodifier slot. After looking at the frequency of common nouns (e.g. *a goods train*) and proper nouns (e.g. *the Bradford team*) as premodifiers, I focus on the semantics of the relation between common-noun premodifiers and their head nouns and the reference of the proper-noun premodifier. The last case study concerns participle clauses as noun-phrase postmodifiers (e.g. *presented in this study* in *the results presented in this study*). Both principles regarding the selection and classification of data and the choice between variationist and text-linguistic perspectives on the incidence of participle clauses are shown to influence the results. In addition, two features of the participle clause – whether the verb phrase includes a present or a past participle and whether the clause is restrictive or non-restrictive – are shown to divide up the data in four categories with partly different characteristics.

The book ends with a concluding discussion in Chapter 9. In this chapter, I return to the aims of the study and demonstrate what light the results shed on LModE and on the historical development of languages in general.

CHAPTER 2

Sociocultural and Linguistic Change in Late Modern English

2.1 Introduction

The present chapter is devoted to the stability paradox, that is, the apparent mismatch between the degree to which English society changes between 1700 and 1900 and the amount of language change that LModE undergoes. While there is general agreement that a great deal of sociocultural change takes place between 1700 and 1900,[1] several linguists point to the comparative lack of structural change in LModE, especially compared with the preceding Middle and Early Modern English periods (see Sections 2.3–2.4). This lack of correlation may seem unremarkable at first glance, as historical linguistics to some extent has a tradition of regarding a language as a self-contained entity or system that undergoes change more or less independently of what its speakers do (Lass 1980: 120). To understand why the lack of correlation between sociocultural and linguistic change is in fact problematic from the perspective of linguistic theory, it is necessary to consider insights gained from research on social networks.

I discuss the general connection made in social-network theory between sociocultural and linguistic change in Section 2.2. Then follow brief surveys of sociocultural (2.3) and linguistic (2.4) change in England between 1700 and 1900. Finally, Section 2.5 synthesizes the conclusions reached in the chapter and discusses why predictions from the perspective of social-network theory appear not to be borne out by empirical linguistic data as regards Late Modern English.

---

[1] I will use *sociocultural change* as a convenient shorthand for changes in society, culture, technology, politics, legislation, and so on that may be hypothesized to have an impact on communicative patterns in the population examined.

2.2 The Connection between Sociocultural and Linguistic Change: The Social-Network Perspective

The inclusion of social networks as an important factor in linguistic variation and change owes a great deal to James and Lesley Milroy's pioneering work on language use in Belfast (e.g. Milroy 1987; Milroy 1992a). Social networks may be more or less close-knit. Close-knit networks are dense (most members have some relationship with one another) and multiplex (contact between members involves several social domains, e.g. the workplace, the neighbourhood, and kinship), and ties between speakers are typically strong; the strength of a network tie is influenced by factors such as duration, periodicity, emotional intensity, intimacy, and reciprocal services (Milroy 1992a: 178; Conde-Silvestre 2012: 333). Members of close-knit networks tend to resist linguistic innovation and maintain conservative forms because they exert pressure on one another to maintain the linguistic status quo. In contrast, loose-knit networks, whose members are characteristically linked through weak ties, facilitate the propagation of innovations (Milroy and Milroy 1985: 355; Conde-Silvestre 2012: 333–4).

Weak network ties can also function as bridges along which linguistic innovations can diffuse between groups (Milroy 1992a: 178–83). If speaker A in network 1 has a weak tie to speaker B in network 2, an innovation – linguistic or otherwise – can spread from network 1 to network 2 via the bridge between speakers A and B. The first user of an innovation in a network (here, speaker B in network 2) is typically a marginal member of that network as well as of other networks, which enhances speaker B's ability to form multiple weak ties (Conde-Silvestre 2012: 334) and means that they have little to lose in terms of network status (Bergs 2005: 29). If the innovation is to spread successfully through network 2, it then has to be adopted by at least one central member of that network (an *early adopter*), who acts as a model for other network members (Milroy and Milroy 1985: 365–7). Central members of the network may have a vested interest in spotting and adopting new trends in order to be regarded as trendsetters (Bergs 2005: 29). Once the new feature has been adopted by one or several core members of the network, it can spread quickly out towards the periphery again, where marginal members who adopt it can spread it to yet other networks via weak-tie bridges (Conde-Silvestre 2012: 334).

Historical linguistic research on social networks faces the difficulty that several of the parameters used to classify network ties, such as intimacy and density, are frequently difficult to recover from the available data. Nonetheless, scholars have shown that the social-network model can be used to explain variation and change in the past. Such research can be divided into what Milroy and Milroy (1985: 370–80) refer to as *micro-level* and *macro-level* studies. Micro-level studies aim at reconstructing one or several historical social networks in order to shed light on language use within that network. For instance, Bergs (2005) examines the language of the Paston Letters from the perspective of what is known about the letter writers' lives in terms of network parameters; Sairio (2009) considers the use of several linguistic features of eighteenth-century English in letters by members of the so-called Bluestocking network. In macro-level studies, which I focus on below, an attempt is instead made to correlate what is known or can be inferred about the strength of network ties in entire populations of varying sizes with known facts about the development of the language(s) used by the relevant speakers.[2]

The underlying assumption behind macro-level studies is that "linguistic change is slow to the extent that the relevant populations are well established and bound by strong ties, whereas it is rapid to the extent that weak ties exist in populations" (Milroy and Milroy 1985: 375). Social conditions where weak ties are likely to be numerous include "[c]ases of conquest and colonization", "the peaceful in-migration of populations who speak other languages or dialects", and "sustained commercial and cultural contact" (Milroy and Milroy 1985: 379–80). However, it is not a requirement that speakers linked by weak ties speak different varieties; for instance, it is claimed that middle-class networks in present-day British society feature a great many weak ties. Trudgill (2020) suggests that the rate of language change that can be expected in a community is affected by the parameters of contact vs. isolation and social stability vs. instability. These perspectives are potentially compatible if it is assumed that the relative prevalence of weak ties is proportional to the amount of contact and instability in a community, which seems broadly reasonable.

Milroy and Milroy (1985: 375–80) use the hypothesized correlation between the strength of ties and the speed of change to explain the historical conservatism and dearth of linguistic variation in Icelandic compared with English. They argue that the geographical isolation of Iceland cannot explain all of the differences found, as greater differences between varieties of Icelandic should then have developed, given that communication between settlements was severely restricted for more than half of the year. Instead, there was little diversification of the variety

---

[2] Both approaches make use of the uniformitarian principle: it is assumed that the linguistic effects of strong and weak network ties were the same in the past as they are now.

combined with a great deal of linguistic conservatism, which indicates that ties between settlements were strong; this is shown to be a likely scenario given the lack of institutional power on the island. England, by contrast, is shown to have had a greater prevalence of weak ties, owing to factors such as the settlement of speakers of Old Norse during the Old English period, strong institutions after the Norman Conquest, and the prominence of London. This difference is argued to account for English displaying more rapid change and more dialectal diversification than Icelandic.

The same macro-perspective can be applied to different historical stages of the same language or variety (Milroy and Milroy 1985: 375), which are then contrasted with one another with regard to the prevalence of language change and weak ties. Lass (1997: 304) points out that "[l]anguages may vary all the time, but they change in bursts"; in this framework, the language or variety is expected to undergo more rapid change during periods characterized by a comparatively large number of weak ties. In addition to the contexts mentioned above, Milroy and Milroy (1985: 370, 380) note that speakers in the middle of the social hierarchy are likely to contract a large number of weak ties in Western societies and that industrialization features social and geographical mobility, which correlates with the dissolution of close-knit networks.

2.3 Sociocultural Change and Weak Ties in Late Modern England

2.3.1 Democratization and Demographics

Shortly before the beginning of the LModE period, one of the outcomes of the so-called Glorious Revolution of 1688–1689 was the Bill of Rights 1689, which entailed a rejection of absolutism and the hereditary right to the throne, and denied the monarch the right to, for instance, raise taxes without parliamentary consent (Langford 1992: 353–5; Beal 2004: 2). Six years later, the Licensing Act lapsed and was not renewed by Parliament, which increased the freedom of the press (Fries 2015: 56). However, while the Bill of Rights contributed to spreading political power to more people (though it deprived Catholics of political rights), the already propertied classes were the main beneficiaries. The right to vote, based on a system of counties and boroughs, remained heavily restricted, extending to only around 10 per cent of the adult male population in England and Wales as late as 1831.

The Reform Acts of 1832, 1867, and 1884 gradually increased the number of voters: while only one man in five could vote after the Reform Act 1832, roughly 60 per cent of the adult male population of England had the vote around the end of the nineteenth century (Lee 1976: 183; Harrison 2018: 147, 172). Women, however, did not benefit from the reforms.[3] Nevertheless, to the extent that the Reform Acts increased communication between different socio-economic sectors of the enlarged electorate, more lines of communication should have opened up between different strata of Late Modern English society in the form of weak links. Joyce (1991: 173) notes that non-standard dialect was "frequently used in the street literature of Victorian political elections", which may be indicative of an increased need to appeal to the recently enfranchised. Such developments are also highly relevant to the process of colloquialization (see Section 4.3.1 and Chapters 5–6).

The LModE period was characterized by population growth; for instance, between 1780 and 1851, the population of England rose from 7.1 to 16.9 million (Harvie 1992: 425). However, the increase was not evenly distributed. The rural population went down in many counties (see Matthew 1992: 475 for the period 1841–1911), and the number of male rural labourers in England and Wales decreased by 40 per cent from 1861 to 1901 (Matthew 1992: 479). Meanwhile, the urban population rose dramatically. Between 1750 and 1800, Birmingham, Leeds, Liverpool, Manchester, Nottingham, Plymouth, Portsmouth, Sheffield, and Sunderland were all among the twenty fastest growing cities in Europe (de Vries 1984: 140). In addition, London continued to grow significantly, reaching a population of 4.5 million in 1911 (outside England, Belfast, Dundee, Glasgow, and Limerick were also among the top twenty, and Dublin, like London, grew considerably). However, towards the end of the LModE period, the bulk of the growth took place in towns surrounding the original centres of the Industrial Revolution, often leading to several urban centres together forming one non-rural area (Matthew 1992: 474), for example Greater London (7.3 million in 1911) and Merseyside (1.2 million).

The massive urbanization described above constituted a dramatic change in population patterns: in the mid-nineteenth century, people living in urban areas accounted for more than 50 per cent of the population of Britain, making that country unique in the world (Beal 2004: 6), and by the beginning of the twentieth century, around 80 per cent of the population of England and Wales resided in urban areas (Harvie 1992: 474). The

---

[3] The Reform Act 1832 explicitly excluded women from the right to vote; before then, a small number of women had been able to vote based on property ownership.

urbanization was paralleled – and in large part caused – by a shift from agriculture to industry, with "the enclosure of common land, the mechanisation of agriculture and the Industrial Revolution" (Beal 2010a: 2) promoting both developments. Agriculture accounted for 53 per cent of male employment in 1760 but only for 29 per cent in 1840, while industry rose from 24 per cent to 47 per cent in the same period (Whyte 2000: 154). However, most of the individual transitions from rural agriculture to urban industry were short distance; with the main exception of London, urban England came to comprise a mosaic of regional economies, with extensive short-distance migration within – but limited migration between – regions (Joyce 1991: 156, 171; Whyte 2000: 140). As I discuss in Section 3.5.1, these conditions stimulated the formation of urban dialects that contained a mixture of features already present in the varieties used in the countryside surrounding urban centres.

The difference between pre-industrial and post-industrial England should not be exaggerated. As Bergs (2005: 47–8, 55) notes, there was early commercialization in the fourteenth century and a great degree of short-range geographical mobility in England from the fifteenth century on; the shift from a mainly rural, agricultural, and feudal society to an urban, industrial, and class-based one can potentially be traced back to 1500. Moreover, people who were members of a generally close-knit village community may still have been loosely affiliated with it. Nevertheless, the industrialization and urbanization of England, together with the increased social and geographical mobility of the population, must have entailed the dissolution of close-knit networks as well as the simultaneous and subsequent formation of new – strong as well as weak – network ties on a different scale (Milroy and Milroy 1985: 354, 366, 370). The new networks formed in the cities are also likely to have been less dense and multiplex on average than the rural ones (Bergs 2005: 58), though especially in working-class communities, close-knit networks are also a feature of urban life (Milroy 1992a: 218). Thus, the overall effect of the industrial transformation and gradual democratization of England on network structure must have been in the direction of weak ties. This emerging picture becomes even clearer when a social-class perspective is added.

2.3.2 A Socio-Economic Perspective on Late Modern England

Much of the eighteenth century was characterized by material growth, but the uneven distribution of wealth, the failure of taxation to redistribute that wealth, and the low wages resulting from population growth and mechanization meant that the extremities on the social continuum nevertheless moved further apart (Langford 1992: 380, 382). However, the Industrial Revolution and the shift from land to money as the basis for the economy increased social mobility in England and made it easier to climb the socio-economic ladder (Beal 2004: 5; Auer 2012: 941, 2014: 152). Somewhat different criteria were now used to define social positions; both wealth and education became important parameters, and a speaker's membership of the gentry no longer depended solely on their position in the status hierarchy (Vartianen et al. 2017: 136–7). Eighteenth-century visitors to the capital frequently remarked on how "[m]iddle-class, even lower-class Londoners aped the fashions, manners, and opinions of polite society" (Langford 1992: 388), which testifies to the relatively porous class boundaries in England compared with much of continental Europe. Although social separation between classes was often commented on, contacts were common between members of different socio-economic groups owing to regular interaction between (i) the upper and middle classes and (ii) domestic servants and tradespeople (Vartianen et al. 2017: 138). Occupational figures for the LModE period still indicate a comparatively stable society – 90 per cent of sons of labourers ended up doing manual work themselves – but the proportion of working-class sons reaching the lower middle classes also increased by 76 per cent between the periods 1839–54 and 1899–1914 (Vincent 1989: 128–30).[4]

Moreover, the middle classes themselves were about to undergo dramatic change. Until the mid-nineteenth century, they constituted "a fairly small and reasonably easily identified group: the professions, business men, bankers, large shopkeepers, and the like" (Matthew 1992: 487). But the last fifty years of the nineteenth century witnessed the emergence of the lower middle class, with the creation of a large number of clerical, bureaucratic, and service jobs in trade as well as a rapidly expanding civil service (Matthew 1992: 487–8; Beal 2004: 5). The expansion of the middle classes is of great importance to a model that draws on social-network theory; as suggested by Milroy (1992a: 213–15), socially mobile groups in the middle

---

[4] Much of the available information is based on male occupations, but women's networks are equally important to trace, not least because, as Labov (2001: 292–3) notes, women are frequently leaders in linguistic change from below. Working-class women were most likely to work, but employment options for urban working-class women were limited. Domestic service was desirable because it offered opportunities for advancement to cook, housekeeper, lady's maid, and so on; other options included sweatshops, laundries, factories, home-assembly work, and cleaning, all of which were poorly paid and involved long hours (Rubenhold 2019: 51–2, 339–40). Nevertheless, some of these occupations would have enabled unmarried women to establish weak network links with fellow workers.

of the hierarchy with a relatively secure financial status are comparatively open to linguistic innovation owing to weak community-based ties. These ties also feature less solidarity than do the multiplex links that characterize upper-class and working-class networks (Bergs 2005: 35). Crucially, the type of innovation such groups are open to tends to conform to the legitimized linguistic code, and, as Beal (2004: 93–4) notes, the linguistic insecurity of the middle classes created a demand for guides to prescribed usage (see Section 3.5.2).

Some urban workers' standard of living gradually began to improve in the second half of the LModE period. Real wages increased by 100 per cent between 1860 and 1914 (Matthew 1992: 481), and towards 1900, a good many working-class speakers could enjoy both some leisure time and a small economic surplus. Nevertheless, many urban workers remained in a state of relative poverty and financial insecurity. This insecurity in turn fostered functional solidarity in the form of close-knit groups that supplied "security and mutual support" (Milroy 1992a: 213).[5] Unlike most middle-class networks that formed during the same period, working-class close-knit groups could be expected to resist external pressure to change. But as I argue in Section 3.5.1, the formation of those networks in itself entailed considerable language change.

2.3.3 Communication

One of the most important areas of change in England during the LModE period is intimately connected to language. Owing to scientific, technological, and sociocultural developments, various new modes of travel and communication became available; in addition, some modes that had existed before came within the reach of more speakers than previously.

To begin with, several developments contributed to making travelling easier in the LModE period. First, the 1730s witnessed the rise of a turnpike system on a national scale, which made it possible to raise money for the maintenance of roads locally with tolls as security. The higher quality of turnpike roads reduced the time it took to travel from London to Manchester from more than three days to just over twenty-four hours

---

[5] The same phenomenon is "reflected at the institutional level" in trade unions (Milroy 1992a: 218); as Matthew (1992: 482–3) notes, trade union activity grew markedly in the late nineteenth century. Trade-union actions made frequent use of dialect features (Joyce 1991: 173), thus demonstrating the link between unions and the close-knit networks of their members, which contributed to imbuing dialect features with covert prestige while signalling linguistic divergence from, for instance, employers.

between 1720 and 1780 (Langford 1992: 374–5). Later in the eighteenth century, transport was greatly aided by the linking of England's important rivers by means of canals (Harvie 1992: 429–30), and the expansion of the railway network, which proceeded at an astonishing pace in the 1830s and 1840s (Beal 2004: 7–8), "created for the first time a nationally integrated economy" (Matthew 1992: 474). Affordable railway tickets became an important means of transport, especially for people from the lower echelons of society (Beal 2004: 8). These and other improvements in travelling made it easier to transport both goods (according to financial transactions) and people. Transport by sea route was also improved; coastal shipping of passengers and cargo continued to be important (Beal 2004: 7–8), and "sailing ships became so sophisticated that they remained competitive with steam until the 1880s" (Harvie 1992: 429). Most ties formed and/or maintained through such communication would have been weak; speakers are less likely to be able to maintain strong personal ties across long distances, and ties involving business and trade tend to be weak (Milroy 1997: 315).

An alternative to travelling for the purposes of communication is to send a message. Although the telephone and the electric telegraph were both introduced in the nineteenth century, the most important mode of communication for maintaining social ties in this fashion during the LModE period was the letter. Letters can be used to maintain ties of any strength, but it is arguably more difficult to duplicate some characteristics of strong ties, such as frequent communication, emotional intensity, intimacy, and reciprocal services, through letters than through face-to-face conversation.

Besides a functional delivery service, which was increasingly provided by the expanded railway system mentioned above (Vincent 1989: 48), successful communication via private letters requires literacy and the financial means to pay for postage. Technically, the literacy involved need not be on the part of either sender or recipient (letters can be dictated and read out loud), but in most cases communication by letter presupposes literate interactants. It is thus highly relevant that literacy increased drastically during the LModE period. Vartianen et al. (2017: 137) cite literacy figures of around 10 per cent for men and 1 per cent for women in 1500; the figures for 1800 are 60 per cent and 40 per cent, respectively. Porter's (1912: 147) data for England and Wales indicate that male literacy in England and Wales increased from 67 to 97 per cent between 1841 and 1900, while female literacy rose even more dramatically, from 51 to 97 per cent.[6] In addition to the gender bias apparent

---

[6] Most of the increase predates the Elementary Education Act 1870, which made basic education generally available. Altick (1957: 171–2) notes that, while the act did not speed up the spread of

from the figures, literacy was socially stratified. The acquisition of reading and writing ability was one of the most important prerequisites for social advancement (Vartianen et al. 2017: 137);[7] in addition, Joyce (1991: 158) argues that, for a child, becoming literate could mean rejecting the home linguistic community. It thus seems clear that, in addition to making the maintenance of weak ties via letter-writing possible, literacy potentially contributed to the establishment of weak ties by upwardly mobile speakers and, perhaps, to the disruption of strong ties with members of the speaker's childhood network. Importantly, the spread of literacy also drastically enlarged the working-class target group for printed matter, leading to popularization (see Section 4.3.1).

As regards the means to send letters, improved standards of living for large parts of the English population constitute an important factor. However, of arguably even greater importance is the 1840 introduction of the Penny Post. Before this reform, postage depended on the distance between sender and receiver, and was more expensive in general: the minimum rate was four pence and the average rate six pence (Vincent 1989: 33–4). Moreover, it was paid by the recipient of the letter (Mugglestone 2006: 276), which made it impossible to anticipate the expense. By introducing uniform, cheap postage paid by the sender, the Penny Post helped to increase the number of items sent from 75–76 million in 1839 via 347 million in 1849 to 3,500 million by 1914 (Vincent 1989: 33; Mugglestone 2006: 276), though much of the increase consisted of corporate correspondence (Vincent 1989: 38). Moreover, the middle classes used the Penny Post more extensively than the working classes (Vincent 1989: 38–41); the halfpenny postcard (introduced in 1870) may have been more instrumental in connecting working-class speakers through writing (Vincent 1989: 51), especially as composition did not become part of the

---

literacy, it did ensure that the increase would continue, as literacy was extended even to the very poor. Literacy was typically higher in towns than in the countryside, and especially high in London (Schneider 2002: 40). Also, figures for England and Wales should not be generalized to other parts of the English-speaking world; for instance, literacy was more widespread in Australia and North America than in England, given the emphasis on education in those regions (Kytö 1991: 24–6; Fritz 2007: 15–16). In contrast, there was concern both in England and elsewhere that the spread of literacy to the lower orders might lead to social unrest (Bailey 1996: 28–30; Williams 2010: 79; Smitterberg 2012a: 954; Auer 2014: 158). Figures are often estimates based on signature literacy, which most likely overestimates the number of proficient writers and underestimates that of readers (see Smitterberg 2012a: 953–5 for more detailed discussion). There was a 3:2 or 2:1 gap between reading and writing in the early nineteenth century, but that gap gradually closed after 1850 (Vincent 1989: 10).

[7] Literacy seems to have been a necessary but not sufficient criterion in this regard. Vincent (1989: 130–2) notes that speakers with working-class backgrounds who reached the lower middle class were more likely to be literate than those who remained part of the working classes; at the same time, new, working-class occupations also arose that incorporated literate speakers but did not offer social advancement, such as post-office workers.

school curriculum until 1871, and even then many children left school without being able to compose coherent texts (Vincent 1989: 89–90). These caveats notwithstanding, the Penny Post was of immense importance in making the production of writing on a regular basis relevant to large numbers of people.

The private letter and the postcard were of course not the only genres that benefitted from societal changes. As a result of a large number of interconnected factors – for example the abolition of paper duties, improved indoor lighting, expanded literacy, increased affluence, and more leisure time – publishing in general, including newspapers (see Section 4.5.2), grew dramatically during the LModE period. While around 100 annual titles, excluding newspapers, were published in the 1750s, the figure rose to 370 in the 1790s, exceeded 500 in the 1820s, and continued to increase; it had passed 6,000 by 1900 (Williams 1978: 42).

2.4 Language Change in Late Modern English

Until relatively recently, LModE was a comparatively neglected field within English historical linguistics. However, LModE studies have been transformed by the increased interest shown in the field since the eve of the millennium (for discussion of the reasons behind this change, see Kytö and Smitterberg 2020b: 1–6). The landmark publication of Romaine (1998a) meant that LModE received the same amount of scholarly attention in the Cambridge History of the English Language series as Old, Middle, and Early Modern English.[8] In 2001, the first conference devoted to LModE was organized in Edinburgh, followed by conferences in Vigo (2004), Leiden (2007), Sheffield (2010), Bergamo (2013), and Uppsala (2017); shortly before I finalized this manuscript, the seventh conference in the series, in Ragusa Ibla, was postponed until 2022 as a result of the Covid-19 pandemic. These conferences have yielded a large number of collections of studies (Dossena and Jones 2003; Pérez-Guerra et al. 2007; Tieken-Boon van Ostade and van der Wurff 2009; Beal et al. 2012; Dossena 2015; Kytö and Smitterberg 2020a). Increasing academic attention was followed by more space being devoted to LModE in undergraduate and graduate curricula, which created a need for specialized textbooks such as Beal (2004) and Tieken-Boon van Ostade (2009). Each of the two centuries

---

[8] The period covered by Romaine (1998a), 1776–1997, is not identical with the typical delimitation of LModE (c.1700–1900), but the coverage is similar enough for the volume to count as a milestone in LModE studies.

traditionally thought to make up the LModE period has also been the subject of separate attention (Bailey 1996; Görlach 1999, 2001; Kytö et al. 2006a; Hickey 2010a; Nevalainen et al. 2018).

Indeed, so much scholarship has been published on LModE in the past twenty-five years that the subject is nowadays too well researched for any concise discussion of language change during this period to aim at comprehensive coverage. I will therefore focus on a number of key trends. Precedence has generally been given to recent sources and to scholarly overviews, in which references to more specific studies can be found. I devote more attention to grammar than to lexis and pronunciation, since the case studies in this book concern changes in grammar.

One of the main reasons why the LModE period was under-researched for a long time was the commonly held assumption that little happened to the English language between 1700 and 1900. More specifically, the underlying *structure* of English was frequently taken to have undergone few changes in the eighteenth and nineteenth centuries: Romaine (1998b: 1) downplays the significance of post-1776 changes in grammar, phonology, and morphology compared with the preceding centuries; Hickey (2010b: xvii) makes a similar claim for eighteenth-century English as a whole; and Bergs (2005: 53), who suggests that English has changed according to a "punctuated equilibrium" model, considers the pace of change to have been slowing down since the beginning of the Early Modern English period (see also Nevalainen et al. 2020b: 8–9).[9] Denison (2003: 67–8) points out that, according to such accounts, change in the history of the language so far actually forms an S-curve, with rapid change in Middle and Early Modern English contrasting with relative stability in Old English and LModE. However, as Denison recognizes, such logic is problematic, as Old English did not come into being out of nowhere; nor are we presumably nearing the end of the English language at present. Biber and Gray (2016: 30–2) suggest that grammatical change since *c.*1700 has mainly concerned the frequency and functions of features rather than the emergence of new categories and that academic writing has been an important locus of this type of change, particularly as regards an increase in phrasal complexity (see Section 4.3.2).

However, it may be unhelpful to attempt to determine the extent and pace of change in LModE as a whole, since different subcomponents of the language may undergo bursts of change at different times (Lass 1997: 304).

---

[9] Dixon (1997: 4, 67) suggests that human language as a whole has been in a state of "punctuation", that is, characterized by quick-paced change, during the last few centuries.

I shall therefore devote separate subsections to LModE lexis, pronunciation, and grammar below.[10] As mentioned above, grammar will be treated in more detail than the other two fields, as the empirical studies in Chapters 5–8 focus on changes in grammar.

2.4.1 Lexis

Additions to the vocabulary of a language are arguably not structural in the same way as, for instance, changes in its phoneme inventory or verbal syntax. However, as English lexis has been shown to have undergone important changes during the LModE period, I will discuss some features of LModE lexical innovation in this section.

Speakers of English in the LModE period were exposed to new experiences in fields including "[t]echnological and scientific inventions, trade, exploration and colonization" (Beal 2004: 14). This impact might be expected to entail a great deal of lexical innovation, as new words from open word classes are needed to identify and describe new referents, processes, and so on. By way of brief illustration, words first attested in 1850 and still current according to the *Oxford English Dictionary* (*OED*) include the following, only some of which may be familiar to most language users: *abalone, campsite, ceramic, dhyana, diethyl, embarcadero, enzyme* ('[t]he leavened bread with which the Eucharist is administered in the Greek Church'; the chemical sense is first attested in 1881), and *jarool*. A quantitative way of charting this type of lexical innovation is to use the "first-cited date" in the *OED* as a rough guide to when a word entered the (written) language. The results of such a search are given in Figure 2.1, which charts the number of first-cited entries per twenty-year period.

Beal (2004: 14) and Tieken-Boon van Ostade (2009: 54) provide data that are comparable to those in Figure 2.1; Beal bases her figure on Finkenstaedt et al. (1970) and provides results per decade, while Tieken-Boon van Ostade uses the *OED*, but considers the first year in each decade only. These minor differences notwithstanding, the three graphs show quite similar developments until *c.*1840: a fairly stable level of moderate lexical innovation until the late eighteenth century, followed by a rise that

---

[10] My account thus leaves important fields such as semantics and pragmatics largely unaccounted for. These fields are of course also relevant to language change; for instance, results presented in Nevalainen and Tissari (2010) and Taavitsainen and Jucker (2010) indicate that the expression of politeness has undergone change between 1700 and the present day. However, most previous research on the pace of change in English has concerned either phonological and grammatical structure or lexis.

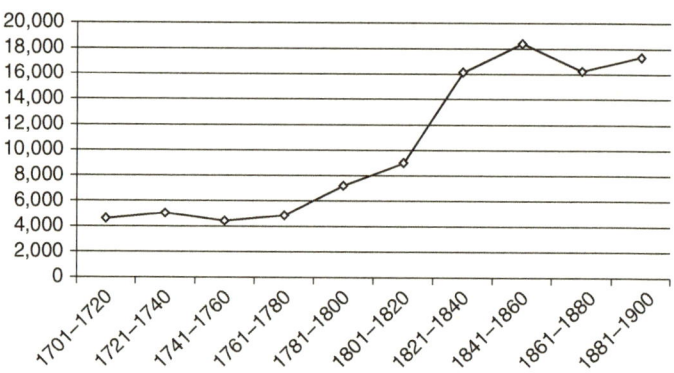

Figure 2.1 Lexical innovation in the *OED* by twenty-year period (data from 2018)

becomes increasingly steep. For the period after 1840, my data suggest fairly stable figures of between 16,000 and 18,000 new lexemes per twenty years; in Beal's figure, the line turns down again after 1840, and there are few new lexemes recorded for especially the last decade of the nineteenth century; conversely, Tieken-Boon van Ostade's results indicate that the rate of innovation continues to increase at least until 1890, after which time there is a sudden drop. Görlach (2001: 146) presents figures for a far longer period (the late fourteenth to the early twentieth century) based on several dictionaries; these data indicate that there have been two main "peaks" in lexical innovation; namely, the time from the late sixteenth century to *c*.1700, and most of the nineteenth century. The eighteenth century, in contrast, forms a "trough" between these two peaks, and the number of new words goes down drastically around 1900.

As regards what can account for these differences across time, Beal (2004: 16) notes that the relative lack of lexical innovation apparent from her late-nineteenth-century data is most likely due to the nature of the data set. The *Chronological English Dictionary* relies for first attestations on the first edition of the *Oxford English Dictionary*, whose coverage becomes notably less extensive in the twentieth century. As regards the lower levels of lexical innovation until *c*.1780, it is likely that several causes are involved. Beal (2004: 17) and Tieken-Boon van Ostade (2009: 53) note that the 1700s follow a period when English was taking over functions that had previously been filled by Latin; there was thus a need to expand the lexicon with words that would enable English to serve such purposes. At the turn of the eighteenth century, this expansion had largely been completed, which may help to explain why lexical expansion slowed down. Beal also suggests that linguistic conservatism may have retarded the pace of innovation during the 1700s.

There are also explanations that are connected to the *OED* as a source of data. To begin with, not all words attested in the dictionary were necessarily ever in current use, which may inflate figures (Tieken-Boon van Ostade 2009: 54–5). Moreover, Görlach (2001: 145) suggests that the *OED*'s coverage of eighteenth-century texts is less comprehensive than for the preceding period, and Mair (2006a: 226–7) shows that the nineteenth century is better documented in the *OED* than are the preceding and following centuries. Brewer (2007) provides an in-depth study of the *OED*'s eighteenth-century coverage and concludes that "it would seem likely that scanty representation of this period is due to the lexicographers (and in some cases, perhaps, the limitations on the material available to them)" (Brewer 2007: 123). She suggests that "consciously or unconsciously, the first-edition editors of the *OED* felt, when shaping the entry for a word, that eighteenth-century quotations were less interesting or important than those from the sixteenth, seventeenth, and nineteenth centuries" and that this is due to "their attitudes to the period". If the 1700s received comparatively scant treatment, this is likely to affect the number of words that are first cited in that century. As Brewer (2007: 129–132) notes, the third edition of the *OED* is a clear improvement in this regard, though some bias remains.

The rapid growth of the English vocabulary raises the question of what the sources of the new words were. Beal (2004: 25–7) has analysed the 350 words first recorded in 1835 according to the *Chronological English Dictionary*. Taken together, Latin and Greek account for 61 per cent of those 350 words (French makes up an additional 17 per cent).[11] (As I will argue in Section 3.3, it is doubtful whether loanwords should be counted as innovations.) In fact, as Görlach (1999: 115) and Beal (2004: 22–4) note, some contemporaries expressed concern about the large number of neologisms based on Latin and Greek, many of which were connected with science and technology, in terms that sometimes echo the Inkhorn Controversy of the Early Modern English period (see, for instance, Rissanen 1975; Nevalainen 1999: 359). There were fears that the lower classes, who had not had access to a classical education, would be excluded from discourse that relied on such words. Fairman's (2006: 77–80) analysis

---

[11] However, several loans considered French by the dictionary originally stem from classical languages, which leads to potential over-representation of French as a source of new words (Görlach 1999: 111).

of early-nineteenth-century letters by minimally schooled and partly schooled writers indicates that such fears were justified. While Latinate words made up 64 per cent of content words in extensively schooled people's letters, the corresponding figure for the minimally schooled and partly schooled group is 25 per cent. In addition, minimally schooled writers often had difficulty spelling words with unstressed first syllables (Fairman 2006: 75–6), presumably because such a word-stress pattern was unfamiliar to writers with a largely Germanic vocabulary; strategies include omitting or detaching the first syllable (e.g. *Grement* for *agreement*; *a prentice* for *apprentice*). The existence of such a "lexical bar" problematizes the issue of what it means to say that a word has been attested in English. As Nevalainen (1999: 342) notes, "[o]nly part of the new vocabulary in any language will find its way into the *common core*, which is shared by the written and spoken medium alike, by all registers, and by all social and regional varieties". An *OED* attestation may not be sufficient to justify counting a word as part of the "English" vocabulary if a large proportion of speakers did not use that lexeme and were unfamiliar with its Standard English representation in writing.

To sum up, it is difficult to reach safe conclusions concerning the eighteenth century. The 1800s, however, were characterized by a remarkable amount of lexical innovation, a significant part of which remained unknown to a sizeable proportion of the English population.

2.4.2 *Pronunciation*

This selective survey of changes in pronunciation focusses on the inventory, distribution, and (to a lesser extent) realization of phonemes, as the phoneme is a unit of obvious structural significance in a language; for changes in stress, intonation, rhythm, voice quality, and so on, see MacMahon (1998: 492–520). The scope is chiefly restricted to the development of speakers from south-eastern England.

As indicated at the beginning of Section 2.4, there were few changes to the inventory of phonemes in LModE. Strang (1970: 78–9) argues that, since *c.*1770, changes in pronunciation have mainly been due "not, as in the past, to evolution of the system, but to what, in a very broad sense, we may call the interplay of different varieties, and to the complex analogical relationship between different parts of the language". Beal (2004: 125–6), however, suggests that the impression of a difference between LModE and earlier periods in what types of change take place may be created by the

2.4 Language Change in Late Modern English

relative richness of the LModE database, which makes systemic changes more difficult to observe.

MacMahon's (1998: 403–4) account suggests that the vowel phonemes present in late-eighteenth-century London speech are also part of present-day Received Pronunciation (though several phonemes were realized differently, and their distribution may have shifted).[12] The main difference in vowel inventory is the appearance of the /ɜː/ monophthong (in the NURSE set) and the centring diphthongs /ɪə/, /eə/, and /ʊə/ (in the NEAR, SQUARE, and CURE sets).[13] The phonemicization of these sounds depends on the loss of non-prevocalic /r/, which had taken place in some varieties of eighteenth-century English (Beal 2004: 154), in combination with compensatory lengthening. The emergence of /ɜː/ is also dependent on the merger of the reflexes of Middle English /ɪ/, /e/, and /ʊ/ before /r/ (as in *fir*, *fern*, and *fur*), which went to completion in most varieties during the LModE period (for details, see MacMahon 1998: 415–18).

The most important shift in the distribution of phonemes probably concerns vowels in what Wells (1982: 133–5) calls the lexical set BATH, which comprises words such as *bath*, *dance*, and *last*. Members of this set originally had the same /æ/ as do members of the TRAP set (e.g. *trap*, *cancel*, and *sad*), but gradually underwent lengthening, lowering, and/or backing in certain phonetic environments, resulting in the BATH/TRAP split, where the BATH set has /ɑː/ and the TRAP set /æ/ in Present-Day Received Pronunciation (see Beal 2004: 138–41 for details).[14] There is little evidence for the split before 1700 (Jones 2012: 829), making this largely a LModE process. Despite initial stigmatization, the new vowel in the BATH set eventually became part of Received Pronunciation. A similar lengthening of the vowels in words like *off* from /ɒ/ to /ɔː/ was reversed; Beal (2004: 141–2) suggests that the use of /ɔː/ by both the upper and the lower echelons of English society may have made the middle classes avoid the long vowel so that they would not be mistaken for working-class speakers.

---

[12] However, there is some doubt about the phonemic status of /ə/ in relation to /ʌ/; see MacMahon (1998: 410–11) and Hickey (2010c: 5).
[13] The emergence and subsequent disappearance of /ɔə/ is treated in MacMahon (1998: 414–15). In Section 2.4.2, I make use of Wells's (1982: 127–68) standard lexical sets and use small capitals for the keywords of such sets.
[14] Lengthening could take place as early as 1700 before some consonants and consonant groups, including /θ/ (*bath*), preconsonantal /r/, /s/, and /n/ (*art, past, dance*), and /lf/, /lm/, and /lv/ (*half, calm, calve*) (Beal 2004: 139). In many environments, for example before final /s/, the split is incomplete and the distribution of /æ/ and /ɑː/ partly dependent on lexis (e.g. *lass* with /æ/ vs. *pass* with /ɑː/). In such contexts, the split constitutes "the ossification of a half-completed sound change" (Wells 1982: 233).

Two other changes in the pronunciation of vowels may be mentioned. The vowels in the FACE and GOAT sets diphthongized and are usually represented as /eɪ/ and /əʊ/ rather than /eː/ and /oː/ in descriptions of Present-Day Received Pronunciation (Beal 2004: 136–8). In various accents in England, the unstressed final vowel in words such as *happy* has been variable between the KIT set and the FLEECE set (so-called happy-tensing) since at least the eighteenth century (Beal 2004: 152).

No new consonant phonemes emerged during the LModE period, but there are differences regarding the distribution of existing phonemes. Arguably the biggest change is the loss of non-prevocalic /r/ in many accents in England (see Beal 2004: 153–7). Although non-rhotic pronunciations were stigmatized for much of the LModE period, they gradually gained ground, and eventually became part of Received Pronunciation. In addition to the phonemicization of the centring diphthongs and /ɜː/, this change also resulted in the introduction of so-called intrusive /r/, as in *Russia and China* /ˈrʌʃər ən ˈtʃaɪnə/; such pronunciations were proscribed during the LModE period and beyond but still appear to have become increasingly common after being first noted in the second half of the eighteenth century (Beal 2004: 156).

The distribution of the phoneme /h/ carried powerful social connotations (see Mugglestone 2003: 95–128 for a detailed account). Prescriptive comments stigmatized /h/-less pronunciations of some words with initial <h>, such as *head*, and also /h/-insertion in words like *orange*, resulting in *a horange* rather than *an orange* (Beal 2010b: 33). The situation was made more complex by the fact that initial <h> was traditionally silent in many French loans, and there was some variation between /h/-less and /h/-ful pronunciations of words such as *hospital* and *humour* (MacMahon 1998: 477–8). It also seems that /h/-ful pronunciations were recommended in some words that had previously been /h/-less (Beal 2004: 159); for instance, Walker (1791: xiii) indicates that *humour* and *humble* lack /h/. While /h/-dropping has never become part of Received Pronunciation, simplifying the initial cluster /hw/ to /w/ – or, alternatively, merging /ʍ/ and /w/ as /w/ – in words in <wh> like *whales* (making it a homophone of *Wales*) gradually became acceptable towards the end of the LModE period (Beal 2004: 158).

Another consonant that was increasingly dropped in LModE is /j/ between a consonant and /uː/, so-called yod-dropping. A /j/ used to occur in clusters where it is not used today, such as /glj/ in *glue* and /rj/ in *rude* (MacMahon 1998: 470–1). In stressed syllables after /r/, yod-dropping appears to have been spreading in late-eighteenth-century

English (Beal 2004: 148). After initial /s/ and /l/ (e.g. *suit* and *lewd*) yod-loss is later, and /j/ is still preserved after the alveolar consonants /t/, /d/, and /n/ in Received Pronunciation (e.g. *tune, due, news*). However, even in this set there has been variation in England; Beal (2004: 149) provides adverse eighteenth-century reactions to London pronunciations of *dew* and *new* without /j/.

The ending *-ing* has had two pronunciations in LModE: /ɪn/ and /ɪŋ/. While /ɪŋ/ appears to have been recommended throughout the period, /ɪn/ was widespread in working-class and upper-class speech. As was the case for /ɒ/ vs. /ɔː/ in *off* and so on, it seems that the middle classes seized upon /ɪŋ/ as the safer option to avoid being perceived as vulgar (Beal 2004: 160–1). The standard spelling with <ng> also indicated /ɪŋ/, which may have been an additional factor (Beal 2004: 161).

To sum up, with the exception of the emergence of several new vowel phonemes in accents that became non-rhotic, the LModE period may appear to witness few changes to the overall phonological system. In addition, many of the changes undergone in south-eastern varieties have not necessarily taken place in other accents. However, as I will argue in Chapter 3, there is a risk of underestimating the change that did take place if we underplay the importance of the individual speaker's role.

2.4.3 Grammar

This brief survey will demonstrate that there was a good deal of grammatical change in LModE. However, apart from a few constructions and patterns which appear to be genuine innovations or which disappear from the language, the period seems mainly to be characterized by shifting frequencies of patterns that were already grammatical by 1700.

The verb phrase is arguably the site of the most radical changes English has gone through since 1700. Rissanen (1999a: 210) argues that "the Present-Day English verbal system" develops in particular between 1600 and 1800, and the verb phrase also witnesses two systemic additions to English grammar during the LModE period (Aarts et al. 2012: 870). The progressive passive, as in *The house is being built*, was first attested in the second half of the 1700s, but became established in English during the nineteenth century, despite being an overtly stigmatized feature for decades (see Anderwald 2014a, 2016: 189–217).[15] This innovation meant

---

[15] As Pratt and Denison (2000: 418–19) and others have noted, the near-simultaneous appearances of the progressive passive and the progressive of the verb BE (e.g. *He was being friendly*) are most likely

that all pairs of English modal, perfect, progressive, and passive auxiliaries could be combined in a verb phrase (Denison 1998: 150), which increased the symmetry of the verbal group.[16] Before the availability of the progressive passive, what Visser (1963–1973: §§1,872–81) refers to as a passival form, that is, a progressive that was active in form but passive in meaning (e.g. *The house is building*), was sometimes used instead. The second addition is the GET-passive, as in *She got fired from her last job*. While isolated examples from Early Modern English can be found (Aarts et al. 2012: 871; see also Fleisher 2006: 227 for a discussion of the origin of this construction), the GET-passive becomes more firmly established during the LModE period and in twentieth-century English (Schwarz 2019), as the general frequency of GET-constructions rises (Hundt 2001: 77). The development of both the progressive passive and the GET-passive has been connected to grammaticalization (Denison 1998: 155; Hundt 2001; Schwarz 2019).

Another important change in the verb phrase is the gradual disappearance of BE as perfect auxiliary with intransitive verbs, as in *I am arrived in Bath* (e.g. Rydén and Brorström 1987; Kytö 1997; McCafferty 2014; Anderwald 2014b, 2016: 131–55; McFadden 2017; Calvo Cortés 2020). The shift from BE to HAVE in this context had begun before 1700, but the bulk of the change is located in the eighteenth and nineteenth centuries (Rydén and Brorström 1987: 232–3). There was also some residual change concerning auxiliary DO. The use of DO-support had not been completely regularized yet by 1700; interrogative and negated contexts that require DO in Present-Day English could still occur without it (e.g. *Know you the answer?* and *I know not the answer*), and there was occasional use of non-emphatic DO in affirmative clauses (Tieken-Boon van Ostade 1987: 123).

The verb phrase has also been the focus of many studies considering quantitative shifts in the frequencies of features. The increase in the frequency of the progressive in general has been well documented (e.g. Hundt 2004; Smitterberg 2005; Kranich 2010; Anderwald 2016: 161; Reuter 2017: 145–98); the phrasal verb, as in GIVE *up*, also increased in frequency in LModE (Smitterberg 2008; Rodríguez-Puente 2019).[17] Both

---

connected, as both involve the sequence BE *being*. In an intricate account, Warner (1997) argues that *being* was re-analysed as a non-auxiliary in the LModE period, which made both progressive passives and progressives of BE possible, as BE was subcategorized for taking non-auxiliary complements.

[16] In contrast, as Denison (1998: 204–5) notes, the near-disappearance of the "double *-ing*" construction, as in *Being reading the paper, I missed the train*, during the LModE period made the paradigm less symmetrical.

[17] Other types of multi-word verbs have also undergone changes. Phrasal-prepositional verbs such as PUT *up with* have increased in frequency (Denison 1998: 223). Many constructions with so-called light verbs, where the added material carries most of the semantic weight of the verb phrase (e.g.

2.4 Language Change in Late Modern English

of these features are associated with colloquialization (but cf. Thim 2012 regarding the historical informality of phrasal verbs). As I will discuss further in Chapter 4, the net result of such changes is that "oral" and "literate" genres move further apart linguistically during the LModE period, which makes the genre parameter increasingly important in the study of morpho-syntactic change between 1700 and 1900.

The use of the subjunctive declined over the LModE period. In nominal clauses, the mandative subjunctive (e.g. *They demanded that he leave the room*) was gradually replaced mainly by *should* + infinitive constructions, though this trend was reversed in the twentieth century, with American English leading the way (e.g. Övergaard 1995; Denison 1998: 263–4; Kjellmer 2009: 247; Leech et al. 2009: 52–61). In adverbial clauses, the subjunctive declined more slowly in LModE (see Schlüter 2009: 281 for conditional clauses); however, this trend has not been reversed, and the indicative rather than constructions with modal auxiliaries took over from the subjunctive (Grund and Walker 2006: 103–4).

The distribution of forms used to express the semantic fields of modality and futurity has undergone several changes since 1700, only a few of which can be mentioned here. MAY has lost ground; for instance, *might* has largely lost the permission-in-the-past sense, as in *The porter might not speak to him* (Denison 1998: 165), where it has been replaced by a paraphrase such as *was not allowed to* or by *could*. In many contexts, CAN has also replaced MAY regarding the expression of permission and possibility, as in *Can I go now?* or *What else can it be?* (Denison 1998: 166). *Must* has largely lost its past-tense uses (Denison 1998: 176). For the expression of futurity, the prescriptive rule that *shall* should be used in the first person and *will* in the second and third persons (see Rissanen 1999a: 211–12 for a discussion of how the distribution originated) was increasingly abandoned, with *will* taking over from *shall* in first-person contexts (Denison 1998: 167–8). The BE *going to* construction also gained ground during the LModE period (Denison 1998: 188). In the field of obligation, HAVE *got* 'be obliged' (e.g. *This has got to be true*) developed after 1600 but did not become common until the nineteenth century (Visser 1963–1973: §§2,011, 2,142). *Used to* 'was/were in the habit of' used to occur in the present tense as well, as in *We*

MAKE *a decision* 'decide') also became more entrenched in English; see, for instance, Denison (1998: 225). However, Claridge (2000: 178) demonstrates that several categories of group verb were relatively stable or went down in frequency in the late seventeenth and early eighteenth centuries; she tentatively attributes a possible decrease in the incidence of phrasal verbs during this time to standardization, stylistic preferences, and prescriptivism.

use to carve a rose on the flat side of the lute, but this usage appears to have died out during LModE (Denison 1998: 175). Variation between uncontracted and *not*-contracted combinations of operator + *not* (e.g. *will not* vs. *won't*) is addressed in Chapter 5.

The LModE period witnesses considerable variation in the form of preterites and past participles. As Lass (1999: 167) notes, there were two main types of variation: some verbs could be either strong or weak, and many strong verbs displayed a great deal of variation in their vowel-grade patterns (and several still do so in non-standard varieties). Several verbs, for example CATCH and TEACH, had alternative, regular preterites and past participles as late as the eighteenth century; for several verbs such as SMELL and BURN, irregular forms in *-t* spread between 1600 and 1800, with subsequent partial regularization (Hundt 2009: 24–7). Mondorf (2012: 844) refers to LModE as "a time of immense variability with rapid morphological change" in past-participle morphology. While there was little variation in the forms of past participles after 1800, preterite forms continued to exhibit formal fluctuation into the nineteenth century (Anderwald 2016: 62–130).

One of the areas where considerable change has taken place is in verb complementation; only a selection of references will be given here. A long-term change in English from finite to non-finite complementation was underway in LModE (Aarts et al. 2012: 878; Denison 1998: 256–7; Cuyckens et al. 2014: 202–3). When *that*-clauses were used as objects, clauses without an overt subordinator (e.g. *He thought Ø the captain was present*) became less frequent during the LModE period, possibly owing to prescriptive pressure (Rissanen 1999a: 284). In contrast, *that* has been lost in several compound (preposition + *that*) conjunctions, such as *besides that* and *for that*; the decrease began in the seventeenth century but continued into LModE (Denison 1998: 294; Rissanen 1999a: 303).

Non-finite complementation is itself an area where a great deal of change took place between 1700 and 1900 (Mair 2006a: 215): *-ing* clauses gradually replaced *to*-infinitive clauses in many contexts (Strang 1970: 100; Fanego 2007, 2010; Mondorf 2012: 851–3) as part of the so-called Great Complement Shift (Rohdenburg 2006: 143); there have also been changes in adjective complementation (see, for instance, Rudanko 2006 on *accustomed*). Sometimes the interplay between these clause types is intricate; for instance, Mair (2006a) demonstrates that, after REMEMBER, *-ing* clauses took over from *to*-infinitive clauses – and possibly also from finite complementation – in retrospective contexts (e.g. *I remembered repairing the engine* vs. *I remembered to have repaired the engine* vs. *I remembered that*

I had repaired the engine). Other factors that have been argued to influence complementation patterns include the main-clause verb, the Complexity Principle – that is, the tendency to prefer more explicit patterns in cognitively complex contexts – and *horror aequi*, that is, the avoidance of repeated forms such as two successive *-ing* forms (see, for instance, Rohdenburg 2003 and Vosberg 2003 for discussion of the latter two factors). In some cases, for example LOOK *forward to* and CONTRIBUTE *to*, reanalysis of *to* from an infinitive marker to a preposition, with a resulting change from infinitive to *-ing* form afterwards, has taken place (Denison 1998: 265–6).

There are also other aspects of variation and change associated with LModE *-ing* forms. The *-ing* form can be clearly nominal (e.g. *the buying of my house*) as well as clearly verbal (e.g. *I cannot avoid hating him*) in both LModE and Present-Day English. However, hybrid forms, which exhibit both nominal and verbal characteristics (e.g. *the gaining her affections*, which combines a definite article with a direct object), were more frequent at least in eighteenth-century English than they are today (Aarts et al. 2012: 879). Many gerundial *-ing* clauses with subjects allow two types of subject heads: objective vs. (dependent) possessive pronouns (*We look forward to them/their spending New Year here*) and common-case vs. genitive nouns (*We look forward to Sue/Sue's spending New Year here*). Preference has increasingly shifted to objective and common-case forms, with nouns and indefinite pronouns being the most advanced types of head in the change (Dekeyser 1975: 180–3; Lyne 2011: 298).[18]

As regards pronoun usage, the LModE period witnessed increased regulation – at least in the standard language – of usage current in Early Modern English as well (Beal 2004: 69–71, 75–7). THOU forms in the second person singular "continued to be used in increasingly restricted contexts" (Beal 2004: 70; see Walker 2007 for a detailed account of the variation up to 1760); similarly, by the eighteenth century *ye* was "relegated ... to special registers" (Lass 1999: 154). Owing perhaps to the lack of number distinctions in the second person (apart from the reflexive paradigm) after THOU forms were no longer in use, alternative strategies developed but did not make the transition to written standard usage, for example *you was* in the singular or alternative plural forms such as *yous* or

---

[18] Personal pronouns also show case variation between subject and object forms in other contexts: in responses (e.g. *Not he/him!*), after words that can be analysed as prepositions or conjunctions, especially *than* and *as* (e.g. *as intelligent as she/her*), and as subject complements (e.g. *It's I/me*). The object form has generally gained ground through LModE (Denison 1998: 107–8).

you all (Beal 2004: 70–1). The use of relative markers also underwent regulatory changes. Although the frequency of relative *which* with human antecedents dropped during the 1600s (Ball 1996: 246), it could still be found among educated writers in the early eighteenth century, and survived longer in non-standard usage and in restrictive clauses (Austin 1985: 18–20). The relative marker *that* was increasingly relegated to restrictive clauses and non-human antecedents in Early Modern English, and this trend also continued into LModE (Ball 1996: 249); the tendency to use *who* was especially strong in subject function (Denison 1998: 278). Johansson (2006: 180) argues that the relative marker *that* was largely restricted to specific syntactic contexts in written nineteenth-century English; Hundt et al. (2012a) show that *which* was increasingly preferred over *that* in restrictive clauses in LModE scientific discourse, though the trend was reversed in twentieth-century American English. *Whom* has been losing ground to *who* as a relative marker as well as an interrogative pronoun (Denison 1998: 246–7). Dekeyser (1975: 190–202) shows that, at least in interrogative contexts, objective *who* is quite frequent in informal nineteenth-century writing. In relative clauses as well as other contexts, prepositions can be stranded (e.g. *the book that I was talking about*) or pied-piped (e.g. *the book about which I was talking*), the latter variant being more formal and prescribed; this too is a field where there is variation in LModE (see Yáñez-Bouza 2014). Regional dialects exhibited greater variation in the range of relative markers, such as *at* in the north, *as* in the Midlands, and *what* in the south-east (Wagner 2012: 929–30).

There were a few developments in the adjective phrase. Lass (1999: 157) argues that the present-day system for the distribution of inflectional (*-er/-est*) and periphrastic (*more/most*) comparison was largely in place by 1750. Contrary to the general trend from synthetic to analytic usage in English, however, the proportion of inflectional comparison increased within the framework of this system during the LModE period (see, for instance, Kytö and Romaine 2006). Mondorf (2009: 117–69; 2012: 863–6) argues that a division of labour has been established in diachrony whereby *more* is favoured in cognitively demanding environments. Double comparison (e.g. *more finer*) became stigmatized in the eighteenth century and is rare in written nineteenth-century English (Kytö and Romaine 2006: 196). The present-day restrictions on adjectives as noun-phrase heads were not fully in place by 1700; adjectives could also appear as heads of noun phrases without the definite article into the eighteenth century (Rissanen 1999a: 192–3, 200, 204).

As regards the noun phrase, the use of increasingly brief modifiers to encode complexity is one of the main topics of the present study and is addressed in detail as *densification* in Section 4.3.2 and Chapters 7–8. But other changes in this phrase type also took place. Occasional plurals in *-n* still occurred in the eighteenth century (e.g. *housen*), as did zero plurals with "[p]otential collectives or mass-like nouns" such as *brick* (Lass 1999: 141). The use of *one* as an anaphoric pronoun in noun phrases underwent some expansion between 1700 and 1900 (Denison 1998: 102–3), with patterns such as *those ones* becoming possible. In some partitive noun phrases, concord has shifted; for instance, a plural verb after *a majority/ number of* + plural noun became more likely during the LModE period, indicating a possible reanalysis of the structure of the phrase so that *a . . . of* functions as a complex determiner and the following plural noun as the head (Denison 1998: 121; Smitterberg 2006: 263–7). In the determiner slot, the combination of demonstrative and possessive determiners (e.g. *this my friend*) was still possible in the eighteenth century (Denison 1998: 114–15).[19]

There have been few developments in clause elements since 1700, but even here some change has taken place. The indirect object has become somewhat more restricted in occurrence. Denison (1998: 217–18) provides several examples of verbs that would not be constructed as ditransitive today, for example *nothing introduces you a heroine like soft musick* and *repeat her some of your own Verses*. Pronominal direct objects preceding indirect objects (e.g. *I gave it him*) seem to have been less marked in LModE than in present-day Standard English (Denison 1998: 239). Reflexive structures also decreased in terms of the number of verbs that are constructed reflexively as well as the number of tokens. American English has been ahead of British English in this process, parts of which took place after the LModE period (Rohdenburg 2009: 180). Other alternatives to reflexives include particles (e.g. BRACE *oneself* > BRACE *up*) and *way* constructions (e.g. WIND *itself* > WIND *its way*) (Mondorf 2012: 848–50).

Given that changes in the incidence of linguistic features are often dependent on genre, cross-genre studies of LModE have become a prominent area of research. The importance of a genre perspective on LModE was highlighted in Biber and Finegan's (1997) factor-score analysis,

---

[19] Although the matter concerns orthography rather than noun-phrase syntax, it should be mentioned that there was fluctuation during part of the LModE period as regards the use of an apostrophe to mark case. In the genitive singular, the apostrophe was regular around 1700, but the use of the apostrophe to signal the genitive plural was settled later (cf. Strang 1970: 109–10; Salmon 1999: 48).

which indicated that linguistic genre differentiation has increased since the seventeenth century. The oral–literate continuum they discuss has been replicated in other factor-score analyses (e.g. Geisler 2002), and in studies of particular linguistic features (e.g. Smitterberg 2008). The distinction between oral and literate styles of course conflates a large number of motives – conscious and subconscious – on the part of writers, editors, publishers, and other stakeholders in written language production. Two such motives are popularization and economy (Biber and Gray 2012). The case studies of colloquialization and densification in the present volume uncover what can be seen as the linguistic effects of these motives (and of other causes, including stylistic trends and sociocultural developments such as language users' access to education and the printed medium).

The grammar of individual LModE genres has also been the subject of scholarly interest. I will restrict attention to three genres here, all of which are important for my own research in this book. Letters are important owing to their comparatively informal production circumstances, which makes their language potentially speech-like even though it is neither speech-based nor speech-purposed (Culpeper and Kytö 2010: 18). Letters are also a useful basis for research within historical sociolinguistics because their language is affected by the relationship between writer and addressee (Görlach 1999: 149); see, for instance, several of the studies in Dossena and Tieken-Boon van Ostade (2008) and in Auer et al. (2015).[20] To the extent that letter writers can be identified and related to one another, their social networks may also be used to shed light on the spread of linguistic features (see, for instance, Pratt and Denison 2000 for suggestions regarding the progressive passive). Especially important for the present study is the window that private letters open on gender differences in LModE syntax, as letters by women have survived in comparatively large numbers.

At the other end of the oral–literate spectrum is academic writing, a category that subsumes a large number of genres and subgenres. This category is important for two main reasons. First, it has been the site of considerable linguistic innovation during and after the LModE period:

---

[20] Like journals and diaries, letters were also written by working-class speakers, and many of those texts have been preserved and are available to us (Mugglestone 2006: 295–6). Such documents help researchers to avoid the bias in favour of Standard English in terms of the available evidence, and can also lead to new research questions (see, for instance, Auer and Laitinen 2014). Although the letters examined in this book were written primarily by well-educated speakers, I will show in Chapter 6 that the survival of an earlier, less sentence-based style of text organization in some private letters affects the results regarding the syntactic units co-ordinated by *and*.

increasing phrasal complexity has resulted in a discourse style that seems to be unprecedented in the history of English (Atkinson 1999: 143–4; Biber and Gray 2012: 315). Moreover, the heterogeneity of academic English has increasingly been recognized. As shown by Biber and Gray (2016: 157–66), academic writing displays increasing syntactic divergence over time. Some of these disciplines have become the subject of separate study, for example Moskowich and Crespo (2012) for astronomy, Moskowich et al. (2019) for history writing, and Taavitsainen and Hiltunen (2019) for medical texts. As the case studies of nominal premodifiers and participle clauses demonstrate, this diversification is clearly noticeable in my data, where Science and History exhibit different trajectories.

The third category singled out for discussion here is newspaper English. Like academic English, this is an umbrella term covering a large number of text categories with different functions and linguistic characteristics, such as editorials, reportage, and advertisements. Newspaper English is important not least because of the mutual influence between newspapers and society in the 1800s: while societal developments such as telegraph networks, rising literacy rates and incomes, and the repeal of taxes gave newspapers new opportunities to spread news and opinions to an ever-widening circle of readers, the newspaper also took up an increasingly central position in nineteenth-century society: the ideas printed in newspapers – and the issue of who had (and should have) access to those ideas – took on new significance (see Section 4.5.2). Partly in response to developments in society, the language of newspapers also changed and diversified. In addition, the narrative conventions of newspaper English influenced contemporary novelists (see Rubery 2009), which shows that conventions from one genre can spread to another. Interestingly, newspaper English is potentially subject to colloquialization as well as densification (Biber and Gray 2012: 326), as both popular appeal and economy of expression became necessary for success. But not all newspapers followed the same trajectory; as I show in Chapters 7–8, the *Poor Man's Guardian*, which had a largely working-class readership, did not participate in the change towards denser modes of expression.

Given that LModE underwent codification from the mid-eighteenth century on (see Section 3.5.2), studies that combine an examination of contemporary normative statements and descriptive analyses of syntax have provided important insights into the role of prescription in language change. Dekeyser's (1975) early study was followed by analyses such as Oldireva Gustafsson (2002) and Anderwald (2016). Research has also focussed on the normative grammars, on the usage guides themselves, and on their authors and readers (e.g. Tieken-Boon van Ostade 2011, 2014b, 2017). The extent to which LModE grammarians were descriptive or prescriptive has been discussed by several authors, for example Beal (2004: 89–123), Tieken-Boon van Ostade (2011), and Anderwald (2016: 237–45). In Chapter 5 and Section 6.3.2, I consider the development of two linguistic features that were stigmatized in normative sources, and demonstrate that proscription affected their genre distribution.

One of the key aspects of the perspective on language and language change outlined in Chapter 3 is the importance of the idiolectal level. Since the idiolect is the only place where a complete version of any language is stored, we need an idiolectal window on language variation and change that can complement the picture of a communal language such as LModE. There has been scholarly interest in individual speakers' usage for some time, as witnessed by studies like Phillipps (1970, 1978) and Clark (1975); more recent additions to this line of research include Mahlberg (2013), who combines a corpus-linguistic and an idiolectal approach, and Tieken-Boon van Ostade (2014a). However, as I argue in Chapter 4, most LModE idiolects that can be studied in this way belonged to comparatively privileged speakers, and results based on those idiolects of course cannot be generalized to LModE as a whole.

Corpora cannot provide linguists with access to more than a minuscule part of a historical language user's idiolect. In addition to the unavoidable absence of a great deal of their spoken production, most corpora cover a few genres only, and a language user is often represented in only one of those genres. In practice, comments on idiolects are thus often based on patterns in individual texts. What we can say is typically that, in comparison with other language users whose texts have been preserved for a particular genre, a given language user is conservative, advanced, or idiosyncratic in some other regard. Generalizations to their entire idiolect are frequently impossible. When I comment on idiolectal patterns in Chapters 5–9, this limitation should be borne in mind.

2.5 Discussion

Macro-level comparisons of sociocultural and linguistic change are necessarily approximations. Data on urbanization, literacy, employment, and so on can give us only a rough guide to real-life network structures (see Conde-Silvestre 2012: 335 for difficulties on the micro level in this regard). Similarly, the relative wealth of linguistic data we have access to for LModE notwithstanding, we remain far removed from actual speakers who were

2.5 Discussion

exposed – and who contributed – to the linguistic reality of England between 1700 and 1900. Nevertheless, as Milroy and Milroy (1985) have demonstrated, the overall link between weak ties and rapid language change is strong enough for a macro-level attempt at correlation to be made.

The picture that emerges raises more questions than it answers, however. On the one hand, the sociocultural developments outlined in Section 2.3 clearly indicate that the trend has been towards more weak ties between speakers. The LModE period should thus on the whole be conducive to widespread language change, compared with several previous periods in the history of the language. On the other hand, it is doubtful whether the linguistic areas investigated in Section 2.4 paint a picture of such pervasive change.

It is true that, at least in the nineteenth century, there appears to have been considerable lexical innovation; as Dossena (2012: 888) points out, sociocultural changes have considerable influence on this aspect of LModE. However, lexical innovation does not alter the structure of the language as clearly as changes in phonology or grammar. (In Section 3.3, I argue that borrowing, which accounts for most of this expansion of the lexicon, is perhaps best regarded as a special case of propagation rather than innovation and thus compatible with weak network ties.) The phonology of LModE does not seem to have gone through major restructuring along the lines of, say, the diphthongization of vowel + glide sequences in Middle English or the Great Vowel Shift. While a number of centring diphthongs – and /ɜː/ – were phonemicized, this involved little actual phonetic shift, and of course affected only speakers who became non-rhotic; no consonant phonemes developed or disappeared in the accent that turned into Received Pronunciation, although the distribution of several consonants shifted. Similarly, with the exception of a few developments in the verb phrase, there were few changes in LModE grammar that added new possible structures to the language. Even with allowance for the fact that gauging the extent of language change in this way is a very difficult and approximate operation, it seems clear that, in terms of macro-level patterns, there is less radical change in the structure of LModE than we would expect from a social-network perspective.

I refer to this apparent lack of correlation between the amount of change in the two fields examined – network ties and LModE – as the stability paradox: LModE appears to be structurally stable when it should exhibit structural change. There are three potential explanations for this discrepancy between network structure and linguistic structure:

1. The positive correlation hypothesized between weak ties and language change is in fact not warranted, either for language in general or for LModE in particular.
2. The LModE period is in fact not characterized by weak ties compared with previous periods in the history of the language.
3. LModE is in fact not characterized by relative linguistic stability compared with previous periods.

More than one of (1)–(3) may of course be true simultaneously.

As regards (1), the overall correlation between social-network structure and language change on the micro level has been attested for twentieth-century English in several studies (see, for instance, Milroy 1992a). The validity of extending these findings to macro-level connections between (i) the distribution of different types of tie and (ii) the incidence of language change is admittedly more difficult to demonstrate empirically, but it is based on extrapolation from attested instances of stability and change, and there seems to be no strong reason to assume that what holds at the micro level should not hold at the macro level as well. As regards accepting the correlation in general but suggesting that LModE should somehow be an exception to it, doing so would refute the uniformitarian principle. Unless independent evidence can show that such special allowance for LModE is warranted, I suggest that we be careful about claiming "exceptional" status for particular language states. There seems to be little reason to abandon the uniformitarian principle in this particular case; rather, we should rely on it more for LModE than for other periods, given the recency of the period studied and the wealth of data available. I am therefore going to provisionally reject (1); however, as I argue in Chapter 3, correlations hold mainly between weak ties and the propagation of changes (as opposed to linguistic innovations).

The next option is to question the connection between the sociocultural changes in England during the course of the LModE period and concomitant weakening of social ties. As I noted in Section 2.3, it is of course true that pre-industrial networks were not uniformly characterized by strong ties (see, for instance, Bergs 2005: 47–8). Similarly, the working-class ties that were forged in the urban areas of industrial England would have had to become strong after some time had passed in order to act as norm-enforcing mechanisms in Present-Day English. However, several aspects of sociocultural change during the LModE period are difficult to dispute:

the urbanization process would in itself have broken strong ties and established new ones that were – at least initially – weak; the development and growth of the middle classes would have added to the number of existent weak ties; increased contact between socio-economic groups in a more densely populated urban setting would have established weak ties along which innovations could be transmitted; and improved communication via travelling as well as sending messages – primarily letters – would have facilitated the establishment and maintenance of predominantly weak ties at a distance. Overall, then, despite likely exceptions to the general pattern, there seems to be no reason to doubt the overall effect of these events on the distribution of strong and weak ties. Option (2) thus seems unlikely.

This leaves only (3), which may seem the least likely option, to be considered. There have been numerous studies demonstrating the relative lack of structural change in LModE. The period is certainly characterized by a great deal of linguistic variation with factors such as genre, medium, and class (Görlach 1999: 71), but changes to the structural system of English do appear to have been rarer and less radical during the period 1700–1900 than before.

Nevertheless, in Chapter 3, I shall argue that option (3) is in fact the (most) correct option that can resolve the stability paradox. My argument will essentially be theoretical, though I will draw extensively on previous research. I will attempt to demonstrate that looking at the communal language as the entity that undergoes change gives us the wrong image of LModE (and, by extension, of any temporally bounded variety of a language seen as an entity). Instead, I will suggest that, from a speaker-based perspective on language change, the period 1700–1900 is indeed characterized by the kinds of widespread changes that we would expect from a time period where weak ties become more numerous.

CHAPTER 3

Aspects of Language Change

3.1 Introduction

There appears to be universal agreement among linguists that a living language – in the sense of 'a language still in vernacular use' (*OED*, s.v. *living*) – must change (see, for instance, Labov 1994: 9; Trask 2010: 1). However, as Kretzschmar (2009: 13) notes, linguistics has yet to reach the type of widespread agreement on basic ideas that characterizes many of the natural sciences; in this case, we do not have complete consensus on (i) what a *language* is and (ii) what it means that it *changes*. I will therefore devote this chapter to discussing these concepts.

The account of language and language change given in this chapter will demonstrate that several factors help to create a false impression that LModE is characterized by relative linguistic stability. At least in the area of grammar, the type of change facilitated by the weak links that characterized many LModE networks does not necessarily lead to the kind of *independent innovation* that is necessary for categorical change (in the sense of 'emergence of new features'). Instead, weak links mainly favour change through the *propagation* of existing features (typically accompanied by *propagation-dependent innovation*). Although a large number of LModE idiolects underwent change, many of those changes are invisible on the communal-language level, because they mainly involve the propagation of features that already existed in some idiolects by 1700. By combining (i) an idiolectal perspective on usage, (ii) a separation of the concept of language change into independent innovation, propagation, and propagation-dependent innovation, and (iii) a recognition that independent innovation, propagation, and propagation-dependent innovation differ in their sensitivity to social factors, I will resolve the stability paradox outlined in Chapter 2.

In this chapter, I first discuss the views of language (Section 3.2) and language change (Section 3.3) that underlie the account in this book. Section 3.4 addresses the role of linguistic and extralinguistic factors in language change. The ensuing section (3.5) compares cases of propagation from above and from below, including the relationship between prescription and actual language use. Section 3.6 summarizes my account in this chapter and briefly addresses two other issues that are relevant to the issue of language change in general.

3.2 Language: Systems and Idiolects

The notion of *language* has been characterized in different ways by scholars; for instance, Bybee (2015: 9) describes language as "an activity that involves both cognitive access (recalling words and constructions from memory) and the motor routines of production (articulation)", while Croft (2000: 26) argues that a language is "the population of utterances in a speech community". However, the most popular hyperonym for *language* is arguably neither *activity* nor *population*, but *system* (Kretzschmar 2009: 1). Labov (1994: 9) conceives of language "as the instrument of communication used by a speech community, a commonly accepted system of associations between arbitrary forms and their meanings". Labov's characterization highlights the existence of a system as well as the use of that system by a community of speakers for the purpose of communication. That double focus is an important reason why language is a difficult entity to describe. On the one hand, language as a system is used for communication *between* speakers; on the other hand, complete versions of the systems themselves exist only *within* individual speakers, in the form of idiolects.[1] (The idiolect of a native speaker who has completed the acquisition process is complete in this sense, but can still undergo change – see Section 3.6.) This relationship between system and use is related to classic distinctions such as *langue* vs. *parole*, *competence* vs. *performance*, and *I(nternal)-language* vs. *E(xternal)-language*.

A great deal of research in linguistics appears to share an underlying assumption about language that has important consequences for the definition of language change. It is often implicitly assumed that

---

[1] There is of course an immense amount of language output stored externally to speakers' idiolects, as recordings, books, corpora, etc.; however, these sources illustrate but do not constitute complete systems. Nor do descriptions of languages in dictionaries, grammars, pronunciation dictionaries, etc. count as full accounts (Kretzschmar 2009: 7), as they are typically incomplete as well as generalized compared with idiolects.

a communal language like English is an independent entity that (first-language) users share. It is recognized that, within this communal language, there is intra-speaker as well as inter-speaker variation in relative preferences for certain linguistic variants, for example *that* vs. *which* (or other options) as subject-position relative markers in restrictive clauses with inanimate antecedents; it is also possible that some speakers of English are categorical in their output and use only one of the options (for instance, *which* is very rare in this context among many American speakers). But in a historical account, the communal language English would typically be considered to "have" both *that* and *which* as relative markers in this linguistic environment if both variants are used by at least some native speakers, which also means that the structure of English as a communal language may be considered unchanged in this regard as long as both *that* and *which* are attested in language users' output. This notion of language tallies with that established by Saussure ([1916] 1986), that is, the sum total of the patterns stored in the minds of linguistically linked speakers. In Saussure's framework, linguistic structure exists outside individual speakers as a "social product" of the language faculty and as "a body of necessary conventions adopted by society to enable members of society to use their language faculty" (Saussure [1916] 1986: 9–10, quoted in Kretzschmar 2009: 42).

The crucial problem for such views concerns the location of this social product. We can only observe language use as output; the underlying systems are stored inside each individual language user. Our impression of the incidence of linguistic features in English is created by the cumulative effect of output from a large number of idiolects; in historical linguistics, this output tends to be heavily biased in favour of the male, the literate, and the wealthy, who were more likely to produce texts, and whose texts are also more likely to have survived (Kytö and Pahta 2012: 125). However, the collected output by several language users taken together is essentially the output of an abstract communal language that never existed as an independent entity, even though, as Johnstone (1996: 11) notes, it is often treated as if it had an independent existence. As mentioned above, this communal language is typically assumed to be structurally intact as long as all features – phonemes, syntagms, and so on – are still present in the cumulative output. Even though a large number of language users may have stopped using a feature (or never used it in the first place), the fact that some speakers whose output has survived used it secures its place in the communal language. In this sense, focussing on cumulative output biases our impressions of languages in the direction of sameness.

3.2 Language: Systems and Idiolects

Any named language or variety is an abstract construct and an observational artefact (Johnstone 1996: 11, 19; Mufwene 2014: 17; Kretzschmar 2015b: 34; Hickey 2020: 48) in that several users' output is considered to represent the same language even though each user's idiolect is unique. Mutual intelligibility does not require identical idiolects (Mufwene 2014: 15), and what we call one language is a little different for each speaker (Johnstone 1996: 3; see Barth and Kapatsinski 2017: 205–6 for examples of such individual differences). The rules of a communal language are constructed by analysts based on after-the-fact extrapolation and generalization (Mufwene 2008: 117; Kretzschmar 2015b: 3). Maguire et al. (2013: 230–1) make a similar distinction for phonology when they point out that phonology is a property of an individual language user and that a property of a speech community (e.g. a merger) is not necessarily shared by all its members. Language users do not command the full range of variation attested in the communal language, as their personal history constrains their repertoires (Nevalainen and Raumolin-Brunberg 2017: 19).

Since communal languages are abstract constructs projected from properties shared among idiolects, the boundaries between them are typically fuzzy (Mufwene 2008: 14). However, regular interaction between speakers and a desire to be understood and to collaborate generally result in idiolectal *convergence* (Johnstone 1996: 5; Mufwene 2014: 19);[2] idiolects become more similar as features are propagated via network links. Communication is further facilitated by the fact that most children acquire a first language based on interaction with adult speakers whose idiolects are similar to those of language users with whom the children will interact later in life. Assessments of linguistic similarity between idiolects therefore typically lead to agreement on who counts as a speaker of a named language, but there are exceptions. For example, speakers along a dialect continuum typically understand one another as long as they have acquired their idiolects in geographical proximity to each other, but this unbroken sequence of mutually intelligible idiolects is at odds with the perception that this continuum is made up of different, discrete languages that are not mutually intelligible.[3] To resolve this paradox, a framework that allows the same individual speaker to exhibit variable linguistic behaviour along what Kretzschmar (2009: 62) calls a *linguistic continuum* is needed. Mutually intelligible idiolects along a dialect continuum can then be mapped onto

---

[2] Communication can of course also result in dissociation, in which case speakers develop features that are different from those used by a group whose usage is considered undesirable (Hickey 2020: 44).
[3] Dixon (1997: 7–8), however, minimizes the problems associated with using mutual intelligibility as a criterion for sameness of language.

different communal languages – say, Portuguese and Spanish – based on factors such as linguistic evidence of similarity and difference, what language the speakers self-report as using, and what standard they aim at in formal styles (if standardization has taken place). Conversely, a Moroccan idiolect and a Jordanian idiolect may be considered to belong to the same language – Arabic – even though they are not mutually intelligible, because the speakers of those idiolects self-report as speaking Arabic (and, in this case, because they may share a diglossic "high" variety, namely Modern Standard Arabic). A similar state of affairs arguably applied to English historically. Knowles (1997: 37) suggests that "[i]n the early twentieth century, forestry workers from Gloucestershire and miners from Durham would have had enormous difficulty in understanding each other"; owing to limitations in the impact of standardization and near-universal schooling, members of such speech communities may have lacked a common standard to switch to in cases of communication breakdown (see also Croft 2000: 16 on *sibling languages* and *polytypic languages*).

As mentioned above, Croft (2000: 26) proposes a different definition of language, namely "the population of utterances in a speech community", and argues that this is "a spatiotemporally bounded set of actual individuals" (i.e. utterances). Those utterances consist of *linguemes*, such as phonemes or expressions of semantic structures, which may undergo replication, and which may have different variants. However, there are a few problems with this perspective. First, although utterances are spatio-temporally bounded entities, it is not clear how long an utterance remains part of the language; for instance, spoken utterances have a very brief existence unless they are recorded, while we still have access to written English from over 1,000 years ago. An idiolect, in contrast, is spatio-temporally bound to an individual with a definite lifespan (although an idiolect can undergo change over time). Secondly, although Croft's (2000) definition of language identifies a spatio-temporally bounded set of tokens, it is difficult to say where such a language is located; as all members of a speech community have unique idiolects, the population of utterances cannot be traced back to any one mind that could have generated all of them.[4] Both the utterance and the idiolect are vital levels of analysis in the sense that they both carry important

---

[4] Croft (2000: 26) requires that the utterances be comprehended in the community for them to belong to the same language. However, as observed by Smith (2007: 12), it is possible for speakers to adopt a feature even though they are ignorant of what its precise meaning was to the speaker(s) who used it first; moreover, knowing whether speakers comprehend an utterance presupposes knowledge of their idiolects, which makes idiolects part of the definition of language regardless.

linguistic information. Moreover, they are in a state of mutual dependence on each other: in order for an idiolect to develop, a language user must be exposed to other language users' utterances and to reactions to his/her own utterances; conversely, the language user's idiolect at any given time constrains the ways in which s/he can, and is likely to, formulate and interpret utterances. However, I argue that, although utterances are what we can actually study, the abstract construct we call English is made up of an accumulation of idiolects, not of utterances. An idiolect is not observable, but we can make careful generalizations from language users' output to their idiolects. In historical linguistics, the most important constraint on generalization is that we have very limited access to spoken output (see Kytö and Walker 2003 for a discussion of this "bad data" problem).

The individual idiolects that are considered to belong to the same communal language may differ quite radically from one another, which makes studying "the history of English" seem problematic; the English language appears to have been reduced to an abstraction that does not constitute a real entity (see Croft 2000: 2). However, this does not disqualify English – or any other language – from linguistic interest as a level of analysis. To begin with, in spite of the fact that it involves abstraction, there is a great deal of common-sense merit in retaining a label like *language* as a hyperonym for a large number of relatively similar idiolects. After all, most speakers instinctively group output as well as the idiolects of the language users who produce it into languages. As Keller (1994 [1990]: 127) puts it, "there is nothing dishonourable in being an epiphenomenon".

Moreover, many of the problems inherent in the notion of *language* are alleviated if communal languages are not regarded as homogeneous, discrete entities. In a useful analogy, Mufwene (2008: 26) likens a communal language to a viral species and idiolects to organisms classified as belonging to that species "based on family resemblance" (but cf. Lightfoot 2003 for a different position). This distinction is of some importance: just as not all organisms classified as belonging to a species have the same DNA, not all idiolects contain all features of the communal language, as mentioned above (Nevalainen and Raumolin-Brunberg 2017: 19; see also Milroy and Milroy 1985: 346–7). That circumstance does not invalidate the notion of a species – or a language – as a category. Unlike a biological organism, whose cells typically have the same DNA, however, idiolects exhibit internal variation (Mufwene 2008: 66). Both the idiolectal level and the language level – and a number of significant levels between them, for example socially based groups of speakers and externally based groups of texts (genres) – are valid objects of inquiry.

In this book, I therefore use convenient labels like *language*, *English*, and *LModE* for communal languages and language states; but the use of such a label does not imply that its referent has clear boundaries, internal homogeneity, or an independent existence. Even more importantly, it does not imply that LModE – or any other language-state – can *change* in itself. This brings us to the notion of language change, which also needs to be discussed from an idiolectal perspective.

3.3 Language Change: Innovation and Propagation

If a language is an abstract construct, as argued in Section 3.2, change in a language is also necessarily an abstraction from the events that are actually taking place. As Croft (2000: 4) puts it, "[l]anguages don't change; people change language through their actions" (see also Fischer 2016: 238–9). Similarly, Milroy and Milroy (1985: 345) argue that "it is not languages that innovate; it is speakers who innovate" and that "[t]he reflexes of speaker-innovations are then observed in language states".

A statement to the effect that a language has changed is typically based on cumulative evidence from output, which in turn is assumed to be indicative of language users' idiolects. Mufwene (2008: 181) argues that histories of languages "have disregarded I-languages (or idiolects), although the immediate causes of changes that cumulate to produce evolution (at the communal level) lie nowhere but in the communicative acts of individual speakers" (see also Joseph 1992: 127). Nevalainen et al. (2020a: 4–5) summarize the three perspectives that have characterized analyses of the rate of change in languages: comparing stages of the language as a whole (e.g. Old vs. Middle vs. Early Modern English); comparing different structural levels (e.g. word order vs. morphology); and comparing different stages in the trajectory of an individual change. All of these perspectives implicitly take the abstraction that is the communal language as the object of investigation.

The concept of the individual language user's idiolect as central to language change is of course not new; for instance, as McMahon (1994: 226) notes, idiolects were important to Paul's ([1891] 1978) views on sound change. What I am trying to add to this perspective is a set of theoretical and methodological principles for how to reconcile an idiolectal view of language change with social-network theory and the corpus-based study of grammar.

3.3 Language Change: Innovation and Propagation

A speaker's idiolect is taken to include knowledge of what is *possible* as well as what is *probable*. Our ability to use (often subconscious) probabilistic thinking about our idiolects allows us to use variable proportions of linguistic features under different linguistic and extralinguistic conditions (see Kroch 1989: 202), in line with what Trudgill (2000: 34–5) calls "inherent variability" in speakers' output. However, in language change from below, the choices speakers make are largely subconscious (Labov 2001: 409–10).

The fact that language change is an abstraction from actual changes in idiolects also helps to explain why it cannot be predicted (on predicting language change, see also Keller 1994 [1990]: 70–1; Lightfoot 2003: 120; Kretzschmar 2009: 179; Kretzschmar 2015b: 1; Mathieu and Truswell 2017: 5; Willis 2017: 493). To begin with, we do not have enough information on idiolectal change to disregard the possibility that at least some changes might be random. Moreover, we would need information on what linguistic and extralinguistic (psychological, sociological, etc.) factors constrain each individual idiolect in order to construct a predictive model, since the variation that underlies change can only be fully explained at the idiolectal level (Johnstone 1996: 8; see Croft 2000: 2–3 for a discussion of whether change could be predicted even in such a best-case scenario).[5] Without the ability to directly observe idiolects and the factors that influence them, we can at best make probabilistic assessments about what types of change are more or less likely (which is nevertheless worth doing).

Moreover, if we look at the language as the unit that undergoes change, there is a risk that change will go unnoticed. Croft (2000: 3) notes that processes of change can be categorized as *inherent change*, where "a single object that exists over time" undergoes change, or as *replication*, where a new entity is created that preserves most, but not all, of the structure of a parent entity. A language has often been treated by linguists as a real entity undergoing inherent change. In reality, however, the entities that undergo change exist at the idiolect and utterance levels, and neither of those levels is necessarily captured in analyses that group several language users' output together. (To take an extreme example, as long as changes cancel one

---

[5] This model would also have to include such information on each speaker whose idiolect does not change in order to fully address the actuation problem, that is, why a change occurs – or does not occur – at a given time and place (Labov 2001: 466; see also Milroy and Milroy 1985: 342 and Mufwene 2008: 22); as Milroy (1997: 313–14) notes, a theory of language change must account for change as well as lack thereof. In the present framework, the actuation problem could be expressed in terms of why a change takes place in one idiolect at a particular time, but not in other idiolects at the same time or in the same idiolect at a different time.

another out in the group of speakers investigated, each individual speaker in the group may in theory change their idiolect without those changes having any impact on the cumulative output.)

There are specific characteristics of LModE that make this variety especially likely to display stability in this regard. I will return to this issue when I discuss propagation from above and below in Section 3.5, but one such characteristic is of more general significance and should be mentioned here: the data set that we have access to. While this data set is rich compared with previous periods, much of it consists of written output that has been affected in one way or another by standardization (see Section 3.5.2). Standard varieties may promote other variants compared with those favoured in most idiolects and styles, for example *whom* rather than *who* as an object pronoun (Kretzschmar 2015b: 102). The features promoted in the standard variety are often conservative; they may also be disfavoured in many other varieties owing to, among other things, clashes between overt and covert prestige. The overall impression researchers get from output affected by standardization is then one of greater stability than what is actually the case, as features that may otherwise have disappeared from the language may be retained in the standard variety, which predominates in the available data set. LModE is in fact at the point where stability is most likely to be claimed for the language on this basis: much of the period 1700–1900 falls between (i) the selection of a standard for educated written usage and (ii) the use of recording technologies to preserve informal spoken usage.

There are two ways in which an idiolect can undergo change. First, a speaker may use a new linguistic feature without having been exposed to that feature in linguistic output before. Following Croft (2000), I refer to this phenomenon as *innovation*. A wide definition of what may count as a new linguistic feature is intended: this may be a wholly new feature, different functions, senses, or realizations of existing features, or the absence of a feature that would previously have been used by the speaker in a given context. As Mufwene (2008: 178) notes, a great deal of linguistic "recycling" takes place as features that are already available in idiolects are used in novel ways; see also Lass (1997: 316–24) on exaptation. In addition, I take the use of a linguistic feature with a higher or lower frequency than previously to indicate language change; indeed, many of the changes studied in Chapters 5–8 involve frequency changes. It is arguable that shifts in frequency do not constitute changes in themselves, but are rather results of changes in the meanings, functions, contexts of use, etc. of the feature (cf. Croft 2000: 57). It may also be difficult to pinpoint at what point a speaker begins to use a feature with a different frequency, and people exposed to, say, a higher frequency of a feature in output may interpret it as a qualitative extension to new contexts (as a type of *propagation-dependent innovation*, which is discussed below). Nevertheless, frequency changes are at least manifestations of language change.

At this level of analysis, the individual language user's linguistic history is what determines whether a change comprises innovation: if the user has not been exposed to output containing the change before they produce such output themselves, innovation has taken place. It is highly likely that the same change will be introduced by a large number of language users independently of one another within a short period of time, as similar factors are likely to act simultaneously on many idiolects (Bergs 2005: 37–8); all such language users are innovators. The entrenchment of one usage in a large number of idiolects may facilitate the development of another, analogical, and/or similar usage, so that usage 1 becoming conventional enables or facilitates usage 2, an extension of usage 1 (De Smet 2016: 99–100). For instance, the establishment of the progressive passive may have facilitated the emergence of the progressive of BE, as both constructions contain the sequence BE *being*.[6] If those constructions were indeed linked, the fact that a great many idiolects had incorporated the progressive passive meant that a large number of language users had also become likely to innovate the progressive of BE independently of one another.

Most innovations die out and are not successful (Milroy 1997: 313; Mufwene 2008: 15, 66), because "deviation from convention" is typically avoided (De Smet 2016: 86), and because pressure to achieve successful communication causes convergence to be favoured (Mufwene 2014: 18). The concept of *success* here is complex. The immediate criterion for success is to be understood, but interlocutors also wish to satisfy, for instance, their material and face needs, and language use is an instrument in this regard (Nevalainen and Raumolin-Brunberg 2017: 240). This function of language puts pressure on language users to speak in such a way that they are not only understood, but also approved of, by their interlocutors.

The second way in which an idiolect can change is through *propagation*.[7] Linguistic output is the medium through which changes spread between

---

[6] The development of these constructions is a much-discussed topic, and other factors may have been at work here (see, for instance, Warner 1997; Denison 1998: 150–8; Pratt and Denison 2000). The argument for surface similarity is based on the progressive passive being attested a few decades before the progressive of BE.

[7] I use *propagation* rather than the alternative term *diffusion* for the transfer of a linguistic feature from one idiolect to another, as diffusion is sometimes understood as the importation of features from

idiolects through propagation; the idiolects themselves are not in contact. Let us assume that feature X is part of some idiolects in a speech community but is not present in idiolect P. The speaker with idiolect P can of course innovate feature X independently, but that speaker is more likely to incorporate it into their idiolect through propagation: the speaker with idiolect P is exposed to output containing feature X and may then – consciously or, more typically, subconsciously – adapt to that output by incorporating feature X into idiolect P. The propagation of feature X becomes noticeable when idiolect P is subsequently manifested in output containing feature X. (As I discuss below, feature X may also be subject to propagation-dependent innovation in this process.)

Not all linguists agree that both innovation and propagation constitute language change (Croft 2000: 5); for instance, Milroy (1992b: 79, emphasis original) argues that "a change is not a change until it has been adopted by *more than one* speaker", that is, change requires propagation. In addition, there seems to be disagreement on how much propagation is required for language change to be said to have occurred. Milroy and Milroy (1985: 347) suggest that we tend not to label innovations as changes until they have undergone propagation both to and beyond a community; Raumolin-Brunberg and Nurmi (2011: 252) suggest that an innovation must have been incorporated by a group of people to be considered language change; and Traugott and Trousdale (2013: 2) argue that innovation is only "potential for change" and that "[f]or an innovation to count as a change, it must have been replicated across populations of speakers resulting in conventionalization, the integration of the innovation in a tradition of speaking or writing, as evidenced by textual materials left to us". Smith (2007: 11), in contrast, argues that change occurs when an innovation is propagated to just one more speaker (see also Nevalainen and Raumolin-Brunberg 2017: 2). If the idiolect is taken as the basis for language and the true locus of language change, Smith's perspective makes more sense: one language user's idiolect is not affected by whether or not a feature that the user has adopted is also adopted into other idiolects. (Whether or not the feature also spreads into other idiolects may affect its fate in an individual idiolect through social pressure to continue or stop using it, but that pressure is external to the idiolect itself.) Moreover, it is difficult to decide how many idiolects, communities, genres, or linguistic contexts must have been affected by

---

other systems, as opposed to *transmission*, which is reserved for parent-to-child transfer of language (see, for instance, Nevalainen and Raumolin-Brunberg 2017: 230).

a linguistic innovation before we can say that the language itself has changed (see Nevalainen and Raumolin-Brunberg 2017: 56).

However, if change in one idiolect through propagation is regarded as language change, innovation should also be counted as change: the innovator's idiolect must have changed for them to be able to produce an utterance containing the innovation. Croft (2000: 5) also argues that both innovation and propagation constitute language change. In addition, there is a practical argument for regarding both innovation and propagation as change: it is impossible to say with certainty whether a change in an idiolect constitutes innovation or propagation, as we can never know whether the new feature had been produced before by someone to whose output the relevant speaker had been exposed (see Milroy and Milroy 1985: 348).

Accepting that the true locus of language change is the idiolect makes it possible to refine the definition of change in the communal language. Communal-language change is an abstraction based on a cumulation of instances of the same change – or very similar changes – which affect idiolects regarded as belonging to the same communal language (cf. Mufwene 2008: 59). As only speaker output can be observed, it is typically assumed that quantitative or qualitative changes in cumulative output are indicative of changes in idiolects – and, conversely, that stability in the cumulative output indicates idiolectal stability. However, especially in historical linguistics, the cumulative output is not always a faithful reflection of developments that took place in idiolects – which are the units undergoing true change.

As mentioned in Chapters 1 and 2, LModE has often been argued to feature less structural change than previous periods. Change that is considered structural is typically categorical; for instance, speakers may replace feature X (say, THOU pronouns) entirely with feature Y (say, YOU pronouns). In this case, histories of English often claim that YOU pronouns have categorically replaced THOU pronouns in the second-person singular, which has led to a loss of number distinctions in English second-person pronouns (except for the reflexive paradigm). Such an analysis ignores varieties and genres where the distinction is maintained, either through conservatism (THOU forms being preserved) or through innovation (alternative plural forms such as *y'all*, *youse*, and *you guys* being used in contrast with singular *you*). Features that are generally regarded as non-standard are more likely to be ignored in this way, as histories of English tend to focus on the development of what became the standard variety.

However, at the true locus of change, that is, an individual language user's idiolect, all that is required for change to have taken place is that the idiolect is different from its previous state owing to innovation and/or propagation. It is irrelevant whether or not the same change leads to structural changes in the communal language to which the idiolect belongs. Moreover, since social networks crucially involve individual language users, and since each individual language user has their own idiolect, language change of the type that is sensitive to speakers' social networks can really be measured only in terms of the number of idiolects that have changed. Given the incomplete nature of the evidence we have at our disposal, such measurements are approximate at best. Language change on the communal level is thus in itself a fuzzy category.

From the perspective of innovation vs. propagation, LModE clearly features a large amount of propagation, which becomes visible to us to the extent that such changes reached communities whose output has been preserved. Some features become more or less frequent in various idiolects and speech communities without any feature disappearing from the communal language. Some changes affect most idiolects, for example the increase in the frequency and uses of the progressive (see Section 2.4.3). In other cases, the result is rather increased differentiation among idiolects, for example the division between rhotic and non-rhotic speakers in Britain. Propagation may also lead to increased variability within idiolects, as certain features come to be associated with particular linguistic or extralinguistic contexts of use; this is the mechanism behind the increased genre differentiation in LModE discussed in Biber and Finegan (1997), which is an important characteristic of LModE; as Görlach (2004: 100) notes, we cannot fully explain the development of English without considering the genre parameter. Several of the case studies reported on in Chapters 5–8 involve features that become increasingly characteristic of particular written genres. These types of propagation may of course co-occur.

Processes of propagation can account for many changes in phonology and grammar that have been attested in LModE. Most changes also involve some measure of innovation while propagation is going on (see below). But what we do not see much evidence of is the appearance of categorical change through innovation. The result gives the impression of relative stability on the communal-language level, despite the large number of idiolects that have undergone change – a number that is the truest measure of the type of language change that correlates with network ties.

LModE lexis, though, seems to exhibit different behaviour in this regard. Although the radical growth of the English vocabulary during part of the LModE period may not constitute structural change, the available evidence indicates that large-scale lexical innovation took place. However, a large number of new lexemes in LModE are borrowings from other languages (see Section 2.4.1). The status of such loanwords as innovations is doubtful, since lexical borrowing presupposes some degree of bilingualism. A speaker who begins to use, say, a French word in English is not an innovator, but rather the locus of a special type of propagation, in which a lexeme that exists in their French idiolect is adopted into their English idiolect, typically with some adaptation to the morphophonology of the target language. (The same applies in principle to cases where there are no native speakers of the donor language, e.g. loans from Classical Greek and Latin in LModE.) This perspective drastically reduces the amount of lexical innovation in LModE. In addition, lexical change is difficult to assess regarding the number of idiolects affected. It is typically assumed that a word is part of English vocabulary when it has been attested in one or several texts produced in English, but as discussed in Section 2.4.1, many new lexemes that were used in some speech communities most likely never reached the majority of idiolects, which means that counting every attestation of a new lexeme as a change overestimates the change on the idiolectal level.

Propagation is involved in all the syntactic changes examined in Chapters 5–8. Language users were exposed to uses of a linguistic feature that were not at the time part of their idiolects, in terms of, for instance, the incidence of the feature in particular genres, and adopted those uses. When a sufficient number of idiolects had changed to incorporate these uses, the results are visible as changes in the genre norms of the communal language. Propagation leads to colloquialization (see Section 4.3.1) if the change in the communal language results in a feature that is characteristic of informal speech increasing in frequency in some but not all written genres; for instance, *not*-contraction (e.g. *They can't sing*; see Chapter 5) was part of a great many language users' idiolects, but with stylistic constraints that appear to have changed across the 1800s. In the case of densification (see Section 4.3.2), features that encode phrasal complexity (e.g. nominal premodifiers; see Chapter 7) instead become more characteristic of output belonging to certain genres with a high informational load.

Innovation that consists in categorical change does occur in LModE; oft-cited cases include the progressive passive and the GET-passive. There are also some features that die out or survive only in restricted contexts, for example BE as a perfect auxiliary and the passival construction in *The house is building* (see Section 2.4.3). Moreover, we typically know only about innovations that were successful in the sense that they underwent propagation to other idiolects; a large number of unsuccessful innovations are likely to have appeared but died out before they showed up in texts that have survived and been studied by linguists. But if we tentatively relate the amount of successful (structural) innovation to that of propagation, LModE may well feature a low innovation-to-propagation ratio compared with other periods in the history of English. In Sections 3.5–3.6, I will discuss some reasons for this possible state of affairs.

So far in this chapter, innovation and propagation have been treated as discrete processes. However, the two are not so easily separated in practice. First, what looks like innovation may in fact be propagation. As discussed above, the introduction of a loanword is in fact a result of intra-speaker propagation between two idiolects belonging to the same speaker. This type of propagation is not limited to lexis. In so-called *linguistic areas*, several languages may come to share the same linguistic feature owing to propagation between bilingual individuals, for example the development of a postposed definite article in several languages in the Balkans (Chambers and Trudgill 1998: 168–70). The feature that undergoes this type of propagation is typically adapted to the structure of the recipient idiolect, which means that innovation and propagation become entangled: the (partly) bilingual speaker is likely to change the feature – and thus innovate in the recipient idiolect – in the process of propagation (see Section 3.6 for further discussion). We therefore need to distinguish *independent innovation*, which is what I have mainly discussed above, from *propagation-dependent innovation*, which takes place during the process of propagation.

Propagation-dependent innovation is not restricted to cases where the donor and recipient idiolects are considered to belong to different languages. Smith (2007: 18–21) notes that sound change may happen because speakers overshoot or undershoot the target (Smith's terms are *hyperadaptation* and *hypoadaptation*) as they attempt to adopt a new phonological system, and suggests that this phenomenon may provide a partial explanation for the Great Vowel Shift (Smith 2007: 132–4). Similar effects are possible in syntax, where several types of language change involve one type or another of *reanalysis*.[8] Many studies of language change point to a stage

---

[8] The status of reanalysis as a process has been the topic of some discussion in recent years. While De Smet (2009) questions whether the concept of reanalysis is needed as a type of change, Traugott and Trousdale (2010: 38–9) claim that reanalysis is the dominant mechanism compared with analogy. In later work, for example Traugott and Trousdale (2013: 21), the term *neoanalysis* is sometimes preferred.

3.3 Language Change: Innovation and Propagation

where output is ambiguous such that a linguistic feature can be seen as having two different functions: the established function A and a new function B. For instance, BE *going to* + [infinitive] as an expression of future (function B) is often assumed to have developed from a construction where BE *going* expressed motion and *to* + [infinitive] purpose (function A).[9] Speaker Y, who is exposed to the ambiguous output by speaker X, may interpret the feature as expressing function B and adopt it as such. In speaker Y's own output, the use of the feature may then be extended to contexts that are compatible only with function B. Here too the line between innovation and propagation is blurred, because we cannot know whether speaker X intended the feature to have function A or function B in the ambiguous output. If the new function B was intended, it is propagated to speaker Y (who merely begins to use it in unambiguous contexts). But if speaker X intended for the feature to have the old function A and merely used it in a context that also allowed an interpretation in terms of the new function B, speaker Y is in fact innovating when using it unambiguously with function B – even though speaker Y is unaware of this innovation. Because idiolects are never themselves in direct contact, the transmission of features between idiolects consists in learning through inference, which may cause interpretation errors (Mufwene 2014: 20). Traugott and Trousdale (2013: 51–3) argue that speakers exposed to a feature attempt to match it with nodes in their idiolects; however, this matching may be different from that of the speaker who used the feature, and there may be no direct match available. Speakers and hearers may thus process the same utterance differently. Mufwene (2008: 2) even suggests that imperfect replication is the default way of copying linguistic structure, partly because speakers are under pressure to communicate and cannot wait until they have gathered sufficient output data on the idiolect that contains the new feature. Most processes of propagation thus involve some measure of innovation as well.

Although innovation and propagation may be difficult to distinguish in practice, they are separate in principle. The distinction between them becomes blurred chiefly because we have access only to linguistic output, not to idiolects, and because linguistic output – unlike, for instance, DNA – is frequently open to different interpretations. Nevertheless, as will become clear in Section 3.4, the difference between innovation and

---

[9] It is likely that reanalysis typically happens in smaller steps (see, for instance, Westergaard 2017 for "micro-cues"); the simplified example here is intended for illustration purposes.

propagation is important because of how these processes of change are conditioned.

3.4 The Role of Linguistic and Extralinguistic Factors in Innovation and Propagation

Most linguists would probably agree that language use and language change are constrained both by factors internal to the language itself (henceforth *linguistic factors*) and by factors external to the language (henceforth *extralinguistic factors*).[10] In contrast, opinions differ regarding the relative weight that should be given to each group of factors. Nor do scholars necessarily agree on what counts as linguistic and extralinguistic; as Willis (2017: 492) notes, calling a change *endogenous* or *exogenous* raises "the question 'endogenous or exogenous to what?' Possible answers include 'to the language', 'to the dialect', 'to the speech community', 'to the linguistic system', 'to syntax' and 'to the individual'." In the present work, I will use the label *linguistic* for factors that are internal to the speaker's idiolect (including any language-universal tendencies that are valid for all idiolects), while *extralinguistic* will be used for other factors.

The distinction between innovation and propagation made in Section 3.3 may shed light on the distinction between these two types of factor. Croft (2000: 8) makes a near-categorical distinction in this respect: functional factors are responsible for innovation, which involves form–function mapping, while propagation takes place via a selection mechanism that is social in nature. Croft's use of *functional* and *social* appears to have close affinities with *linguistic* and *extralinguistic* as used in this work.

It seems intuitively reasonable to assume that independent innovation is not typically caused by extralinguistic factors. Since independent innovation is by definition nonconformist – a speaker is producing something that they have never been exposed to in output – a desire to identify with others would be unlikely to lead to independent innovation.[11] Extralinguistic factors may of course play a role at the independent-innovation stage if speakers consciously or subconsciously innovate owing to a desire to distance themselves from other speakers, but that would account for only a small minority of changes. However,

---

[10] In accepting that linguistic factors play a role in change, I am not arguing that language change makes the language "better" as such (cf. Milroy 1997: 321 on perfectly adapted languages).

[11] Terms like *desire* should be taken to apply subconsciously here; as Mufwene (2008: 2) points out, speakers do not typically plan to change idiolects – their own or other speakers' – through innovations (except presumably in cases of change from above).

Fischer (2016: 242) argues that innovation in phonology and lexis is more likely to be socially motivated than innovation in grammar, as morphosyntax is more dependent on multi-speaker innovation and on analogy. These three areas of language should thus perhaps be considered separately.

It is likely that lexis differs from phonology and grammar, owing to the relative prevalence of conscious, independent, lexical innovation, for example the introduction of new terms for recently discovered phenomena and avoidance of offensive language. The reason that these types of independent innovation can be extralinguistically motivated is thus that they often constitute change from above the level of social awareness. As regards phonology and grammar, the question arises whether it really is independent innovation that is extralinguistically motivated. It is impossible to be certain without access to the innovation stage, but my assumption is that, in change from below, independent innovation does not take place for extralinguistic reasons; rather, independent innovations that happen to make speakers' idiolects more similar to idiolects that they wish to emulate are more likely to be propagated – for extralinguistic reasons. (Owing to imperfect replication, such propagation may also involve unintentional, propagation-dependent innovation.)

If we accept that most independent innovation in phonology and grammar is unlikely to be governed by extralinguistic factors, there are three options: independent innovation may be random, it may be caused by linguistic factors, or it may be due to a combination of the two. Random independent innovation would provide an appealing analogy with genetic mutation. However, certain types of linguistic change show that intralinguistic factors are likely to play a part in innovation. Focussing on grammar, De Smet (2016: 86) argues that though innovation is intrinsically unlikely, the probability of innovative use increases when this use deviates minimally from convention and there are well-established, analogically related conventional expressions in the speaker's mental retrieval. The speaker's current idiolect thus constrains their potential for innovation. How strict these constraints are is a matter of some debate among linguists. Mufwene (2014: 22) argues that speakers are constrained by their current idiolect as well as "their cognitive capacity", and Milroy and Milroy (1985: 381) claim that linguistic constraints "sharply limit the class of possible innovations". In contrast, Bergs (2005: 44) argues that no type of change is impossible, though some are very unlikely. This position tallies with the occurrence of counter-examples to several types of change that have been hypothesized to be unidirectional; as Traugott (2003: 124) puts it, "no change is likely to be exceptionless. Unidirectionality is a strong tendency manifested by particular sets of changes." A combination of linguistic and random – or at least unidentified – factors may be the most likely cause of innovation.

As regards the propagation stage, Croft (2000: 39) argues that this phase, which is equivalent to evolutionary selection, "is governed largely if not exclusively by social forces". However, there are good grounds for considering linguistic factors as potentially involved in this area as well.[12] To begin with, if linguistic factors were involved only in innovation, and their influence was not absolute, we might expect to see more counter-examples to grammaticalization and related changes. Linguistically unlikely innovations that do occur could be selected by language users for social reasons, leading to less clear tendencies in language change than we actually find. Secondly, if linguistic factors are connected with language users' idiolects, they would be expected to be involved in propagation as well as innovation, because the recipient's idiolect takes part in propagation: the recipient has to adopt the innovation for propagation to take place.[13] This adoption may be partial only, owing to imperfect replication, in which case the recipient both propagates and innovates (see Section 3.3). But since the recipient has to incorporate (part of) the innovation into their idiolect, it makes sense that the current make-up of that idiolect will also affect the likelihood of incorporation. Denison (2003: 58) points out that propagation would not take place unless there was some social or functional advantage to the new form (see also Keller 1994 [1990]: 118 on costs and benefits). Thus features that are "a good fit" for the hearer's idiolect arguably stand a better chance of being adopted. If a feature that is a candidate for propagation into an idiolect converges on or reinforces a feature that already exists in that idiolect, the likelihood of propagation increases, while non-convergent features have smaller chances of success (Mufwene 2008: 173; De Smet 2016: 86).

In addition, speech communities that feature regular interaction are likely to consist of speakers with similar idiolects, owing to convergence (Mufwene 2008: 15; Kretzschmar 2015a: 253) and the process by which we acquire our native language(s). This would in turn lead to inter-idiolectal similarities in the types of innovation and propagation that occur in the community: a feature that is "a good fit" for the community linguistically would be more likely to be independently innovated as well as propagated.

---

[12] I am grateful to Sarah Schwarz for drawing my attention to this possibility.
[13] This example sketches a scenario where a recipient adopts a feature that has just been innovated, but the mechanism would be the same if, for instance, the feature had been innovated some time ago and was being propagated through a new community.

3.4 Linguistic and Extralinguistic Factors

A language user who lacks the feature in question would undergo repeated exposure to it, which increases the social advantage of undergoing propagation and adopting it. Propagation-dependent innovation is also likely to occur; for instance, language users who are exposed to *not*-contractions (see Chapter 5) in a written genre where they have not encountered them before may attempt to imitate this usage in their own idiolects. When they do so, they may produce *not*-contracted forms that occur in a wider range of linguistic contexts than those in which they occurred in the target output. Speech sounds are likely to be affected by such processes before grammatical structures, as more minute variation is possible in phonetics than in grammar, and as sounds are more frequent than grammatical structures and may thus more easily become targets of accommodation (Hickey 2020: 43–4). But the general mechanism seems applicable to change in grammar as well. This type of propagation-dependent innovation may involve both linguistic and extralinguistic causes: as in all innovation, language users are to some extent constrained by their present idiolect; but they are also more likely to "overshoot the mark" in propagation-dependent innovation if they have strong social reasons to accommodate to the language user(s) with the idiolect(s) whose feature is being adopted.

However, conformity with the hearer's idiolect is not a requirement in propagation. A speaker's main goal may well be to achieve success in communicative situations (see Keller 1994 [1990]: 143), and "a successful innovation needs to be evaluated positively, either overtly or covertly" (Milroy and Milroy 1985: 368); social factors may thus override linguistic factors. Inertia and ability to communicate with speakers who have not gone through the change are also likely to exert influence on speaker choice (Denison 2003: 58), so a new feature would most likely need to confer social advantages on the speaker in order to be propagated.

To sum up, the present state of our knowledge does not allow us to state with any degree of certainty how large a part linguistic and extralinguistic factors play in propagation (see Blythe and Croft 2012: 273) and in propagation-dependent innovation, though it seems likely that a combination of the two is involved. However, the main argument I wish to make for the purposes of the present study is that extralinguistic factors are unlikely to play a part in independent innovation in grammar (and, probably, phonology).

This view makes it possible to refine our picture of language change in LModE. We should not necessarily expect sociocultural change to co-occur with categorical, or structural, change in grammar (unless such changes are due to propagation from other languages or varieties – see Section 3.6); such change is predominantly due to independent innovation, which is not extralinguistically motivated. Changes in grammar through propagation and propagation-dependent innovation, in contrast, should multiply during periods of social upheaval that leads to the disruption of strong social networks and the formation of weak ones (see Section 2.3): changes in contexts of occurrence, functions, stylistic associations, and so on can all be expected to be frequent and to co-occur with frequency changes. This description appears to fit LModE well. There is clearly widespread propagation of changes among idiolects. In addition, propagation-dependent innovation occurs owing to imperfect replication in speaker contact. But neither propagation nor propagation-dependent innovation necessarily brings about the type of structural or categorical change whose rarity in LModE has been pointed out by scholars.

3.5 Propagation in Change from Above and in Change from Below

Labov (2001: 274, 279) makes an important distinction between change from above, which takes place at a high level of social consciousness, and change from below, in which idiolects are undergoing change below that level. In this section, I briefly consider one example each of these important types of language change in LModE, both of which predominantly involve propagation and contribute to the impression that there is little categorical change in the period: the development of urban dialects (3.5.1), which mainly comprises change from below, and standardization (3.5.2), which involves a great deal of change from above. These changes also mainly involve the propagation of existing features together with propagation-dependent innovation (for instance, hypercorrection by middle-class speakers aiming at standard usage). Language users affected by these changes were socially and/or geographically mobile and bound together by comparatively weak ties during the time when their idiolects went through the changes, which made comparatively rapid change possible despite social and geographical distance in some cases (Milroy and Milroy 1985: 370; see Sections 2.2–2.3).

3.5.1 Propagation from Below: Urban Dialects

An indirect result of the large-scale urbanization that took place in England in the LModE period (see Section 2.3.1) was that the distribution of dialects changed dramatically. England before the Industrial Revolution was dialectally diversified to a high degree; for instance, Joyce (1991: 156) reports that at least twenty different dialects were in use in Lancashire, many of them associated with individual towns. As large numbers of speakers relocated to industrial centres and the metropolis, there was a great deal of concern that rural dialects were going to die out and that they needed to be recorded and catalogued before they disappeared (Beal 2010a: 2–3). Dixon (1997: 104) also argues that developments in transport and media after 1830 began to narrow the dialectal diversity of languages. The English Dialect Society, founded in 1873, and other scholarly efforts thus focussed on traditional rural dialects. However, at the same time, new, urban dialects emerged, and while these varieties did not attract the same interest among contemporary dialectologists, they represent one of the most important results of idiolectal change in LModE.

As the urbanization of the workforce between 1700 and 1900 was mainly regionally based (see Section 2.3.1), many of the new inhabitants in industrial centres had idiolects associated with related but distinct regional dialects. In such contexts, *levelling* typically takes place, whereby linguistic features that are more localized and/or less widespread than others tend not to be selected for inclusion in the emerging urban variety (Beal 2010a: 73). This process is an instantiation of the general tendency for communication between speakers to trigger mutual accommodation that causes idiolectal convergence (see Mufwene 2008: 15–16; in the case of urban varieties, the relevant changes frequently consisted in the non-use of a feature associated with one or several rural varieties in the surrounding area). The spread of urban varieties was facilitated by the network structure of the urban centres: network ties established between speakers who had recently relocated were (at least initially) weak compared with those previously forged in the countryside.

The typical result of these developments was a hybrid variety, as speakers selected features from the available feature pool and incorporated them – with some modification owing to propagation-dependent innovation – into their own idiolects (cf. Mufwene 2008: 117). Each idiolect was also a hybrid resulting from piecemeal acquisition, but the end result was widespread convergence on a number of features that together characterized the new urban variety, which contained a mixture of features from surrounding dialects (Joyce 1991: 156) but was linguistically different from all input varieties (Hickey 2003: 214). As a result, present-day urban varieties in England are recognized as distinct from the varieties used in surrounding areas, which would not have been the case before 1800, with the exception of Cockney (Beal 2010a: 6). However, post-levelling features of the new urban variety may subsequently spread to smaller nearby urban centres, villages, and finally the countryside (Beal 2010a: 78).

There are a number of reasons why the emergence of urban dialects has not traditionally received widespread attention in studies of change in LModE. To begin with, they disrupted what was regarded as a clear "line of descent" from the regional dialects of Middle English to the rural dialects of LModE (Beal 2010a: 6), which meant that they were of less interest to early dialectologists. Nor did they typically fit neatly into accounts of the development of Received Pronunciation during this time (see Section 2.4.2). In terms of grammar, output from LModE urban varieties is comparatively rare in corpora, which limits the amount of scholarly attention paid to them in corpus studies.

Moreover, to some extent the new urban dialects were also "negatively defined" in that, compared with the varieties used in the surrounding countryside, their most salient characteristic may have been what features of those rural varieties did *not* become part of the urban variety. As a rule, levelling does not bring about the appearance of new linguistic features. This circumstance may have contributed to a sense that the new urban varieties were in fact nothing new. Although propagation-dependent innovation most likely occurred, the impression at the communal level is that little or no categorical change was involved: even the linguistic features from neighbouring rural varieties that died out in the urban variety still lived on in the communal language, provided that the rural varieties themselves continued to exist. Although the formation of LModE urban varieties involved changes to a very large number of idiolects, these developments have not significantly altered the image of LModE as a period of stability in the history of English. The magnitude of the change is severely downplayed in relation to the number of idiolects that underwent change.

3.5.2 *Propagation from Above: Standardization*

Although it is not easy to define a standard, a standard language is typically "a linguistic norm which a very large speech community overtly adheres to" (Smakman and Nekesa Barasa 2017: 23). Increasing adherence to such a shared norm has far-reaching consequences for the study of LModE.

By 1700, educated London English had, to a large extent, been selected as the variety that would form the basis for the standard (Beal 2010b: 22; Hickey 2010c: 15), but this variety had not yet been extensively codified, with the exception of printed orthography, where widespread uniformity had been reached (Auer 2012: 942). This lack of codification led to concern

3.5 Propagation in Change from Above and Below

about the neglect and decay of the language, which in turn was linked to "other forms of degeneration" (Auer 2012: 941). The Acts of Union 1707, which united England and Scotland, also contributed to the formation of an ideal of a single, stable form of English (Hickey 2010c: 9). The suppression of regional variation thus became an important goal (Hickey 2010c: 13; Beal 2010b: 32). While no English Academy was established to maintain the language, the eighteenth century, and especially its second half, is characterized by codification (Joyce 1991: 158; Auer 2012: 940–1), as evidenced by the publication of influential works such as Johnson (1755), Lowth (1762), and Walker (1791). This development was facilitated by what Lewis (2012: 902) refers to as "[t]he increased accessibility of print, and the generalization of the print culture". By 1800, a written variety of English had been established which was "associated with the political, commercial, and academic centre of London" and "clearly distinct from colloquial or ordinary language usage" (Auer 2012: 941). While the main reason for proscribing pronunciation before 1750 had been deviation from the written word (Beal 2010b: 23), comments became increasingly judgemental in the second half of the century, when attempts at standardization were made (Auer 2012: 944), and a prestigious accent acquired social value and came to be "a prerequisite for social advancement" (Hickey 2010c: 15–16). Orality in writing was also increasingly disparaged among social aspirers during this time (Lewis 2012: 902).

The normative trend continued into the nineteenth century. Bailey (1996: 215) argues that "[a]ttitudes toward grammar ... hardened into ideology"; Beal (2004: 116) notes the correlation between the emergence of the linguistically insecure lower middle class, whose members "needed accessible guides to help them avoid social embarrassment", and the popularity of usage guides addressing grammar, word usage, and pronunciation. Print culture continued to spread to new sections of society, aided by technological advances in printing as well as tax cuts on newspapers and paper (see Section 4.5.2). The introduction of universal education with the Elementary Education Act 1870 helped to promulgate the perceived superiority of written Standard English, since regional linguistic features were discouraged by schoolteachers (Beal 2010a: 3). The emergence of Received Pronunciation as an elite accent in the nineteenth century (Beal 2010b: 21) further increased the social consequences of using a particular accent. Joyce (1991: 158) emphasizes the increased correlation between social class and dialect in the 1800s, and Lewis (2012: 902) argues that regional speech became strongly stigmatized during the same time.

The late-eighteenth and nineteenth centuries witnessed a veritable explosion of grammars, pronunciation dictionaries, usage guides, and so on; for instance, while around 50 grammars were published in the period 1700–50, over 200 were put on the market during the following half-century (Beal 2004: 90). Such a prolific supply of course presupposes demand. As Auer (2012: 941) notes, the process of codification is linked to increased opportunities for social advancement in a money-based economy (see Section 2.3). People belonging to the middle classes became interested in grammars, usage guides, elocution lessons, etc. owing to the linguistic insecurity that characterizes socially mobile speakers (Labov 2001: 277–8; Beal 2004: 94, 168–9): instruction in linguistic matters was seen as necessary in order to benefit fully from opportunities to advance socially (Tieken-Boon van Ostade 2014b: 147). Some of the supply of normative works that arose to meet this demand was also aimed at ordinary people for the first time (Wagner 2012: 916). This plethora of advice on linguistic behaviour is one aspect of the market for etiquette guides of various kinds that flourished in the period (Beal 2004: 179; Lewis 2012: 911), as linguistic behaviour was considered indicative of social propriety.

The middle classes were thus the main target for books promulgating standard usage; within this large group, the emerging lower middle class represented a target group for simpler guides that taught readers to avoid stigmatized usage (Beal 2004: 116, 179). A large number of books were also produced for women and children (Hickey 2010c: 7–8). The growing market for books for children tallies with the increased importance of the teaching of English in school during the LModE period (Beal 2004: 101–5). As regards books aimed at women, standards of propriety, including language, were arguably even stricter for women than for men, owing to the inequality of gender roles in the LModE period. Women were presented as guardians of manners and morals, and propriety in language was seen as indispensable in a wife – and in a mother, who was in a position to transfer her impeccable language to her offspring (Mugglestone 2003: 138–62). The lower classes had limited access to the standard owing to lack of education (Auer 2012: 940) and the financial means to purchase guides to standard usage (Hickey 2010c: 8). This class difference also means that the relationship between the speech used by the working classes and the types of writing typically preserved in corpora becomes increasingly problematic after the emergence of standardization and a literary culture (Durrell 2015: 16).

Bergs (2005: 54–5) argues that the establishment of a codified standard affected the overall result of language change mediated through weak ties. Before standard usage had been codified and become available to a significant proportion of the population, loose-knit networks mainly promoted change that increased linguistic diversity. However, in the LModE period, members of loose-knit networks, which were characteristic above all of the middle classes, were easily influenced by pressure to conform to standard usage. Loose-knit networks thus instead came to facilitate the adoption of pre-existing usage norms by large numbers of speakers. We do not of course know to what extent such conformity spread to these language users' informal conversation, but even if standard patterns were adopted more or less consciously and may mainly have been a feature of planned production, they must be part of the feature pool of a language user's idiolect in order to be used at all.

As was the case regarding the formation of urban dialects, the number of idiolects that changed by adopting standardized patterns, largely through propagation, was very large. But because features that made up the target norm were already part of English as a communal language, there are few traces of this widespread idiolectal change in the overall structure of English. The feature pool of the communal language remained intact, since there were standard as well as non-standard users both before and after the relevant idiolects were affected by standardization; moreover, since most written – especially printed – documents were produced in Standard English already, there were few noticeable effects in the texts from the period. Like urban varieties, Standard English is also to some extent negatively defined, though in a slightly different way: while urban varieties can partly be described in terms of what features of the varieties used in the surrounding areas did not become part of the urban variety, the standard can be seen as what remains of the feature pool after features deemed unacceptable have been removed (Kretzschmar 2009: 18; Hickey 2010c: 16).[14] The main differences between urban-variety formation and standardization are (i) that the emerging urban variety was to a greater extent a new variety and (ii) that standardization is, to a greater extent, a change from above. As the large market for normative works indicates, speakers are likely to be aware that there is an overtly prestigious variety to aim for, and while some changes in output as speakers approach standard usage may be due to a subconscious desire to emulate Standard English patterns, many of the idiolectal changes will have been aided or caused by conscious decisions to accommodate to standard usage.

---

[14] Because the standard is an institutionalized construct, it may promote and demote variants in terms of their frequency compared with their incidence in the communal language as a whole (Kretzschmar 2015b: 102).

The brief account above is of course a simplification. Standard English is not a static entity but a moving target (Hickey 2012: 15–16). As shown in Section 2.4, some features that would not have been part of accepted usage around 1800 are now uncontroversial (e.g. the progressive passive or /ɑː/ in the BATH set), and other features that were previously considered normal in educated usage are no longer current (e.g. BE as perfect auxiliary or using /ɔː/ in words like *off*). In addition, when a large number of people began to produce spoken and written output that approximated Standard English more closely than previously, the boundaries of what counted as standard output are likely to have been affected as a result. Indeed, colloquialization is due in part to this type of interchange, whereby features previously characteristic of informal speech became more frequent and/or acceptable in some types of writing (see Section 4.3.1 for fuller discussion). This process was doubtless assisted by the fact that speakers who adopted standard patterns did not typically lose the variety they had previously used; instead, their idiolects came to encompass a wider range of registers, with potential for interchange between them. However, standardization typically minimizes variation in form concerning language structure (Lange 2012: 995); as Milroy (1997: 313) notes, a standard variety is typically more uniform than any other variety of the language.

As mentioned above, the actual effects of normative statements on actual usage are debatable (see Auer 2012: 946–8). Curzan (2014: 24) defines *standardizing prescriptivism* as "rules/judgments that aim to promote and enforce standardization and 'standard' usage"; the codification of English is thus seen as belonging to one strand of prescriptivism.[15] However, prescriptivism has often been regarded as a failure, largely because of its inability to stop language change (Curzan 2014: 2–3). Dekeyser (1975: 276) claims that, with regard to the number and case relations he surveyed, normative works had "no effect worth mentioning, if any at all" on nineteenth-century English; Bailey (1996: 260) argues that normative grammarians were "almost entirely unsuccessful" in their efforts to eradicate what they regarded as erroneous usage;[16] and Anderwald (2016: 245) suggests that, as regards the grammar of the verb phrase, "both the

---

[15] As regards grammar, twentieth-century views on the codifiers of the 1700s often focussed on their prescriptive nature and their unwillingness to accept language change and social dimensions of usage. However, the twenty-first century witnessed a more nuanced attitude, in which grammarians like Lowth were partly re-evaluated (Beal 2004: 105–15); for instance, see Tieken-Boon van Ostade (2012: 46–8) for a discussion of Lowth (1762) from this perspective.

[16] In a later work, Bailey (2010: 189) argues that the "explosive growth in the publication of grammar books had some influence" in the direction of increased uniformity of English in the 1800s, though he still gives more weight to migration patterns.

prescriptive nature and the prescriptive impact of nineteenth-century grammar writing on actual language change have been greatly overestimated". Summarizing the findings of several studies, Percy (2012: 449–51) discusses a complex picture where natural standardization sometimes preceded proscription, which in turn makes some prescriptive comments seem more descriptive; nevertheless, some temporary influence can be traced to prescriptivist trends.

This type of reasoning is necessarily speculative, as it presupposes that we know what would have happened if standardization had not taken place and normative works had not been published (cf. Bailey 1996: 261). For example, the occurrence of proscribed usage such as *who* as an object relative marker in texts that are assumed to aim at standard usage may be taken as evidence of the failure of normative efforts, but we cannot know how frequent objective *who* would have been if there had been no normative works in the first place; as Hickey (2020: 57) points out, the survival of objective *whom* may itself be due in part to normative statements. There are suggestions in research that some normative statements did have an impact on usage; for instance, Sairio (2009: 213) suggests that normative works did play a part in the increased preference for pied piping over preposition stranding in her eighteenth-century material, and Auer and González-Díaz (2005) argue that a temporary revival of the subjunctive in adverbial clauses in the late eighteenth and early nineteenth centuries was influenced by this feature being recommended in normative works. Against this background, it seems likely that normative pronouncements did have some effect on the idiolects especially of socially mobile speakers, who also constituted a larger part of the population of England than ever before. In addition, what Percy (2012: 449) calls "'natural' standardization" doubtless had an impact on the language of many documents that have been included in corpora; for instance, as Percy notes, multiple negation began to disappear from educated usage before it was explicitly proscribed.

Neither standardization nor the publication of normative works could of course eradicate non-standard varieties; but those varieties are not predominant in the texts that have formed the basis for most corpora of LModE. Even though a great many language users who learnt the basics of the emerging standard variety between 1700 and 1900 doubtless preserved their native non-standard usage, their idiolects also came to include some ability to produce texts in Standard English – which means that those idiolects changed. (Many printed texts also went through an editing process that further enforced standardization.) The fact that Standard

English predominates in most corpora of LModE is both a problem for scholars who wish to paint a complete picture of the language of the period and an indication of the influence of standardization.

3.6 Summary and Discussion

I have demonstrated in this chapter that a large number of interacting factors create the impression that LModE is characterized by relative linguistic stability, because widespread change on the idiolectal level – the true measure of language change – remains largely invisible on the communal-language level. First, at least in grammar, the type of change facilitated by the weak links that characterized many LModE networks consists in the propagation of existing features, with concomitant propagation-dependent innovation resulting from imperfect replication. Weak links do not correlate with independent innovation, which is often responsible for most structural changes in the communal language. Examples of changes that affect a great many LModE idiolects but need not lead to the emergence of new features include the development of urban varieties and standardization. The combination of the dominance of texts influenced by standardization in the surviving evidence and the lack of access to colloquial speech makes LModE appear even more homogeneous compared with Early Modern and Present-Day English.

I will devote the rest of this section to discussing three issues which have not been addressed in this chapter, but which are important in order to connect my account of LModE to more general frameworks of language change. First, I shall discuss why LModE may feature comparatively little independent innovation compared with previous periods; then I will touch on scenarios where propagation may in fact correlate with structural change. The end of the section will be devoted to the issue of what speakers are responsible for language change.

The fact that LModE should feature a great deal of propagation does not entail that it should not *also* feature independent innovation, and my suggested explanations for the apparent rarity of independent innovation remain speculative. First, it is possible that language users may reach a "saturation point" with regard to how many changes their idiolects are likely to undergo simultaneously. If a large number of features are being propagated via weak network links at a given time, this may decrease an innovation's likelihood of success. Features that are being propagated are likely to have a quantitative advantage over innovations in terms of which of them are selected for further propagation, because the former are used by

3.6 Summary and Discussion

a larger number of speakers already, thus increasing both language users' exposure to the new feature and the social advantages of adopting it. In this scenario, it is thus not necessarily the case that LModE features less innovation as such; rather, the innovations that do occur are less likely to be picked up and propagated because of competition with the large amount of propagation that is already taking place.

Another factor that may be influential is the scope of each speaker's idiolect. Owing to advances in literacy, communications, etc. (see Section 2.3), a large number of LModE speakers were exposed to varieties other than those they were familiar with from growing up – including the standard variety. This situation would make it necessary for them to incorporate a wider range of registers into their idiolects than previously; Biber and Finegan's (1997) analysis of the growing linguistic diversity of written English since the seventeenth century is a clear indication of this. Such demands on speakers may also set a limit on the acceptance of new innovations. This line of reasoning is mainly limited to written language – we know far less about register differences in speech – but writing is also our main source of evidence.

If we compare LModE to previous periods in the history of English, it becomes important to acknowledge an exception to the principle that weak links – and thus widespread propagation of linguistic features – do not correlate with the emergence of new features in a communal language: cases of language contact leading to widespread second-language learning, bilingualism, language shift, substratum influence, etc. in an area. In such a situation, intra-speaker propagation between idiolects belonging to speakers who are bilingual to a greater or lesser extent is likely to be a far more significant factor in language change than it was in LModE. Syntactic and phonological features will be involved (Filppula et al. 2008: 2), and propagation-dependent innovation will occur as features from the donor idiolect are being propagated: these features will be imperfectly replicated (which typically involves simplification) and/or adapted to the structure of the recipient idiolect. Since the idiolects that the propagated feature spreads between are mapped onto different communal languages, the change will be perceived as a structurally new feature emerging in the recipient language, which is otherwise associated mainly with independent innovation, even though propagation between two idiolects within the same speaker combined with propagation-dependent innovation is the actual source of the change.

This argument has potential repercussions for how we regard the earliest recorded stage of the English language, that is, Old English. It is usually implicitly assumed that most language users during the Old English period had idiolects whose output would have been structurally similar to what we see in surviving texts. However, Trudgill (2010: 1–35) argues that most idiolects underwent many of the changes typically associated with the transition between Old and Middle English before the Middle English period; in Trudgill's account, the Old English documents that have come down to us represent the learnt language of a literate, elite minority. If this argument is correct, in terms of grammar, most language users' output during the Old English period was more similar to Middle English output (Tristram 2004: 106). In this scenario, language contact with Celtic – and possibly North Germanic – languages would have been an important factor in the early development of English (Trudgill 2010: 1–35; see also Milroy 1996 on a possible Anglo-Danish koiné). Language contact may thus help to explain why the transition between Old and Middle English appears to feature more structural change than, for instance, LModE. Most Old English idiolects would already have been similar in structure to Middle English owing to widespread propagation of features from Celtic (and later North Germanic) idiolects to Old English idiolects; this propagation would have involved considerable amounts of propagation-dependent innovation in the form of imperfect replication and simplification in the West Germanic varieties that ended up forming the basis for first-language idiolects in England.[17] What happened in the transition from Old to Middle English was then mainly that speakers ceased to produce texts in classical Old English, not that their idiolects quickly underwent massive language change. While Trudgill's (2010) theory is necessarily speculative, it matches the account of independent innovation, propagation, and propagation-dependent innovation sketched in this chapter.

If we consider only propagation and propagation-dependent innovation, the amount of change in a communal language may be due mainly to two parameters:

1. The number of idiolects that undergo propagation and propagation-dependent innovation (which in turn is related to factors such as the intensity of the contact and the strength of the network ties that exist in the community).
2. The degree of linguistic similarity of the idiolects belonging to the speakers who are in contact with one another.

---

[17] The fact that people living in north-eastern England were exposed to contact with both Celtic and North Germanic speakers may help to explain why those dialects appear to be more advanced in the changes that characterize Middle English texts. There were of course regions that were characterized by language contact and shift to English between 1700 and 1900 (e.g. much of Ireland). But English already had a large native-speaker population and a near-standardized version by 1700, which would reduce the amount of structural change LModE underwent in this process.

3.6 Summary and Discussion

Language change in a linguistically homogeneous community characterized by strong network ties would then be expected to be very limited, as the idiolects in contact are similar to begin with and the pressure to converge high. LModE would feature a great deal of change according to parameter (1), but the perceived effects on the communal language would be limited because the idiolects involved were comparatively similar, because most features of these idiolects had already been attested in linguistic research, and because the surviving LModE texts that have been subjected to analysis are heavily biased towards standard usage.

This situation is clearly different from the scenario outlined above, in which a large number of Celtic and Old Norse speakers shifted to English during the Old English period. Language shift to English (for instance, from Irish on Ireland and from a great many languages spoken by Native Americans, enslaved people, and migrants in the United States) of course occurred between 1700 and 1900 as well. The English idiolects of speakers who underwent such shifts were doubtless affected by those processes, and in some cases, the shift is very likely to have affected the resulting regional, social, ethnic, etc. variety of English. But the existence of an influential and relatively focussed Standard English variety in the LModE period, and the dominance of this variety in the preserved output, are likely to have constrained the long-term effects on surviving output in the communal language.

The amount of change that has taken place in English since 1700 is also a matter of perspective. If a variety like African American Vernacular English were granted the same importance in descriptions of the communal language as Standard English is, Present-Day English would arguably be considered to "have" copula deletion as a rare optional feature. For reasons that have little to do with linguistics, this is not usually the account given in descriptions of this particular communal language.

At this point, it may be argued that independent innovation is perhaps not a necessary mechanism for language change at all. If even far-reaching structural changes can be the indirect result of language contact, perhaps all language change can be reduced to propagation and propagation-dependent innovation? However, there are good grounds for assuming that independent innovation is a factor in language change. Most importantly, there are clear tendencies as regards what changes tend to take place in communal languages. Perhaps the best-known example is grammaticalization, where a very strong tendency towards unidirectionality has been found. Changes tend to be in the direction of more abstract, less specific meaning; for instance, future markers often develop from motion verbs (e.g. BE *going to* in English or *kommer att* in Swedish), but the opposite development is vanishingly rare (see, for instance, Hilpert and Correia Saavedra 2016: 357–8). Strong tendencies of that type become a great deal easier to explain if it is assumed (i) that speakers can produce independent linguistic innovations and (ii) that those innovations are constrained by linguistic factors.

Finally, the issues of who can innovate and where innovations are stored are matters of debate among linguists. In generativist approaches, it is often assumed that adult speakers' language undergoes only peripheral changes (often referred to as changes in E-language), which may be unpredictable, "represent chance, contingent factors" (Lightfoot 2003: 120), or be due to migration, innovation, or sociocultural factors (Yang 2000: 237). Children exposed to input including such changes then reset rules to make their underlying system (their I-language) compatible with the input as a repair strategy (Bickerton 2014: 194; Potsma 2017: 76–7). Similarly, Newmeyer (2014: 44–5) suggests that new types of utterances in adult output may be stored outside adults' grammatical competence proper and are only integrated into it by the next generation.

A number of potential problems with this framework have been pointed out. These problems include why there would be changes in adults' E-languages without change in their I-languages (Westergaard 2017: 457), how such change would be directional if differences in the E-language input children receive are accidental (Croft 2000: 50), and how innovations would be propagated by children, who are not typically influential members of speech communities (Cournane 2017: 11), while members of the speech community old enough to be influential have typically stopped producing the novel constructions used during their language-acquisition process (Croft 2000: 48). Differences have also been argued to exist between the types of phenomena attested in language change and first-language acquisition (Croft 2000: 46–7); even when differences between children's and adults' first-language output seem parallel to language-change phenomena, the similarities have been argued to be attributable to "different processes and factors" (López-Couso 2017: 345). Widespread inter-person variation seems to exist in the process of first-language acquisition, where the Universal-Grammar model would predict homogeneous trajectories (López-Couso 2017: 340). Cournane (2017) constitutes a recent attempt to address some of these issues; Westergaard (2017) attempts to reconcile the abrupt changes predicted by theories of parameter resettings in first-language acquisition with the seemingly gradual nature of much attested language change. Nevertheless, a large number of linguists maintain that language change does take place in adults' idiolects; one source of such change is language contact between adults (Roberts and Sneller 2020: 197), which may be relevant mainly to propagation and propagation-dependent innovation.

It has been suggested that the groups which undergo language change may vary with the type of linguistic feature studied. Labov (1994: 84) argues that change in phonology and morphology is characterized by maintained frequencies in individual speakers and that the community's language changes because speakers adopt increasingly advanced options, often in generational increments; in syntax and lexis, by contrast, all community members typically undergo the change together. However, Nevalainen and Raumolin-Brunberg (2017: 88, 97) argue that, at least as regards morphology, the expected stability of speakers does not appear from their studies, and that their results rather suggest differences among speakers as well as among instances of language change regarding generational vs. lifespan change. Raumolin-Brunberg (2005) identifies both generational difference and lifespan change in the shift from *-(e)th* to *-(e)s* in the third person present singular indicative. Nahkola and Saanilahti (2004) suggest that idiolects are unlikely to undergo change with regard to features that are acquired as categorical, while lifespan changes are likely when what is acquired is rather a variant field with true competition between variants. Petré and Van de Velde (2018) also find evidence of both types of change in their analysis of the BE *going to* future expression: speakers with an entrenched representation of *going* as a lexical verb were unable to fully adopt new patterns, but conversely, speakers who have fully grammaticalized the construction were limited in what they could communicate successfully by what uses were conventionalized in their speech communities, so that "actual linguistic behavior is a trade-off between entrenched cognitive schemas and social accommodation" (Petré and Van de Velde 2018: 890–1).

Another distinction argued to be relevant is whether the motivation for the change is linguistic or extralinguistic. Hickey (2020: 45) suggests that internally motivated and externally motivated change may be linked mainly to childhood and adulthood, respectively, although language-shift scenarios can involve internally motivated change for adults as well. Sankoff (2013: 274) argues that there is evidence for "grammatical malleability" in adolescents and young adults, while adulthood is mainly characterized by stability and more or less conscious changes towards a community-based, supra-local, or standard norm. (The role assigned to linguistic and extralinguistic factors in language change in my framework was discussed in detail in Section 3.4.)

The mechanism of change itself may also constrain what can be propagated. Labov (2010: 311) argues that abstract structural patterns such as rules and constraints are less likely to be affected by propagation across speech communities, as the contact that enables propagation takes place mainly between adults, who do not acquire the abstract features as easily and accurately as children do. However, as Labov (2007: 347) acknowledges, the dichotomy between changes that are due to transmission (acquisition of a first language by a child) and diffusion (contact between – mainly adult – members of different speech communities) is to some extent an idealization, as most speech communities are not homogeneous entities with clear boundaries.

In sum, there is no clear consensus regarding whether transmission or diffusion is the more important mechanism in language change or whether all changes take place via the same mechanism. In principle, the framework outlined in this chapter is compatible with a scenario where features that are innovated or propagated are stored peripherally by adults and are fully integrated into idiolects only by the next generation's children when they are exposed to output containing the new features (see Blythe and Croft 2012: 277). However, my assumption is that change does occur in adults' idiolects (for similar views, see Denison 2003: 61; Bergs 2005: 264; Beckner et al. 2009: 14; Traugott and Trousdale 2013: 21). The changes examined in Chapters 5–8 all result in frequency shifts in patterns that were already available to most speakers; such changes may be especially easy to undergo as an adult, because little structural modification of the idiolect is required. Colloquialization and densification are assumed to occur mainly through the propagation of changes in genre norms through adult output. However, it is also possible that some of the change is due to generational transmission, as part of a more general tendency in English as a whole. As shown in Chapter 7, some of the increase in nominal premodifiers appears to be more general in my material, and not restricted to informational language. Similarly, Leech et al. (2009: 219n22, 234–5) note that late-twentieth-century speech may be following a trend set by writing in this regard.

The case studies in Chapters 5–8 all employ a corpus-linguistic perspective on propagation and propagation-dependent innovation. This choice of methodology may seem unexpected, given that corpus linguistics does not typically focus on the idiolectal level, which has been foregrounded in this chapter. I will therefore devote part of Chapter 4 to demonstrating why a corpus-linguistic framework can provide us with important insights into language change.

CHAPTER 4

Methodological Framework

4.1 Introduction

In this chapter, I treat aspects of methodology that, taken together, form a conceptual bridge between the theoretical account of language change in Chapter 3 and the four empirical case studies. I begin by looking at the framework of historical corpus linguistics, which will be applied in all case studies, and at how this framework is compatible with the perspective on language change outlined in Chapter 3 (Section 4.2). I then focus on the two types of syntactic change in communal languages that are examined in the case studies, namely, colloquialization and densification (Section 4.3). This account is followed in Section 4.4 by a discussion of frequency, one of the most important concepts in corpus linguistics. Next, I describe CONCE and CNNE, the two corpora that are the main primary sources for the case studies (Section 4.5); special attention is paid to CNNE, which has not previously been described in published research, and to how its periodization reflects changes in the newspaper market in nineteenth-century England. A brief summary closes the chapter in Section 4.6.

4.2 Corpus Linguistics as a Methodology for Studying Language Change

As Biber and Reppen (2015: 1) note, the relationship between *corpus* and *linguistics* in *corpus linguistics* differs from that between, for example, *socio-* or *psycho-* and *linguistics* in *sociolinguistics* or *psycholinguistics*. Unlike sociolinguistics and psycholinguistics, corpus linguistics is not usually regarded as a theoretical domain, but rather a methodological approach in which it is considered "possible to actually 'represent' a domain of language use with a corpus of texts, and possible to empirically describe linguistic patterns of use through analysis of that corpus" (Biber and Reppen

2015: 1). Corpus techniques thus do not constitute a theory, but the use of corpora may enable researchers to answer theoretical questions about language. In particular, they can reveal systematic patterns in usage that may easily escape notice in intuition-based analyses (Biber and Reppen 2015: 2). Using corpus data also facilitates addressing the "when" and "how" of language change (Hilpert and Mair 2015: 199).

I shall devote this section to two aspects of corpus linguistics that have important consequences for the case studies of variation and change reported on in the following four chapters. First, some characteristics of historical corpus linguistics will be discussed. I will then address how the idiolect-based model of language change outlined in Chapter 3 can be reconciled with a corpus-based approach where the goal is typically to represent a domain of use rather than one or several idiolects.

4.2.1 *Historical Corpus Linguistics*

Historical linguistics differs from the analysis of present-day languages in that we have little access to native-speaker intuitions about idiolects, because the idiolects we are interested in belong to native speakers who are no longer alive. Present-day intuitions are sometimes used to shed light on historical language, but this practice is controversial; as McEnery et al. (2006: 96) point out, "the intuitions of modern speakers have little to offer regarding the language used hundreds or even tens of years before". However, the reliability of intuition is likely to vary with the type of phenomenon investigated. Most historical grammarians use their intuitions and their knowledge of the present-day language as a guide to classifying historical data (or to devising tests that can be used to classify the data), and this is arguably acceptable as long as caution is exercised and expert knowledge of the language of the period is used (see Denison and Hundt 2013 for a critical discussion of this procedure for classifying relative clauses). We do have access to some cases where past speakers have recorded their opinions about language in grammars, usage guides, and so on, and this type of evidence becomes more plentiful than previously during the LModE period. Such sources can be of great value, but they need to be examined critically. The relationship between the opinion expressed and actual language use may be problematic, especially if the author's aim was prescription rather than – or as well as – description; there is also the question of whose language was intended to be described by the statement.

The historical study of English grammar is thus based mainly on evidence presented by actual usage, that is, surviving texts, which are grouped together into corpora in corpus linguistics. Such evidence inherently limits the scope of investigation to the language represented in preserved texts, which means that male, literate, and wealthy speakers' English is over-represented (see Section 3.2). But within those constraints, corpus linguistics has enabled us to chart variation in usage with accuracy.

The study of LModE syntax is particularly well suited to corpus-based analysis. As discussed in Chapter 3, a large proportion of linguistic changes in LModE feature the propagation of changes that become visible in texts through shifts in frequency patterns. Because such changes are less salient than those that involve the emergence of new features, they are less likely to be noticed without quantitative scrutiny. Historical corpora offer researchers a way to examine and quantify such shifting patterns (Gray and Biber 2018: 125) with reliability and precision according to various linguistic and extralinguistic parameters.

As regards extralinguistic parameters, variation with *genre* has been in focus in many studies (Nevalainen and Raumolin-Brunberg 2017: 2). Genres (e.g. letters, depositions, or science texts) can be broadly defined as text categories that are established based on text-external, extralinguistic considerations, such as the function and purpose of the text (Claridge 2012: 238).[1] Genres lend themselves well to the investigation of linguistic variation, as no circularity is involved in the analysis: the distribution of linguistic features in a text often correlates with the genre to which the text belongs but is not part of the definition of any genre. Linguistic genre differences in the past provide a window on the systematic linguistic variation that characterized past language states. Genres vary in how "agile" or "uptight" they are in adopting incoming features (Hundt and Mair 1999), and a genre is often agile with regard to some features but uptight with regard to others (see, for instance, Biber and Gray 2012).

The examination of genres that are related to speech can give us an idea of what past speech was like, even though we lack direct access to informal conversation. Because much of the innovation and propagation that took place in past idiolects occurred in speech, this opportunity to approach spoken language is of considerable importance. Genres may be

---

[1] There is some variation among studies in what term is used for text categories established on such grounds; other terms used for similar categories include *register* and *text type*. I will use *genre* throughout the present study, including cases where I cite scholars who have used other terms. The purpose of a text is a vital component of Swales's (1990) definition of genre, but as Ljung (2000: 144) notes, other criteria may be needed for genres such as newspaper texts.

speech-related in several ways: they may (purport to) contain speech taken down verbatim, for example cross-examinations at trials (speech-based genres); they may be written in order to be read aloud, for example plays (speech-purposed genres); or they may be speech-like by virtue of informal production circumstances, for example private letters to people with whom the letter writer was on an intimate footing (Culpeper and Kytö 2010: 17–18). However, hypotheses about past speech are also strengthened by the inclusion of non-speech-related genres, as we may then be able to extrapolate towards informal speech from linguistic differences between speech-related and non-speech-related language (Rissanen 1986: 98). In addition, written texts – speech-related or non-speech-related – are worthy objects of study in their own right, and innovation is not limited to spoken language; as Biber and Gray (2011) demonstrate, the trends towards densification (see Section 4.3.2) that are noticeable in LModE are led by written genres.

Two important goals that compilers of historical corpora attempt to reach are *representativity* (also known as *representativeness*) and *comparability*. If a corpus is representative of a language variety, the study of that corpus can "stand proxy for" the study of that variety (Leech 2007: 135). Representativity is thus about making the corpus similar to the total output of a communal variety, so that analysis of the corpus can reveal shared patterns in idiolects that belong to speakers of that variety. However, representativity is difficult to operationalize. The problem concerns both what genres should be sampled and how much should be sampled from each genre. Biber (1993), who also makes a sophisticated attempt to assess representativity, argues that truly proportional sampling of a variety would lead to conversation accounting for most of the corpus, but other genres may be of great linguistic significance. Leech (2007: 138) suggests that texts from some genres, for example various mass-media texts, should be given greater relative weight in representative corpus compilation than should conversation, as the former have far more receivers. While this is certainly true, a counterargument may be that mass-media texts, most of which are received as part of one-way communication, are unlikely to be as influential on speakers' idiolects as habits picked up in more personal communication. Váradi (2001: 590) notes that fully representative sampling is essentially impossible to achieve, as it requires such extensive knowledge about the target population that, if we had that knowledge, we might not need a representative sample in the first place. We are thus left with approximations of representativity. In historical studies, a further problem is that we lack access to the language of many idiolects (e.g. most illiterate speakers). For these reasons, statements about representativity need to be hedged carefully when applied to historical language varieties. Variables such as gender and socio-economic group interact with ongoing changes (see, for instance, Labov 2001), and the extent to which we have access to varied samples of data in this regard affects how detailed our accounts can be.

At the same time, the unattainability of perfect representativity is not an excuse not to attempt to attain it. The combination of CONCE and CNNE (see Section 4.5) was considered suitable from this perspective, as genres with different relationships to informal speech are sampled and both public and private writing are included. Moreover, three genres of special importance to the present study are sampled extensively: private letters and trial transcripts, which provide insights into speech-related language and women's voices, and newspaper writing, which has been argued to be hospitable to both colloquialization and densification.

While representativity concerns the relationship between the texts in a corpus and the variety represented by the corpus, comparability holds between two or more sets of texts in corpora: if such sets differ with regard to only one feature (e.g. time), they are comparable (Leech 2007: 141). Leech (2007) discusses comparability between different corpora; I focus on comparability between period samples of the same corpus. The goal in achieving comparability in that sense is that only texts that had comparable counterparts in the other period(s) sampled should be included in the sample for any one period. As was the case with representativity, perfection is difficult to achieve for historical corpora.

As Leech (2007: 142–3) notes, comparability and representativity can come into conflict in diachronic investigations, especially when genre evolution has taken place. Genres are not static entities but change in response to external influence. Such change leads to the existence of texts from one period that lack clear counterparts in another period and/or shifts in the relative distribution of texts belonging to different genres over time. Such situations present corpus compilers with a difficult choice. On the one hand, each period sample can be made maximally representative of the language of its period; but then the comparability of the period samples decreases, as not only time, but also the effects of genre evolution, will differentiate the samples. On the other hand, only texts that have counterparts in all periods sampled may be included (and in the same proportions), which makes the samples comparable; but each period sample will then be less representative of the textual universe of its period.

Newspaper writing (see Section 4.5.2) provides a good example of genre evolution; for instance, some types of newspaper were available only in one of the periods covered by the corpus. The existence of a stamp duty on newspapers in period 1 meant that there was a division between papers that were stamped and legal and papers that were unstamped and illegal; this division is irrelevant to period 2. The best fit for comparability might be to include only legal papers from period 1 (as newspapers in period 2 were legal by default in this regard), but that solution would ignore a very important segment of the early-nineteenth-century radical press. In such cases, I generally favoured representativity: it was considered more important to provide a representative image of what newspaper texts in England looked like in 1830–50 and 1875–95, respectively, than to make sure that two – less representative – period subcorpora could be compared. This choice should be borne in mind when results based on CNNE are interpreted.

Another important pair of concepts is *recall* and *precision*, which, however, have to do with corpus analysis rather than corpus compilation. Potential data are typically retrieved automatically from a corpus: software (in my case studies, WordSmith Tools) is used to retrieve all tokens of certain strings of characters. The goal at this stage is typically to achieve high recall: a large proportion of relevant tokens should be retrieved. Manual analysis may then be necessary in order to achieve precision, that is, to ensure that the retrieved tokens that remain in the database are relevant (Ball 1994: 295). Details on how recall and precision were achieved in each case study are given in Sections 5.2, 6.2, 7.2, and 8.2.

If the relevant tokens can be retrieved using lexical searches only, the corpora can be used as regular text files. This is the case for the studies reported on in Chapters 5 and 6: provided that spelling variants are included in searches, both negations with *not* or *-n't* and co-ordinations with *and* can be retrieved with high recall through simple searches for these strings. The studies in Chapters 7 and 8, by contrast, required more complex retrieval procedures. As there are no morphemes in English that unambiguously identify nouns, past participles, and so on, recall could not be guaranteed through lexical searches for nouns as noun-phrase premodifiers or for past-participle clauses as noun-phrase postmodifiers. Instead, I relied on grammatically annotated versions of CONCE and CNNE,[2] which enabled direct retrieval of syntactic features on the word level, for example a noun followed immediately by another noun. However, errors in tagging may lead to relevant tokens not being retrieved, which has

---

[2] CONCE was tagged using the EngCG–2 tagger, while the Machinese Phrase Tagger was used for CNNE.

a negative effect on recall. For parts of CONCE, the tagging has been checked manually with regard to some tags that are frequently problematic, such as the distinction between past tenses and past participles (see Smitterberg 2005: 50–3 for details). I therefore used the manually checked subset of CONCE rather than the whole corpus for some searches. In addition, a few corpus texts were checked manually in order to estimate recall for all searches that were based on corpus annotation.

4.2.2 Reconciling the Idiolectal Model with Corpus Methodology

In Chapter 3, I argued that the idiolect is the true locus of language change: change in the abstraction that is the communal language is a result of idiolects undergoing change. However, this perspective does not entail that idiolects necessarily constitute the best data for the *study* of language change. On the contrary, corpus linguistics offers researchers a solid empirical foundation – in many cases, the most solid empirical foundation – for statements about language change in grammar, even though corpora are not usually sampled on an idiolectal basis.

Our knowledge of the circumstances surrounding historical texts that have survived and become subject to linguistic analysis is often incomplete.[3] Metadata on the speakers who produced the texts and their network ties to other speakers are sometimes absent, which makes it difficult to say something meaningful about individual idiolects and may preclude applying techniques such as social-network analysis (Milroy 2000: 220). This means that, in historical linguistics, it is frequently necessary to use a lower level of granularity than in analyses of Present-Day English; for instance, Nevalainen and Raumolin-Brunberg (2017: 136) note that coarser models of social stratification yield clearer results for past societies. It is true that LModE is close enough to the present for idiolectal analyses to be possible in some cases; but such studies would limit the scope of inquiry to texts with identifiable speakers whose output has been preserved in large amounts, which would bias our knowledge of LModE even more in the direction of the male, literate, and well-to-do than is already the case. This bias becomes even more apparent if it is assumed that idiolects change during an adult speaker's lifetime (see Section 3.6), since evidence of usage by the same individual at several points in time would then be required. While

---

[3] There are even changes that need to be inferred from texts produced after the changes had gone to completion, for example prehistorical sound changes such as Grimm's Law.

analyses of that type are clearly valuable, restricting scholarly attention to such texts in order to maintain a strictly idiolectal perspective would be counterproductive. The lower level of granularity that most corpora offer is better suited to making meaningful generalizations about linguistic and extralinguistic constraints that operate in the communal language as a whole.

The reason why the focus can frequently be moved from the idiolect to the corpus is *convergence*. Communication between speakers with similar idiolects typically triggers mutual accommodation, which causes convergence between their systems (Mufwene 2008: 15–16); that convergence makes the representation of communal languages in corpora a legitimate object of study. This legitimacy is increased further by the fact that the communal language exhibits structure; see, for instance, Weinreich et al. (1968) on orderly heterogeneity, Beckner et al. (2009) on language as a complex adaptive system, and Kretzschmar (2015b) on speech as a complex system. As noted by Roberts and Sneller (2020: 190), language typically exhibits more regularity on the community level than on the idiolectal level, and it is also possible to demonstrate correlation between linguistic behaviour and factors such as gender and socio-economic group.

There are clear indications in the scholarly literature that convergence is in fact considerable. Gries and Hilpert's (2010: 307) binary logistic regression model correctly predicted the choice between *-(e)th* and *-(e)s* as the third person singular present indicative inflection (e.g. *she playeth* vs. *she plays*) in the period 1417–1681 in 86 per cent of cases. When they used generalized linear mixed-effects modelling that took the behaviour of individual authors as well as individual verbs into account, the accuracy rose to 94 per cent. While the inclusion of an idiolectal factor thus contributed to improving accuracy, the model's predictive power was already considerable (see also Barth and Kapatsinski 2017 for mixed-effects models).

Owing to widespread inter-speaker convergence, the lower granularity afforded by corpus studies does not preclude significant generalizations about language change being made. What is important is to be aware of – and explicit about – what can and cannot be studied. From a macro-level perspective, confident extrapolation to the entire communal language is often not possible: we can typically generalize results from corpora only to speech communities with which the language users who produced the corpus texts would have interacted regularly (with the usual caveats about writing representing speech, etc.) and to text categories that are similar to those included in the corpus.[4] Hypotheses about the linguistic behaviour of groups of speakers and/or texts not represented in the corpus remain speculative to some extent. One well-known limitation in historical linguistics is our lack of access to spoken texts, which precludes obtaining a complete picture of the spoken interaction of the past, although significant advances have been made in recent years (see, for instance, Culpeper and Kytö 2010).

From a micro-level perspective, we cannot assume that the linguistic behaviour of an individual language user matches the patterns in the corpus as a whole. Individual corpus texts that deviate linguistically from otherwise similar texts should be studied carefully and not discarded as outliers. They may shed light on how speakers used resources available to them to create unique, idiolectal voices (Johnstone 1996: 56); they may also provide clues to what characterized advanced and/or conservative language users with regard to the change examined. We need to consider idiolects, including outliers' idiolects, as well as aggregates in order to fully understand linguistic variation and change (see, for instance, Labov 2001: 466–97; Nevalainen and Raumolin-Brunberg 2017: 202–14). In Chapters 5–8, I will draw attention to language users that appear to be outliers where relevant.

Finally, collections of preserved texts such as corpora are not necessarily good tools for gauging the extent of language change taking place in idiolects at a given time (see Chapter 3). This limitation is particularly important for the study of a historical period like LModE, which predates the advent of sound recording of informal speech, and which is characterized by the development of a standard variety that is often privileged in corpus compilation and contains features that were already current in parts of the population. Large numbers of idiolects can change towards the standard variety without the changes being visible in corpus data, as texts sampled were comparatively likely to feature what was to become standard usage even before the shift took place for most speakers, and because no new features necessarily emerged in the process. For the changes that are charted in Chapters 5–8, however, corpus linguistics remains a very suitable methodological framework as long as the necessary limitations are kept in mind. If the genres included are sampled carefully, we can typically assume that, say, an increase in *not*-contraction in a speech-related written genre

---

[4] A possible exception to this rule may be corpora that contain speech-purposed texts which purport to reflect the speech of characters from other groups faithfully, for example comedies. However, such claims of authenticity must be examined carefully.

represents increased acceptance of that feature in that genre, which in turn implies that idiolectal genre norms for the use of that feature underwent change.

Convergence results not only in similar idiolects, but also in similarities in changes that idiolects go through. This similarity is due to shared characteristics of (i) the idiolects themselves and (ii) the interaction that members of the same speech community experience (although, again, outliers are of importance and should not be disregarded). Similarities can be established with regard to both linguistic and extralinguistic parameters.

From a linguistic perspective, the original similarity of the relevant idiolects increases the chances that near-identical innovations will occur independently at roughly the same point in time in different idiolects within a community. Furthermore, when a linguistic innovation is being propagated across the community, it is likely to take hold in similar linguistic contexts in different speakers' idiolects, owing to a "snowball effect". Speakers are more likely to produce the innovation – say, DO-support – in certain linguistic contexts than in others, and hearers are more likely to internalize the innovation when it occurs in much the same contexts, because their idiolects are similar enough to favour and disfavour the innovation in similar linguistic environments. There is empirical support for the assumption of such convergence in change; for instance, De Smet (2016) found that the behaviour of individual speakers with regard to the development of adjectival uses of *key* largely matched the trends in the corpus as a whole.

Diachronic studies tend to uncover clear tendencies regarding the way in which a change is propagated through linguistic contexts; for instance, as shown in Chapter 5, the proportion of *not*-contraction must have increased with present-tense operators before past-tense operators. The process can also be considered from the opposite perspective: features that are, to some extent, being replaced by innovations may become associated with one or several linguistic contexts, and their entrenchment in such contexts may retard the overall change (Nevalainen and Raumolin-Brunberg 2017: 98).

The importance of considering linguistic contexts of change has been discussed from different scholarly perspectives. Denison (2003: 58; see also Denison 1999) links the frequent S-curve pattern of change in a community to tiny shifts in statistical preferences for one construction or another, which add up over time to language change.[5] Similarly,

---

[5] As noted by Nevalainen and Raumolin-Brunberg (2017: 79), the S-curve pattern does not always occur on the macro level. Some such exceptions are most likely due to the fact that S-curves are essentially extrapolations from a large number of idiolectal changes. As Denison (2003: 61) notes, we do not know whether the S-curve phenomenon occurs on the idiolectal level as well or whether it is

4.2 Corpus Linguistics and Studying Language Change

Aitchison (2001: 92–3) suggests that the S-curves we notice in language change are actually made up of smaller, overlapping S-curves representing different linguistic environments undergoing the change. Lass (1997: 281–8) discusses the loss of non-prevocalic /r/ in non-rhotic varieties of English in terms of several partly overlapping "micro-stories" of weakening, loss, and lengthening of preceding vowels, which together stretch across almost 500 years and call into question what type of object the resulting "macro-story" is. De Smet (2016: 85, 100) argues that the different steps in the process of change may require one another, as an incoming expression spreads to new linguistic contexts in a stepwise fashion in which each step enables the next one through analogical extension. In De Smet's (2016: 86) view, innovation is "intrinsically unlikely", but its likelihood increases if there are already well-established constructions in the language to which the new, unconventional expression can be related through analogy; thus "shifts in what is conventional change also what is conceivable". In an attempt to reconcile the abrupt changes in idiolects predicted by generative theory with the apparent gradualness of change in the communal language, Westergaard (2017) suggests that change proceeds in a large number of "micro-cues", that is, small, abrupt steps in a speaker's idiolect. Micro-cues include the linguistic context covered by the change and come from the speaker's knowledge of the relevant language, not from Universal Grammar (Westergaard 2017: 460).

Extralinguistic factors also exert pressure on members of the same speech community in broadly similar ways, leading to idiolectal convergence. These factors can be divided into two main groups: speaker-related parameters (e.g. gender and socio-economic group) and text-related parameters (mainly genre). These parameters are sometimes reflected in corpus compilation: aiming at consistency over time in the selection of language users and genres helps to increase the comparability of the data.[6]

---

a cumulative effect of another type of change making its way through a large number of idiolects at different times. Moreover, differences which obtain between the idiolects sampled but which are not taken into account in corpus compilation may distort the overall picture. Labov (1994: 65–6) provides an explanation for the frequent appearance of the S-curve based on contact, exposure, and pressure to change; Blythe and Croft (2012) argue that the prevalence of the S-curve indicates that change is typically propagated through differential weighting of linguistic variants. In Blythe and Croft's framework, the weighting is transferred from a speaker (group) to the variant they favour.

[6] In diachronic analyses, some of these parameters may themselves undergo structural change over time, which complicates comparisons; for instance, as Nevalainen and Raumolin-Brunberg (2017: 137) note, there is no one model of social hierarchy that appropriately describes all historical stages of English society. (See Section 4.2.1 for genre evolution.)

To begin with speaker-related factors, an incoming feature will be more or less strongly associated with the same gender, the same socio-economic group, the same type of prestige (e.g. overt vs. covert), and so on across a large speech community, because of convergence within smaller groups – ultimately, social networks – that together make up the community. In these cases, convergence does not necessarily lead to more homogeneous language within the community as a whole. If an incoming feature comes to be associated with, say, working-class, male language users, its adoption by that group but not by others may increase linguistic differentiation; for instance, there is anecdotal evidence that some female LModE speakers used a raised vowel in the BATH set to avoid the stigma associated with the "vulgar" incoming variant, that is, a pronunciation that was lengthened, lowered, and/or backed towards [ɑː] (Beal 2004: 141). What is important is that language users agree on the sociolinguistic *evaluation* of the feature.

A change undergoing propagation will also be linked to much the same values with regard to text-linguistic parameters across language users, because convergence will lead to agreement regarding the appropriate use of the incoming feature in different genres and styles. Frequency patterns in genre-stratified communal language output emerge as a result. However, such association patterns are open to change. Colloquialization (see Section 4.3.1) is the net result of a large number of idiolectal changes in such patterns, whereby the stylistic evaluation of some linguistic features associated with informal speech is adjusted so that the features become increasingly available for deployment in (some) written genres.

Functional and social pressure on idiolects may coincide. Densification (see Section 4.3.2) leads to certain linguistic features becoming frequent in, for instance, newspaper language. This increase in frequency presumably happens partly because the features are functional in informational writing: they permit language users to economize on space by taking advantage of readers' (general and/or subject-specific) ability to process phrasal complexity. However, genres also undergo densification because they become associated with a stylistic ideal that includes such features, and convergence then promotes idiolectal conformity with that ideal regardless of the function of the feature.

While the linguistic factors relevant to the propagation of change vary depending on the incoming feature, two extralinguistic parameters are central in several of the case studies in Chapters 5–8: gender and genre. Gender is important because of Labov's (2001: 292–3) "gender paradox", which predicts that women should be leaders in language change from below, except when the incoming variant receives overt (negative) sociolinguistic evaluation. Consistent gender differences in the data that reflect whether women's or men's idiolects are more advanced overall can thus be a valuable indication about the normative connotations of the change. I will therefore comment on gender variation in the results wherever relevant. Coding for gender as a binary parameter (women vs. men) is problematic, since a person's gender identity in fact tends to occupy a position on a continuum (Romaine 1999: 8), and this position represents a construct that is subject to change. However, the binary coding was the most reliable option given the limited information offered by historical data.

The genre concept is of central importance to the case studies. While speaker-centred parameters are about differences among idiolects, genre variation is fundamentally concerned with variability *within* idiolects: it is assumed that language users employ different features – and different proportions of features – depending on the genre their communication occurs in. Owing to idiolectal convergence, such variation manifests itself in a corpus as statistical differences in the distribution of linguistic features across genres. Historical studies have demonstrated that such variation occurred in the past as well; for instance, Raumolin-Brunberg (1991) and Evans (2013) demonstrate that both Sir Thomas More and Elizabeth I varied their language use according to genre. However, as discussed in Section 4.3, the importance of the genre parameter is likely to have increased since 1700; as a result, genre is "a strong predicting factor" in the study of grammatical variation (Biber 2012: 23), which makes it necessary to consider genre differences carefully in studies of LModE. Change is also frequently "genre-graded" in that it occurs in some genres before others (which may or may not take part in the change later on); as Devitt (1989) and Smitterberg (2009) demonstrate, it may even be possible to draw S-curves with genre rather than time on the X-axis, with advanced genres corresponding to later stages in the change.

4.3 Types of Change Considered

The four linguistic features studied in Chapters 5–8 – *not*-contraction, the co-ordinator *and*, nouns as premodifiers in noun phrases, and participle clauses as postmodifiers in noun phrases – were all established features of English syntax by 1800. However, their distribution changed through propagation in terms of idiolectal adjustments in contexts of occurrence, frequency levels, and so on. (As explained in Section 3.3, propagation also involves propagation-dependent innovation through imperfect replication.) In the case studies, the main effects of propagation are expected to be rising frequencies of *not*-contraction and clause-level *and* (colloquialization) and of nominal premodifiers and participle-clause postmodifiers (densification). In addition, it can be expected that these frequency increases will be mediated through specific linguistic and extra-linguistic contexts.

One of the main characteristics of LModE is the increasing linguistic diversification of written English. Biber and Finegan (1997) demonstrate that late-seventeenth-century texts are comparatively uniform in terms of their distribution of linguistic features, while by the end of the 1800s a far more heterogeneous pattern had been established. "Oral" genres like drama had adopted increasingly speech-like patterns with high frequencies of progressives, contractions, and semi-modals, while "literate" genres such as science had become more distant from spoken communication by employing, for instance, phrasal modifiers (Biber and Gray 2011: 226). This development meant that many language users had to control a wider range of linguistic variation in writing than before.

These trends are closely linked to the two types of change investigated in this volume. Colloquialization leads to features common in informal speech increasing in frequency in some written genres; informational genres that undergo densification make more extensive use of phrasal or non-finite structures that compress semantic content. Colloquialization and densification are indications that genre norms are being renegotiated. In colloquialization, a large number of idiolects undergo change whereby linguistic features that were previously associated with occurrence mainly in informal speech also become available for (more extensive) deployment in some written genres. These shifts manifest themselves as a change in genre norms for those written genres in the communal language (see Mair 2006b: 187). In the case of densification, the more frequent use of phrasal and non-finite complexity in informational writing does not appear to have a model in other genres (Biber and Gray 2012: 315), but the relevant genre norms change nonetheless. These changes are not mutually exclusive;[7] for

---

[7] For some features, there is arguably a more direct, inverse relationship between colloquialization and densification. Several features that are involved in colloquialization – such as the progressive, phrasal verbs, and *not*-contraction – are tied to the verb phrase and thus to clausal units, while many features contributing to the densification of written discourse (e.g. nominalizations, nouns as premodifiers, and prepositional phrases as postmodifiers) are noun-phrase constituents. To some extent, there is an inevitable trade-off between the use of phrases and the use of clauses to express the same semantic content: texts belonging to a genre that undergoes colloquialization may thus be less likely to exhibit densification and vice versa. However, Biber and Gray's (2012) findings regarding newspaper language indicate that this trade-off is not absolute.

instance, Biber and Gray (2012) demonstrate that, to some extent, newspaper writing underwent both developments in the LModE period. However, most genres are likely to be subject to one of the processes to a greater extent than the other.

From a methodological perspective, colloquialization and densification are ideal topics for corpus-based investigations, because our limited access to spoken data is not a serious drawback. Colloquialization involves the spread of oral features into some written genres; we thus do not need access to speech itself as an object of study as long as we can assume that a given feature – say, *not*-contraction – was more frequent in informal speech than in writing before the change took place (investigations of Present-Day English are useful in order to corroborate such hypotheses in analyses of LModE). And unlike many other linguistic changes, densification is typically assumed to have originated in informational writing and then spread to other genres, which means that spoken language is not immediately relevant to the change.

4.3.1 Colloquialization

The label *colloquialization* was, to my knowledge, first used in Siemund (1995) and Mair and Hundt (1995); it received greater prominence in Mair (1997) and Hundt and Mair (1999). Mair (2006b: 187) defines colloquialization as a stylistic change "away from a written norm which is elaborated to maximal distance from speech and towards a written norm that is closer to spoken usage" and "away from a written norm which cultivates formality towards a norm which is tolerant of informality and even allows for anti-formality as a rhetorical strategy".[8] A large number of linguistic features that have increased in frequency in recent English are likely to be involved in colloquialization, for example the progressive (Mair and Hundt 1995) and *not*-contraction (Hundt and Mair 1999: 228). However, decreases in the frequencies of features that are common in formal writing but rare in conversation may also be indicative of colloquialization; examples include the preposition *upon* (Hundt and Mair 1999: 234) and the BE-passive (Hundt and Mair 1999: 231–2; Leech et al. 2009: 148–54).

Colloquialization is sometimes distinguished from similar types of language change such as democratization and informalization.

---

[8] Mair (1997: 205) distinguishes "genuine" informality, which consists of features of informal speech being subconsciously used in writing, from anti-formality, which is the result of the conscious use of certain constructions in a text in order to reduce its formality.

Fairclough (1992: 201) considers "five areas of discursive democratization: relations between languages and social dialects, access to prestigious discourse types, elimination of overt power markers in institutional discourse types with unequal power relations, a tendency towards informality of language, and changes in gender-related practices in language". It is mainly the fourth area and, to some extent, the first and third areas that are relevant to colloquialization. Informality of language is the main indication of colloquialization, but the process can be stimulated by a wider range of sociolects becoming accepted in writing and by a wider range of language users becoming able to contribute texts to prestigious written genres. Farrelly and Seoane (2012: 393) define "democratization proper" as "the phasing out of overt markers of power asymmetry with the aim of expressing greater equality and solidarity", while informalization is used for "a tendency toward informality in language" and colloquialization covers shifts towards more speech-like styles. However, they admit that these three processes are closely related (and sometimes difficult to separate) and subsume them under the common label "discursive democratization".

Distinguishing Farrelly and Seoane's (2012) notions of informalization and colloquialization, which appear to be largely subsumed by the same area of discursive democratization in Fairclough's (1992) account, is potentially difficult. To begin with, Mair's (2006b) influential definition of colloquialization specifically includes informality. Furthermore, the main distinction Farrelly and Seoane make between the two processes appears to be that informalization is not limited to popular written registers but also affects expository writing such as journalism and scientific texts. However, Hundt and Mair (1999) show that newspaper texts and academic writing behaved differently with regard to colloquialization in the late twentieth century, which complicates lumping these genre clusters together. Farrelly and Seoane (2012: 395) interpret Westin's (2002) finding that the *Guardian* was ahead of other British upmarket papers in its acceptance of informality in editorials as indicating that informalization is spreading upward to formal writing; but as Hundt and Mair (1999) have demonstrated that newspapers are responsive to colloquialization, this could also be seen as a process of colloquialization in which different newspapers participate to varying degrees. (As I will show in Chapters 7 and 8, such differentiation is in evidence as regards densification as well.) Perhaps the strongest case for separating informalization and colloquialization comes from the finding that the BE-passive does decrease drastically in – especially American – academic writing, while other features that might indicate colloquialization remain rare (see Seoane and Loureiro-Porto 2005); this result might indicate that the change is an instance of informalization but not colloquialization (Farrelly and Seoane 2012: 396). However, the BE-passive in scientific writing is perhaps best regarded as a special case, given the crusade against the use of the construction in the late twentieth century (see Leech et al. 2009: 151–2), which would make its decrease a potential result of prescriptivism (Schwarz 2018: 55–6). In addition, to some extent, a decline in BE-passives may be a consequence of a development that would be a clear case of colloquialization, namely an increased use of first-person subjects in active clauses (Leech et al. 2009: 152). For these reasons, I will let the label *colloquialization* subsume all cases where forms hypothesized to have been common in informal speech increase in frequency in (some) written genres and, conversely, where forms avoided in informal speech decrease in frequency in writing.

Mair's definition of colloquialization pertains to twentieth-century English, but the phenomenon is argued to be "in evidence to a greater or lesser extent in different communities synchronically, and at different times diachronically" (2006b: 187). I have shown elsewhere (Smitterberg 2008, 2012b, 2014; see also Kytö and Smitterberg 2006) that colloquialization occurred in nineteenth-century English. Biber and Gray (2012) also consider the period 1800–1985 in their discussion of popularization and economy, and Biber and Finegan (1997) uncover long-term trends towards orality in their diachronic material. There can thus be little doubt that features of informal speech have been spreading into writing for a long time.

An important question regarding colloquialization is what drives it. Although Mair's (2006b) definition of colloquialization does not include causation, similar causes should ideally be identified for the linguistic developments in nineteenth-century and twentieth-century English in order for us to be certain that we are dealing with the "same" development. To some extent, it can be regarded as a natural development that changes which originate in speech gradually spread into writing, but since the speed at which such developments take place seems to vary over time, more specific causes that may characterize particular periods should also be identified. Biber and Gray (2012: 315) focus on popularization, that is, the fact that "written texts are required for an increasingly wide readership" owing to developments such as increases in literacy and near-universal access to education; Hundt and Mair (1999: 235–6) interpret the colloquialization of late-twentieth-century newspaper English in terms of sensitivity to market forces. From these perspectives, the LModE period is clearly of interest to colloquialization research, as both literacy and access to education spread in England during this time, while market forces also had considerable influence on society. As noted by Milroy (1998: 59), *literacy* frequently meant functional literacy only: the ability to process linguistically complex writing would have been limited on the part of a section of the population classified as literate, which may further have stimulated the production of more speech-like written texts. In addition, several sociocultural and technological developments pertaining to specific genres contributed to making the production and consumption of written language increasingly accessible in England during the nineteenth century (see Sections 2.3 and 4.5).

There are also interpretations of colloquialization in terms of power and hegemony. Fairclough (1992: 205) notes that informality may be "simulated for strategic reasons", which is related to hegemonic struggle. Hegemony is achieved through "integrating rather than simply dominating subordinate classes, through concessions or through ideological means, to win their consent" (Fairclough 1992: 92), and "discursive practice ... is a facet of hegemonic struggle" (Fairclough 1992: 93). In a similar vein, Mair (1997: 203) argues that the social transitions of the late 1960s and early 1970s in the Western world may be interpreted either as a genuine shift towards democracy or as a veiling of pre-existing hierarchies "through the promotion of an egalitarian and informal public atmosphere". In nineteenth-century Britain, the issue of how to "incorporate" especially the industrial working class in society was frequently discussed, and there was also some fear of revolution (Harvie 1992: 439, 451, 459–62). In such a societal context, ceding some elements of discursive practice – in this case, allowing the spoken mode to become more prevalent in some written texts – may have been one discursive result of hegemonic tension. Joyce's (1991: 173) statement that non-standard dialect features were often employed in street literature connected with elections in Victorian Britain is an indication of this tension. It was also argued that the same "ignorance" that fostered belief in things such as witchcraft bred resentment towards the rich, and that these problems could be reduced by (i) increasing the amount and breadth of the literature aimed at the poor and (ii) simplifying its language (Vincent 1989: 174). In this context, colloquialization is linked with the continuation of the then current social structure.[9]

The rise of the lower middle class in especially the nineteenth century may also be an important conditioning factor. As discussed in Section 3.5.2,

---

[9] There were also voices arguing for the continuation of this structure through excluding the poor from the written word altogether; both the cost of schooling and the risk that working-class readers would be exposed to texts that made them dissatisfied with their station in life were causes for concern (Bailey 1996: 28–30).

members of this group were typically anxious to achieve propriety in speech, which would have promoted formal usage. However, at the same time, many speakers belonging to this category are likely to have begun to use written English more than previously, as writing came to play an increasingly central role in LModE society. Under these circumstances, features of their hitherto mainly oral communication may have subconsciously spread into their writing even while they made conscious attempts to model their usage on prescribed patterns (Smitterberg 2008: 283–4) as the scope of their idiolects grew in order to accommodate a wider variety of registers.

The two features that may indicate colloquialization examined in the present study are *not*-contraction (Chapter 5) and *and* as a clausal rather than phrasal co-ordinator (Chapter 6). These features were chosen because they can be expected to exhibit different behaviour with regard to their genre distribution (see also Smitterberg 2014). Since *not*-contraction was a stigmatized feature of written LModE, its deployment in texts is likely to have been the result of at least partially conscious choice; in Mair's (2006b) terms, it would then be an expression of anti-formality. In contrast, with the exception of sentence-initial position, there was no proscription against *and* being used to co-ordinate either phrases or clauses. For this reason, the proportion of co-ordination that takes place above the phrase level in LModE texts is likely to be the result of largely subconscious choices on the part of writers. The two features studied can thus be argued to represent the two groups Hundt and Mair (1999: 226) identified: those whose occurrence is due to a conscious attempt at involved style and those that do not involve conscious decision-making. Contrasting these features may shed light on how language users negotiated tensions between pressures towards popularization and perceived propriety in language.

4.3.2 Densification

Leech et al. (2009: 206) use the label *densification* to denote "an overall pattern of condensation of information in the noun phrase", with the result that fewer words than previously are used to express the same semantic content, for example, *a goods train* instead of *a train for goods*.[10] Features associated with densification include nominalizations and premodifying

---

[10] Leech et al. (2009: 210) technically look at densification from the opposite perspective, that is, that "more information content" is packed "into a given number of words". However, if two constructions such as *a goods train* and *a train for goods* are compared, it seems more relevant to assume that the semantic content is kept constant while the number of words goes down if the former is used instead of the latter.

nouns. Densification implies a variationist perspective on variation (see Section 4.4.1), in which the same meaning can be expressed by two or more linguistic units; however, as will be made clear in Chapters 7 and 8, applying a variationist perspective to densification is not a straightforward procedure.

The genres that tend to be mentioned as receptive to densification are news and scientific writing. As Biber and Gray (2011: 223–5, 2016: 32–9) point out, it is a fairly common assumption – implicit or explicit – in linguistics that language change takes place mainly in spoken interaction, from which it may later spread to writing as speakers whose idiolects have incorporated a new feature produce written texts containing that feature. While colloquialization fits neatly into that expected pattern, densification does not. Biber and Gray (2012: 315–16) argue that densification is a more significant change than colloquialization, as the former results in "completely new linguistic styles of discourse" that are not modelled on or spreading from other genres, and as newspapers, which should be subject to both types of influence, show clearer tendencies towards densification than colloquialization. On the other hand, densification arguably affected fewer writers and readers than colloquialization did in the nineteenth century, given that access to the production and, to a lesser extent, reception of informational texts was limited for large segments of the population. Nevertheless, the idiolects of language users who produced or read newspapers and/or academic texts must have changed by adopting new norms for the expression of structural complexity: phrasal and non-finite structures were increasingly favoured over finite structures for this purpose.

As regards the causes of densification, Biber and Gray (2012: 315) discuss the influence of *economy* on usage: increased specialization and an "information explosion" have put a premium on conciseness in informational genres. Densification is to some extent also made possible by specialization, as well as by assumed knowledge on the part of readers: texts written by and for experts on a topic can leave more semantic relationships unexpressed (Biber and Gray 2016: 183–4). Biber and Gray (2012) demonstrate that academic writing has been undergoing densification since 1800. The combination of an informational purpose, writers as well as readers with specialist knowledge, sufficient time to edit documents, and constraints on publication that promote economy is likely to foster such phrasal discourse styles (Gray and Biber 2018: 124).

The connection between densification and academic writing notwithstanding, the process is not limited to scientific and scholarly genres:

densification can take place in any genre characterized by an increased informational load over time. As mentioned above, both newspaper writing and science prose underwent densification between 1800 and the late twentieth century (Biber and Gray 2012). The need for condensed forms of expression in newspaper writing presumably outweighed the time constraints under which news articles were produced and the more general nature of the shared knowledge relied on by journalists compared with scholars and scientists. Genres and subgenres of academic writing also vary as regards both the extent to which they undergo densification and the types of densification that take place (Gray and Biber 2018: 118–19); as will be shown in Chapters 7 and 8, Science and History in CONCE display very different trajectories. Leech et al.'s (2009) analysis of late-twentieth-century English reveals that densification may spread to additional genres. The main growth in noun + common noun sequences during this time took place in genres other than press and academic prose, where they nevertheless remain most frequent (Leech et al. 2009: 218); these results suggest that newspapers and academic texts were in the vanguard of the development and that other genres were "catching up". Moreover, noun + noun sequences may be on the increase even in spoken genres, thus reversing the direction of genre diffusion in colloquialization (Leech et al. 2009: 219n22, 234–5). As I suggest in Chapter 7, this finding may also indicate that densification is not the only mechanism involved in the spread of nominal premodifiers. Against this background, an examination of nineteenth-century English that covers a wide variety of genres is called for.

Two linguistic features that are potentially characteristic of densification will be examined in the present study. These features are nouns as noun-phrase premodifiers (e.g. *goods* in *a goods train*; see Chapter 7) and participle clauses as noun-phrase postmodifiers (e.g. *reached by the jury* in *the verdict reached by the jury*; see Chapter 8). These features were selected because they may pattern differently across the genre parameter. Noun premodifiers are a central feature of densification that can be expected to increase in frequency based on previous research (see Leech et al. 2009: 217–18; Biber and Gray 2012: 323), while participle-clause postmodifiers present a less clear picture (see, for instance, Biber and Gray 2012: 323; Hundt et al. 2012a: 231). Any increase in the frequency of participle clauses is thus likely to be limited – and/or confined to a small set of genres – in comparison with noun premodifiers. Participle clauses are also a less obvious candidate for densification linguistically: although they form part of noun phrases, they constitute clausal units, and the most conspicuous changes in densification involve phrasal features (Biber and Gray 2012: 325). As Biber and Gray (2016: 62) note, noun premodifiers are phrasal in two respects: they both comprise and function inside phrasal structures.

However, the two features also have important characteristics in common that make them suitable candidates for inclusion in the study. Most notably, they are characterized by informational compression compared with some alternative expressions, such as prepositional phrases (e.g. *for goods* in *a train for goods*) and finite relative clauses (e.g. *that was reached by the jury* in *the verdict that was reached by the jury*); see Biber and Gray's (2016: 207) "cline of compression" for noun-phrase modifiers. In addition, they are both underspecified in comparison with these alternatives: the relationship between the two nouns in *a goods train* is not made explicit, and information on parameters such as tense (and, for present-participle clauses, aspect) is missing from participle clauses. The use of these constructions thus places more interpretive responsibility on the reader. As Biber and Gray (2016: 18) note, the stereotype that academic writing is maximally explicit does not tally with the frequent use of features such as these in several academic subgenres, as they actually reduce explicitness. The use of features that indicate densification thus presupposes other interlocutors' ability to manage underspecification for communication to be successful.

4.4 Frequency Data in Corpus Linguistics

In this section, I first examine the essential choice researchers have to make in order to measure the incidence of linguistic features in corpora (Smith and Rayson 2007: 134), namely whether to employ a variationist or a text-linguistic perspective. While the variationist framework (Section 4.4.1) considers the frequency of a feature in relation to those of other features that could express the same meaning, text-linguistic approaches (Section 4.4.2) focus on the rate of occurrence of a feature independently of the use of other features (see Biber 2012; Biber et al. 2016). Both perspectives will be employed in Chapters 5–8, where discussions of case-study-specific advantages and drawbacks complement the more general account given here. Finally, in Section 4.4.3, I discuss the use of statistical tests to identify significant differences between frequencies in corpus linguistics.

4.4.1 The Variationist Framework

The concept of the *linguistic variable* lies at the heart of the variationist framework. A typical definition of the linguistic variable is "two or more ways of saying the same thing" (see, for instance, Tagliamonte 2012: 2). The different ways are the *variants* of the variable. A more comprehensive definition of the variable includes several additional requirements; for instance, the variants must constitute "a linguistically defined set of some type", for example, a morpheme or a syntactic relationship; "must have a structurally defined relationship" in the idiolect(s) considered; and "must also co-vary, correlating with patterns of social and/or linguistic phenomena" (Tagliamonte 2012: 5). Variants must be interchangeable without a change of meaning, and the unit of analysis in this framework is the individual, interchangeable token (Biber et al. 2016: 356–7).

The most important frequency measure in variationist analyses is the relationship between (i) the number of tokens of each variant and (ii) the sum total of all tokens of all variants. The incidence of each variant can then be expressed as a percentage of that *envelope of variation* (also known as the *variable context*). However, the proportions of the variants of the linguistic variable also correlate with other variables. These variables may be linguistic (e.g. whether a *not*-contraction has a present-tense or a past-tense operator) or extralinguistic (e.g. the genre provenance of the text or the gender of the writer) and are often referred to as *independent variables* (or, in sociolinguistics, factors); the linguistic variable is called the *dependent variable*. These labels imply hypothesized causality: it is assumed that the direction of influence is from the independent to the dependent variable.

The variationist framework presents researchers with a number of challenges. To begin with, deciding what should be included in the envelope of variation can be a difficult endeavour. On the one hand, researchers want "the whole truth", that is, complete recall of the relevant tokens of all variants. On the other hand, in terms of precision, the goal is to include "nothing but the truth", which makes it necessary to exclude (i) all linguistic forms that do not constitute relevant variants and (ii) any tokens of relevant variants where the co-text is categorical, that is, environments where there is no variation between the variants.[11]

---

[11] To take an example from Present-Day Standard English, the relative marker *that* is limited mainly to restrictive relative clauses; an analysis of variation between *that* and other markers should thus exclude non-restrictive clauses.

On the one hand, the envelope of variation can be defined narrowly. In grammar, a problem arises regarding what counts as sameness of meaning, because morpho-syntactic variants have cognitive meaning (Romaine 1984: 411). As exact synonymy is rare or non-existent in language (Rydén 1979: 17), the assumption of sameness of meaning is thus potentially problematic. Tagliamonte (2012: 237) argues that "the interpretive component of Variationist Sociolinguistics comes to the fore in the analysis of linguistic variables above and beyond phonology" in terms of circumscribing the variable context; Denison (2003: 67) suggests that the assumption of semantic equivalence is especially difficult to make for syntactic structures, as opposed to phonology, morphology, or even lexis. The importance attached to such problems varies among scholars. Weiner and Labov (1983: 30–1, 36) start out from truth-conditional sameness of meaning, which leads them to assume that an agentless passive is semantically equivalent to its active transform with a generalized subject pronoun (e.g. *The car had been stolen ~ Someone had stolen the car*) in the vast majority of cases. Grund and Walker (2006: 92) specifically note that they "adopt a fairly wide definition of semantic equivalence" in their variationist study of the choice between subjunctives, indicatives, and verb phrases with modal auxiliaries in adverbial clauses. Variationist scholars often proceed from a weaker notion of equivalence, namely descriptive synonymy (Rosenbach 2019: 789); see also Walker (2010: 69–77) for form-based vs. function-based approaches.

On the other hand, the envelope of variation can be regarded as very large. There are constructions which can potentially express similar meanings, but which are not clear variants of the same variable. It is therefore a relevant question how different in form two interchangeable features can be while still being considered variants. Kretzschmar (2015b: 28–32) argues that there are typically a large number of variants of a given variable, though only a few frequent ones are considered "normal" while most of them are infrequent. Romaine (1984: 422–3) suggests that, in the appropriate context (one in which a speaker desires someone else to close a window), *It's cold in here*, *I'm cold*, *Are you cold?*, *Would you close the window?*, and *Close the window!* might all be "ways of 'saying the same thing', loosely speaking". Retrieving corpus data for such variables becomes problematic, as it is difficult to specify lexical or grammatical search frames that would catch all tokens of all variants. In addition, if the variable includes more than two variants, the problem arises that, for instance, a token of variant 1 might be interchangeable with variant 2 but not with variant 3 in the particular linguistic environment in which it occurs (see Biber et al. 2016 for a discussion of this problem).

In practice, corpus researchers typically limit the envelope of variation to relevant tokens of a relatively small number of variants to make retrieval and analysis manageable. For instance, by including three variants that may express genitive meaning – noun + noun sequences (e.g. *the book cover*), *s*-genitives (e.g. *the book's cover*), and *of*-phrases (e.g. *the cover of the book*) – Szmrecsanyi et al. (2016) and Biber et al. (2016) are more inclusive than several other scholars, who restrict retrieval to two constructions. Nevertheless, Szmrecsanyi et al. (2016: 24–6) acknowledge that their study may be considered both too inclusive (because they included tokens that were deemed interchangeable with one other variant but not both) and not inclusive enough (because prepositional phrases with prepositions other than *of*, which may be interchangeable with one or several of the variants included, were not considered). What is sometimes treated as a simple binary choice is in reality a highly complex "web of variation, with different degrees of interchangeability among the variants that make up that web" (Szmrecsanyi et al. 2016: 25). I discuss similar problems in Chapters 7 and 8.

Historical linguists face additional difficulties. Partly because introspection is not available when deciding what type of variation is possible in historical data, it is difficult to reach certainty that all possible variants have been identified, and string-based corpus searches will miss variants not covered by the search strings (Enrique-Arias 2018: 264–5). This can sometimes be alleviated by using a "bottom-up" method where part of the corpus is examined manually to see what features might be added to those already selected for the corpus search (Whitt 2018: 6). In addition, if the scope of the investigation is diachronic, not all variants may be valid options at all times; the many ways in which future time has been expressed in the history of the English language – including the simple present tense – is a good example. In addition, new variants may appear through the occurrence of ambiguous tokens, compatible with both an old and a new meaning or function, but the feature is only a variant if it expresses the new meaning or function; see, for instance, Traugott (2016: 380–3) for a discussion of ambiguous cases in the development of BE *going to* into a future auxiliary. As we shall see in Chapter 8, one context – non-restrictive postmodification of nouns – causes a great deal of ambiguity even though it does not involve the emergence of new functions.

The variationist perspective also needs to be examined on the level of the individual token. Even if two variants are in principle different ways of saying (roughly) the same thing, individual tokens of those variants may not offer the language user any choice because features of the co-text rule out one of the variants. Tokens that are subject to such knock-out factors must be excluded from the counts (Tagliamonte 2012: 10–11) in order to achieve acceptable precision. Researchers must thus examine each token of every variant. However, not all contexts enable clear-cut decisions: deciding whether a variant that was not used *could* have been used may be a difficult task. We have access to no native speakers who could provide acceptability judgements, and present-day intuition must be used with caution and becomes less reliable the further back in time the text is from (see Denison and Hundt 2013). An approach that does not require native-speaker competence is to make an assessment based on whether similar tokens of the other variant(s) occur in other contemporary texts. However, as discussed in Chapter 3, we have access only to an incomplete and biased selection of texts, based on which we have to make responsible decisions. While we can arguably conclude that a variant that occurred in a text from a given period would also have been an option in other texts from the same period, the opposite does not hold: the non-occurrence of a feature in a corpus is not sufficient evidence that it could not occur (Bergs 2005: 14; Romaine 2016: 34; but cf. Kroch 1989: 200).[12]

Although the variationist approach is potentially problematic, this framework has a great deal to offer historical linguistics. Important insights have been reached into the nature of linguistic variation and change using variationist methods. Nevertheless, even the most advanced statistical techniques cannot compensate for deficiencies in validity that result from imperfect selection of data. It remains the responsibility of the scholar to assess and justify the most appropriate envelope of variation for each study (see Raumolin-Brunberg 1988: 141).

4.4.2 Text-Linguistic Approaches

The main alternative to variationist investigations is to calculate the frequency of the feature analysed separately from those of other features.

---

[12] There is also a mismatch inherent in assessing the interchangeability of features in an entire (sub)corpus. In doing so, researchers are essentially deciding on whether a feature is possible in a communal language; but the acceptability of a given feature is a characteristic of each idiolect. In many cases, this complication is likely to be of little consequence, as populations establish norms for language use (Traugott 2016: 378) based on convergence. But in some situations – for instance, if the variant is a very recent addition to the communal language, or if texts by writers with widely differing regional and/or sociocultural backgrounds are included in the same (sub)corpus – there may be reason to believe that not all idiolects in the corpus would have agreed on whether or not a variant is possible (and/or semantically equivalent to other variants).

Frequency is thus not operationalized as a proportion of a variant field; instead, normalization is used to make the frequency independent of the length of the texts examined. In corpus linguistics, normalized frequencies tend to be based on the orthographic word as a unit, and common choices include occurrences per 1,000 words or per million words.

Biber et al. (2016: 357–8) argue that, while each relevant token is treated as an observation in variationist approaches, the text-linguistic framework considers either a text or a (sub-)corpus as an observation. However, a text-linguistic framework does not preclude coding each token for a number of linguistic and extralinguistic features in a manner similar to similar to common practice in variationist research. For example, Leech et al. (2009: 126–7) are able to show that much of the recent increase in the frequency of the progressive in written British English has taken place in present-tense contexts and that writing is becoming more similar to speech, where present-tense uses predominate, on this parameter. Such an approach can provide valuable clues to what contexts – linguistic and extralinguistic – are connected with changes in the frequency of forms (see, for instance, Section 7.3).

The text-linguistic approach is in some ways a safer choice than a variationist approach. In many cases, it might be difficult to establish a variant field with certainty for all or parts of the data (see Sections 4.4.1, 7.2, and 8.2). For some linguistic features, it may even be difficult to reach reliable conclusions regarding what a variant field would potentially comprise. Conjuncts, also known as linking adverbials, are a case in point (see, for instance, Grund and Smitterberg 2014). To study conjuncts from a variationist perspective, researchers would need to broaden the definition of *variant* to encompass structures containing the features rather than merely the features themselves; for instance, two main clauses linked by a conjunct such as *however* or *though* might correspond roughly to (i) two main clauses linked by *but* or (ii) a complex sentence containing a subordinate clause introduced by *(al)though*. Moreover, the corresponding structures would vary with the conjunct examined; a conjunct such as *for instance* would instead need to be checked against the occurrence of structures with *such as* and *like*. It is even arguable that a conjunct may vary with zero; for instance, the linguistic context may make it so clear that a sentence is intended as exemplification that a sentence-initial conjunct like *for instance*, while fully possible to insert, does not add much to the overall meaning of the text (this might be true of the present sentence). Texts would then need to be gone through manually to find places where a conjunct could have been inserted without changing the meaning of the text, which would be a time-consuming – and not easily reproducible – process. In such cases, reporting on frequencies per 1,000 words is methodologically safer, since no assumptions about an envelope of variation need to be made.

From the perspective of the idiolect as the locus of language (and of language change), text-linguistic perspectives are also safer options. If a speaker's idiolect does not contain a certain feature, this will be visible in the results as a frequency of zero in the relevant text(s). If texts differ with regard to their normalized frequency of a feature, an analysis of the linguistic environment of each token can reveal environments that co-occur with the feature in question only in some texts, which may in turn be indicative of inter-idiolectal variation in the propagation of the feature. However, importantly, in terms of both overall occurrence and occurrence in particular contexts, absence from texts does not entail absence from idiolects (see Section 4.4.1).

There are certain limitations associated with a text-linguistic approach. Most importantly, while word counts are easily retrievable automatically, the orthographic word is frequently not the most suitable unit of normalization. As Ball (1994: 297) notes, a relative frequency should measure the number of tokens that do occur in relation to the number of tokens that could have occurred; but linguistic features typically are not a possible substitute for any word in language, because their occurrence is structurally constrained. The slots available for progressives, for instance, are a subset of the number of verb phrases (further restrictions apply regarding *Aktionsart*, mood, and other factors) in a text. Texts differ with regard to the number of verb phrases per 1,000 words; for instance, academic writing tends to contain fewer verb phrases than trial proceedings (see Smitterberg 2005: 64 for data on finite verb phrases). As such discrepancies are not taken into account in the normalization procedure, the frequency of progressives in academic texts might be under-reported in comparisons with trial proceedings. This may in return affect statistics that test for differences between text categories. As implied in the example, such problems are particularly significant when texts or subcorpora from different genres are compared (see Ball 1994: 297–9 for a similar example regarding *it*-clefts). Like the variationist approach, text-linguistic research thus has its own advantages and drawbacks.

Several of the case studies make use of text-linguistic approaches and present results as normalized frequencies (per 1,000 words). When such results are given, raw frequencies are always provided (typically in tables), while normalized frequencies are sometimes provided in figures only. In such cases, the exact frequency per 1,000 words can be easily calculated based on the raw-frequency counts in the corresponding table and the word counts given in Section 4.5.

4.4.3 The Use of Significance Testing

The last few decades have featured increasingly extensive use of statistics in corpus linguistics. In particular, significance testing is commonly carried out to help researchers to decide whether a difference in frequencies between samples is likely to be due to random fluctuation. This practice is potentially very valuable, as it provides researchers with an objective method of evaluating differences. However, the practice of significance testing has also come under attack. Kilgarriff (2005: 264) notes that language is never random; provided that we have enough data, the null hypothesis can thus always be rejected – even when two corpora set up to be identical are contrasted (see also Hilpert 2020: 9–10 for the danger of using large corpora). Gries (2005) notes that Kilgarriff's doubts partly echo those from several other fields but also suggests several ways in which linguists can improve on the situation, such as considering effect sizes and corrections for post hoc testing. At the end of the article, Gries (2005: 284) asks whether, owing to the problems associated with null-hypothesis significance testing, corpus linguists should give up on this practice.

Recently, Koplenig (2019) returned to this question and claimed that it should be answered in the affirmative: as the assumptions that allow us to infer something about a language based on corpus-linguistic samples of that language are not fulfilled, linguists should not test differences for significance. From a theoretical point of view, Koplenig (2019: 329) argues that, as I-language is "a cognitive phenomenon and ... not directly observable", more research is needed on the link between linguistic output stored in corpora and cognitive processes in language users' minds.[13] (In addition, as discussed in Chapter 3, since each language user's idiolect is unique, what corpora based on several users can represent is always an abstraction from individual idiolects.) Other arguments raised by Koplenig (2019: 331–7) include problems with defining the population the corpus

---

[13] The types of evidence Koplenig (2019) suggests should complement corpus-linguistic evidence – for example psycho-linguistic experimentation, elicitation, and neurolinguistic experimentation – are largely unavailable to historical linguistics, given the lack of native speakers of historical language states. Language historians thus need to extrapolate from information culled from present-day language users when they can, and otherwise restrict themselves to the analysis of E-language.

sample is intended to represent and the subjectivity that is consequently inherent in balancing a corpus. These problems are argued to invalidate significance testing.

Given the weight attached to the outcome of significance tests in corpus linguistics and the particular nature of language output as data, these objections need to be addressed. In particular, a difference need not be linguistically important merely because it is statistically significant. As the assumptions of randomness and independence are not met by corpora, statistical tests can only indicate that a development may be important, and the linguist's interpretation remains irreplaceable. In the present study, I will where relevant apply significance testing (chi-square and, in Section 5.3.2, binary logistic regression) to the results of variationist analyses where a choice between options can be assumed to have been made; however, significant differences alike will also be discussed critically.

4.5 The Corpora Used in the Case Studies

The case studies in Chapters 5–8 are based chiefly on two corpora: a Corpus of Nineteenth-Century English (CONCE; see Section 4.5.1) and the Corpus of Nineteenth-Century Newspaper English (CNNE; see Section 4.5.2). Together, these corpora contain roughly 1.3 million words, which is a modest size compared with modern corpora of LModE such as the Corpus of Late Modern English Texts (CLMETEV 2006; 15 million words), the Old Bailey Corpus (OBC 2012; 14 million words), and, in particular, the Corpus of Historical American English (COHA 2010–; 400 million words).[14] Studying nineteenth-century English using corpora such as CONCE and CNNE may potentially seem a somewhat dated endeavour now that far larger sources of data are electronically available.

However, there are also several advantages to using smaller corpora. To begin with, the sampling procedure may have been more careful. Although representativity and comparability are goals that are difficult to reach (and sometimes mutually exclusive – see Section 4.2.1), it is arguably easier to come close to attaining them with a small corpus whose texts have been selected carefully. Very large corpora may also feature errors owing to uncorrected OCR (Optical Character Recognition) or typing mistakes, which have typically been corrected in smaller corpora. Similarly, tagging

---

[14] Word counts were taken from the corpus entries in the Corpus Resource Database (CoRD), maintained by the Research Unit for Variation, Contacts and Change in English at the University of Helsinki. Further details are available at www.helsinki.fi/varieng/CoRD/index.html.

problems may be possible to address for small corpora (Hundt and Leech 2012: 179). For instance, the tagging of the subset of CONCE used for the study of participle-clause postmodifiers (see Chapter 8) had been manually checked for whether a verb form was tagged as a past tense or a past participle; this greatly facilitated the retrieval of past-participle clauses for that study.[15] Moreover, the size of the material is ultimately of less importance than the size of the database resulting from the retrieval process. Provided that the feature investigated is sufficiently frequent, a small corpus may provide enough data to enable a reliable analysis. The size of CONCE and CNNE was deemed sufficient to achieve robust results as regards the four case studies in this volume.

One important desideratum when selecting corpora for a study is to capture any important genre variation in the distribution of the linguistic feature studied. Patterns of use attested for an entire corpus represent a conflation of results for individual genres that often have very different linguistic characteristics, and the overall results for the corpus or corpora used may not accurately represent any one genre (Biber 2012: 9). This factor is arguably more important for LModE than for preceding periods in the history of English, as increased linguistic genre differentiation characterizes the period (see Biber and Finegan 1997). As the spread of features between genres is an integral part of colloquialization and densification, genre variation is especially important in the case studies.

4.5.1 CONCE

A Corpus of Nineteenth-Century English (CONCE) was compiled by Merja Kytö (Uppsala University) and Juhani Rudanko (University of Tampere). As CONCE has been described in relative detail in previous publications (Kytö et al. 2000; Smitterberg 2005; Kytö et al. 2006b), the present discussion focusses on aspects of the corpus that are immediately relevant to the case studies in Chapters 5–8, with special reference to genre characteristics.

The texts in CONCE, all of which contain British English, are grouped into three periods: 1800–30 (period 1), 1850–70 (period 2), and 1870–1900

---

[15] These potential advantages of small corpora in no way imply that very large corpora like COHA are not of immense value in historical linguistics. They enable linguists to ask research questions that were previously virtually unanswerable, and they can also be adapted to be suitable for the study of frequent features; for instance, the retrieved output can be thinned randomly in order to provide researchers with a suitable number of tokens. The point made here is merely that the corpora chosen, which are described in the following subsections, were suitable for the concerns of the present study.

(period 3). In some of the case studies, only parts of the corpus will be drawn on for data. Of special importance in this regard is the "S-coefficient subcorpus" (Smitterberg 2005: 52, 271–5). This subcorpus comprises parts of the tagged version of CONCE where all tags that were ambiguous between non-finite and finite verb forms have been manually disambiguated, which proved important especially for the analysis in Chapter 8.

One of the features that make CONCE a particularly attractive choice of corpus is the wide range of genres sampled. Seven genres are included in the corpus: Debates (recorded debates from the Houses of Parliament), Drama (prose comedies or farces), Fiction (novels), History (historical monographs), Letters (personal letters between relatives or close friends), Science (monographs pertaining to the natural or social sciences), and Trials (trial proceedings in dialogue format) (Kytö et al. 2000: 88). Word counts for the different samples of the corpus are given in Table 4.1; Table 4.2 provides corresponding word counts for the S-coefficient subcorpus. The total word count for the entire corpus, which excludes elements such as stage directions (Drama), speaker information (Drama and Trials), chapter titles (Fiction, History, and Science), and sender and addressee information (Letters), is just under 1 million words.

Another important issue is the number of texts sampled per cell in Table 4.1. For some genres, this factor is of lesser importance, as a corpus text comprises samples from several language users' output: this holds true for Debates and Trials in particular. The Letters genre was sampled more extensively than the other genres in the corpus, with nine or ten texts (four or five by men and four or five by women) per period/genre subsample; in addition, each Letters text contains a large number of separate letters. In Drama, Fiction, History, and Science, however, each such subsample contains texts by three writers only,[16] which makes it possible for individual texts to influence results. I will discuss such effects in the data where relevant in Chapters 5–8. In keeping with the idiolectal perspective on language change adopted in this study (see Chapter 3), individual outliers will not be seen as problems of sampling, but as important windows on language variation and change.

Geisler's (2002) factor-score analysis of CONCE reveals that the seven genres fall into two main groups based on their linguistic characteristics in

---

[16] In Drama and Fiction, it is of course possible for authors to use language to differentiate characters, narrators, etc., which may lead to more linguistic heterogeneity within texts (in addition to the overall difference between narrative and dialogue passages in Fiction).

Table 4.1 Word counts for period and genre subsamples of CONCE

Period	Debates	Drama	Fiction	Letters	History	Science	Trials	Total
1	19,908	31,311	42,032	121,624	30,904	38,037	62,360	346,176
2	19,385	29,543	39,045	131,116	30,504	31,679	60,570	341,842
3	19,947	29,090	30,113	90,891	30,564	30,603	67,588	298,796
Total	59,240	89,944	111,190	343,631	91,972	100,319	190,518	986,814

Table 4.2 Word counts for period and genre subsamples of the S-coefficient subcorpus

Period	Debates	Drama	Fiction	Letters	History	Science	Trials	Total
1	19,908	31,311	42,032	52,164	30,904	38,037	62,360	276,716
3	19,947	29,090	30,113	37,728	30,564	30,603	67,588	245,633
Total	39,855	60,401	72,145	89,892	61,468	68,640	129,948	522,349

4.5 The Corpora Used in the Case Studies

terms of the dimensions of variation established in Biber (1988). The non-expository group, which is closer to the "oral" end of the relevant dimensions, comprises Drama, Fiction, Letters, and Trials, while Debates, History, and Science make up the expository group, with texts that are closer to the "literate" end of the same dimensions. The divide between expository and non-expository genres is thus not one of medium alone: the speech-based Debates genre patterns with the written, non-speech-related genres Science and History; even though the texts in Letters are neither speech-based nor speech-purposed, they display similarities with those in Drama (speech-purposed), Fiction (partly speech-purposed), and Trials (speech-based). Geisler (2002) also presents information on the development of the genres on four of Biber's dimensions of variation, some of which is potentially relevant to hypotheses about whether or not they underwent colloquialization and/or densification. This concerns in particular Dimensions 1 ("Involved vs. Informational Production"), 3 ("Elaborated vs. Situation-dependent Reference"), and 5 ("Impersonal vs. Non-impersonal Style"). Significant changes on these dimensions can, broadly speaking, be in "oral" or "literate" directions, where a change towards orality can be assumed to tally with colloquialization. In addition, some of the linguistic features that load on these dimensions are directly relevant to these types of change, for example contractions (Dimension 1; colloquialization), nouns (Dimension 1; densification), nominalizations (Dimension 3; densification), and passives (Dimension 5; colloquialization).[17]

Within the non-expository group, Drama is one of the most informal genres in CONCE. It is speech-purposed, that is, Drama texts were "designed to produce real-time spoken interaction" (Culpeper and Kytö 2010: 17), although there is of course no guarantee that such speech representation was – or was intended to be – wholly successful. As the texts included belong to the subgenre of drama comedy, and the setting of the plays is frequently domestic (Kytö et al. 2000: 88), the characters can be expected to use comparatively informal language. This characteristic would make comedies an excellent vehicle for colloquialization. Smitterberg (2008, 2012b) also shows that phrasal verbs, the progressive, and *not*-contraction, three features associated with colloquialization, rise in frequency in the Drama genre. In contrast, as Drama texts are written

---

[17] A few features listed in Biber (1988) that would be relevant to colloquialization and densification were not included in Geisler's (2002) analysis because they resisted automatic retrieval, for example present-participle and past-participle clauses (see Chapter 8) and clausal and phrasal co-ordination (see Chapter 6).

mainly for aesthetic and entertainment purposes, they are less likely to have undergone a general increase in information density. Geisler (2002) found that Drama remained stable on Dimensions 1 and 3 but became more oral on Dimension 5. This development may be expected to co-occur with colloquialization; several of the features that would have decreased in frequency as a result are passives, and a decrease in passive verb phrases has been suggested to be a "negative manifestation of colloquialization" (Leech 2004: 73).

Fiction is more difficult to describe in terms of its relationship with speech, as it is essentially a mixed genre. Fictional dialogue may have affinities with drama dialogue linguistically, though the settings of the dialogue are more varied in novels than in the plays sampled, while narrative sections typically feature less orality. Fiction is also the least involved of the non-expository genres in Geisler's (2002) factor-score analysis of CONCE. However, there are some tendencies towards colloquialization in Fiction: *not*-contraction and phrasal verbs both become more frequent across time in this genre (Smitterberg 2008: 276, 2012b: 199). The progressive appears not to take part in this development, but instead increases in frequency between periods 1 and 2 only to decrease again between periods 2 and 3 (see Smitterberg 2005: 69–72 for discussion). Fiction also patterns with Drama in Geisler's (2002) factor-score analysis in that it changes towards orality on Dimension 5 but is stable on Dimensions 1 and 3. It is difficult to link such developments directly to wider sections of society reading novels in nineteenth-century England. While large portions of the working classes were able to spend some money on purchasing fiction by the end of the nineteenth century, which might have created market forces favouring colloquialization, new full-length fiction largely remained a middle-class market owing to high prices (Vincent 1989: 211–13). There is little reason to expect densification in Fiction, partly because the purpose of Fiction texts did not change in the direction of increasing their informational load (Biber and Gray 2012: 316).

The Letters genre is unique in several ways. To begin with, the private letters sampled for CONCE are stratified into letters written by women and men. This feature enables a gender perspective on linguistic variation. Moreover, the private letter is typically seen as a speech-like genre without being either speech-based or speech-purposed (Culpeper and Kytö 2010: 17–18), owing to the informal production circumstances of most private letters that were sent to people who knew the letter writer well. The Letters genre also emerges as oral on Dimension 1 of Biber's (1988) factor analysis, and Nevalainen and Raumolin-Brunberg (2017: 43) note that letters share

4.5 The Corpora Used in the Case Studies

features with colloquial speech. The Letters genre clearly undergoes colloquialization with regard to phrasal verbs and the progressive (Smitterberg 2008: 276), and in fact displays the highest frequencies in CONCE of both features in period 3. Private letters were also subject to an important sociocultural change in nineteenth-century England: the 1840 introduction of the Penny Post (see Section 2.3.3) made the sending of letters considerably simpler and cheaper than it had been previously. In fact, the impact of this reform may have caused private letters to undergo "de-densification" during the 1800s: after 1840, it became less important to economize on words when writing private letters in order to keep down the number of letters sent as well as postage costs. Again, like Drama and Fiction, the Letters genre changes significantly only on Dimension 5 in Geisler's (2002) analysis, which tallies with an interpretation in terms of colloquialization but not densification taking place.

Trials, finally, is a speech-based genre: the published accounts of courtroom dialogue supposedly constitute a verbatim account of what was actually said. However, such faithfulness is rare or non-existent in practice. As there were sophisticated shorthand systems around after the 1750s (Smith 1978: 162), the content of what was said was potentially taken down with a great deal of accuracy, but false starts, repair strategies, etc. may have been omitted (but cf. Kytö and Walker 2003: 224–8). As the corpus files were based on printed reports of the trials, there is also scribal as well as editorial interference to consider (Kytö and Walker 2003: 241); however, an attempt was made to limit editorial change by basing the transcriptions on trial proceedings that were printed soon after the trials took place. Also, even faithful records of trials do not give us access to informal speech, as several factors – for example the formal atmosphere of the courtroom and the possibility that several of the lawyers' questions would have been partly prepared in advance – constrain the naturalness of the exchanges. These caveats notwithstanding, trial records are an important source for past speech, and they also represent a wider variety of idiolects than most genres, as they contain testimony by women, illiterate speakers, and so on. The notion of colloquialization is arguably difficult to apply to a speech-based genre like Trials: since verbatim accounts of speech were aimed at, the written norms for this genre should already be tolerant of spoken usage. However, there are a number of ways in which such change may nevertheless occur. First, features that were stigmatized in writing but normal in speech may become more acceptable in speech-based writing over time. Secondly, though Mair's (2006b) definition of colloquialization pertains only to writing, other scholars have explored the possibility that conversational style influences other spoken genres; for instance, Fairclough (1992: 204) suggests that "conversation is . . . a powerful model for other types of spoken discourse", and Kytö and Smitterberg (2019) discuss possible colloquialization in the OBC. It is possible that the formality of the courtroom setting decreased with time, leading to more colloquial features actually being uttered by the participants in the trial, although no such trend was noticeable in Smitterberg's (2008, 2012b) analysis of progressives, phrasal verbs, and *not*-contraction. The relationship of Trials to densification is also unclear and requires further investigation. In Geisler's (2002) factor score analysis, Trials is stable on Dimension 5 (unlike Fiction, Drama, and Letters) but instead becomes more oral on Dimension 1. This change may indicate colloquialization but constitutes a weak argument against densification, as two literate features on this dimension (nouns and prepositions), which may thus be increasingly disfavoured in Trials, are involved in densification.

The expository Debates genre is similar to Trials in that the speech-based nature of the genre complicates hypotheses regarding colloquialization. Nevertheless, there are some tendencies towards colloquialization in Debates: the frequency of the progressive more than doubles across the century, and there is also a possible increase in the incidence of phrasal verbs (Smitterberg 2008: 276–7). In contrast, *not*-contraction is absent from Debates (Smitterberg 2012b: 194). However, the interpretation of developments in this genre is complicated by a change in the mode of speech representation between periods 1 and 3: while indirect speech is predominant in period 1, most debates are rendered as direct speech in period 3. The fact that the Debates genre becomes more oral across the century in Geisler's (2002) factor-score analysis – it undergoes significant change on Dimensions 1 and 3 – is most likely partly due to this period difference in speech representation: several of the oral features indicating involved production, for example first-person pronouns and present-tense verbs, must have increased in frequency as a result of a shift from indirect to direct speech. It is more difficult to make hypotheses concerning densification, but, as mentioned above, the Debates genre becomes less literate on Dimensions 1 and 3. Nouns, prepositions, and nominalizations all load on the literate end of Dimension 1 or Dimension 3 (Geisler 2002: 251); a change towards orality here may thus indicate a change away from densification.

CONCE contains two genres that represent academic writing: History and Science. These genres are writing-based, writing-purposed, and non-speech-like in Culpeper and Kytö's (2010: 18) framework. Interestingly, despite their similarity, History and Science do not display the same linguistic development. While *not*-contraction does not occur in either genre (Smitterberg 2012b: 194), the progressive, and possibly also phrasal verbs increase in frequency in History, while their incidence remains unchanged in Science (Smitterberg 2008). Despite these increases in frequency, Geisler's (2002) analysis provides no indication that History undergoes colloquialization.[18] On the contrary, there is a weak indication of densification in that History moves towards the "literate" end of Dimension 3; one of the "literate" features with significant loadings on that dimension is nominalizations, a rising frequency of which is a feature of densification. Science remains stable on every parameter: frequencies of progressives and phrasal verbs are stable (Smitterberg 2008: 277), *not*-contraction is absent (Smitterberg 2012b: 194), and the genre does not exhibit change on any dimension of variation (Geisler 2002: 269). However, given that Biber and Gray (2012: 316, 326) suggest that scientific writing became increasingly specialized and acquired a heavier informational load during the LModE period, and that these developments are taken to indicate linguistic densification, there is still some reason to assume that densification will manifest itself in the Science data. As will become clear in Chapters 7 and 8, History and Science do not display parallel developments, despite their similarities as written, non-speech-related, academic genres.

4.5.2 CNNE

Newspaper English is a very important genre to include in the study of nineteenth-century English. First, according to Lee (1976: 18), the press "was the most important single medium of the communication of ideas" during the 1800s. Secondly, technological and societal developments fuelled considerable changes in the newspaper industry during this time; indeed, the concept of *the news* as such can be argued to have arisen between 1800 and 1900 (Brown 1985: 1). The number of newspapers in England and Wales grew from 267 in 1821 to 563 only 30 years later. Sales also increased dramatically; between 1855 and 1880, circulation rose by 600 per cent (Bös 2015: 93). The immense increase both in the amount of newspaper English produced and in the number of people who were exposed to news text means that newspaper English most likely had a greater impact on nineteenth-century idiolects than

---

[18] Smitterberg (2005: 101) suggests that the increase in the frequency of the progressive in History is connected to an increase in narrativity in Geisler's (2002: 259) analysis. While this correlation is clearly present in the data, it is difficult to connect to either colloquialization or densification.

most other written genres, especially towards the end of the century. Any reasonably comprehensive account of nineteenth-century English thus needs to consider newspaper language.

Newspaper English is also of particular importance for the case studies in Chapters 5–8, as previous work (e.g. Mair 1997; Hundt and Mair 1999; Leech et al. 2009; Biber and Gray 2012) indicates that the language of newspapers is affected by colloquialization as well as densification. In a process driven by popularization, nineteenth-century newspapers increasingly located their appeal between elite and popular knowledge and gradually underwent a transition from aiming to enlighten to aiming to represent their readers (Conboy 2010: 79), which is likely to have had an effect on linguistic choices as writers increasingly accommodated to the perceived linguistic preferences of their readers. At the same time, journalists needed to communicate an increased informational load in a limited space (Biber and Gray 2012: 316), under time pressure, and with limited opportunities for revision (Görlach 1999: 146). The combination of these factors makes newspaper English an interesting object of study.

The Corpus of Nineteenth-Century Newspaper English (CNNE) was compiled in order to enable the study of variation and change in the language of newspapers published in England. The compilation was based on converting PDF images of news texts from digital newspaper archives (ProQuest Historical Newspapers, The Times Digital Archive, and Nineteenth Century British Library Newspapers) into text files with the aid of OCR software (ABBYY FineReader). The resulting files were manually checked against the originals. Articles that seemed suitable for OCR processing were given precedence in selection; texts that featured torn paper, blots, smudged ink, and so on were excluded. The size of CNNE is 323,658 words.

Metropolitan as well as provincial newspapers were sampled for CNNE. Both dailies and weeklies were included, owing to the great importance of Sunday papers for the development of the nineteenth-century newspaper: Sunday papers had a larger number of – and more socially diversified – readers than dailies did from the start of the nineteenth century (Williams 1978: 41, 48), and aspects of the Sunday press spread to dailies after the repeal of the Taxes on Knowledge (Conboy 2017: 124). Two periods were drawn on for material: 1830–50 (period 1: 159,881 words) and 1875–95 (period 2: 163,777 words).[19] There were two main reasons for the choice

---

[19] Millar (2009: 193, 207–8) criticizes the practice of basing hypotheses about language change on two temporal snapshots only; as many changes are not unidirectional, looking at only two chronological points may lead to incorrect generalizations. While this limitation should certainly be borne in mind, the features studied in CNNE have been found to take part in change across longer time

4.5 The Corpora Used in the Case Studies

of periodization. First, I wanted the time span separating the periods to be longer than that covered by either period, so that, for instance, all texts from period 1 are closer in time to other texts from period 1 than they are to any text from period 2. Secondly, the periods were chosen to reflect a number of important extralinguistic developments that may be hypothesized to have had an effect on newspaper language; these are summarized below.

Although period 1 begins some time after the first paper claiming to speak for the working classes had been established, namely the *Twopenny Trash* in 1816 (Vincent 1989: 242), the main growth of the radical press belongs to the 1830s (Asquith 1978: 106). Papers such as the *Poor Man's Guardian* and the *Northern Star*, which represented a compromise between newspaper and spokesperson (Vincent 1989: 249), radicalized the emergent working-class movement. At the same time, the Reform Act 1832 enfranchised more middle-class voters, and these new voters were also targeted by newspapers (Conboy 2010: 78). As early as the 1830s, there were thus papers aimed at different classes in society, so this decade was taken as a suitable point of departure for sampling. Another reason for drawing the line around 1830 is the increasingly rare use of prosecution for libel after the mid-1820s (Asquith 1978: 111), one indication of the decline in government ability to control newspapers. This decline was to some extent a delayed consequence of the Libel Law 1792; this law put decisions regarding libel in the hands of a jury rather than a judge (Bös 2015: 92).

A large number of important developments separate periods 1 and 2. Perhaps most importantly, the abolition of the so-called Taxes on Knowledge (especially the stamp duty on newspapers, abolished in 1855, but also the advertisement and paper duties, removed in 1853 and 1861 respectively) contributed to radically changing the newspaper landscape in Britain. In period 1, newspapers had to carry a stamp that cost 4d. until 1836, when it was reduced to 1d. (Curran 1978: 56). This artificially raised the price of newspapers, making daily papers unaffordable for many members of the working classes. However, a number of illegal, unstamped newspapers that were aimed at a working-class readership, for example the *Poor Man's Guardian*, were published as a countermeasure, and by 1836 the radical unstamped papers outsold the legal ones (Curran 1978: 62).[20] After the reduction in the stamp duty in 1836, working-class readers would often

---

frames in previous work (see Chapters 5–8), which decreases the risk of identifying false positives with regard to language change.

[20] In 1834, a jury found that the *Poor Man's Guardian* did not count as a newspaper and that people could thus not be prosecuted for selling it (Hollis 1970: 53; Claridge 2017: 139).

combine together to buy stamped radical papers like the Chartist *Northern Star*.

The abolition of the stamp duty in 1855 made a penny daily paper a possibility (Brown 1985: 4), which vastly increased the circulation of papers; the first successful London daily priced at 1d. was the *Daily Telegraph* (Conboy 2010: 91).[21] It also enabled the introduction of the rotary press, developed in 1846, which greatly increased printing speed; as the stamp duty had required separate stamping for sheets of paper, continuous rolls of papers could not be used before the duty had been abolished (Schneider 2002: 22). At the same time, technological innovations resulting from the industrialization of the press – as well as rising operating costs and reduced retail prices – increased the amount of capital needed to start a newspaper. These developments, which meant that higher circulation figures were required in order to break even (Curran 1978: 68), put running a newspaper beyond the means of many independent editors (Bös 2015: 97) and made it more important for proprietors to protect their investments. Market forces thus turned out to be a more effective weapon against the so-called pauper press than the stamp duty had been (Vincent 1989: 234; see also Bös 2015: 92). The importance of attracting advertisements also limited the financial appeal of radical papers, which were discriminated against by advertisers owing to the limited purchasing power of their readers (Curran 1978: 60, 69; Williams 2010: 76). Partly for these reasons, and unlike radical papers from period 1, popular papers from period 2 tended to stress identification with the existing social system rather than, for instance, class solidarity (Curran 1978: 72), as the market favoured a broadly liberal position (Conboy 2010: 79). Working-class attitudes also shifted to some extent from conflict to consensus after the 1850s (Williams 2010: 95).

The period 1860–1910, which encompasses period 2 in CNNE, is sometimes regarded as the "golden age" of newspapers (Fries 2012: 1,067). While the mid-1840s development of the telegraph "revolutionised the transmission of news" (Asquith 1978: 102), actual access to such news was greatly facilitated by the formation of the Press Association in 1868 (Brown 1985: 4). The Press Association secured a monopoly outside London on news from the Reuters news agency (established in 1851) (Brown 1985: 121–2). The availability of such a cheap news service to

---

[21] Another factor affecting the price of newspapers was paper costs. Changes in the raw material used – from rags via esparto grass to wood pulp – further lowered the cost of newspapers (Schneider 2002: 22–3).

4.5 The Corpora Used in the Case Studies

provincial papers enabled them to compete with metropolitan newspapers, as international news reached the countryside in provincial papers before metropolitan papers could be delivered there (Clarke 2004: 130). The transatlantic cable (1866) and the use of telephones for news reporting (from 1878) further facilitated news gathering (Schneider 2002: 22) for metropolitan and provincial papers alike. Meanwhile, London papers benefitted from the expansion of the railway network, which made it easier to distribute copies of metropolitan papers to the countryside quickly; by 1875, London morning papers could be purchased in, for instance, Birmingham and Bristol when business hours began (Lee 1976: 59).

Commercialization caused newspapers to be regarded as businesses rather than political investments (Wiener 1988b: 56, 62; Boyce 1978: 25). As the predominant function of the newspaper gradually shifted from the political to the commercial sphere (see Conboy 2010: 79–80), newspaper ownership was concentrated into fewer hands (Bös 2015: 95). Although only *The Times* could be regarded as a national paper by 1900, there was a clear trend towards centralization (Lee 1976: 73). The role of advertising became increasingly central for revenues; for instance, *The Times* made £94,463 from sales and £104,766 from advertising in the second half of 1867, and the gap was even wider for the *Manchester Guardian* (£35,866 from sales and £54,208 from advertising) twenty-one years later (Xekalakis 1999: 43). Papers now sold for less than they cost to produce, which made attracting advertisers a requirement for success (Curran 1978: 69). Although there was no real market research in the 1800s, the increasing dependence on advertisement revenue meant that knowing what a paper's readership was became more important (Lee 1976: 38).

The practice of newspaper reading also changed dramatically. On average, each copy of an early-nineteenth-century newspaper was probably read by between ten and thirty people (Asquith 1978: 101); newspapers might be read in clubs or pubs, hired per hour, or circulated among joint rural subscribers (Lee 1976: 35–6). Some papers, for example the *Northern Star*, which was designed to facilitate this practice (Williams 2010: 80), were often read aloud to listeners (Lee 1976: 27; Brown 1985: 50–1). In contrast, in the late 1800s individual purchases were the norm (Schneider 2002: 23), owing to factors such as increased affluence, the poor quality of most newsprint, and falling prices. This difference had been foreseen as a positive development by members of the ruling classes, who were concerned that the phenomenon of members of the working classes coming together to share and read the same copy of a paper might fuel social unrest (Vincent 1989: 235).

Influential London dailies in period 2 included conservative papers such as the *Standard* as well as liberal ones like the *Daily News* (Schalck 1988: 74). Outside London, provincial dailies, which had been rare before 1855, were now a familiar feature (Lee 1976: 68). In addition, the first successful mass-circulation papers – Sunday papers such as *Lloyd's* and *Reynolds's* – were an established feature of the market (Brown 1985: 27; Conboy 2010: 86). Members of the working classes, for whom a penny daily was still too expensive, could afford a Sunday paper, which gave them access to newsprint even before the introduction of halfpenny evening papers (Brown 1985: 30–1).[22] Sunday newspapers had thus largely taken the place of the radical papers aimed at the working class from the 1840s on (Wiener 1988b: 60); however, their contributors, owners, and editors were less concerned with radical social reform (Berridge 1978: 254–5). Their success was due to the combination "of (mild) pro-working class positions", "the expanded use of sensationalism", "new business techniques", and "country-wide advertising" (Bös 2015: 97).

Significant developments also took place between 1875 and 1895. A number of novelties known collectively as New Journalism developed during period 2 (Lee 1976: 70), including the interview, an increased liveliness and directness of style, typographical changes that increased readability, more illustrations, use of the front page for news, more sensational content, sports reporting, and investigative journalism (Lee 1976: 120–5; Wiener 1988b: 55; Xekalakis 1999: 18). There was also an increased focus on human interest and on news rather than opinion (Bös 2015: 99), which had often been the focus of mid-Victorian papers; in addition, news was more clearly separated from the expression of political opinions (Wiener 1988b: 53; see also Matheson 2000: 561). One of the main early examples of New Journalism is Stead's evening paper the *Pall Mall Gazette*, which was pioneering in its use of interviews and of investigative journalism, most famously in the "Maiden Tribute of Modern Babylon" story about the prostitution of teenage girls (Conboy 2010: 108).[23]

The dramatic developments during the 1800s notwithstanding, newspapers from period 2 were not wholly "modern". Period 2 ends the year

---

[22] Halfpenny evening papers, which began to be published in 1870, mainly compiled telegraphed news and sometimes formed partnerships with morning papers (Lee 1976: 126, 1978: 122; Brown 1985: 33–4); for these reasons, they were not included in CNNE.

[23] The interviews in the *Pall Mall Gazette* are also indicative of women's greater role in journalism, as Hulda Friederichs was "Stead's chief interviewer" (Conboy 2010: 108).

4.5 The Corpora Used in the Case Studies

before the appearance of the halfpenny morning paper the *Daily Mail* in 1896. The *Daily Mail* can be seen as one of the "roots of modern popular journalism" (Bös 2015: 105), and it took several aspects of New Journalism further: its prose was seen by some as simplistic (Lee 1976: 130), and it featured extensive rewriting and shortening by editors (Clarke 2004: 265). In contrast, the extensive process of interpreting, editing, and summarizing the news that characterizes twentieth-century journalism was largely absent in the 1800s, when letters, speeches, correspondents' reports, and the like were typically printed in their entirety with little or no editorial interference (Schalck 1988: 76; Matheson 2000: 562–3). As a result, a nineteenth-century paper contained a mixture of several different styles and voices rather than a standard, journalistic voice (Matheson 2000: 564), though the New Journalism movement did initiate a process of change in this regard (see Bös 2015: 100 for examples). The "inverted-pyramid" writing style is also largely a twentieth-century development (Fries 2012: 1,070). Schneider (2002: 22) refers to the period 1850–1900 as a time of transition leading to, for instance, the establishment of the distinction between "quality" and "popular" papers; Matheson (2000: 558) sees the period 1880–1930 as witnessing "the birth of the modern newspaper primarily as a matter of writing style".

In order to include a sufficient number of papers in CNNE to represent several aspects of the nineteenth-century newspaper market, I selected ten newspapers per period, and sampled ten texts for each newspaper and period. The sampling set-up is given in Table 4.3, which also provides the codes for newspapers used in corpus examples.

Similar or identical texts frequently appeared in several nineteenth-century newspapers owing to, for instance, papers sharing information (and sometimes proprietors), the same journalist working for several papers, and news agencies selling the same information to several papers (Brown 1985: 114–21). Texts were therefore checked to eliminate duplicates. Articles that consisted only of more or less verbatim reports of, for instance, political speeches were excluded from the corpus, as were advertisements, letters to the editor, and so on. In contrast, news articles were included regardless of whether they originated with the paper sampled or not; as nineteenth-century journalism was frequently anonymous (Brown 1985: 3), it would be difficult, if not impossible, to ascertain that a given article was original to the newspaper. Moreover, it would make samples of especially late-nineteenth-century provincial newspapers less representative; as mentioned above, cheap telegraphed news was an important ingredient in such publications. Both information-based "hard news" and "soft news"

Table 4.3 *Newspapers included in CNNE*

Paper	Code	Period
Birmingham Daily Post	BDP	2
Daily News	DN	1 + 2
Examiner	EX	1
Leeds Mercury	LM	1 + 2
Liverpool Mercury	LIM	2
Lloyd's Weekly London Newspaper[a]	LL	1 + 2
Manchester Guardian	MG	1 + 2
Morning Chronicle	MC	1
Northern Echo	NE	2
Northern Star and Leeds General Advertiser	NS	1
Pall Mall Gazette	PMG	2
Poor Man's Guardian	PG	1
Reynolds's Weekly Newspaper	RW	1 + 2
The Times	TT	1 + 2

[a] This paper was originally called *Lloyd's Illustrated London Newspaper*.

such as human-interest stories were included (see Fries 2015: 83 for this distinction). As one effect of the New Journalism was the inclusion of more human-interest material in papers, limiting CNNE to hard news would have made the corpus less representative of the late-nineteenth-century newspaper landscape.

A difficult question concerns whether to attempt to separate news from editorials or leading articles. The fact that these texts may differ linguistically as a result of their genre affiliation is an argument for separating them (Wang 2017: 99). However, the two genres were nowhere near as distinct, especially in the early nineteenth century, as they are now. There was no clear distinction between the genres in the early eighteenth century (Milic 1977: 36), their form and length had not yet fully stabilized by the late 1700s (Liddle 1999: 5), and it was not until "well into the nineteenth century" (Wang 2017: 99–100) that the editorial was clearly established as a genre in Britain. Stylistically, editorials did not begin to separate from, for instance, feature articles until after 1855 (Conboy 2010: 80). Indeed, in the period 1830–50, several important radical newspapers did not necessarily attempt to distinguish objectively represented news from opinion pieces. Example (4.1), from the *Poor Man's Guardian*, is a case in point.

(4.1) Mr. W. L. WELLESLEY was summoned before the Court, and committed, for not choosing to inform it where his child was concealed; – for, not answering the questions of this Court, is what is called a high contempt, and is very severely punishable: why, or wherefore, ask the "law." "The Chancellor" admitted that the act was an amiable one – and yet, for an amiable act, though a mere formal "legal" offence, was a man summarily deprived of his liberty – without the Freeman's boast, as Mr. O'Connell calls it, trial by Jury! Are we such slaves that we must deliver up our very children to the care of strangers, against our own and their own consent; that we must stifle all our feelings as men, or, in default, commit "a contempt of Court," and without trial, be summarily condemned to prison! is this the land of liberty?   (CNNE: 1830–50, PG0002)

Many articles in the *Poor Man's Guardian* begin with the phrase *Friends, Brethren, and Fellow-Countrymen*, which might be taken to imply that the newspaper's voice is being heard in an editorial. The extract in (4.1) also clearly expresses an opinion in a way that is different from what would be expected of a neutral news article, and it contains several features that suggest a subjective, involved viewpoint, for example the first-person pronoun *we*, exclamations, and scare quotes. However, excluding articles in the *Poor Man's Guardian* that express opinions from CNNE would decrease the representativity of the selection, as it was a clear goal of the paper to educate its readers (Claridge 2017: 142); see also Claridge (2017: 140n3) on the subjectivity involved in distinguishing editorials from reportage in the *Poor Man's Guardian*. An alternative might have been not to include papers with blurred distinctions between editorials and reportage in CNNE, but again, this would have decreased representativity, especially in period 1, in which the distinction was not always made. I therefore followed Wang (2017) and included both editorials and reportage in CNNE.

The possible occurrence of colloquialization and densification in CNNE remains to be commented on. Some sources suggest that differences between upmarket and downmarket papers were less significant in the 1800s than they are today and that the gap between papers narrowed over the century (e.g. Brown 1985: 100, 125). Such uniformity may limit the extent of colloquialization. In addition, radical papers from period 1 such as the *Poor Man's Guardian* and the *Northern Star* were written in a style that was suitable for reading aloud (Brown 1985: 50–1; Clarke 2004: 235), which may have facilitated the use of oral features in period 1 compared with period 2, when individual reading was more frequent. However, the Sunday papers (e.g. *Lloyd's* and *Reynolds's*) from period 2 were "written in a more accessible style" than were papers aimed at the middle class (Clarke 2004: 246), which may result in colloquialization; *Reynolds's News*, especially, was a champion of working-class interests and retained some of the demotic style and direct address that had characterized the early radical press (Vincent 1989: 252–3). The New Journalism of the late 1800s was criticized for, among other things, its effect on grammar (Lee 1976: 130) and vocabulary (Bös 2015: 100), which may indicate that late-nineteenth-century papers which feature such styles contain more colloquial language. Wiener (1988a: xix) hypothesizes that New Journalism may have represented "an uneasy compromise between oral and written culture". Schneider (2002: 98–100) notices a drop in sentence length in newspapers from 1700 to 2000 and suggests that this development may be due in part to a more speech-like style becoming dominant over time. Westin's (2002) analysis of twentieth-century editorials in upmarket papers indicated that colloquialization took place at least in the following century (see also Hundt and Mair 1999). Bös (2015: 143) notes that "as regards popularization processes, the nineteenth century appears to be a particularly interesting phase of transition". Overall, there is thus somewhat conflicting evidence as regards the occurrence of colloquialization in newspaper prose, which is also reflected in the features examined in the present study (see Chapters 5 and 6).

Based on previous work, densification can clearly be expected in nineteenth-century newspaper writing. Leech et al. (2009: 218) report that the frequency of (noun + common noun) structures, an indicator of densification, rose in late-twentieth-century British English; however, the increase was less pronounced in genres where the feature was most common, namely press and learned writing. They interpret this result in terms of fiction and general prose catching up with developments that had already taken place in newspapers and academic writing, which makes newspapers from the 1800s a potential source for early densification. As Biber and Gray (2012: 316) note, this parallel development in two genres is due to an increase in informational load in academic as well as journalistic prose; their corpus investigation also reveals several indications of densification in newspapers between 1800 and 1985, for example an increase of most types of phrasal modification in the noun phrase. There are several extralinguistic indications of this increase in informational load. The number of topics typically included in a paper grew over time, which decreased the amount of space devoted to each topic (Brown 1985: 87). The sheer volume of information arriving at a newspaper office increased dramatically in the second half of the nineteenth century (Clarke 2004:

254), and as the amount of incoming news increased, a shift in focus took place, from filling up the space available to selecting what to include and what to leave out (Bös 2015: 99). Owing to the cost of sending telegrams, the establishment of telegraphic links also favoured brevity in foreign and war correspondence (Brown 1985: 228).[24] Agencies like the Press Association frequently concentrated incoming dispatches, and subeditors at newspapers increasingly reduced their length further to fit them into the space available (Wiener 1988b: 54). All of these developments are likely to have promoted densification. However, as mentioned above, nineteenth-century newspapers featured less editing, condensation, and so on than is the case today (Brown 1985: 253–4); for instance, connected news items were frequently printed piecemeal rather than merged into one coherent text. Taken together, these indications make the investigation of densification in nineteenth-century news writing an area where more research is needed.

4.6 Concluding Summary

Chapter 4 has provided an analytical framework that forms a bridge between the theoretical account of language change in Chapter 3 and the empirical case studies in Chapters 5–8. Section 4.2 was devoted to the framework of historical corpus linguistics and to reconciling the corpus-linguistic framework of the case studies with an idiolect-based perspective on language change. I argued that, owing to limitations of the available evidence and widespread inter-speaker convergence, corpus-based analyses are often the most suitable method for reaching significant generalizations about historical change in communal languages. The importance of considering linguistic and extralinguistic conditioning factors (e.g. genre) and of being aware of the limitations of a corpus-linguistic approach was also discussed. In addition, the value of an idiolectal perspective on usage was highlighted: examining individual usage in detail can provide a window on past language that complements the aggregate impression gained from corpus data.

In Section 4.3, I introduced the two kinds of language change that the case studies are devoted to, namely colloquialization and densification. Both types of change exemplify the increased linguistic genre

---

[24] In contrast, on the – fairly rare – occasions when metropolitan papers sent reporters out of the capital, their reports tended to be verbose, although limited reduction is noticeable towards the end of the 1800s (Brown 1985: 250).

differentiation which characterizes LModE. (The increase in linguistic differences among written genres in LModE, which made it necessary for literate language users to command a larger array of registers, was also discussed in Section 3.6 as a potential reason why there appear to be few successful structural innovations in LModE.) Section 4.4 was devoted to a critical discussion of the two main ways of measuring frequency in studies of grammar – the variationist framework and the text-linguistic framework – and of the appropriateness of testing differences in frequency for statistical significance. Finally, CONCE and CNNE, the two corpora on which my results are based, were introduced in Section 4.5.

Taken together, Sections 4.1–4.5 enable a realistic view of what the corpus-linguistic case studies in Chapters 5–8 can be expected to reveal. While independent innovation is relatively unlikely to be present in the corpus texts, such corpus analyses offer researchers a reliable window on language variation and change on a lower level of granularity than the individual idiolect. This level permits significant generalizations to be made about the trajectory of a change through a community, as long as the limitations of the approach are kept in mind. One very important limitation concerns what genres are represented in the corpora that form the basis for the case studies. Colloquialization and densification are two types of change whose trajectories are particularly suitable for corpus-based study, as they become visible in texts as shifting frequencies of linguistic features in written genres for which there is plenty of evidence from the LModE period. Since frequency shifts are at the heart of the case studies, it was crucial to discuss critically how frequency measures will be treated.

CHAPTER 5

Colloquialization I: Not-*Contraction*

5.1 Introduction

This chapter is concerned with contractions of an operator + *not*, for example *don't* in (5.1), which alternates primarily with uncontracted forms such as *do not* in (5.1'):

(5.1) [$Trus.$] Though you may draw very well, I *don't* pour freely. (CONCE: Drama, 1800–30, Poole, p. 30)
(5.1') [$Trus.$] Though you may draw very well, I *do not* pour freely.

The contracted pattern illustrated in (5.1) is often called not-*contraction* or *negative contraction* in the literature; I shall use the former term in this chapter. The relevant operator and *not* will be italicized in numbered corpus examples.

The nature of the available evidence makes it difficult to know for certain when forms that were intended to represent *not*-contraction appeared in writing. The first tokens of orthographic -*n't* or -*nt* appeared in drama texts in the early seventeenth century (Brainerd 1989 [1993]: 181). However, *not*-contraction occurred in speech before it was overtly represented in writing: Lass (1999: 180) shows that some Shakespearean uncontracted spellings must have represented spoken *not*-contractions for metrical reasons. Moreover, Rissanen (1994) lists sixteenth-century instances in which uncontracted *not* occurred in the position where -*n't* rather than *not* would be used today (e.g. *dyd not I send unto yow one Mowntayne that was both a traytor and a herytyke*; cf. today's contracted *didn't I send* vs. uncontracted *did I not send*). Such cases may represent an early stage of reduction of *not*, possibly corresponding to spoken /nət/, which in that case happened quite soon after *not* had grammaticalized in the late fifteenth century (Rissanen 1999b: 199). Similarly, Denison (1998: 195) suggests that *not*-contractions may have been regularly used in speech as early as the late sixteenth century. *Not*-contractions were common in Restoration comedies, and contraction seems to have been the more frequent option in speech in the early 1700s (Lass 1999: 180).

While contractions were very rarely proscribed before 1700 (Haugland 1995: 171), the eighteenth century witnessed a "war upon contractions" (Leonard 1929: 170), fuelled by Swift's and Addison's attacks on reduced forms in 1710 and 1711, respectively (Haugland 1995: 172; see also Percy 2002). *Not*-contractions were among the most heavily criticized contracted forms (Haugland 1995: 170; see Sundby et al. 1991: 162–3 for examples). There was some recognition of differences with genre and medium; for instance, contractions might be deemed acceptable in speech, familiar writing, or poetry (Leonard 1929: 171–2; Haugland 1995: 173, 176). Phillipps (1984: 68–70) demonstrates that prescriptive condemnation continued in the 1800s, when normative sources sometimes considered *not*-contractions inappropriate even for conversation.

An examination of twentieth-century and early-twenty-first-century sources indicates that modern opinions are more accepting, but also that contractions are still felt to be an oral feature. Millar (2009: 210–12) shows that *not*-contractions expanded at the expense of uncontracted forms in *TIME* magazine between the 1920s and the 2000s, and this increase is also reflected in attitudes; for instance, *The Chicago Manual of Style* (2017, §5.105) suggests that contractions are suitable for most prose styles. Nevertheless, in Biber's (1988, 2003) factor analyses, contracted forms are clearly associated with involved production and oral discourse, respectively. Contractions are also said to be less frequent in formal English (Quirk et al. 1985: §10.55; Huddleston and Pullum 2002: §3.1.9),[1] statements that are borne out by the genre distribution of *not*-contraction (Kjellmer 1998: 170–1; Biber et al. 1999: Appendix; Castillo González 2007: 389). Hundt and Mair (1999: 227–8) demonstrate that the frequency of *not*-contraction rose between the early 1960s and the early 1990s in both newspaper English and academic writing, but contraction ratios remain far higher in newspapers. Yaeger-Dror et al. (2002: 96) found that carefully scripted speech was less likely to feature contraction than other spoken texts, and uncontracted forms still predominated in written texts in the late twentieth century (Castillo González 2007: 393). Overall, the combination

---

[1] Huddleston and Pullum (2002: §3.1.9) argue that forms like *don't* in (5.1) should be considered one single word – an operator with negative inflection – rather than a contraction of two words in Present-Day English (see also Zwicky and Pullum 1983). The status of *-n't* as clitic vs. affix is relevant to discussions of how far the unit has grammaticalized (Mazzon 2004: 105), but accounting for it falls outside the scope of the present study.

of connotations with speech in Present-Day English and historical prescriptive opposition makes *not*-contraction a good candidate for a study of colloquialization in nineteenth-century English; indeed, Leech et al. (2009: 240) consider contractions the "paradigm case of colloquialization".

In addition to *not*-contraction, English also allows operator contraction with some operators (e.g. *we're* in alternation with *we are*). It is beyond the scope of this case study to address operator contraction in any detail. However, the availability of operator contraction is discussed in Section 5.2, and I comment briefly on the occurrence of operator contraction in linguistic environments that allow both *not*-contraction and operator contraction in Section 5.3.1.[2]

5.2 Method

The selection of material for the analysis of *not*-contraction was governed by (i) the occurrence of a sufficient number of contracted tokens in the genre and (ii) the reliability of the genre data. I have shown elsewhere (Smitterberg 2012b) that *not*-contraction is absent from the expository genres – Debates, History, and Science – in CONCE. The absence of contracted forms in History and Science is unsurprising given the genre distribution of *not*-contraction in eighteenth-century and Present-Day English (see Section 5.1); as regards Debates, it seems likely that the original speech events included contractions that were expanded to uncontracted forms in the published accounts. Similarly, as shown in Smitterberg (2014), *not*-contraction is very rare in CNNE: the search retrieved twenty-four *not*-contracted forms, most of which occurred in oral and/or informal contexts. This leaves the non-expository genres in CONCE – Drama, Fiction, Letters, and Trials – as potential candidates for inclusion. However, as the Letters genre in CONCE is based on published editions of private letters, there is a risk that the letters included in the corpus were edited prior to publication. This is not an important concern as regards the other features studied in this book; nominal premodifiers and participle clauses

---

[2] The comparison in Section 5.3.1 considers only variation according to the operator itself. Several other factors have been investigated by scholars with regard to their possible influence on the choice between operator contraction and *not*-contraction, including region, variety, genre, speaker age, type of subject, and various features of the linguistic environment (e.g. Kjellmer 1998; Westergren Axelsson 1998; Tagliamonte and Smith 2002; Yaeger-Dror et al. 2002; Walker 2005; Grieve 2011); as the present study focusses on *not*-contraction, these parameters will not be included in the comparison. Nor will I address factors that influence the choice between operator contractions and uncontracted forms (e.g. McElhinny 1993; MacKenzie 2013; Barth and Kapatsinski 2017; Thoms et al. 2019).

were not targets of prescriptive condemnation, and, with the possible exception of sentence-initial *and* (see Section 6.3.2), nor was co-ordination; moreover, substituting other constructions for those features would require extensive rewriting of sentences. But *not*-contractions were both stigmatized and comparatively easy to replace with uncontracted forms,[3] which means that we cannot wholly trust the corpus texts to represent actual nineteenth-century usage in informal letters (Smitterberg 2012b: 194; see Tieken-Boon van Ostade 2014a: 16–17 for a discussion of the authenticity of spelling regarding contractions in Jane Austen's letters). The Letters genre was thus excluded from analyses, and the quantitative analysis reported on in Section 5.3 was based on three genres from CONCE: Drama, Fiction, and Trials.

As Haugland (1995: 166) recognizes, the notion of contraction implies a variationist perspective in that "an uncontracted counterpart is presupposed". Since virtually all *not*-contractions can be replaced with uncontracted forms, as in (5.1) vs. (5.1'), I aimed mainly at comparing the incidence of those two variants in contexts where both of them were possible. A detailed account of what strings were retrieved and what tokens were included is given in Smitterberg (2012b: 194–7), a study that used the same set of *not*-contracted and uncontracted forms that is subject to more detailed analysis here. My discussion below focusses on two areas where scholars' decisions as regards what tokens to include in the counts may differ.

First, uncontracted tokens like (5.2), where the subject of a question intervenes between the operator and *not*, receive different treatments in previous research.

(5.2) [$Mrs. Fer.$] *Did* you *not* hear me, Sir? (CONCE: Drama, 1800–30, Morton, p. 25)

While, for instance, Westergren Axelsson (1998: 130) includes tokens like (5.2), they are excluded by Kjellmer (1998: 176) and by López-Couso (2007: 303), who argues that the intervening subject blocks contraction. However, as both (5.2) and the uncontracted variant with *not* adjacent to the operator

---

[3] Texts in Drama, Fiction, and Trials may of course also have been edited so that, for instance, contractions in the original texts or speech events were turned into uncontracted forms before publishing. However, those changes would have been made shortly after the texts were written (Drama and Fiction) or the speech events took place (Trials – see also note 7 for the possible influence of shorthand writers in this regard), so they would still represent nineteenth-century norms for written texts. In contrast, some of the collections of private letters drawn on for CONCE were published some time after the letters were originally written, making it unclear what genre norms were adhered to.

(*Did not you hear* ...) can be argued to be in variation with a *not*-contraction expressing the same meaning (*Didn't you hear* ...), (5.2) was included in the counts as an uncontracted token.[4]

Secondly, some linguistic environments permit two different contractions: *not*-contraction, as in (5.3), and operator contraction, in which the operator is cliticized onto a host, as in (5.3').

(5.3) [$Inez.$] Perhaps the Divorce Court *isn't* the best place to learn what unsuspected depths and treasures there are in woman's nature. (CONCE: Drama, 1870–1900, Jones, p. 29)

(5.3') [$Inez.$] Perhaps the Divorce Court*'s not* the best place to ...

The availability of operator contraction depends on the operator: HAVE, present-tense forms of BE, *will*,[5] and *would* are subject to contraction (Biber et al. 1999: §3.8.2.5). However, there are several additional factors that block operator contraction (Westergren Axelsson 1998: 50–63); for instance, had (5.3) been a *yes/no*-question, with the operator preceding the subject, operator contraction would not be an option (*'s the Divorce Court perhaps not* ...). Not all *not*-contracted and uncontracted tokens with the relevant operators can thus be transformed into operator contractions.

One way of tackling such a data set would be to restrict the analysis of *not*-contraction to those contexts that permit all three variants (see Varela Pérez 2013: 265 for this approach to Present-Day English). Such a study would reveal factors influencing speaker choice among all three variants; however, it would reduce the data set greatly, as several frequent operators, including DO, *can*, and *could*, do not permit operator contraction. As the main focus of the present study is to chart the distribution of *not*-contraction as an indication of colloquialization, removing a great many relevant tokens from the counts was undesirable. Alternatively, operator contraction could simply have been removed from the counts; this was the procedure followed by Walker (2005: 7) and in Smitterberg (2012b), where I focussed on the total incidence of *not*-contraction relative to that of uncontracted forms. However, as I consider the operator as a parameter in the present study, ignoring operator contractions would distort the results: operators that can be contracted may

---

[4] Following Westergren Axelsson (1998: 130–1), I excluded instances where an adverbial separates operator and *not*, for example *They are certainly not the same* (CONCE: Trials, 1870–1900, Tichborne, p. 2,410), as the scope of the adverbial may change if a *not*-contracted form is substituted.
[5] See Quirk et al. (1985: §4.57) for the choice to regard *-'ll* as a contracted form of *will* only and not of *shall*.

display lower proportions of *not*-contraction because operator contraction was chosen instead in some cases. Moreover, the relevant operators have been shown to differ with regard to their relative preference for operator contraction and *not*-contraction. Several studies indicate that present-tense forms of BE favour operator contraction, while HAVE, *will*, and *would* promote *not*-contraction, in Present-Day English (Kjellmer 1998: 181; Anderwald 2002: 75–6; Valera Pérez 2013: 261). López-Couso's (2007: 311–12) results for BE and HAVE indicate that a similar distribution may have characterized LModE, though the tendency for present-tense BE to favour operator contraction and HAVE *not*-contraction has become more pronounced over time (Valera Pérez 2013: 261).

Faced with this complex variant field, I opted for separate analyses. In Section 5.3.1, I consider overall results for *not*-contraction vs. uncontracted forms, and also include operator contraction in the data to be able to compare the distributions. In addition, I briefly account for the choice between *not*-negation (e.g. *They did not see anything*) and *no*-negation (e.g. *They saw nothing*) in this section. These analyses are followed in Section 5.3.2 by a multivariate analysis that considers only those operators that cannot be contracted, where the most relevant choice is thus between *not*-contracted and uncontracted forms. (Section 5.3.3 is concerned only with a subset of the *not*-contracted forms.)

5.3 Results

5.3.1 Overall Results

In Smitterberg (2012b), I showed that there was an overall increase in *not*-contraction compared with uncontracted forms between periods 1 and 2 in CONCE, while no change was noticeable between periods 2 and 3. The overall stability after 1850 was largely due to two developments cancelling each other out: while both Drama and Fiction featured more *not*-contraction in period 2 than in period 1, there was a decrease in contraction in Drama (from 82 to 72 per cent) but an increase in Fiction (from 29 to 49 per cent) between periods 2 and 3. Trials displayed a low and stable *not*-contraction ratio (between 8 and 9 per cent) throughout the century.

However, as discussed in Section 5.2, to get a complete picture of contraction in clauses negated by *not*, we also need to take operator contraction into account. Table 5.1 presents the distribution of *not*-contraction, operator contraction, and uncontracted forms in *not*-negated clauses.

Table 5.1 *Not*-contractions, operator contractions, and uncontracted forms in Drama, Fiction, and Trials by period (not-negated clauses)

Genre	Period	*Not*-cont. #	*Not*-cont. %	Oper. cont. #	Oper. cont. %	Uncont. #	Uncont. %	Total
Drama	1	128	34.5	17	4.6	226	60.9	371
	2	352	74.6	43	9.1	77	16.3	472
	3	319	67.7	28	5.9	124	26.3	471
	Total	799	60.8	88	6.7	427	32.5	1,314
Fiction	1	14	4.2	1	0.3	316	95.5	331
	2	108	28.8	7	1.9	260	69.3	375
	3	129	48.7	4	1.5	132	49.8	265
	Total	251	25.8	12	1.2	708	72.9	971
Trials	1	66	9.4	0	0.0	633	90.6	699
	2	81	8.8	0	0.0	837	91.2	918
	3	77	7.7	0	0.0	922	92.3	999
	Total	224	8.6	0	0.0	2,392	91.4	2,616
All genres	1	208	14.8	18	1.3	1,175	83.9	1,401
	2	541	30.7	50	2.8	1,174	66.5	1,765
	3	525	30.3	32	1.8	1,178	67.9	1,735
	Total	1,274	26.0	100	2.0	3,527	72.0	4,901

The addition of operator contraction to the distribution does not alter the overall impression from Smitterberg (2012b). Drama remains the genre most hospitable to contraction, followed by Fiction and Trials. Operator contraction is less common than *not*-contraction in *not*-negated clauses and displays no clear trend in diachrony. Operator contraction is also entirely absent from *not*-negated clauses in Trials. The overall results indicate that Drama and Fiction underwent colloquialization in nineteenth-century English as regards *not*-contraction (the decrease between periods 2 and 3 in Drama notwithstanding), while the Trials genre does not appear to take part in this change.

Several studies have shown that English operators favour contraction to different degrees (see Westergren Axelsson 1998: 171 for late-twentieth-century figures) and that these preferences have changed over time; for instance, Denison (1998: 167) comments on the increasing rarity of *mayn't* in twentieth-century English. It is therefore of interest to consider individual operator + *not* combinations. (See Section 5.3.2 for multifactorial data on those verbs that do not feature operator contraction.) For this analysis, tokens of *ain't* (34 ×) were counted as *not*-contracted variants of the uncontracted operator that would have been used in Standard English (for instance, *I ain't happy with this* would be counted as a contraction of *am* + *not*); tokens of *don't* with singular subjects were counted as *do* + *not*. (I devote special attention to the distribution of these non-standard forms in Section 5.3.3.) As one of my aims was to compare present-tense and past-tense contexts, I also excluded imperative contexts (175 *not*-contracted and 63 uncontracted tokens, with a contraction ratio of 73.5 per cent); see Section 5.3.2 for a discussion of imperative clauses.

The results are given in Table 5.2.[6] Operators where operator contraction is not considered possible have dashes in the cells where the raw frequencies of operator contraction would appear (and empty percentage cells). The table lists primary verbs before modals and semi-modals. (For the purposes of these analyses, I treat modal-auxiliary pairs like *can/could* as present and past tenses of the same verb; see Section 5.3.2 for further discussion.)

Findings from previous research regarding the distribution of *not*-contraction and operator contraction according to verb (see Section 5.2) are partly supported by the results in Table 5.2 in that operator contraction is more common with BE than with HAVE and WILL. However, *not*-contraction is the more frequent option with all operators except *am*, where there is no readily available *not*-contracted variant in present-day Standard English (Quirk et al. 1985: §3.32nc). Conclusions regarding the choice between *not*-contraction and operator contraction cannot be drawn with any certainty based on these data, as *not*-contractions that could not have been replaced with operator contractions are included in the counts. López-Couso (2007: 307, 311) demonstrates that this factor affects the frequency relationship between the two contraction types in the 1800s: *not*-contraction outnumbers operator contraction if all tokens are considered, while the opposite is the case when only tokens that admit both contraction strategies are included. For the purposes of the present study, the most important consideration was to present as complete a picture as possible of contraction in *not*-negated clauses, given that both contraction strategies are more colloquial than the uncontracted variant.

---

[6] A small number of tokens that could not unambiguously be assigned to one particular operator were excluded from the counts in Table 5.2.

Table 5.2 Not-*contractions, operator contractions, and uncontracted forms in Drama, Fiction, and Trials by operator and verb* (not-*negated clauses*)

Verb	Operator	Not-cont. #	Not-cont. %	Operator cont. #	Operator cont. %	Uncont. #	Uncont. %	Total
BE	am	7	4.9	31	21.8	104	73.2	142
	is	52	15.3	32	9.4	256	75.3	340
	are	16	16.5	11	11.3	70	72.2	97
	was	24	6.7	–		334	93.3	358
	were	2	2.5	–		79	97.5	81
	Total	101	9.9	74	7.3	843	82.8	1,018
DO	do	455	49.7	–		460	50.3	915
	does	22	24.7	–		67	75.3	89
	did	73	9.1	–		733	90.9	806
	Total	550	30.4	–		1,260	69.6	1,810
HAVE	have	31	20.5	6	4.0	114	75.5	151
	has	16	30.8	0	0.0	36	69.2	52
	had	17	7.7	0	0.0	204	92.3	221
	Total	64	15.1	6	1.4	354	83.5	424
CAN	can	131	25.2	–		389	74.8	520
	could	39	13.9	–		241	86.1	280
	Total	170	21.3	–		630	78.8	800
DARE	dare	4	36.4	–		7	63.6	11
MAY	may	3	16.7	–		15	83.3	18
	might	1	5.6	–		17	94.4	18
	Total	4	11.1	–		32	88.9	36
MUST	must	19	35.2	–		35	64.8	54
NEED	need	8	36.4	–		14	63.6	22
OUGHT	ought	0	0.0	–		4	100.0	4
SHALL	shall	14	40.0	–		21	60.0	35
	should	15	18.5	–		66	81.5	81
	Total	29	25.0	–		87	75.0	116
WILL	will	110	58.8	12	6.4	65	34.8	187
	would	39	23.2	0	0.0	129	76.8	168
	Total	149	42.0	12	3.4	194	54.6	355
Total		1,098	23.6	92	2.0	3,460	74.4	4,650

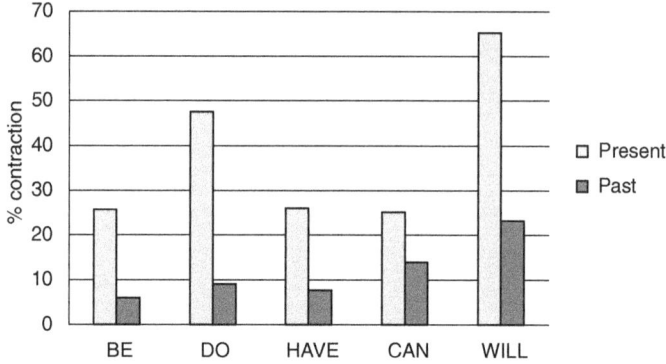

Figure 5.1 Contraction ratios for present-tense and past-tense forms of BE, DO, HAVE, CAN, and WILL in Drama, Fiction, and Trials (*not*-negated clauses)

The results also indicate that the present tense promotes contraction. For each verb that has distinct present-tense and past-tense forms, the total contraction ratio is higher in the present tense. In addition, in the CONCE data, the verbs whose past-tense operators can be contracted – HAVE and WILL – only display operator contraction in the present tense. This finding helps to explain the rarity of operator contraction in Fiction and Trials (see Table 5.1); as the past tense predominates in narrative genres, there are fewer opportunities for operator contraction to occur in such texts if it is available mainly in the present tense. The tense difference is further illustrated in Figure 5.1, which plots contraction ratios for the operators whose present-tense and past-tense forms both add up to > 100 tokens. (Note that *not*-contraction and operator contraction are conflated for BE, HAVE, and WILL in the figure.)

One potential reason for the high proportion of *don't* is token frequency: combinations of operator + *not* that occur often may be more likely to be reduced (Kjellmer 1998: 158; see also, more generally, Bybee and Thompson 2000: 379), and *do* + *not* is the most frequent such combination in CONCE. However, token frequency cannot explain why the ratio of *won't* is even higher than that of *don't*, as *will* is less frequent than *do* as an operator in the corpus.

The difference between present-tense and past-tense operators is less apparent in similar analyses of twentieth-century English; for instance, Kjellmer (1998: 170) found that *do* and *will* were the most frequently *not*-contracted operators, but *could*, *would*, and *did* also displayed high contraction ratios. Westergren Axelsson's (1998: 171) results indicate that change may have taken place in this regard during the 1900s, as these three past-tense operators all change significantly towards more *not*-contraction in her late-twentieth-century data. It is thus possible that increasing integration of *not*-contraction into written English resulted in past-tense operators becoming more compatible with contraction; I will return to this issue in Section 5.3.2.

In the remainder of this section, I will briefly consider four parameters that will not be included in the multifactorial analysis in Section 5.3.2. These parameters are gender, the function of the operator, word order in questions, and *no*-negation, which will be treated in that order.

A gender perspective on the variation in the data is of interest, since Labov's (2001: 292–3) "gender paradox" suggests that women would normally be leaders in language change from below, but also that women conform more closely to sociolinguistic norms that are overtly specified. As *not*-contraction was a proscribed incoming form, we might expect women to use a lower ratio of contraction than men. However, coding reliably for gender represents a problem in the three genres on which my analyses are based. Fictional dialogue in Drama and Fiction has at least two "speakers": the fictional character who is speaking and the author of the text (fictional narrators who are separate from the author may be an additional complicating factor). In Trials, the original speech events have undergone mediation via shorthand writers, editors, and publishers, most of whom were male. For these reasons, gender is not included as a parameter in the multifactorial analysis in Section 5.3.2, but I will devote some attention to gender variation as represented by authors (in Fiction) and witnesses (in Trials) here.

Interestingly, the two women authors in Fiction, period 1, Jane Austen and Mary Shelley, are very restrictive in their use of *not*-contraction (2 × for Austen and 0 × for Shelley, compared with 12 × for Theodore Edward Hook). The pattern is repeated in period 2, where the two women authors sampled – Elizabeth Gaskell (15 per cent) and Charlotte Yonge (28 per cent) – also display lower proportions of *not*-contraction than the only male writer in this period sample, Charles Dickens (44 per cent). In the sample from period 3, Mary Braddon (39 per cent) falls between Walter Besant (28 per cent) and Thomas Hardy (60 per cent), but the overall picture, albeit based on limited evidence, is still one where women writers are more reluctant to use *not*-contraction. *Not*-contraction in Fiction is largely limited to dialogue: only nineteen tokens were attested outside quotation marks, and most of those occur in passages that are otherwise marked for orality, such as first-person accounts of experiences. In (5.4), for instance, a narrator retells his experiences of a night when he was under the influence of alcohol:

(5.4)   There was an abundance of bright lights, and there was music, and there were ladies down in the boxes, and I *don't* know what more. (CONCE: Fiction, 1850–70, Dickens, p. 255)

The distribution of narrative and dialogue does not explain the gender differences: men writers display a higher contraction ratio in both dialogue (51 vs. 29 per cent) and narrative (9 vs. 3 per cent). This correlation between gender and contraction ratio needs to be re-examined based on a larger sample of writers and an even distribution of writers per period, which is why I refrain from testing the differences for significance.

In Trials, three main groups of speakers are represented: members of the legal profession (who were all male), female witnesses, and male witnesses. To avoid the role of the speaker as a witness or a member of the legal profession influencing results, I will focus on *not*-contraction in witness statements. Here too gender is an influential parameter: women's operator + *not* combinations display contraction in 6 per cent of tokens (43 *not*-contracted vs. 698 uncontracted forms), while male witnesses use *not*-contraction nearly twice as often, in 10 per cent of cases (90 *not*-contracted vs. 791 uncontracted tokens). This gender difference is more reliable owing to the larger number of male and female witnesses in Trials compared with the number of male and female authors in Fiction, and a chi-square test reveals that it is significant (d.f. = 1; χ^2 = 10.41; p = 0.001).

Taken together, the gender differences attested in Fiction and Trials tally with Labov's (2001: 292–3) gender paradox. Since *not*-contraction was an incoming feature that received overt (negative) evaluation, we would expect women to use it less. As the CONCE data show, this is supported by data for fictional authors as well as trial witnesses. We cannot know for certain whether these gender differences are based entirely on the authors' original texts (in Fiction) and the original speech events (in Trials), or whether they are partly the result of a subsequent editing process; nevertheless, the results indicate that there were differences between men's and women's usage regarding how appropriate *not*-contraction was believed to be in the 1800s.

Two of the operators – BE and HAVE – can function as auxiliaries as well as main verbs, while the remaining operators are always auxiliaries. Most previous research appears to indicate that verb function does not influence either contraction ratio or the choice between operator contraction and *not*-contraction (e.g. Westergren Axelsson 1998: 148; Tagliamonte and Smith 2002: 276; Varela Pérez 2013: 277–8), though Kjellmer (1998: 172–3) argues that main-verb BE is less likely to be *not*-contracted. I will examine the distribution briefly here. All uncontracted and *not*-contracted tokens of BE and HAVE + *not* were classified according to whether the operator functioned as an auxiliary or a main verb. Operators in reduced forms and tag questions were given the same function as their unreduced counterparts; *were* in (5.5) was thus classified as an auxiliary and *had* in (5.6) as a main verb. Tokens of BE and HAVE in structures classified as modal idioms (e.g. *had better* and BE *to*) and semi-auxiliaries (e.g. BE *going to*) by Quirk et al. (1985: §3.40) were considered auxiliaries, for example *hadn't* in (5.7).

(5.5) [$Q.$] They were crying, I believe, *were* they *not*? (CONCE: Trials, 1800–30, Angus, p. 34)

(5.6) [$Q.$] Had you any conversation with James Bowditch then? [$A.$] No, I *had not*. (CONCE: Trials, 1800–30, Bowditch, p. 41)

(5.7) [$Mr. Gibson [nervously].$] *Hadn't* I better have assistance within call? (CONCE: Drama, 1850–70, Taylor, p. 312)

Quirk et al.'s (1985: §§3.74–8) passive gradient was used to categorize BE + past participle combinations as either passive (Quirk et al.'s central passives), in which case BE is an auxiliary, or main-verb BE + adjectival participle (Quirk et al.'s semi- and pseudo-passives). Table 5.3 presents *not*-contraction ratios for BE and HAVE by verb function; a small number of tokens that resisted classification are absent from the counts. Main-verb function appears to promote *not*-contraction compared with auxiliary function for both verbs, but neither difference is statistically significant (for BE, d.f. = 1; χ^2 = 2.020; p = 0.155; for HAVE, d.f. = 1; χ^2 = 1.449; p = 0.229). I therefore regard the results as inconclusive on this parameter.

Direct questions and tag questions with uncontracted *not* exhibit word-order variation: *not* is placed either where *-n't* would have occurred, as in (5.8), or after the subject, as in (5.8'). Based on the constituents in (5.8), I will refer to the three resulting options as the *would not she*, *would she not*, and *wouldn't she* patterns in the discussion below.

(5.8) Poor Miss Charlecote! *would not* she miss her little moonbeam? (CONCE: Fiction, 1850–70, Yonge, p. II.50)

(5.8') Poor Miss Charlecote! *would* she *not* miss her little moonbeam?

As discussed in Section 5.1, Rissanen (1994, 1999b) argues that the early appearance of the *would not she* type may suggest reduction of *not*. It is thus possible that, in LModE, *would not* in (5.8) was a way of rendering /wʊd

Table 5.3 Not-*contracted and uncontracted forms in Drama, Fiction, and Trials by verb function*

Verb	Function	Not-contracted		Uncontracted		Total
		#	%	#	%	
BE	Auxiliary	12	7.5	149	92.5	161
	Main verb	88	11.2	695	88.8	783
	Total	100	10.6	844	89.4	944
HAVE	Auxiliary	44	13.8	276	86.2	320
	Main verb	19	18.6	83	81.4	102
	Total	63	14.9	359	85.1	422

nət/ or even /wʊdnt/, that is, the *not*-contracted pronunciation, in writing, without the stigma attached to contraction; but this option existed only in cases where the position of *not* was variable. In the present study, *would not she* tokens were counted as uncontracted, but the two word orders were given separate codes in the database, enabling a variationist perspective on word-order choice.

In Drama, part of the dramatic change between periods 1 and 2 appears to consist of a shift from the *would not she* to the *wouldn't she* pattern: in period 1, the *would not she* pattern accounts for 29 per cent of tokens, while it is very rare (3 ×) after 1850. This finding needs to be substantiated by more data, but it supports Rissanen's hypothesis that sequences like *would not she* might have been used as a way of representing *wouldn't she*, in this case as late as the early nineteenth century. The *would not she* pattern might then have been a more acceptable way to render a spoken *not*-contraction in writing. Raw frequencies in Fiction are quite low, but at least one author appears to have used a similar strategy: Jane Austen uses only one *not*-contraction in questions of this type, but the *would not she* pattern occurs six times, and is even used in a tag question:

(5.9) "I do remember it," cried Emma; "I perfectly remember it. – Talking about spruce beer. – Oh! yes – Mr. Knightley and I both saying we liked it, and Mr. Elton's seeming resolved to learn to like it too. I perfectly remember it. – Stop; Mr. Knightley was standing just here, *was not he?* – I have an idea he was standing just here." (CONCE: Fiction, 1800–30, Austen, p. III.54)

As in Drama, the *would not she* pattern declines in frequency after period 1 in Fiction, perhaps because actual *not*-contraction became a more acceptable part of fictional dialogue.

The Trials genre displays a different pattern: interrogative sentences are frequent in Trials, as much of a cross-examination typically consists of questions from lawyers, and the *would not she* pattern helps to explain the seeming lack of change in the genre. Two of the files that have very low frequencies of *not*-contraction in questions – the trial of William Palmer (period 2; 0 x) and the Tichborne vs. Lushington case (period 3; 1 x) – also have the two highest percentages of *would not she* patterns in the genre (57 and 63 per cent, respectively). As in Austen's fiction, the pattern is also used in tag questions, where *not*-contraction in speech seems likely, as in (5.10):

> (5.10) That was in the newspapers, *was not* it? – Yes.
> Then you had read it? – I had heard of it.
> I suppose you thought that was a strong thing, *did not* you? – Yes, I did. (CONCE: Trials, 1870–1900, Tichborne, p. 2,165)

The *would not she* strategy is not prevalent in all trials; for instance, in the trial of John Singleton Copley Hill, 87 per cent of the relevant tokens are of the *would she not* type, which is the norm even in tag questions (5.11). Such differences may be due to several factors, such as shorthand systems used and editorial decisions.[7]

> (5.11) [$Defendant to Mr. Pole$] – When I called upon you the second time, on Tuesday, the 16th, I showed you a printed document, *did I not*? – I said nothing about the second time. (CONCE: Trials, 1850–70, Hill, p. 28)

Nevertheless, from a quantitative perspective, this parameter can help to explain why the Trials genre appears not to exhibit change. If we contrast the *would she not* pattern with *wouldn't she* and *would not she* taken

---

[7] Several Trials texts indicate that the published version was based on shorthand notes, but as nothing is said about what systems were used, it is impossible to say to what extent shorthand writers distinguished *not*-contracted and uncontracted forms. For instance, Pitman's system, which came to be widely used after it was introduced in 1837, was based on phonetics, which makes it possible to represent the difference between, say, *will not* and *won't*; but the negator *not* was also a "grammalogue", that is, a word represented by its own symbol (Pitman 1852: §110). The *not*-contracted or uncontracted form that eventually appeared in the Trials text may thus be due to a number of choices: a speaker's choice during the original speech event, the shorthand writer's choice of representation (which may be dependent on the system used), and choices made when the shorthand account was expanded and edited for printing. What can be said is ultimately that the end product on which the corpus text is based represents genre norms for nineteenth-century trial proceedings; the relation to the original speech event is potentially indirect.

together, the proportion of *would she not* goes down consistently over time: from 74 per cent in period 1 via 72 per cent in period 2 to 52 per cent in period 3. While *not*-contraction does not appear to have been considered acceptable in printed trial proceedings, *would not she* word order may have been a way to represent spoken *not*-contraction in writing when there was a word-order choice. In sum, then, *would not she* tokens declined in frequency in Drama and in fictional dialogue, where they were probably replaced by actual *not*-contraction; this tallies with Rissanen's (1999b: 199–200) suggestion. In contrast, the *would not she* pattern became increasingly popular in Trials, where the relative formality of the dialogue and/or shorthand conventions may have been more powerful constraints on the use of actual contraction.

The final parameter to be discussed in this section concerns an additional possible variant. *Not*-contracted, operator-contracted, and uncontracted forms in my dataset are all types of what Biber et al. (1999: §3.8.2) refer to as "*not*-negation", and several studies have applied a variationist perspective to the variants available within the *not*-negated paradigm. Grieve (2011: 518) argues that *not*-contraction and operator contraction "are relatively uncontroversial examples of linguistic variables ... as they involve alternations between two phonologically (and orthographically) distinct yet synonymous constructions" and that "contracted and full forms vary with relative freedom in English discourse". This is also the main perspective I take in this chapter. However, it is a further requirement of variationist analyses that all variants should be included. Some clauses can also be negated using other negative forms, for example *no* and *nothing*, an option often called "*no*-negation" (Biber et al. 1999: §3.8.3). Compare the *not*-negated (5.12) with the *no*-negated counterpart in (5.12'):

(5.12) "Oh! I *don't* know any thing about that," said Apperton. (CONCE: Fiction, 1800–30, Hook, p. II.70)
(5.12') "Oh! I know nothing about that," ...

No-negation accounts for a larger share of negation in writing than in speech in Present-Day English (Biber et al. 1999: §3.8.4.2), and Leech et al.'s (2009: 241–2) results indicate that *no*-negation was on the retreat in the late twentieth century. *No*-negation thus potentially has the status of an additional, formal variant; a rising proportion of uncontracted *not* may even indicate colloquialization if it coincides with a decrease in *no*-negation.

However, including *no*-negation in a variationist analysis is problematic. First, there are contexts where *no*-negation and *not*-negation are not wholly semantically interchangeable (Biber et al. 1999: §3.8.3). Secondly, the two options cannot always replace each other grammatically. Roughly 80 per cent of *no*-negated clauses can be rewritten as *not*-negated ones (exceptions include pre-verbal *no*-forms, e.g. *Nobody has seen the film*). But the opposite replacement only works in *c.*30 per cent of cases, as there has to be "some other form which can incorporate the negative element" in the clause if *not* is not present (Biber et al. 1999: §3.8.4.1); for instance, a *not*-negation like *She doesn't play the piano* lacks a readily available *no*-negated equivalent.[8] Including *no*-negation in the analysis would thus drastically reduce the number of relevant tokens. Instead, by way of a rough approximation, I will compare the normalized frequencies of (i) the total number of *not*-negated – uncontracted, *not*-contracted, or operator-contracted – forms and (ii) the total number of the following negative items: *no, none, nobody, nothing, nowhere,* and *never*.[9] As a tagged version of the corpus was necessary in order to exclude tokens of *no* as an adverb, the comparison is based on texts in the S-coefficient subcorpus only.

The raw frequencies of *not*-negation and *no*-negation, as defined here, are given in Table 5.4. *Not*-negation consistently outnumbers *no*-negation, by a factor of roughly 2.5 in Drama, 1.5 in Fiction, and 3.1 in Trials. These ratios mirror the orality of the three genres: while the Trials genre is speech-based and Drama is speech-purposed, Fiction is only partly speech-purposed (dialogue passages).

---

[8] By contrast, if the direct-object noun phrase had been indefinite, *no* could have replaced *not + a*: *She does not play an instrument ≈ She plays no instrument* (Biber et al. 1999: §3.8.4.1). Another complication is that operator contraction and *no*-negation can co-occur in Standard English (e.g. *She's found nothing so far*); in varieties that feature multiple negation, other co-occurrence patterns are also possible (e.g. *She hasn't found nothing so far*).

[9] The number of *not*-negations in this analysis is slightly higher than that given in Table 5.1, as some variants of *not* or *-n't* (e.g. *na*) are included as unambiguous *not*-negations even though they were not included as clear uncontracted or *not*-contracted forms. The selection of *no*-negation items was based on the lists in Quirk et al. (1985: §10.60), Tottie (1991: 106), Biber et al. (1999: §3.8.3), and Leech et al. (2009: 242). In this regard, I follow Leech et al. (2009: 242n5) in excluding *neither . . . nor* as a rare alternative of *not + either . . . or*, and I also exclude *nor* as an alternative to *and + not* (cf. Biber et al. 1999: §3.8.3), as *neither* and *nor* also have other functions. There are no tokens of the spellings *noone* or *no-one* in CONCE, so the search for *no* automatically captures *no one*. The status of *never* as a *no*-negation is somewhat debatable. *Never* accounts for *c.*40 per cent of the *no*-negated tokens in Table 5.4, but the *not*-negated equivalent *not + ever* is never used in place of it in the material. Pragmatically, *never* is arguably not equivalent to *not + ever* but is rather used in speech-related texts as a more forceful version of *not* (see, for instance, Mazzon 2004: 115n1), as in *We were parted immediately afterwards, and we have never met since* (CONCE: Drama, 1870–1900, Gilbert, p. 24). However, as *never* differs syntactically from *not* (for instance, *never* cannot be contracted and does not occur in the *would not she* pattern discussed above), it was nevertheless counted as a *no*-negator in this study.

Table 5.4 Not-*negation and* no-*negation in Drama, Fiction, and Trials by period (raw frequencies in the S-coefficient subcorpus)*

	Drama		Fiction		Trials	
Period	*Not*	*No*	*Not*	*No*	*Not*	*No*
1	384	193	331	226	699	241
3	503	168	265	164	999	301
Total	887	361	596	390	1,698	542

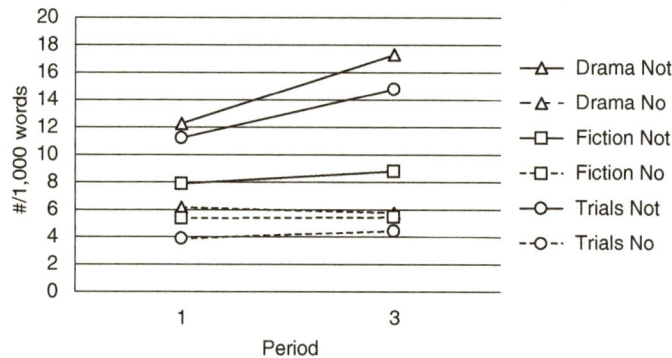

Figure 5.2 *Not*-negation and *no*-negation in Drama, Fiction, and Trials by period (frequencies per 1,000 words in the S-coefficient subcorpus)

I do not present percentages in Table 5.4, because the data do not represent the outcome of a variationist choice: as discussed above, it cannot be assumed that the tokens are interchangeable and semantically equivalent. However, juxtaposing the frequency developments of the two types of negation may still shed light on colloquialization patterns in nineteenth-century writing. Following Leech et al. (2009: 242), I therefore present the normalized frequencies of the two strategies by genre and period in Figure 5.2.

Negation becomes more frequent overall in Trials, but *not*-negation increases more than *no*-negation (by 32 vs. 15 per cent). Fiction, which displays the smallest frequency difference between the two strategies, also displays more *not*-negation over time (+ 12 per cent), while there is virtually no change in the frequency of *no*-negation. Drama, finally, combines a considerable increase in *not*-negation (41 per cent) with a far smaller decrease in *no*-negation (6 per cent). Overall, these findings support the hypothesis that colloquialization is taking place in the genres, albeit in a different way compared with Leech et al.'s (2009) results for late-twentieth-century English: Leech et al. found no pronounced change in the frequency of *not*-negation in British English but a clear decrease in *no*-negation; in my material, *no*-negation is comparatively stable while the frequency of *not*-negation rises in all genres (and increasingly differentiates the genres examined). In both cases, the more oral strategy is gaining ground relative to the more literate one.

5.3.2 Binomial Logistic Regression Analysis

In this section, I restrict the envelope of variation to combinations of operator and *not*-negation where the operator itself cannot be contracted. In addition, it will be assumed that a decision not to use *no*-negation has been made,[10] which restricts the language user's choice to two main variants: *not*-contracted and uncontracted forms. This analysis enables a detailed look at the independent effects and interplay of the factors that potentially condition that choice. In what follows, I will first account for the factors considered and then present the results of a multifactorial analysis. After the exclusion of tokens that were indeterminate with regard to one or several of the parameters, the number of relevant tokens on which a binary logistic regression analysis was based was 2,904.

In addition to time and genre, which are the most relevant parameters from a colloquialization perspective, I include several linguistic variables in the analysis. These variables were coded for to enable me to demonstrate whether period and genre have an independent effect on contraction ratios or whether what looks like a change in contraction ratio over time in a given genre is in fact due to shifts in the incidence of linguistic contexts that promote or disfavour *not*-contraction.

---

[10] We do not at present know whether such decisions are made in sequence by language users or whether a more complex set of interacting parameters are involved (or even whether decisions are made in the same way in all idiolects). However, if a sequential model is assumed, it makes intuitive sense that the choice between *no*-negation and *not*-negation should be made before the choice between an uncontracted and a *not*-contracted form, as the former involves more drastic differences in structure.

In order to rule out operator contraction, the analysis is restricted to tokens with an operator other than HAVE, BE, and WILL (see Section 5.3.1). The remaining operators that occur with *not*-contraction in the material are (in alphabetical order) *can*, *could*, *dare*, *did*, *do*, *does*, *may*, *might*, *must*, *need*, *shall*, and *should* (see Table 5.2). As I was interested in the influence of the tense parameter on the choice between *not*-contracted and uncontracted forms, I further excluded *must*, which does not show formal tense distinctions, and *dare* and *need*, which only occurred with *not*-contraction in the present tense. The four verbs considered are thus DO, CAN, MAY, and SHALL. Even within the group of remaining operators, results presented in previous research (e.g. Westergren Axelsson 1998: 171–3) and in Section 5.3.1 indicate that the likelihood of contraction varies with the operator, so the verb itself was included as a parameter.

As I showed in Section 5.3.1, present-tense operators promote contraction compared with past-tense operators. This difference should be included in the multifactorial analysis, in order to ascertain whether it is an independent effect of the tense variable or a result of variation on other parameters. I therefore coded each operator based on what type of finiteness it displayed: past-tense, present-tense, or imperative operators.[11] Imperative clauses have been shown to favour *not*-contraction in previous work (e.g. Kjellmer 1998: 177), and the fact that imperative mood, past tense, and present tense are mutually exclusive categories makes it possible to capture this influence on one and the same parameter.

The subject of the negated verb phrase has also been shown to be a relevant factor in previous work: pronoun subjects are more likely to co-occur with *not*-contraction, and first- and second-person pronouns promote contraction more than other pronouns (e.g. Westergren Axelsson 1998: 173–5). I therefore coded all subjects as first-person (*I* and *we*), second-person (*you* as well as zero subjects of imperatives),[12]

---

[11] I have coded modal auxiliaries as present or past, although English modals do not fit easily into a tense system. Biber et al. (1999: §6.2.1) classify modality as separate from tense, while Huddleston and Pullum (2002: §§3.2, 3.9.8.4) list modals as lexemes with preterite forms, though they admit that the analysis is problematic for *should* and *might*. However, as the analysis in Section 5.3.1 indicated that the forms labelled present-tense exhibited higher contraction ratios than their past-tense counterparts regardless of whether the verb was a modal auxiliary or a primary verb (where the tense distinction is uncontroversial), maintaining tense as a label seemed defensible for the purposes of this study.

[12] As Quirk et al. (1985: §11.25) and Huddleston and Pullum (2002; §10.9.2.1) note, imperatives typically imply *you* as subject, as can be seen from tag questions (e.g. *Grab the bag, will you?*), reflexive pronouns (e.g. *Get yourself a beer!*) and the possibility of inserting stressed *you* (e.g. *'You grab the bag!*). The imperative sentences were checked manually to ensure that *you* rather than a third-person subject (as in *Somebody open the door!*) was understood.

third-person pronominal (e.g. *she*, *nobody*, and *they*), and other (noun-headed noun phrases and nominal clauses).

The type of sentence used appears to affect *not*-contraction ratios: interrogatives and imperatives display higher contraction ratios than declaratives (e.g. Kjellmer 1998: 175–7; Westergren Axelsson 1998: 177–8). As imperative sentences had already been identified on the finiteness parameter, I classified the syntactic main clauses in my material as interrogative and non-interrogative (the latter comprising declarative as well as imperative sentences) according to Quirk et al.'s (1985: §11.1) framework (the very few exclamative main clauses were excluded). As syntax was the basis for my classification, declarative questions, as in (5.13), were considered non-interrogative.

(5.13) [$Q.$] You tried to speak loud and *could not*? (CONCE: Trials, 1800–30, Bowditch, p. 33)

However, the immediate clause in which *not* is the negator may be a subordinate clause that in turn is part of the main clause which is classified as interrogative or non-interrogative; in (5.14), for instance, *didn't* occurs in a non-interrogative main clause, but it is immediately situated inside a subordinate (relative) clause:

(5.14) "Always," interrupted the major. "I never heard any man speak of a school-fellow, who *didn't* make the same observation – curious – odd – strange – hey, Palmer! – wonderful! – surprising – eh?" (CONCE: Fiction, 1800–30, Hook, p. I.237)

Since whether or not an operator + *not* combination occurs in a main or subordinate clause might also influence contraction ratios, I classified the tokens according to whether their immediate clause was main or subordinate.

In the above classifications, clause fragments were coded as belonging to the same category that the full clause would have instantiated whenever this information was recoverable from the co-text. However, the fact that operators can occur in reduced clauses, where the rest of the verb phrase – as well as any objects, complements, etc. – has been elipted but is typically recoverable from the previous co-text (see Quirk et al. 1985: §3.26), as in (5.15), is also of potential interest.

(5.15) [$Har.$] Pshaw! Will you, or will you not comply?
[$Gold.$] Tell'ee I *can't*. Have a better scheme! (CONCE: Drama, 1800–30, Holcroft, p. 8)

Varela Pérez (2013: 273–4) demonstrates that such reduced contexts favour *not*-contraction in comparison with uncontracted and, in particular, operator-contracted forms in Present-Day English. I therefore classified all tokens into two categories depending on the status of the clause in which they occurred: (i) reduced clauses, which contained only the operator + *not* combination, a subject (if present), and any non-obligatory adverbials, and (ii) non-reduced clauses. The reduced category thus also contains tag questions such as (5.5) and (5.9–11).

The variants were relevelled so that uncontracted forms and the variants of independent variables that, based on previous research and my own monofactorial analyses, were expected to favour uncontracted forms were turned into the reference levels. The original model included the following categorical variables, together with the labels they were given in the statistical analysis (when these are not transparent) and reference levels: period (reference: period 1),[13] genre (reference: Trials), subject (= Subj.3, reference: Other), main-clause type (= Sen.2, reference: nq = non-interrogative), immediate clause (= Cla.2, reference: s = subordinate), verb (reference: MAY), type of finiteness (= Tense, reference: past), and reduction (= Code; reference: n = no reduction). In addition, interactions between the period variable and all other independent variables were included, as one of the most important questions for the analysis concerns change over time. After such a glm model had been fitted, non-significant interactions and variables were removed from the model until all variables included had a significant effect in themselves and/or participated in at least one significant interaction. The final model is given in Table 5.5.

As regards the assumptions of the model (Levshina 2015: 271–3), the observations cannot be considered wholly independent of one another; for instance, each text, speaker, etc. often contributes several tokens to the data. There are no quantitative predictors, so it is not necessary to test the assumption of linear relations between the logit and such predictors. No serious problems were reported when the predictors were tested for multicollinearity. The model was also tested for overfitting (Levshina 2015: 274), which did not reveal high optimism (e.g. Slope optimism = 0.0346). The high C value indicates that the model discriminates very well, that is, it

---

[13] The use of the period in CONCE as a categorical variable is potentially questionable. Time is a numeric, continuous variable, and some information is lost when such a variable is divided into groups (see Plonsky and Oswald 2017: 582–3 for criticism of this practice when using ANOVA). However, because the CONCE data are based on time periods (1800–30, 1850–70, and 1870–00) rather than exact points in time, and because these time periods correspond partly to a number of extralinguistic events of importance (Smitterberg 2005: 18–20), this practice was deemed defensible for the purposes of the present study.

5.3 Results

Table 5.5 *The final glm for Drama, Fiction, and Trials*

Coefficients	Estimate	Std. Error	z value	Pr(>|z|)	
(Intercept)	-8.859234	1.105150	-8.016	1.09e-15	***
PeriodSecond	0.008882	0.958114	0.009	0.99260	
PeriodThird	1.954571	0.927122	2.108	0.03501	*
GenreDrama	1.765594	0.267408	6.603	4.04e-11	***
GenreFiction	-1.044946	0.402687	-2.595	0.00946	**
Subj.3First	0.743602	0.628801	1.183	0.23698	
Subj.3 Second	0.952341	0.657527	1.448	0.14751	
Subj.3Third	0.488226	0.742294	0.658	0.51071	
Sen.2q	0.553642	0.203454	2.721	0.00650	**
Cla.2 m	0.558404	0.186784	2.990	0.00279	**
Verbcan	1.566566	0.740366	2.116	0.03435	*
Verbdo	2.996846	0.737672	4.063	4.85e-05	***
Verbshall	1.363786	0.792766	1.720	0.08538	.
TenseImp	3.704514	0.650705	5.693	1.25e-08	***
TensePresent	4.033726	0.536416	7.520	5.49e-14	***
PeriodSecond: GenreDrama	2.844250	0.373227	7.621	2.52e-14	***
PeriodThird: GenreDrama	1.797328	0.341118	5.269	1.37e-07	***
PeriodSecond: GenreFiction	3.620973	0.475803	7.610	2.74e-14	***
PeriodThird: GenreFiction	4.109048	0.480129	8.558	< 2e-16	***
PeriodSecond: Subj.3First	1.860556	0.772072	2.410	0.01596	*
PeriodThird:Subj.3First	-0.175545	0.752996	-0.233	0.81566	
PeriodSecond: Subj.3 Second	1.623242	0.822324	1.974	0.04839	*
PeriodThird: Subj.3 Second	0.185610	0.797672	0.233	0.81600	
PeriodSecond: Subj.3Third	1.371402	0.891226	1.539	0.12386	
PeriodThird: Subj.3Third	-0.777791	0.890325	-0.874	0.38233	

Table 5.5 (cont.)

Coefficients	Estimate	Std. Error	z value	Pr(>|z|)	
PeriodSecond:TenseImp	−1.986243	0.791255	−2.510	0.01206	*
PeriodThird:TenseImp	−2.647264	0.770434	−3.436	0.00059	***
PeriodSecond:TensePresent	−2.419783	0.578347	−4.184	2.86e-05	***
PeriodThird:TensePresent	−2.799320	0.581314	−4.816	1.47e-06	***

Deviance Residuals: Min −2.8548, 1Q −0.5476, Median −0.2278, 3Q 0.4150, Max 3.5835; R^2 = 0.592; C = 0.912; AIC = 2069.6

predicts a higher probability of the variant that was actually used (a *not*-contracted or uncontracted form) 91 per cent of the time.

The output reveals several interesting things about the distribution of *not*-contraction that would not be clear from monofactorial analyses. To begin with, time period interacts with several other parameters. The interaction between time and genre demonstrates that the increase after period 1, which constitutes colloquialization, is dependent on genre, with the interactions between (i) Drama and Fiction and (ii) periods 2 and 3 displaying high z values. (As shown in Section 5.3.1, Trials did not display any increase across time.) The type of subject is not a significant parameter in itself, but there are significant interactions favouring *not*-contraction between first- and second-person subjects and period 2. Finally, the finiteness parameter is of interest. While the imperative and the present tense favour *not*-contraction compared with the past tense, the association becomes weaker across time; *not*-contractions are virtually restricted to the imperative and the present tense in period 1 – see Figure 5.3 as well as the discussion of outliers below – but co-occur more regularly with the past tense in periods 2 and 3. The relationship between finiteness and *not*-contraction over time in the data is illustrated in Figure 5.3.

The remaining parameters did not interact significantly with the period variable, but three of them had a significant effect on contraction ratios in themselves. Interrogative main clauses favour *not*-contraction significantly compared with non-interrogative clauses; occurrence in a main clause promotes contraction; and among the verbs included, CAN and, in particular, DO are more likely to be contracted than MAY, while results for SHALL are not significant. This result is indicative of a trend that

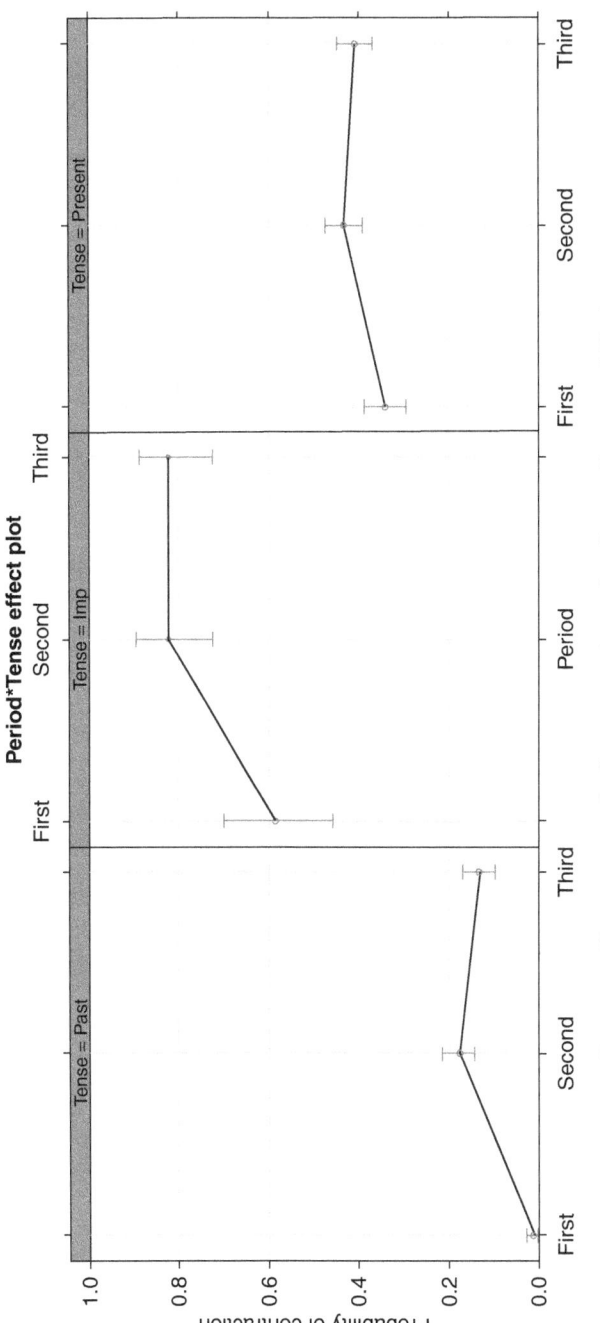

Figure 5.3 *Not*-contraction by finiteness and period in Drama, Fiction, and Trials

accelerated in twentieth-century English, where *mayn't*, *mightn't*, and *shan't* are rare or non-existent in many (sub)corpora (Kjellmer 1998: 170; Westergren Axelsson 1998: 26–7; Biber et al. 1999: Appendix). Of particular interest is perhaps the result that main clauses are more hospitable to contraction than subordinate clauses, as this parameter has not been in focus in previous research. Even though we know today that spoken complexity is frequently encoded through clausal subordination (Biber and Gray 2016: 92), Drama and Fiction writers may have connected hypotaxis with formality and thus been less likely to use *not*-contraction in complex sentences.

Finally, whether or not the clause was reduced was neither significant in itself nor part of a significant interaction with the period variable (hence the absence of the code parameter from Table 5.5). A brief look at contraction ratios per period suggests that there is no clear difference between these two categories in any of the three periods, but that reduced tokens display a clearer pattern across time, with a consistent increase in *not*-contraction ratios from period 1 to period 3. If that trend was continued into the 1900s, it is possible that the association between reduced clauses and *not*-contraction grew stronger in twentieth-century English, resulting in a statistical correlation that was not present in my nineteenth-century data.

The function influencePlot() in the car package was used to identify outliers and overly influential tokens. There were three tokens with high studentized residuals (> ±2) and large Cook's distance values, all of which were *not*-contractions in unexpected contexts: two from Hook's novel *Maxwell* (period 1), one of which was given in (5.14), repeated here as (5.16), and one from Robertson's comedy *Society* (period 2; see 5.17):

(5.16) "Always," interrupted the major. "I never heard any man speak of a school-fellow, who *didn't* make the same observation – curious – odd – strange – hey, Palmer! – wonderful! – surprising – eh?" (CONCE: Fiction, 1800–30, Hook, p. I.237)

(5.17) [$Chodd Jun.$] Mr. Sidney Daryl may lose, and, perhaps, Mr. Sidney Daryl *mayn't* show. After that ball – (CONCE: Drama, 1850–70, Robertson, p. 79)

Example (5.16) and the other unexpected token from Hook's novel are the only *not*-contractions in the past tense in period 1, and (5.16) also occurs in a subordinate clause. Example (5.17) stands out from all other tokens in CONCE by allowing *not*-contraction with a noun-headed noun-phrase subject and with *may* as operator; it also has the highest leverage of the three tokens, indicating that it has more influence on the fitted values. All three tokens occur in speech-purposed text.

In sum, the binary logistic regression both supports the hypothesis that colloquialization occurs in the material and underscores the importance of the genre parameter in colloquialization. The importance of verb, finiteness, and sentence type is also highlighted by the results, and clause type is added as an influential parameter. In contrast, subject type has comparatively little explanatory power as an independent variable and is influential mostly in period 2, and reduced clauses do not increase the likelihood of contraction in my nineteenth-century data.

5.3.3   Non-Standard Patterns: A Qualitative Perspective

Before leaving the presentation of results, I will devote some attention to *not*-contractions that are typically not considered part of Standard English today. The most important of these are *ain't*, which can stand for any present-tense form of BE and HAVE + *not*, and singular *don't* (i.e. *don't* with a third-person singular subject). The occurrence of such tokens in writing may indicate orality even more strongly than other *not*-contractions do. I will first discuss *ain't* and singular *don't*, before considering other *not*-contractions that would not normally be found in the standard language today, such as *warn't*.[14]

At least in writing, *ain't* dates from the eighteenth century (Lass 1999: 180). Clark (1975: 36–7) and Phillipps (1978: 121), who base their conclusions on fiction by Anthony Trollope and William Thackeray, respectively, argue that *ain't* was acceptable in familiar educated speech from the time, though Clark's (1975) findings suggest that *ain't* was less generally accepted for *is* + *not* than for *am/are* + *not*. In the CONCE data, there are thirty-four tokens of *ain't*, plus one *a'n't*, given in (5.18), where the contraction may represent either *ain't* or *aren't* since the subject is *I*:[15]

(5.18)   [$Tyke.$] [$Starting up.$] For what? is not father dead? – *a'n't* I a thief – cursed – hated – hunted? ... (CONCE: Drama, 1800–30, Morton, p. 43)

---

[14] As mentioned in Smitterberg (2012b: 196–7), tokens where negation was represented by *na* or *no* (e.g. *dunno* and *is na' born* corresponding to uncontracted Standard English *do not* and *is not born*) were not included in the counts of contracted or uncontracted forms; these forms are therefore not commented on in Section 5.3.3.

[15] Phillipps (1984: 69) cites a nineteenth-century prescriptive source which considers *a'n't it* particularly objectionable and notes that it is usual for *a'n't* to be pronounced as to rhyme with *faint*.

The colloquial status of *ain't* is shown by its being almost wholly restricted to Drama; the only exception concerns three tokens in fictional dialogue, two of which are spoken by the nurse in Charlotte Yonge's *Hopes and Fears*, who also uses multiple negation and singular *don't* in the same utterance:

> (5.19) Nurse winked knowingly at the housemaid. "Yes, yes, my darling, no one likes to hear who is to come after them. Don't you say nothing about it; it *ain't* becoming; but, by and by, see if it don't come so, and if my boy *ain't* master here." (CONCE: Fiction, 1850–70, Yonge, p. I.113)

As shown in (5.19), *ain't* is not restricted to clauses with *I* as subject, where there is no available standard *not*-contraction: only nine tokens co-occur with *I*. Instead, third-person-singular subjects predominate (19 ×), and there are eleven tokens of *it* + *ain't*. The only token where the underlying operator is clearly HAVE is given in (5.20):[16]

> (5.20) "I seed her father married," mumbles the old man, without taking his pipe out of his mouth; "that'll do for me. I seed her mother buried; that was a rare sight, that was – sixteen murning curches. That'll last my time. Miss has got my blessing wherever she goes; but I *ain't* got strength for no more sight-seeing." (CONCE: Fiction, 1870–1900, Braddon, p. II.71)

There is no consistent diachronic trend in the incidence of *ain't/a'n't* (1 × in period 1, 26 × in period 2, 8 × in period 3); it appears to be available as a marker of non-standard speech especially in mid-century.

Singular *don't* is attested from the 1660s (Lass 1999: 180). It was "common in dialogue" between roughly the mid-eighteenth and mid-nineteenth centuries (Denison 1998: 196) and acceptable in colloquial speech somewhat later (Phillipps 1984: 69). Brainerd (1989 [1993]: 186) links singular *don't* to the decline of the subjunctive, where *do* would have been used throughout the present tense. In my data, singular *don't* occurs almost exclusively in Drama – the only exception is given in (5.19) above – but has a lower frequency than *ain't* overall and is only found in periods 2 (12 ×) and 3 (5 ×). Most subjects are pronominal, as in (5.21–22):

> (5.21) [$HANNAH.$] No, I never ask Noah nothing about Queen's business. He *don't* want two women over him! (CONCE: Drama, 1870–1900, Pinero, p. 103)

---

[16] In *I say, don't cry, granny, we ain't come to skilly yet* (CONCE: Drama, 1850–70, Taylor, p. 297), *ain't* might represent either BE or HAVE + *not*.

(5.22)   [$Lady P.$] Money can do everything.
         [$Maud.$] Can it make me love a man I hate?
         [$Lady P.$] Yes; at least if it *don't*, it ought. I suppose you mean to marry somebody? (CONCE: Drama, 1850–70, Robertson, p. 71)

In three of the seventeen tokens, including (5.22), *don't* occurs in an adverbial clause where the verb can be interpreted as subjunctive, which would make *don't* rather than *doesn't* the expected form. If the possibility of subjunctive readings is taken into account, the number of relevant tokens is fourteen.

As regards other tokens that do not conform to present-day standard usage, the use of the apostrophe to signal cliticization of *not* is not quite universal even in printed texts: there are a total of thirty-five tokens without an apostrophe in -*n't*, most of which have the forms *dont* (27 ×) and *wont* (4 ×). *Wont* occurs only in Yonge's novel *Hopes and Fears*; *dont* occurs almost exclusively in the Trial of Mr. Jeremiah Smith (period 2), where *don't* is not used. There is also one token each of *dont'e* and *dont'ee*, where -(*e*)*e* represents a second-person subject, as in (5.23), one *did nt*, and one *hav'nt*, where the apostrophe seems to represent the word boundary.

(5.23)   [$HANNAH.$] Oh, *dont'ee* trust to Nick, Noah dear – he's such a vicious brute. Kitty's safer in the cart. (CONCE: Drama, 1870–1900, Pinero, p. 107)

Some *not*-contractions have an apostrophe in -*n't* but feature other differences from their typical present-day spelling. Several cases appear to be attempts to spell phonemically or to represent the absence of sounds that are potentially present in the uncontracted variant: *musn't* (1 ×), probably representing the pronunciation /mʌsnt/ or /mʊsnt/; *arn't* (2 ×), possibly representing /ɑːnt/; *sha'n't* (1 ×), with the first apostrophe presumably representing the /l/ in *shall* (and, possibly, a lengthened and/or backed vowel); and three representations of /h/-dropping, namely *'asn't* (1 ×) and *'aven't* (2 ×). There are also three tokens where *n't* or *nt* occurs as a separate orthographic word (*did nt*, mentioned above, *is n't*, and *do n't*). The older pattern where the pronoun *it* is cliticized onto the operator is found in *'tisn't* (2 ×) and *'twasn't* (1 ×).

Finally, a few tokens that occur once in the material may represent regional varieties: *warn't* with a singular subject, which may represent *was* + *not* or *were* + *not* (Brainerd 1989 [1993]: 189), *dursn't* 'dare not', *maun't* (5.24), which may represent *must* + *not* (cf. Upton et al. 1994: 500), and one *bain't* for *be* + *not* (5.25):

(5.24) [$TREVOR.$] Well, thou knows best, Lily; but I *maun't* have thee overset or flurried. (CONCE: Drama, 1850–70, Marston, p. 24)

(5.25) "I believe she did .... Ma'am, shall I call Liddy? You *bain't* well, ma'am, surely? You look like a lily – so pale and fainty!" (CONCE: Fiction, 1870–1900, Hardy, p. II.130)

As Hardy's *Far from the Madding Crowd* is set in a fictional Wessex, *bain't* may represent contemporary south-western usage (cf. Brainerd 1989 [1993]: 181).

To sum up this brief discussion, apart from tokens with no apostrophe in -*n't* from Trials (where in one case the *nt* is printed as a separate word), *not*-contractions with forms that are not in use in present-day Standard English are a feature of Drama and of fictional dialogue. They arguably add yet another qualitative level of colloquialization to the material.[17] They occur predominantly in periods 2 and 3, which means that their distribution broadly matches that of *not*-contractions in the data in general, although a tendency towards a decrease between periods 2 and 3 can be noted.

5.4 Discussion

The analyses in this chapter clearly demonstrate that colloquialization occurred in the CONCE material as far as *not*-contraction is concerned. While the three expository genres did not contain *not*-contracted tokens, the monofactorial analyses in Section 5.3.1 showed that the proportion of *not*-contraction was low and stable in Trials (speech-based) but increased in Drama (speech-purposed) and Fiction (partly speech-purposed). The result is an increase in linguistic genre differentiation (cf. Biber and Finegan 1997): an indicator of orality becomes more integrated into some but not all written genres. There were also pronounced differences in contraction ratios between different operators, and present-tense operators were consistently more likely to co-occur with *not*-contraction.

A number of features that were not included in the multifactorial analysis were also considered in Section 5.3.1. As might be expected when a stigmatized feature is studied, there were tendencies in the material towards women using lower proportions of the incoming form (see Labov 2001: 292–3). This tendency was visible for both women authors

---

[17] To some extent, this interpretation is dependent on authorial intentions. For instance, if dialect forms are used to portray fictional characters negatively as ignorant or uneducated, their occurrence does not illustrate genuine tolerance of those forms. Nevertheless, their mere occurrence in written texts testifies to their availability for characterization.

5.4 Discussion

in Fiction and women witnesses in Trials. In contrast, whether BE and HAVE were auxiliaries or main verbs did not have a clear influence on contraction ratios. A separate analysis of word order in questions indicated that the word order in *Would not she have noticed it?* (as opposed to *Wouldn't she have ... ?* or *Would she not have ... ?*) developed in two different directions. In Drama and Fiction, it became less frequent over time and was probably replaced by *not*-contracted forms. Conversely, the *would not she* pattern increased in prominence in Trials, where it may have been used as a more acceptable way of rendering questions that had featured *not*-contraction in the original speech events; alternatively, the occurrence of *not* in the position where *-n't* could have occurred may be due to a lack of distinction between *-n't* and *not* in the shorthand system used for a particular trial. Finally, the variationist perspective was problematized by considering the occurrence of *no*-negation in the material. The incidence of *no*-negation was largely stable, while *not*-negation became more frequent across time, which results in what looks like an increasing preference for *not*-negation over *no*-negation in writing. Such a development would tally with tendencies towards colloquialization, as *not*-negation is more prevalent in speech than in writing, but that hypothesis must remain speculative since the substitutability of the *not*-negated and *no*-negated constructions was not examined.

The importance of the genre parameter was further underscored by the multifactorial analysis in Section 5.3.2. Hundt and Mair (1999: 236) argue that their findings regarding colloquialization in recent English require a model where grammatical change is perceived "as mediated through genre". The multifactorial model provides part of such a picture, where the interaction between period and genre is necessary to get a full picture of developments even after several linguistic parameters have been taken into account. Powerful interactions between (i) periods 2 and 3 and (ii) the genres Drama and Fiction favoured *not*-contraction in comparison with Trials and period 1. There were also interactions between (i) periods 2 and 3 and (ii) imperative or present-tense finite verbs; here, the dominance of imperative and present-tense operators became less marked over time, as past-tense operators increasingly participated in *not*-contraction. While the role of the subject was less important in the multifactorial analysis than previous research has indicated, there were interactions with lower z values between first- and second-person subjects and period 2 favouring *not*-contraction. In addition, several parameters that did not interact with the period variable had an independent effect on contraction ratios: occurrence in questions, main clauses, and with DO or CAN (as opposed to MAY) as operator all favoured *not*-contraction. Such significant effects indicate that, as idiolectal norms for some genres began to allow increased use of *not*-contraction, the new usage was sensitive to the linguistic environment of the negation.

A brief look at non-standard *not*-contraction patterns indicated that, with the exception of absent apostrophes in a few Trials texts, non-standard spellings were confined to speech-purposed text in Drama and Fiction. Like *not*-contraction in general, these spellings occurred mainly in periods 2 and 3; perhaps the increased use of *not*-contraction in general in these two genres stimulated the occurrence of forms that were even more marked for orality, as a second layer of colloquialization. A few regional forms, such as south-western *bain't*, could also be observed in the data.

In sum, the present study has produced several types of evidence that colloquialization was taking place. Most importantly, the multifactorial analysis of *not*-contracted and uncontracted forms clearly demonstrates that colloquialization was underway in the material, but also that this process was dependent on the genre parameter. Several other results reached in the chapter lend additional support to the conclusion that *not*-contraction is an indicator of colloquialization: women used the stigmatized incoming variant less; *no*-negation, which is less oral than any *not*-negated variant, did not increase in the material; the marked *would not she* word order in questions became rarer in Drama and Fiction (where it may have been being replaced with *not*-contraction) but commoner in Trials (where it may have been used instead of *not*-contraction); and *not*-contractions with non-standard forms were least frequent in period 1.

A number of minor indications in the data would be worth pursuing in studies of early-twentieth-century English. To begin with, *not*-contraction in the past tense appears to have been more marked in the 1800s; studies of the first six decades of the 1900s would be valuable in tracing the gradual disappearance of this possible constraint. Other tendencies may instead have become stronger since the nineteenth century; for instance, whether or not the negated clause was reduced was not found to have an effect on contraction ratios in my material.

The present study has not exhausted the topic of *not*-contraction in LModE. Analyses of very large corpora may add further to our knowledge of variation in negation. COHA may contain enough material to allow for including only contexts that also permit *no*-negation and/or operator contraction in addition to the variants in focus here, thus widening the variant field. A look at Fiction in COHA and at the OBC would also be valuable from a gender perspective, to see whether the tendencies attested in this study are borne out when more data are included.

5.4 Discussion

In addition, the linguistic factors studied here were mainly morpho-syntactic, but other types of variable may also be of interest. While prosodic features like pitch are near-impossible to reconstruct from written material, aspects of semantics and pragmatics may shed further light on the choice between *not*-contracted and uncontracted forms. Yaeger-Dror's (1997) Social Agreement Principle suggests that face-threatening negatives should be more likely to be contracted in order to minimize or de-emphasize unsupportive information; Varela Pérez (2013: 274–7) finds that both the status of the operator as discourse-old or discourse-new and the status of the negation as an explicit denial, implicit denial, or corrective may influence the choice between *not*-contracted, operator-contracted, and uncontracted forms; Walker (2005) reports that non-stative verbs favour *not*-contraction over operator contraction in early African American Vernacular English. Tagliamonte and Smith (2002: 264–5) and Beal (1993: 202–4) argue that the type of answer required or expected may affect *not*-contraction ratios for questions in Scottish and Northern Irish English and tag questions in Tyneside English, respectively.

While we still need further work on how the different types of negation available in LModE idiolects were distributed across linguistic and extralinguistic contexts, the present study has demonstrated that the nineteenth century is a pivotal period in the emergence of *not*-contraction as a vehicle for colloquialization. The identification of independent effects in a multifactorial analysis and the contextualization of the results relative to other negation strategies as well as the gender parameter shed light on the complex way in which *not*-contraction was gradually integrated as a colloquial feature of written LModE. Idiolects whose norms for certain genres became increasingly tolerant of *not*-contraction as an indication of colloquialization did not simply go through the change as a homogeneous shift towards higher contraction ratios. Instead, speaker-related parameters such as gender and several features of the linguistic environment continued to condition the choice between *not*-contracted and uncontracted forms in idiolects even as the overall proportions of those options were undergoing change.

CHAPTER 6

Colloquialization II: Co-ordination by And

6.1 Introduction

The co-ordinator *and* can link units on many different levels of syntactic structure. Following Quirk et al. (1985: §2.10), I will refer to the units linked by *and* as "conjoins".[1] Examples (6.1–3) illustrate three types of conjoins: individual words, as in (6.1), where only the head words of the noun phrase are co-ordinated; phrases, for example the noun phrases in (6.2); and clauses, such as the two main clauses in (6.3).

(6.1) He put it to their lordships, whether, under such circumstances, for this was not a mere technical objection, it was not due to the *gravity* **and** *dignity* of their own proceedings, to take some decisive step with respect to this bill. (CONCE: Debates, 1800–30, p. XV.437)

(6.2) *The royalists,* **and** *the king himself,* exclaimed against this as the most audacious treason, though it may be reckoned as a very natural consequence of the state in which the parliament was placed; ... (CONCE: History, 1800–30, Hallam, p. II.222)

(6.3) *Of course I refused,* **and** *she quitted me telling me that she would devote her life to finding you out.* (CONCE: Drama, 1870–1900, Gilbert, p. 30)

In numbered corpus examples, I italicize the conjoins and put *and* in boldface. In many studies of co-ordination, conjoins are often grouped

---

[1] While Quirk et al. (1985: §2.10) and Biber et al. (1999: §3.3) treat the co-ordinator as conjoin-external, Huddleston and Pullum (2002: §15.1.1) argue that syntactically it forms a constituent together with the second conjoin (called a *coordinate* by Huddleston and Pullum). One of Huddleston and Pullum's reasons for this analysis is the ability of co-ordinators to link sentences, in which case they are always placed at the beginning of the second conjoin/sentence. This difference in analysis is not of great significance to the present study, but when discussing conjoins and representing them in examples, I will treat *and* as conjoin-external. Sentence-initial *and* is discussed separately in Section 6.3.2.

6.1 Introduction

into two main categories, which are typically called *phrasal* or *phrase-level* and *clausal* or *clause-level*, respectively (e.g. Biber et al. 1999: §2.4.7.3; Culpeper and Kytö 2010: 158–83). I use a modified version of this framework in the present study (see Section 6.2).

There is also variation among texts in the distribution of functions filled by the *conjoint item*, i.e. the structure that comprises the two conjoins together with *and* (Quirk et al. 1985: §2.10). Syntactically, the conjoint item has the same status as either conjoin (Quirk et al. 1985: §§2.10, 13.49), but it is also possible to see what function that item fills in the larger phrasal or clausal structure. In (6.1) the conjoint item is a noun-phrase head, in (6.2) it is a subject, and in (6.3) a sentence. This chapter focusses on variation among different types of conjoins, but I will occasionally comment on conjoint items where relevant to the discussion.

The relevance of co-ordination to colloquialization is implied in Biber's (1988, 2003) factor analyses of Present-Day English, which establish a positive correlation between the orality of a genre and the proportion of clausal co-ordination. In Biber (1988), clausal co-ordination loads as an involved feature on Dimension 1, "Involved vs. Informational Production", the most powerful dimension in the analysis, and one of the three that, taken together, represent an oral vs. literate divide in Biber and Finegan's (1997) diachronic factor-score analysis. The factor analysis of academic genres in Biber (2003) identifies one single dimension that separates oral from literate discourse; on that dimension, phrasal co-ordination loads as a "literate" feature and clausal co-ordination as an "oral" feature. In Present-Day English, the relative proportions of phrasal and clausal conjoins of *and* thus seem to be one indication of how oral a given genre is. Clausal and phrasal co-ordination by *and* is related to the different ways in which oral and literate genres encode linguistic complexity: while conversation favours clausal features such as subordinate clauses, expository writing condenses information by means of phrasal units like premodifying nouns (Biber and Gray 2016: 91–2). This difference has probably been part of the language for a long time.

Literate genres have contained more phrasal co-ordination than oral genres for centuries; for instance, Lehto (2013: 247) found that 70 per cent of tokens of *and* in Early Modern English proclamations, a formal written genre, were phrasal, while the proportion in direct speech from the Corpus of English Dialogues (CED) from roughly the same period was 40 per cent (Culpeper and Kytö 2010: 178). However, the relative proportions of phrasal and clausal conjoins in different genres are subject to change over time, and previous research indicates that these proportions have become increasingly different during the Modern English period. Culpeper and

Kytö (2010: 165) show that the considerable differences between oral and literate genres established for Present-Day English by Biber et al. (1999: §2.4.7.3) were far less pronounced 300 years ago. Culpeper and Kytö (2010: 167–8) argue that the incidence of clausal *and* has decreased in written texts and link this decrease to the gradual development of the syntactic sentence as a major unit of textual structure in writing. As the division of the text into sentences became a more important aspect of structuring writing during the mid-to-late seventeenth century, the need for other markers of clausal division, such as *and*, may have decreased. This shift would be part of a change from oral to literate styles in such genres.

However, research on LModE also points to changes in the opposite direction, whereby written genres that underwent colloquialization during the nineteenth century may display an increase in the proportion of clausal conjoins of *and*. I have shown elsewhere (Smitterberg 2014: 323) that the proportion of clausal conjoins in CNNE increased during the nineteenth century; in the present chapter, those results are discussed in more detail, and comparable data from CONCE are presented. Kytö and Smitterberg (2019) demonstrate that even speech-based language changed in this regard: clausal co-ordination became increasingly dominant in witness statements from the OBC between the periods 1753–85 and 1850–81.

There may thus be two separate and potentially conflicting developments regarding conjoins of *and* during the Modern English period. On the one hand, an increase in the importance of the sentence as a unit in some written genres may lead to a decrease in the proportion of clausal *and*, as the need for clausal demarcation by co-ordinators decreased. On the other hand, colloquialization may manifest itself as an increase in clausal conjoins of *and*. As will be shown in this chapter, there is evidence for both types of development in the nineteenth century.

My account focusses on *and* to the exclusion of the other two central co-ordinators, namely *but* and *or*. The reason for restricting the scope of the investigation to *and* is twofold. First, the correlation between clausal co-ordination and orality established in Biber's (1988, 2003) analyses was based on co-ordination by *and* only; there is thus less empirical support for assuming that oral styles will feature more clausal conjoins with *but* and *or*. Secondly, including *but* and *or* would have necessitated obtaining separate data sets for each co-ordinator, as they behave differently with regard to the proportions of clausal conjoins; for instance, *but*, which is also less central a co-ordinator than *and* and *or* (Quirk et al. 1985: §13.16), is used mainly at the clause level (Biber et al. 1999: §2.4.7).

As mentioned in Section 4.3.1, the co-ordinator *and* was a perfectly acceptable feature of LModE with virtually all types of conjoins. Any changes towards less phrasal co-ordination in the overall quantitative results (presented in Section 6.3.1) would thus be likely to indicate that informality was more or less subconsciously deployed in texts. However, sentence-initial *and*, which was overtly proscribed in contemporary sources, is an exception; I therefore devote special attention to this feature in Section 6.3.2.

6.2 Method

The intermediate position of news texts in Biber et al.'s (1999) analysis of phrasal vs. clausal co-ordination and the openness to change of newspaper language noted by Hundt and Mair (1999) indicate that it may be especially relevant to chart possible changes in newspapers. All relevant occurrences of *and* in CNNE were therefore included in the analysis. I restricted the scope of the investigation of CONCE to periods 1 and 3 and included all texts from these periods in the searches. For each genre except Letters, 400 randomly chosen examples per period were selected for analysis; given the importance of charting gender differences in usage, I analysed 400 random tokens by women and 400 by men from each period of the Letters genre.[2]

Lexical searches were run for *and*, *an'*, and *&*.[3] For CNNE, the entire concordances were used. For CONCE, each period/genre sample was first examined in order to eliminate clearly irrelevant examples, where tokens of *and* occurred inside corpus codes indicating that they were part of stage directions, chapter headings, and so on. After this initial step, the resulting concordances were randomly pared down to 400 tokens per sample using the "Reduce to N ... " feature in WordSmith Tools.

The steps described above yielded a total of 10,033 relevant tokens of *and* from CNNE and 6,400 from CONCE to be analysed. However, the actual number included in analyses is somewhat lower, as some occurrences of *and* resisted classification or turned out to be irrelevant on close inspection;

---

[2] The restriction to 400 instances per sample was due partly to a desire to obtain a sufficient number of examples while keeping the study within manageable proportions and partly to the fact that there were 403 relevant instances of *and* in the period/genre sample that yielded the smallest number of tokens (Debates, period 1).

[3] To see whether *an*, without an apostrophe, occurred as a variant of *and* in the material, 200 randomly selected instances of *an* from the material were examined manually. As none of those examples represented *and*, this search word was not included in further searches, given the large amount of work that would be necessary to eliminate the occurrences of indefinite articles from the concordances and the unlikelihood that any relevant instances would be found.

for instance, cases where *and* was part of a proper name were excluded, as in *the new Redruth and District Bank* (CNNE: 1875–95, BDP0002). The total number of examples that were included in the counts was 9,642 for CNNE and 6,133 for CONCE.

In previous research, conjoins are often divided into two main categories, for example "phrasal" vs. "clausal" (Culpeper and Kytö 2010) or "clausal" vs. "subclausal" (Huddleston and Pullum 2002). However, as the results in Smitterberg (2014) showed that over 5 per cent of tokens in CNNE were difficult to classify with certainty within a binary framework, I recognize a third, intermediate category. Each occurrence of *and* was classified as belonging to one of three main categories based on its conjoins: phrasal, intermediate, and super-phrasal.[4] Where relevant, I will also comment on patterns involving more specific conjoin categories when the results are presented.

The first step in the procedure consisted in classifying the conjoins; for instance, the conjoins in (6.1–3) in Section 6.1 were identified as two nouns, two noun phrases, and two main clauses, respectively. In cases where there were more than two conjoins, as in (6.4), only the two conjoins immediately before and after *and* were counted.

(6.4) The M'Connell Family, ranking amongst the most popular artists who are engaged from time to time at the "Star," made a welcome reappearance last evening, delighting a numerous audience with an entertainment which was refined, *attractive,* **and** *original*. (CNNE: 1875–95, LIM0004)

In the vast majority of cases, identifying the conjoins was straightforward, as they comprised the immediately preceding and following syntactic material. However, in a few instances this was not the case, particularly in Trials texts, which are frequently characterized by short question/answer sequences where lawyers control the structure of the exchange; in such contexts, *and* may link lawyers' questions to one another rather than connecting a question to the witness's answer to the preceding question, as in (6.5):

(6.5) [$Q.$] *Afterwards did they go to Merton Cottage?* – [$A.$] Yes.
[$Q.$] **And** *you continued to visit them there?* – [$A.$] Yes. (CONCE: Trials, 1870–1900, Bartlett, p. 110)

---

[4] I prefer the term *super-phrasal* to *clausal* since, as will be illustrated below, not all conjoins in this category comprise complete clauses. Huddleston and Pullum (2002: §15.1.3.1) instead reserve the label *clausal* for tokens when both conjoins are full main clauses, as in (6.3), and refer to all other tokens as *subclausal*. However, such a set-up would not be suitable for a study of colloquialization, as oral genres frequently make use of clausal material below the level of a full main clause, such as subordinate clauses, to encode complexity in texts.

6.2 Method

In cases such as (6.5), I interpreted the first conjoin to be not the immediately preceding linguistic item (i.e. the witness's answer), but rather the last question asked by the same lawyer.

In the second step, the classification of the two conjoins was used to assign a structural level to the co-ordination as a whole. In phrasal co-ordination, both conjoins are on or below the level of a noun phrase, adjective phrase, adverb phrase, or prepositional phrase. Examples (6.1) and (6.2) in Section 6.1 and (6.4) above were thus all classified as phrasal, as their conjoins are parts of noun phrases, full noun phrases, and full adjective phrases, respectively. In addition, conjoins that comprised less than a full verb phrase and contained no other linguistic material, for example the main verbs in (6.6), were classified as phrasal.

(6.6) These same facts have been *arranged* **and** *rearranged* by each successive interpreter; ... (CONCE: Science, 1870–1900, Bateson, p. 13)

In some cases, the conjoins consisted of different syntactic structures. For instance, the verb BE may be followed by noun phrases, adjective phrases, and prepositional phrases, and if such complements are co-ordinated, the conjoins may belong to different categories (Huddleston and Pullum 2002: §15.3.2), as in (6.7), where an adjective phrase and a noun phrase are co-ordinated. The two conjoins may also strictly be non-parallel, as in (6.8), where the second conjoin is the noun-phrase complement of the preposition *of*, even though *of* is, strictly, part of the first conjoin. As shown in (6.8), tokens where *and* was reinforced by *both* were included in the counts.

(6.7) The foreman, Jos. Dangerfield, has left a wife and seven children; William Wells, a wife (pregnant) and one child; Samuel Appleton, a wife and nine children, – his wife is *pregnant* **and** *a cripple*; ... (CNNE: 1830–50, NS0005)

(6.8) They had had some relief from the board, but were in a very destitute condition, requiring the immediate attention both *of the relieving officer* **and** *the surgeon*. (CNNE: 1830–50, MG0001)

Instances such as (6.7) and (6.8) were classified as phrasal, as both conjoins in each token constitute phrases.

The super-phrasal category includes tokens that meet two criteria:

1. Each conjoin includes more linguistic material than can be included in a single noun, adjective, adverb, verb, or prepositional phrase.
2. Each conjoin includes at least part of a (finite or non-finite) verb phrase.

The instance of *and* in (6.3) in Section 6.1, where the conjoins are main clauses, was thus classified as super-phrasal. Occurrences of *and* with conjoins such as finite or non-finite subordinate clauses or whole sentences, as in (6.5), also belong to this category. In addition, cases where *and* co-ordinates two predicates, as in (6.9), were classified as super-phrasal, as were cases such as (6.10), where part of a verb phrase as well as one or several other clause elements makes up each conjoin.

(6.9)   We *are all flourishing,* **and** *send our best love to Jack and you.* (CONCE: Letters, 1870–1900, Huxley, p. 312)

(6.10) When the law had been so mercifully extended to them, he hoped they would prove their gratitude by a change in their conduct, and that upon being released they would return to their work, and that their masters would *receive them into their employment again* **and** *forget what was past*; ... (CNNE: 1830–50, NS0004)

Conjoins were classified as subordinate clauses even if the subordinating element was outside the conjoins, as in (6.11), or if one or several adverbials were external to the conjoins.

(6.11) I think it would take time and labour; and because I think that, I complain that it was not done when *the seats were being redistributed* **and** *the votes were being dealt with.* (CONCE: Debates, 1870–1900, pp. IV.1,198–9)

A similar solution was applied to gapped clauses in which all or part of the verb phrase is absent and has to be understood from a previous conjoin, as in (6.12):

(6.12) More destruction followed in the reign of Charles I., when *the old central tower was taken down,* **and** *the present mean but picturesque tower of red brick built.* (CNNE: 1875–95, PMG0003)

In the second conjoin of (6.12), the auxiliary *was* has to be inferred from the first conjoin. Gapped clauses of this type were treated as if they were full clauses in the present study (cf. Huddleston and Pullum 2002: §15.4.2). Occasionally, the conjoins themselves resisted easy classification in terms of syntactic structure but included more material than one phrase and at least part of a verb phrase, as in (6.13):

(6.13) [$Q.$] Now, Miss Glenn, how long before you returned home were you told; – *I am told*, **and** *I suppose it to be correct*, that you returned home to your uncle's on the 2d of September? (CONCE: Trials, 1800–30, Bowditch, p. 21)

Such tokens were also classified as super-phrasal.

6.2 Method

The third, intermediate category was used for cases that could not be safely assigned to either the phrasal or the super-phrasal category. To begin with, when the conjoins consisted of different syntactic structures, one of which was phrasal and the other super-phrasal, as in (6.14) and (6.15), the token was considered intermediate.

(6.14) Lord BROUGHAM may remember *the QUEEN'S Trial,* **and** *how, with the Country at his back, he 'fluttered their Volscians.'* (CNNE: 1830–50, EX0003)

(6.15) Did the policeman *intervene* **and** *say there must be no conversation?* – Yes. (CONCE: Trials, 1870–1900, Maybrick, p. 66)

In (6.14), the first conjoin is a noun phrase and the second a subordinate clause. The first conjoin in (6.15) constitutes only part of a verb phrase and is thus phrasal according to the criteria used in the present study, while the second includes another clause element – a direct object – and is therefore clausal. The intermediate category was also used for cases where one or both conjoins comprised full verb phrases but no other linguistic material, as in (6.16):

(6.16) [$Trus.$] As usual, sir, she *questioned* **and** *cross-questioned* me as to whether you had faithfully abided by the conditions of a certain arrangement between you. (CONCE: Drama, 1800–30, Poole, p. 8)

Culpeper and Kytö (2010: 161–4) discuss how instances such as (6.16) can be classified as either phrasal or clausal in their framework, depending on whether the actions denoted by the verb phrases are considered to represent one activity or two. While that distinction is potentially valuable, applying such a semantic criterion to my material would have increased the subjectivity of the classification. Instead, I relied only on syntactic surface structure and thus grouped instances such as (6.16) together with the other intermediate cases. Finally, examples where at least one conjoin contained more linguistic material than one syntactic phrase but did not contain any part of a verb phrase were included in the intermediate category, as in (6.17), where each conjoin consists of a noun phrase + a prepositional phrase:[5]

(6.17) When this Bill passes the law will be reduced to an absurdity, because there will be *one law for the rich landlord* **and** *another for the poor retailer and tenant.* (CNNE: 1875–95, RW0012)

---

[5] It might be argued that the prepositional phrases in (6.17) are noun-phrase postmodifiers rather than adverbials, and that each conjoin thus consists only of a noun phrase. However, the mobility of the prepositional phrase in similar sentences (e.g. *For the rich landlord there will be one law, and for the poor retailer and tenant there will be another*) makes an adverbial interpretation more likely.

The introduction of an intermediate category made it possible to avoid excluding intermediate tokens while relying solely on syntactic criteria, which, it is hoped, increased the replicability of the classification process.

While I will consider proportions of occurrence of these three categories of conjoins, this method does not imply a variationist framework. Speakers are unlikely to first choose to use *and* and then decide whether to use the co-ordinator with phrasal, intermediate, or super-phrasal conjoins. Instead, *and* is one way of organizing the intended message on any of these levels, and alternatives to *and* vary greatly depending on the conjoins; they include conjuncts (e.g. *in addition*), hypotactic structures (i.e. subordination rather than co-ordination), and asyndetic co-ordination, where the conjoins are juxtaposed without an overt marker (Quirk et al. 1985: §13.1). It is beyond the scope of the study to chart variation in this regard. It is also arguable that *and* itself does not fill the same function in phrasal and super-phrasal contexts. When the conjoins are full main clauses or even sentences (see Section 6.3.2), the syntactic–semantic function of *and* as a co-ordinator may be backgrounded in favour of a pragmatic, textual function as a discourse organizer (Dorgeloh 2004: 1,762). In Biber's (1988) factor analysis, clausal and phrasal co-ordination do not in fact load on opposite ends of the same dimension, but on two different dimensions, another indication that their functions are not identical. However, as clausal co-ordination loads as an oral and phrasal co-ordination as a literate feature respectively, the basic premise that an increase in the proportion of super-phrasal *and* might indicate colloquialization still holds, although the connection between that proportion and the orality of the text is more indirect than would have been the case if the proportion had represented the outcome of variationist choice. The method, where a form (*and*) is retrieved and the different types of co-ordination it carries out are mapped, rather has affinities with form-to-function mapping in historical pragmatics (see Jacobs and Jucker 1995).

6.3 Results

6.3.1 Overall Results

The results by period for CNNE and CONCE are given in Tables 6.1 and 6.2.[6] The results seem to indicate that the proportion of super-phrasal co-ordination increases in nineteenth-century English, whereas that of phrasal

---

[6] The results for CNNE are identical with those presented in Smitterberg (2014).

6.3 Results

Table 6.1 *Co-ordination by period in CNNE*

Period	Phrasal		Intermediate		Super-phrasal		Total
	#	%	#	%	#	%	
1	2,375	46.9	304	6.0	2,382	47.1	5,061
2	1,984	43.3	224	4.9	2,373	51.8	4,581
Total	4,359	45.2	528	5.5	4,755	49.3	9,642

Table 6.2 *Co-ordination by period in CONCE (periods 1 and 3)*

Period	Phrasal		Intermediate		Super-phrasal		Total
	#	%	#	%	#	%	
1	1,288	42.4	179	5.9	1,573	51.7	3,040
3	1,275	41.2	198	6.4	1,620	52.4	3,093
Total	2,563	41.8	377	6.1	3,193	52.1	6,133

co-ordination goes down. However, this difference is statistically significant only for CNNE (d.f. = 2; χ^2 = 23.4; p < 0.001). As I showed in Smitterberg (2014), four of the six newspapers that were sampled for both periods in CNNE also displayed change in diachrony, while two exhibited stability; the trend seen in the whole corpus is thus mainly supported when individual newspaper trajectories are plotted. The most frequent conjoin pairs in CNNE are main clauses in both periods, with noun phrases in second place. However, the distance between them as measured in number of tokens grows between the two periods (1,037 × vs. 1,022 × in period 1; 1,203 × vs. 982 × in period 3), which mirrors the overall development towards more super-phrasal co-ordination in the corpus.

Given Biber et al.'s (1999: §2.4.7.3) finding that there is extensive genre variation regarding the proportions of phrasal and clausal co-ordination in Present-Day English, it is of interest to present comparable data for the 1800s. I provide results by genre for CONCE in Table 6.3; in the table, the Letters genre is split into private letters written by women and men.

The genre parameter clearly influences the distribution of conjoins in nineteenth-century English; the difference in the proportion of super-phrasal co-ordination between Science and Trials amounts to 17 percentage points. The genre pattern seems to be based on medium as well as

Table 6.3 *Co-ordination by genre in CONCE (periods 1 and 3)*

Genre	Phrasal #	Phrasal %	Intermediate #	Intermediate %	Super-phrasal #	Super-phrasal %	Total
Debates	342	43.6	36	4.6	407	51.8	785
Drama	257	35.4	61	8.4	407	56.1	725
Fiction	337	43.8	52	6.8	380	49.4	769
History	397	50.3	28	3.5	365	46.2	790
Letters (women)	286	37.0	58	7.5	430	55.6	774
Letters (men)	293	38.0	47	6.1	432	56.0	772
Science	398	52.6	37	4.9	322	42.5	757
Trials	253	33.2	58	7.6	450	59.1	761
Total	2,563	41.8	377	6.1	3,193	52.1	6,133

formality. The two written expository genres in CONCE, History and Science, display the highest percentage of phrasal co-ordination in the corpus. At the other end of the spectrum, the speech-related genres Drama and Trials, and informal private letters written by women and men, exhibit more than 55 per cent super-phrasal co-ordination. Fiction, which comprises a mixture of dialogue and non-speech-related text, and the speech-based but expository Debates genre form a middle ground, with roughly half of all occurrences of *and* being super-phrasal; CNNE as a whole would also belong to this category, though the periodization of that corpus is not identical with that of CONCE. The distribution of the genres in CONCE tallies with an interpretation of the change attested in CNNE in terms of colloquialization.

Cross-genre differences in CONCE are less pronounced than was the case for Present-Day English in Biber et al.'s (1999: §2.4.7.3) results, where clausal co-ordination accounts for between *c.*35 (academic prose) and *c.*80 (conversation) per cent of tokens. Biber et al.'s analysis of fiction points to a proportion of clausal co-ordination of almost 70 per cent, *c.*20 percentage points higher than Fiction in CONCE; at the same time, the proportion of clausal co-ordination is lower in their sample of academic prose than in either Science or History. Biber et al.'s classificational framework may of course differ from that used in the present study, but it nevertheless seems clear that cross-genre differentiation on this parameter increased between the nineteenth and late twentieth centuries. Co-ordination by *and* thus fits into a pattern that has been attested in several studies of LModE, including multi-feature/multidimensional analyses like Biber and Finegan (1997) and studies of individual features such as Smitterberg (2008): written English genres become increasingly different in their linguistic make-up as they tend towards increasingly oral or literate styles. This development would in turn have made it necessary for idiolects to incorporate a wider range of linguistic variation in written output as speakers adjusted their usage to the increasingly varied norms of the genres they communicated in.

Genre differences are also visible in the relative frequency of different conjoin pairs and conjoint items. In Debates, Drama, and women's letters, the most frequent conjoin pairs are main clauses in both periods, as in (6.18).[7]

> (6.18) *The county of Lancaster, for instance, is divided into twenty-three electoral districts,* **and** *I am told that there is more than one case of a firm of brewers who, by virtue of their public-houses scattered all over the county, have a large number of qualifications in a large number of different constituencies.* (CONCE, Debates, 1870–1900, p. IV.1,185)

In Debates, there is a clear increase in the proportion of such conjoins between the period samples (80 × in period 1 vs. 137 × in period 3); as will be shown below, this increase parallels a change towards more super-phrasal coordination.

In Fiction and Science, in contrast, the most frequent conjoin pair is a pair of noun phrases in both periods. Noun-phrase conjoins make up conjoint items that fill a varied range of functions; the most frequent function in both genres is prepositional complement. In Science texts, noun conjoins that make up noun-phrase heads as conjoint items, as in (6.19), are also frequent (78 ×).

> (6.19) It may be said then of two countries possessing precisely the same quantity of all the *necessaries* **and** *comforts* of life, that they are equally rich, but the value of their respective riches would depend on the comparative facility or difficulty with which they were produced. (CONCE: Science, 1800–30, Ricardo, p. 384)

Such complex noun phrases are signs of an informational focus in the Science texts; nouns are the informational feature with the highest factor score on Dimension 1 in Biber's (1988) factor analysis.

---

[7] In tokens like (6.18), each conjoin was coded as a main clause (and the conjoint item functions as a sentence). If there had been a full stop between *districts* and *and*, each conjoin would instead have been coded as a sentence (with the conjoint item operating on the paragraph level). However, in speech-based genres, the decision to represent tokens such as (6.18) as one sentence rather than two rests to some extent with transcribers, editors, and/or printers rather than speakers, as the same syntactic material can be presented in both ways on the printed page.

Like Debates, some genres in CONCE display period differences in the proportions of conjoins. In History, the commonest conjoin-pair category is noun phrases (93 ×) in period 1 but main clauses (103 ×) in period 3. However, this shift in distribution is not mirrored by an overall change towards more super-phrasal co-ordination (see Table A.3 in the Appendix). In men's letters, noun phrases (83 ×) and main clauses (82 ×) top the list in period 1, followed by predicates (44 ×); but in the late nineteenth century, both main clauses (105 ×) and predicates (77 ×) are more frequent than noun phrases (68 ×). As will be shown below, this period difference does reflect significant change towards super-phrasal co-ordination. There is also some variation in what conjoins are preferred in the two period samples from Trials. In period 1, the most frequent conjoin pairs are main clauses (79 ×), followed by predicates (75 ×) and noun phrases (64 ×). In period 3, by contrast, sentences are in fact the most frequent pairs (76 ×), followed by noun phrases (69 ×) and main clauses (62 ×). While there is no overall change in the proportions of phrasal, super-phrasal, and intermediate co-ordination in Trials (see Table A.5), this development is connected to the use of sentence-initial *and*, as will be shown in Section 6.3.2. When the conjoins are sentences, *and* is used sentence-initially to link two units presented as sentences on the printed page, and that usage becomes more characteristic of Trials over time.

When developments in phrasal vs. intermediate vs. super-phrasal co-ordination are analysed at the level of individual genres (and in Letters, male and female writers), only three of the eight samples – Debates, letters by women, and letters by men – exhibit clear and significant change. In this section, I focus on those three samples; period frequencies for the remaining five are given in Tables A.1–A.5 in the Appendix.

The development in Debates is presented in Table 6.4. This genre exhibits a significant shift towards less phrasal and more super-phrasal co-ordination across the period covered by CONCE (d.f. = 2; χ^2 = 9.70;

Table 6.4 *Co-ordination by period in Debates (periods 1 and 3)*

Period	Phrasal		Intermediate		Super-phrasal		Total
	#	%	#	%	#	%	
1	192	49.0	18	4.6	182	46.4	392
3	150	38.2	18	4.6	225	57.3	393
Total	342	43.6	36	4.6	407	51.8	785

$p = 0.008$). To put this difference in perspective, while the debates from period 1 have roughly the same distribution of phrasal and super-phrasal co-ordination as does the History genre as a whole, the sample from period 3 is similar to the overall figures for private letters written by men (see Table 6.3). The change coincides with a shift in the dominant mode of speech representation in the debates: most samples for period 1 comprise indirect speech, whereas direct speech is the norm for the debates taken down for period 3. In some cases, this shift leads to near-automatic changes in the incidence of linguistic features such as tense (from the past to the present) and personal pronouns (from the third to the first person). However, a shift from indirect to direct speech should not in itself affect the proportions of phrasal and super-phrasal conjoins. Instead, there seem to be two possible reasons for the change (which may be combined):

1. The shift to direct speech co-occurred with – and may have caused – a more verbatim rendering of the debates as they were originally spoken in period 3 than in period 1, including a change in the direction of super-phrasal co-ordination.
2. There was an actual shift towards more super-phrasal co-ordination in the original speech events between periods 1 and 3.

As Kytö and Smitterberg (2019) demonstrate, a speech-based genre where the speech events were formal, such as courtroom interaction, can undergo genuine change in the direction of orality.

The results for women's letters are given in Table 6.5. Interestingly, private letters by women show the opposite tendency compared with CNNE and Debates: there is a statistically significant decrease in the proportion of super-phrasal *and*, coupled with an increase in the percentages of phrasal and, above all, intermediate instances (d.f. = 2; χ^2 = 12.18; p = 0.002). This development would imply that women's private letters

Table 6.5 *Co-ordination by period in women's letters (periods 1 and 3)*

Period	Phrasal		Intermediate		Super-phrasal		Total
	#	%	#	%	#	%	
1	137	35.8	17	4.4	229	59.8	383
3	149	38.1	41	10.5	201	51.4	391
Total	286	37.0	58	7.5	430	55.6	774

became less oral over time, which seems unlikely given the many indications to the contrary in, for instance, Smitterberg (2005) and Kytö and Smitterberg (2006). Instead, the decrease in super-phrasal *and* in women's letters is perhaps related to what Culpeper and Kytö (2010: 167–9) argue may have been the cause of the decrease in the frequency of super-phrasal *and* between Early Modern and Present-Day English, namely an increased reliance on the sentence as a syntactic unit. An illustrative example from Mary Shelley's letters (period 1), which display a high ratio of super-phrasal *and* (forty-four of seventy tokens) is given in (6.20). Because there are several relevant occurrences of *and*, some of whose conjoins overlap syntactically, in (6.20), the conjoins in (6.20) and similar examples have not been italicized.

(6.20) **And** now tell me how your headachs are **and** if any thing has disturbed you since our departure – If nothing new has happened – pray remember – sufficient for the day is the evil thereof – **and** do not disturb yourself by prognostics – This may be a difficult but I believe it to [\be\] an attainable art **and** surely it is very desirable – Believe me, my poor Mary Anne, all your fears **and** sorrows shall fly when you behold the blue skies *&* bright sun of Marlow – **and** feel its gentle breezes (not winds) on your cheeks – We enjoy in this town a most delightful climate – **and** rivers – woods **and** flowering fields make no contemptible appendage to a bright sky. (CONCE: Letters, 1800–30, Shelley, p. 20)

As in many private letters, sentence division and punctuation in (6.20) do not follow conventions for printed Standard English; in particular, the dash is a multi-purpose punctuation mark, while the syntax-based Standard English sentence delimitation, the full stop, does not seem to be as important. The letter quoted in (6.20) makes use of an alternative pattern of textual organization, in which extensive use is made of super-phrasal co-ordination (often combined with punctuation) to divide up the written discourse. Four of the tokens in (6.20) occur immediately after a punctuation mark (in addition to the three tokens after dashes, the first *and* follows a full stop in the corpus text), as if to underscore the structural division of the text. It is of course not the case that the women letter writers in CONCE who make frequent use of dashes and super-phrasal *and* in period 1 – Sara Hutchinson, Mary Shelley, and Mary Wordsworth – did not master conventions for printed text; rather, they chose an alternative type of clausal linkage in their private letters. This practice represents a survival of the older style of structuring written text mentioned by Culpeper and Kytö (2010: 167–9), in which clause-level connectors were more important – and sentence boundaries less important – than is the case

Table 6.6 *Co-ordination by period in men's letters (periods 1 and 3)*

Period	Phrasal		Intermediate		Super-phrasal		Total
	#	%	#	%	#	%	
1	161	42.3	18	4.7	202	53.0	381
3	132	33.8	29	7.4	230	58.8	391
Total	293	38.0	47	6.1	432	56.0	772

today. The private letters by women sampled for period 3 do not give the same impression: dashes occur in these texts as well, but the letters by and large adhere to present-day Standard English conventions concerning sentence structure. More research on a larger number of letter writers is needed to suggest reasons underlying this trend, but women's greater ability to style-shift in their use of language (Chambers 1995: 131–7) may have enabled them to move more effortlessly between a printed style and a private style while the latter remained an option.

As shown in Table 6.6, men's letters evince quite a different development. Both super-phrasal and intermediate co-ordination become more prevalent in men's private letters, whereas the proportion of phrasal co-ordination decreases by more than eight percentage points. The differences in Table 6.6 are statistically significant (d.f. = 2; $\chi^2 = 7.13$; $p = 0.028$). Private letters written by men thus undergo the opposite development compared with women's letters. However, there is little indication that this change is due to the style of the letters moving towards less dependence on the sentence as an important structural unit. Even the sample with the highest proportion of super-phrasal co-ordination, a collection of Samuel Butler's letters (30 phrasal, 8 intermediate, and 84 super-phrasal tokens),[8] makes use of fairly standard sentence structure, as illustrated in (6.21):

(6.21) I have finished my translation of Von Hartmann on Instinct. It is odious, but I am very glad to have done it *&* can now read German tolerably easily. You mention cuckoos in your letter: in the course of what I am doing I have had occasion to investigate a fact about about

---

[8] Two collections of Samuel Butler's letters were sampled for period 3; the collection not illustrated in (6.21) also has a high proportion of super-phrasal *and* (thirty-four phrasal, nine intermediate, and fifty-eight super-phrasal tokens).

> them, *&* was introduced by Mr. Garnett to the gentleman who attends to birds in the British Museum **and** who I understand is the best authority we have on ornithological subjects. (CONCE: Letters, 1870–1900, Butler, Samuel [2], pp. 83–4)

Although all three occurrences of *and* in (6.21) are super-phrasal, the organization of the extract is different from that in (6.20): (6.21) is clearly divided into three sentences. Thus whereas (6.21) is oral rather than literate in that conjoins tend to be super-phrasal units, orality is deployed within the bounds allowed by the written sentence unit of Standard English. This sort of interplay between written and spoken norms is what might be expected to occur in texts undergoing colloquialization, as the incoming spoken norms are mediated and contested by the written norms for the genre that predominate at the time. The result of such tension and renegotiation in idiolectal genre norms then becomes visible in output stored in corpora.

Interestingly, the male letter writer in period 1 whose texts have the highest proportion of super-phrasal co-ordination (thirty-two out of fifty-two tokens), John Keats, is also the only male letter writer who evinces a tendency towards relying on a non-sentence-based structure in his letters, as illustrated in (6.22):

> (6.22) Now Fanny you must write soon – **and** write all you think about, never mind what – only let me have a good deal of your writing – You need not do it all at once – be two or three or four day[s] about it, **and** let it be a diary of your little Life. You will preserve all my Letters and I will secure yours – **and** thus in the course of time we shall each of us have a good Bundle – which, hereafter, when things may have strangely altered **and** god knows what happened, we may read over together **and** look with pleasure on times past – that now are to come. (CONCE: Letters, 1800–30, Keats, p. 28)

As in (6.20), one function of super-phrasal *and* in (6.22) appears to be to highlight the organization of the text; the two tokens that follow dashes in (6.22) may seem redundant syntactically, but arguably fill an important textual function. Keats's letters have been noted for their speech-like style, which features an extensive use of dashes (Barnard 2014: 17). Keats is thus similar to the women letter writers discussed above in making use of strategies characteristic of an earlier, less sentence-based written style, which survived as an option in private documents. As Barnard notes, this was a choice on Keats's part, since there is evidence that he uses print-like punctuation in fair copies, etc.

In sum, three samples from CONCE undergo significant change during the nineteenth century: super-phrasal co-ordination becomes increasingly characteristic of Debates and men's private letters (which thus develop in the same direction as newspaper texts), while women's private letters change in the opposite direction. I suggest that these changes can be interpreted in terms of colloquialization and changes in written sentential style, respectively. As regards Debates, if the change is due to reports of the speeches becoming more faithful to the original speech events, the development is clearly a case of colloquialization: the written norm for parliamentary reporting moved towards orality. On the other hand, if the speeches themselves changed, we potentially have a case of colloquialization of a spoken genre: the norm for delivering a parliamentary speech became more similar to that of informal conversation, a shift which was then reflected in the written reports. (Both changes may of course have taken place simultaneously.) Colloquialization has hitherto been discussed in terms of written genre norms becoming more similar to those for conversation (see Mair 2006b: 187). However, extending the scope of the term also to encompass cases where norms for a spoken genre become less formal and approach those prevalent in informal conversation seems potentially justified. The change in men's letters tallies with several other ways in which the genre develops in the direction of orality. In this context, the Penny Post, introduced in 1840 (see Section 2.3.3), may have been of importance. The availability of cheap and uniform postage paid by the sender may have made an individual private letter appear less special to letter writers, and if, after the reform, letters were written on topics that would previously not have been deemed worth the cost of postage, the tone of private letters may have changed so that their genre norms came to approach those of informal speech more closely.

The development in women's private letters, in contrast, is unlikely to be connected to colloquialization. It makes little sense to assume that such letters would have become less colloquial during the period studied, especially given the many changes in the other direction that have been observed for the same texts (see, for instance, Kytö and Smitterberg 2006; Smitterberg 2008). Rather, we appear to be observing the increasing obsolescence of an earlier mode of written communication where the sentence was of lesser importance as a syntactic unit, and where texts were instead structured to a large extent using dashes and co-ordinators. Further research on nineteenth-century private letters is needed to clarify whether the gender differences attested in the CONCE data are representative of the genre as a whole.

6.3.2 Sentence-Initial And

As mentioned in Section 4.3.1, a good reason for contrasting *not*-contraction and co-ordination with *and* as indicators of colloquialization is that they are likely to receive different prescriptive evaluations. Whereas contractions were overtly frowned upon, both phrasal and clausal co-ordination were recognized as integral parts of Standard English. However, one aspect of *and* usage is relevant to analyse from the perspective of prescriptivism, namely occurrence in sentence-initial position.[9]

The controversy surrounding the use of sentence-initial co-ordinators is frequently discussed in normative works. Straaijer (2018: 24) notes that, even though the usage guide "is a strongly author-driven genre, which means that there is much variation in form and content within its boundaries", the propriety of starting a sentence with *and* or *but* is commonly included as a topic. Style guides for Present-Day English typically take up the pattern mainly to point out that it is considered acceptable (e.g. Butterfield 2015: s.v. *and*), though Tieken-Boon van Ostade (2020: 152) notes a negative comment from the 1990s.

Dorgeloh (2004: 1,769–70) argues that sentence-initial *and* is typically used to increase coherence in narrative text and that it came to be proscribed in scientific writing as the narrative style common in older texts gave way to the modern organization of academic discourse (see Atkinson 1999: 145). This growing aversion to sentence-initial *and* is noticeable in history and science texts from the Early Modern English part of the Helsinki Corpus, while biblical, biographical, and autobiographical texts do not display a decrease (Dorgeloh 2004: 1,771). Sentence-initial *and* was also quite common in Early Modern English proclamations (Lehto 2013: 249), the formality of the genre notwithstanding. Any rise in the frequency of sentence-initial *and* in LModE – and connections between such a rise and colloquialization – must therefore be interpreted against the background of this style-based proscription. Cotter (2003) examined twentieth-century newspapers from Redding, California, and documents a rising use of sentence-initial *and* and *but* that she connects to factors such as the emergence of light news and the need to establish a closer connection with the reader.

---

[9] As noted by Dorgeloh (2004: 1,762) among others, *and* can be considered a (pragmatic and textual) connector rather than a (semantic and syntactic) co-ordinator when it links units across sentence boundaries (see also Biber et al. 1999: §2.4.7.4; Cotter 2003: 47–8; Haselow 2015: 193). Sweetser (1990: 86–93) discusses uses of *and* in the content, epistemic, and speech-act domains in terms of pragmatic ambiguity. In the interest of brevity, I nevertheless refer to all tokens of *and* as co-ordinators in the present study.

In Present-Day English, sentence-initial *and* is most frequent in conversation, where it accounts for over 20 per cent of tokens (although it may be difficult to apply the concept of the sentence to spoken communication – see below). In fiction, sentence-initial *and* comprises less than 10 per cent of tokens, while in news and academic texts *and* is very rarely sentence-initial (Biber et al. 1999: §2.4.7.4). Dorgeloh (2004: 1,774) notes that tabloids favour sentence-initial *and* compared with upmarket newspapers; if this difference is the result of a change towards increased sentence-initial use in tabloids, Dorgeloh's results would tally with an interpretation in terms of colloquialization. In Hundt and Mair's (1999: 228) study of late-twentieth-century English, sentence-initial *and* increased in frequency in American but not in British newspapers, while results for academic writing indicated stability over time. Haselow (2015: 202) demonstrates that sentence-initial *and* was more common in British news texts in 2013 than in 1900, although its frequency remains low.

Sentence-initial *and* actually decreases in frequency over time in CNNE: there are 31 tokens in period 1 and 14 tokens in period 2, corresponding to raw frequencies of 0.2 and 0.1 tokens per 1,000 words, respectively. This finding tallies with Smitterberg's (2014: 328) suggestion that nineteenth-century newspaper English underwent colloquialization with regard to linguistic features that were not stigmatized, such as super-phrasal *and* in general and the progressive, but did not typically adopt overtly proscribed usage, for example *not*-contractions and sentence-initial *and*. No single newspaper or text stands out as promoting sentence-initial *and*, with the exception of one outlier from the *Daily News* in period 1, in which *and* appears to have a particular rhetorical function, exemplified in (6.23):

> (6.23) While the Corn Bill moves too slowly for England, any movement of the Coercion Bill will be too rapid for Ireland. **And** to rule in the whirlwinds of these elements of confusion and mischief, there is only a Government so weak that at every step it must bribe a band of deserters, or appeal to the sympathy of opponents. (CNNE: 1830–50, DN0006)

The sentences in (6.23) form the end of a paragraph, and the writer frequently uses sentence-initial *and* to present the conclusion of the paragraph in this way: six of the tokens begin either the last or the penultimate sentence in a paragraph.

The genres in CONCE vary greatly in their relation to speech. In some speech-based or speech-purposed genres, the relevance of the sentence as a syntactic unit and of Standard English norms for punctuation and capitalization may be limited. But as all CONCE texts were printed with the intention that they should be able to be processed as written texts, it still makes sense to examine the occurrence of sentence-initial *and* in the corpus. To that end, I defined sentence-initial *and* as any token that (i) co-ordinated linguistic units across a sentence boundary and (ii) was written with an upper-case initial *A*.[10] Not all such tokens co-ordinate full sentences from a syntactic point of view; consider (6.24):

> (6.24) Had you heard before then *that Roger Tichborne had come home?* – I believe it was.
> **And** *that he had grown very stout?* – Yes. (CONCE: Trials, 1870–1900, Tichborne, p. 2,406)

In (6.24), the conjoins are really nominal *that*-clauses, unless *had you heard before then* is assumed to be ellipted in the second conjoin. The token of *and* in (6.24) was nonetheless classified as sentence-initial.

According to this definition, there are 311 relevant tokens in the samples from CONCE. However, these are only the tokens that occurred in the samples of 400 random tokens per text category and period that were used for the study, which means that they cannot in themselves form the basis for normalized frequencies. Instead, approximate normalized frequencies were calculated on the following principle. In the total sample from Trials, period 1, there were 1,066 tokens of *and*. In the 400 randomly selected tokens of *and* from that sample, 30 were sentence-initial. The approximate number of tokens of sentence-initial *and* in the entire sample is then (30 / 400) × 1,066.[11] This measure is not reliable for comparisons of text categories where this use of *and* is rare, but it can still give a rough idea of the frequency of the feature in the corpus.

Table 6.7 presents (i) the raw frequencies of sentence-initial *and* in the samples, (ii) the percentage of all tokens in each sample that received a classification as phrasal, intermediate, or super-phrasal that they account for, and (iii) the approximate normalized frequency of sentence-initial *and* in the relevant part of the corpus. Sentence-initial *and* clearly becomes a more prevalent feature in CONCE over time, as regards both its frequency and its proportion of all *and* tokens. However, the distribution is highly

---

[10] In twelve cases, for example *Ah! how! where?* – [$*Tyke, shuddering, points up to heaven*$] – *Damnation!* – *baffled* – *trod on by this wretch!* – *and must I stoop to dissemble?* (CONCE: Drama, 1800–30, Morton, p. 71), a potentially sentence-initial token was not capitalized, which made its status doubtful; these twelve tokens were not included in the counts.

[11] See Schwarz (2017: 313–14) for the application of the same method to an estimation of the frequency of BE- and GET-passives in the TIME Magazine Corpus.

Table 6.7 *Sentence-initial* and *by period and genre in CONCE (periods 1 and 3; raw frequencies and percentages of all relevant tokens in each sample)*

	Period 1			Period 3			Total		
Genre	#	%	Freq.	#	%	Freq.	#	%	Freq.
Debates	2	0.5	0.10	6	1.5	0.38	8	1.0	0.24
Drama	40	11.5	2.13	58	15.3	4.40	98	13.5	3.22
Fiction	9	2.3	0.76	16	4.2	1.29	25	3.3	0.98
History	2	0.5	0.16	11	2.8	0.75	13	1.6	0.45
Letters (women)	2	0.5	0.15	5	1.3	0.57	7	0.9	0.32
Letters (men)	5	1.3	0.42	8	2.0	0.63	13	1.7	0.51
Science	4	1.1	0.29	3	0.8	0.17	7	0.9	0.23
Trials	30	7.9	1.28	110	29.0	5.29	140	18.4	3.37
All genres	94	3.1	0.66	217	7.0	2.05	311	5.1	1.31

dependent on genre: Drama and Trials together account for 77 per cent of tokens. The low proportions and frequencies in History and Science are expected, as academic English still shows sensitivity to the prescription against sentence-initial *and* in Present-Day English (Biber et al. 1999: §2.4.7.4). The slightly higher figures for History in period 3 are largely due to Walpole's *History of England*. Walpole makes use of *and* to increase coherence in largely narrative passages (see Dorgeloh 2004: 1,769) or to initiate a new topic (Biber et al. 1999: §2.4.7.4); several tokens occur either at the beginning of a paragraph or near its conclusion, a use reminiscent of (6.23) from CNNE. It is possible that, as Dorgeloh (2004) suggests, this usage represents the remnant of a narrative textual organization in scholarship. Culpeper and Kytö (2010: 166, 175) link the fairly high frequency of clausal *and* in Early Modern English history texts to narrative features of this genre and to shifts between narrative and authorial comment.

In Drama, where the percentage of sentence-initial *and* is roughly half of what Biber et al. (1999: §2.4.7.4) found for present-day conversation, sixty-seven of the ninety-eight tokens occur immediately after a stage direction or speaker indication, as in (6.25):

(6.25) [$Lucien.$] *You said I was not to write.*
[$Lady S. [Reproachfully.]$] **And** *you obeyed me!* (CONCE: Drama, Jones, 1870–1900, p. 34)

Sentence-initial *and* is thus typically used either in connection with a change of speaker or immediately following some type of non-verbal action (e.g. a character sitting down). This use of *and* may underscore the connection between the preceding line in the play and what follows *and* in spite of the extra-textual event reported on in the stage direction.

The Trials genre displays similar frequencies, and even higher percentages, of sentence-initial *and* when the period samples are conflated. In Trials, sentence-initial *and* is clearly used as a cohesive device by lawyers to control the course of the cross-examination by linking one of their questions to the preceding one, as in (6.26), where the answer regarding the location of the bed provides the background for the question about the stool or chair:

(6.26) [$Q.$] *Was that bed near the fireplace?* – [$A.$] Yes.
[$Q.$] **And** *was there often a stool or chair at the bottom of the bedstead?* – [$A.$] No, sir; the piano was mostly there at the foot of the bed. (CONCE: Trials, 1870–1900, Bartlett, p. 59)

Content-wise, the most relevant conjoins are thus the two questions, and the witness's answer is outside the conjoint item (see also 6.24). *And* in effect creates a larger sequence of linked questions in cases like (6.26), as noted by Culpeper and Kytö (2010: 171). Schiffrin (1987: 147) argues that this use of *and* signals that what follows the co-ordinator is regarded by the speaker as a continuation of the interaction. The vast majority of the sentence-initial tokens in the random samples from Trials (129 out of 140) begin a question from a lawyer or from the court. The results in Table 6.7 indicate that the proportion and frequency of sentence-initial *and* rose sharply between periods 1 and 3 in this genre. One Trials text from period 1 (*The Trial of James Bowditch and Nine Others*) in particular is notable for its dearth of sentence-initial *and* (3 ×). Given the prevalence of this feature at the start of questions elsewhere in the trials sampled, some of the actual questions, such as those given in (6.27), may have contained tokens of sentence-initial *and* that were either not taken down in shorthand or removed from the published versions of the trials at a later stage – arguably because the feature was thought too oral for printed text. If so, the increase in sentence-initial *and* in Trials would be an example of colloquialization in that an oral feature became more accepted in writing within the scope of a particular genre norm.

(6.27) [$Q.$] I believe you married a sister of Mrs. Glenn, who is now living at St. Vincent's?
[$A.$] I did.
[$Q.$] Can you tell us what her name is?

> [$A.$] Mary Fenton Glenn.
> [$Q.$] Has she a daughter of the name of Maria Glenn?
> [$A.$] She has.
> [$Q.$] What is her age?
> [$A.$] I cannot tell within a month or two; but she is not seventeen. Certainly not more than seventeen at this moment. (CONCE: Trials, 1800–30, Bowditch, p. 17)

This hypothesis must remain speculation, but as several of the questions in (6.27) are closely connected so that one question builds upon or follows from the previous one, sentence-initial *and* could have been used in several places in the extract.

A similar omission of sentence-initial *and* may be behind the low frequency of this feature in Debates, but there are also further possibilities. Members of Parliament could prepare parts of their speeches in advance; this circumstance reduces the orality of the text and thus the likelihood of sentence-initial *and*. Moreover, in Debates most potential occurrences of sentence-initial *and* would not occur in conjunction with a shift between speakers, as in Drama and Trials, but inside a speaker's long turn. Of the 800 randomly selected tokens of *and* in Debates, 217 have main-clause conjoins, and *and* follows a heavy punctuation mark (typically a semicolon) in 60 of those 217. If a full stop had been substituted for the heavy punctuation mark in the transcription (and the following *and* capitalized), such a token would instead have been sentence-initial. To some extent, the decision to use sentence-initial *and* in Debates is thus editorial. Consider the extended example (6.28), in which only the relevant instance of *and* appears in boldface:

> (6.28) But it is wrong likewise that within the confines of England eleven boroughs with a Member each should only have an electorate of 33,000, whilst Bristol, with 39,000, has only four Members; Bradford, with 35,000, has only three; and Newcastle, with 32,000, has only two. There you have a grievance greater than the over-representation of Wales, or even of Ireland; **and** yet the hon. Member comes forward with this Amendment, and proposes to cross a great and complete reform like this with a mere re-adjustment of representation between the countries, the nations, the provinces – whatever he prefers to call them – that constitute this Kingdom. (CONCE: Debates, 1870–1900, p. IV.1,216)

There is nothing unidiomatic about the semicolon before *and*, as the two main clauses are clearly connected; but a full stop would also have been fully possible, depending on the transcriber's or editor's interpretation of the speech event. In Drama and Trials, by contrast, sentence-initial *and* typically begins a new turn or follows a stage direction, in which case there is no alternative to letting it begin a sentence except omitting it.

The low frequency of the feature in the two remaining non-expository genres, Fiction and Letters, is most likely due to partly different reasons. In Fiction, sentence-initial *and* is clearly associated with dialogue, which accounts for twenty-one out of twenty-five tokens;[12] in eleven of these, *and* begins an utterance, which resembles its use in Drama. In non-dialogue passages, it is likely that the proscription of sentence-initial *and* was stronger, which led to avoidance of the feature. In Letters, it is possible that sentence structure may underlie the low frequencies. As was shown in Section 6.3.1, some letter writers in period 1 tend to use very long sentences (according to present-day definitions of the sentence) in which sequences of main clauses are linked by dashes and co-ordinators rather than split into separate sentences. This structure naturally leads to a low frequency of sentence-initial *and*, as there are fewer opportunities for the feature to occur. Even in period 3, when the sentence structure of private letters was more similar to present-day conventions, punctuation and co-ordination are frequently used as an alternative to sentence division, as in (6.29), in which, again, only the relevant instances of *and* are in boldface:

(6.29) You walk through a great blowing wind into a mist, and across a moor with brown cropping cows, and a horn blowing out of the sea, with rocks flinging out quite black, and all sorts of currents and waves streaming in from the horizon, **and** then you come to a most detestable little object called Bude, with a dripping man on horseback riding down the street, **and** then you are quite wet through and come home in a little thing called a Jingle: **and** then you go out again next day into another sort of wind, capricious without any rain. (CONCE: Letters, 1870–1900, Thackeray Ritchie, p. 158)

In this passage, *and then* preceded by punctuation seems to underscore the chronological structure of the narrative as an alternative to sentence division.

In sum, the present analysis has shown that sentence-initial *and* became increasingly available during the 1800s mainly in non-expository texts that were speech-purposed or speech-based. In these contexts, it is an indication of colloquialization, as an oral strategy for achieving coherence became more frequent in texts which were written to be read aloud or which purported to be speech taken down.

---

[12] It is possible that part of the increase in the frequency of sentence-initial *and* visible in Table 6.7 is due to a larger proportion of dialogue in period 3; in period 1, dialogue accounts for 30 per cent of the word count, compared with 42 per cent in period 3 (see Smitterberg 2005: 70 for word counts for dialogue and non-dialogue passages in Fiction).

6.4 Discussion

In this chapter, the distribution of the co-ordinator *and* has been analysed from two perspectives. The proportions of phrasal, intermediate, and super-phrasal co-ordination in CNNE and in random subsamples of CONCE data were considered in Section 6.3.1. CONCE was found to display considerable cross-genre variation, with proportions of super-phrasal co-ordination varying from a little over 40 to almost 60 per cent. However, results presented in Biber et al. (1999: §2.4.7.3) point to even more pronounced cross-genre differences in Present-Day English, indicating that genre differentiation continued after 1900.

As previously reported in Smitterberg (2014: 321–4), there is a clear overall increase in the proportion of super-phrasal co-ordination in CNNE; moreover, this increase is paralleled by most of the individual newspapers sampled for both periods. However, this increase was not mirrored in all CONCE genres, most of which displayed stability in this regard. However, Debates and men's private letters changed towards more super-phrasal co-ordination across time, which was interpreted as indicative of colloquialization. For Debates, the change may concern both the way in which the original speech events were transferred to printed English and the structure of the speech events themselves (see also Kytö and Smitterberg 2019), as the mode of speech representation underwent change between the periods examined. In men's letters, several other features characteristic of colloquial texts have been shown to increase in frequency over the nineteenth century, which strengthens a hypothesis about colloquialization. Women's letters, by contrast, developed in the opposite direction, featuring less super-phrasal *and* over time. This change appears to reflect changing conventions of discourse organization: the syntactically defined and orthographically marked sentence gradually became the main way in which text was structured below the paragraph level in private letters, which co-occurred with a decrease in the use of *and* as a reinforcer of inter-clausal connections.

Unlike *and* in general, one specific use of the co-ordinator was stigmatized in nineteenth-century English and thus singled out for special attention in Section 6.3.2, namely sentence-initial *and*. As might be expected given the prescriptive opposition to starting written sentences with co-ordinators, sentence-initial *and* was rare in CNNE as well as in the expository genres in CONCE, where two speech-related genres – Drama (speech-purposed) and Trials (speech-based) – accounted for the bulk of tokens. In both genres, the frequency of the feature also increased over time, which was regarded as an indication of colloquialization. In a speech-purposed genre like Drama, written norms may increasingly have allowed an overtly conversational feature like sentence-initial *and* in writing (cf. the results for *not*-contraction presented in Chapter 5). In Trials, sentence-initial *and* may have been part of the original speech events in both periods and may have been edited out – or not taken down – to a greater extent in period 1 than in period 3. If so, an increase over time would reflect increasing acceptance of preserving a spoken feature in a text purporting to be a "true" or "verbatim" account of speech events. The rarity of sentence-initial *and* in Fiction and Letters, two non-expository genres that may otherwise have been expected to contain a certain amount of informality, was explained in genre-specific terms. In Fiction, this use of *and* was largely restricted to dialogue; proscription on its use was apparently too strong for widespread occurrence in non-dialogue passages, where the author's own voice is more apparent. Nineteenth-century private letters frequently featured very long orthographical sentences, where punctuation marks other than the full stop were used together with *and* to structure the texts. Such discourse does not present many opportunities for sentence-initial *and* to occur, as there are fewer sentence boundaries marked off by full stops.

The present chapter has shown that *and* is a multilayered linguistic feature. The syntactic level on which it links units does not carry great stylistic significance in itself but nonetheless helps to create an impression of a genre as oral vs. literate. These characteristics make co-ordination by *and* a useful indication of comparatively non-intrusive, subconscious colloquialization, particularly in comparison with an overtly stigmatized feature such as *not*-contraction. The separate analysis of the one use of *and* that was proscribed in LModE, namely its occurrence in sentence-initial position, revealed a very different genre pattern, where two overtly speech-related genres, Drama and Trials, accounted for the bulk of tokens as well as noticeably increased use. Specific textual, discourse-organizing functions of sentence-initial *and* were also identified in the two genres.

A common characteristic of the features studied in Chapters 5 and 6 is that genre diversity in the distribution of *not*-contraction, co-ordination by *and*, and sentence-initial *and* becomes more pronounced across time. The nineteenth century is part of a long-term trend towards more pronounced linguistic genre differentiation, which meant that idiolects' written genre norms diversified as many literate language users needed to command a wider range of usage in writing. This and the previous chapter considered influence from oral modes of communication in this regard; the next two chapters are devoted to developments that most likely began in informational writing.

CHAPTER 7

Densification I: Nouns as Premodifiers in Noun Phrases

7.1 Introduction

The increased use of nouns as premodifiers in noun phrases, for example *telegraph* in (7.1), is one of the most drastic quantitative changes in LModE syntax. I shall refer to nouns like *telegraph* in (7.1) as *premodifying nouns* or *nominal premodifiers* in this chapter. In most analyses, these terms cover only nouns in the common (as opposed to the genitive) case.[1] Unless stated otherwise, the relevant noun phrase is italicized and the premodifying noun(s) rendered in boldface in numbered corpus examples.

(7.1) *The **telegraph** wires* had been cut by the falling building, and had it not been for his expeditious arrival at Church Street it is difficult to say what might not have happened. (CNNE: 1875–95, BDP0001)

In Raumolin-Brunberg's (1991: 199–201, 308) analysis of Sir Thomas More's sixteenth-century English, adjectives were nearly ten times more frequent than common-case nouns in pre-head position, and virtually all such nouns were titles or title-like words. By contrast, nouns account for 30–40 per cent of all premodifiers in Present-Day English noun phrases in news and academic prose (Biber and Clark 2002: 46), and perceived overuse of the pattern has been associated with newspaper texts (Denison 1998: 129). In 1970s engineering English, nominal premodifiers even outnumbered attributive adjectives (Varantola 1984: 117–18).[2]

---

[1] *Common case* is the term used in Quirk et al. (1985: §5.112) and Biber et al. (1999: §4.6) for nouns without genitive marking; Huddleston and Pullum (2002: §5.16.1) use *plain case* for the same category.
[2] This change is not due to premodifying nouns simply replacing attributive adjectives, as the frequency of the latter has been fairly stable since 1800 (Biber and Gray 2016: 144). The increase in premodifying nouns forms part of a general trend towards increased productivity in the premodifier slot in LModE and twentieth-century English; for instance, complex prenominal adjective phrases such as *a difficult to explain phenomenon* have also become more common (see Günther 2019).

Like many other changes in LModE, higher frequencies of nominal premodifiers result in increased genre differentiation, as not all genres take part in the shift to the same extent. Biber and Clark (2002: 52) show that minor increases between the eighteenth and nineteenth centuries in the frequency of noun–noun sequences in fiction and news texts gave way to dramatic rises in frequency after 1800, especially in medical and news writing. Similarly, Biber et al. (2016: 372–3) found minor increases in personal letters, newspapers, and scientific articles between the eighteenth and nineteenth centuries, but while letters continue to display a modest rise in frequency, there are remarkable increases in both newspaper and scientific prose between the 1800s and 1900s. Scientific prose lags behind newspaper writing somewhat until the early twentieth century, when science research articles display a pronounced increase in the frequency of premodifying nouns; there is also a minor but steady increase in novels, while drama does not seem to take part in the development (Biber and Gray 2011: 231–2, 2012: 323, 2013: 107–9). In Leech et al.'s (2009: 217–18) analysis of late-twentieth-century English, the increase was most marked in genres other than press and academic prose (the two genres where the feature was the most frequent); this finding led them to suggest that these other genres were catching up with developments that had already taken place in newspapers and scholarly texts.

As discussed in Section 4.3.2, the rise in frequency of premodifying nouns is a sign of densification: meaning that could have been expressed by a larger linguistic unit – for example a relative clause like *that transmit telegraph messages* in example (7.1) – is compressed into a single noun. There is a trade-off between such compression of expression and explicitness of meaning (Biber and Clark 2002: 63): because there is no overt marker of the semantic relation between the two nouns in (7.1), readers may need to draw on the meaning of the two nouns, the co-text, and their extralinguistic knowledge to arrive at the appropriate connection. Indeed, specialist knowledge may be necessary for full comprehension (Gray and Biber 2018: 122), as the mere juxtaposition of two nouns is arguably "maximally *inexplicit* in meaning" (Biber and Gray 2016: 222, italics original). Biber and Gray (2011: 238–40) argue that the range of possible semantic relations between such nouns has expanded over time. In addition, there has been a statistical shift in the reference of premodifying nouns whereby animate referents have become more common (Rosenbach 2007); this shift has also affected proper nouns in the premodifier slot (e.g. *the Obama administration*), which have been the subject of a great deal of recent interest (see, for instance, Breban and Kolkmann 2019). To fully understand the increased preference for nominal premodifiers in LModE syntax, it is necessary also to consider these semantic developments. I will thus examine both overall frequencies (Section 7.3.1) and semantic aspects of premodification (Section 7.3.2).

The use of titles such as *Mister* is often treated in studies of premodifying nouns. However, their status as premodifiers is debatable: they are sometimes treated as premodifiers (e.g. Raumolin-Brunberg 1991: 210; Biber and Gray 2011: 236) but have also been regarded as forming a single proper noun together with the names that follow (e.g. Keizer 2007: 57–9). Moreover, changes in titular usage are unrelated to densification: titles are either used or not used, rather than replacing – or being replaced by – shorter expressions. For this reason, titles were excluded from the analysis of nominal premodifiers in this case study.

7.2 Method

Previous work (see Section 7.1) has established that a wide range of genres is required in analyses of nominal premodifiers, as frequency developments display considerable genre diversity. It is reasonable to assume that the news texts in CNNE and, to a lesser extent, Science in CONCE will exhibit the most advanced usage, while the remainder of CONCE is a useful control corpus. Given that nominal premodifiers can be identified easily by searches for noun–noun sequences, I made use of tagged versions of the two corpora in retrieval; this meant that the CONCE material was restricted to the S-coefficient subcorpus (see Section 4.5.1).

In CNNE, I searched for (i) noun-phrase heads preceded by nouns and (ii) premodifying nouns preceded by nouns. The latter search captured tokens where nominal premodifiers occurred in succession, as *iron* and *partition* do in (7.2):

(7.2)   Messrs. W. B. Whittingham and Co. write to the effect that *the **iron partition** doors* have saved their premises at No. 3, White Hart-court, so that they are able to carry on their printing business as usual. (CNNE: 1875–95, DN0014)

Iron and *partition* in (7.2) were thus included in the counts as two separate premodifier tokens. In CONCE, the basic search was for any noun preceded by any other noun, as the tagger used does not analyse noun-phrase structure. Additional searches retrieved nouns in *-ing* used as heads, for example *meeting* in (7.3), and as premodifiers, for example *hunting* in (7.4), as such forms were typically assigned the "_ING" tag rather than a noun tag.

(7.3) [$A.$] Yes, it was ordered at *that **prayer** meeting*, as the class leader was not there, that he should officiate. (CONCE: Trials, 1800–30, Martin, p. 40)

(7.4) What time in 1849? – I think just the beginning of *the **hunting** season*. (CONCE: Trials, 1870–1900, Tichborne, p. 2,413)

Taken together, these searches resulted in 24,232 hits from CNNE and 22,480 hits from CONCE, which were gone through manually to exclude false positives.

As this word-based retrieval method implies, orthography was used as the main criterion for separating premodifier–head sequences from compounds; if the noun + noun pair was written as two orthographic words, the first noun was typically taken to be a potential premodifier. Though orthography is not a wholly reliable criterion (see Huddleston and Pullum 2002: §5.14.4), the correspondence between orthographic separation and premodification is robust enough for the purposes of the present study. Jucker (1992: 67–8), Biber et al. (1999: §8.3), Rosenbach (2007: 161–2), and Leech et al. (2009: 215) also used orthography as a basis for their classifications, though several of them admit that this procedure imposes a binary categorization on what is actually a gradient or cline. I return to this matter in Section 7.4.

While most hits returned by the searches proved easy to classify, it was occasionally difficult to decide whether a premodifier was a noun or an adjective. The premodifier was typically considered a noun if (i) dictionaries such as *Longman* and the *OED* indicated that the potentially adjectival form occurred only before a noun (occurrence in predicative position would have made the form clearly adjectival) and (ii) its potentially adjectival meaning was closely related to that of the noun. Thus *infant* in (7.5) was classified as a noun and included in the analysis, but *summary* in (7.6) was considered adjectival and excluded from the counts, as the relevant adjective sense 'done immediately, and not following the normal process' (*Longman*, s.v. *summary*, adj.) is clearly distinct from that of the noun *summary*. Similarly, Rosenbach (2007: 147) regards the modifiers she analyses as nouns rather than adjectives "[u]nless there is clear indication to the contrary".

(7.5) [$Lord Avon.$] ... She lived in profound retirement – I could seldom see her; but her regret at my absence was softened by the endearments of *our **infant** son*. (CONCE: Drama, 1800–30, Morton, p. 73)

(7.6) That would be equivalent, as things go, to being careless about the administration of the criminal law, for every year the area of *summary convictions* is extended. (CNNE: 1875–95, TT0012)

These criteria were more difficult to apply to *-ing* forms, however. These forms can often occur after BE (as adjectives or parts of progressives), and their senses are frequently related to those of their corresponding verbs. The relationship between the *-ing* form and the head of the noun phrase was therefore used as the most important criterion instead. If the [*-ing* form + noun] sequence could be rewritten such that the noun functioned as the antecedent of a relative clause in which the *-ing* form became either a verb or a subject complement, the participle was excluded as non-nominal. For instance, *trifling act* in *this one trifling act of disobedience* (CONCE: Drama, 1800–30, Poole, p. 25) does imply 'one act that is trifling', and *working men* in *a meeting of gentlemen, representative working men and others interested in the relief of the poor* (CNNE: 1875–95, LL0020) implies 'men who work'; these sequences were thus excluded from the counts. In contrast, *the smoking room* (CONCE: Drama, 1870–1900, Jones, p. 36) was included in the counts, as a *smoking room* is '[a] room in a house, hotel, club, etc., set apart as a place for smoking in' (*OED*, s.v. *smoking-room* [n.]), and not 'a room that smokes' or 'a room that is smoking'.

While scholars may disagree on the classification of individual cases, the criteria outlined above were comparatively straightforward to apply and enabled me to make the data set internally consistent.[3] Six files from CNNE and two files from CONCE were randomly selected for manual checking to estimate recall. The checking round revealed that recall was 95.0 per cent, which was considered sufficient.[4]

Once the relevant tokens had been selected, the question arose how best to represent the frequency of nominal premodification. As mentioned in Section 4.3.2, a variationist framework is implicit in the notion of densification if it is assumed that the meaning expressed by the feature examined

---

[3] Noun + noun sequences where the relationship between the two nouns was clearly appositive, for example *the girl Terry* (CNNE: 1875–95, BDP0010), were not included (but see Chapter 9 for brief discussion of apposition, which also contributes to densification). Following Breban and De Smet (2019: 881), I include cases where "the second noun provides a hyperonymic classification of the [proper noun]", for example *Rowley village* (CNNE: 1875–95, BDP0003), although for some of these tokens the relationship can arguably be considered apposition as well as premodification.

[4] The checking was based on all tokens that were, or would have been, classified as a common, proper, genitive, or temporal noun premodifying a common noun (see Section 7.3.1). The recall rate was similar in CNNE (59 of 63 tokens, or 93.7 per cent) and in CONCE (54 of 56 tokens, or 96.4 per cent), which indicates that the results for the two corpora are comparable despite the fact that different taggers were used for them.

(here, nominal premodifiers) could instead have been expressed by other structures that contain more linguistic material. A study that aims at demonstrating with certainty whether densification takes place as the frequency of nominal premodifiers increases should then ideally also chart the frequency development of all other variants and relate these frequencies to one another.

However, such a study would be virtually impossible to carry out in practice. Kretzschmar (2015b: 21, 32) argues that the number of variants available to language users is typically larger than is usually assumed, although "the long tail of infrequent variants" may not be recognized as such; Ström Herold and Levin (2019) demonstrate that premodifying proper nouns in English correspond to a wide range of syntactic features in translations into Swedish and German. Even a study that was limited to the most obvious near-equivalents of a noun–noun sequence such as *ocean life* would need to chart the frequency development of attributive adjectives (e.g. *oceanic life*) and prepositional phrases (e.g. *life in the ocean*). In other cases, one might imagine equivalence with a clausal postmodifier; for instance, *our infant son* in (7.5) above might correspond roughly to *our son, who was an infant*. Studies such as Rosenbach (2019) have focussed on variation between nominal premodifiers and genitive determiners, as in (7.7); such analyses may also include postmodification by prepositional phrases headed by *of* (see Biber and Gray 2016: 171–4).

(7.7) The **police** version is that about 300 persons who had started from Poplar reached Southampton-row, Holborn, at half-past three. (CNNE: 1875–1895, LL0019)

(7.7') *The police's version* is that ...

Decisions on what variants to include may affect the outcome of the analysis; for instance, Biber et al. (2016: 355–6, 374) note that conclusions regarding the expansion of the genitive and the decline of the *of*-construction are affected by the inclusion of premodifying nouns, which have increased in frequency compared with both structures.

Moreover, as discussed in Section 4.4.1, not all tokens have the same set of variants. A few examples may suffice. Owing to the greater explicitness of the prepositional phrase compared with the premodifying noun, there are prepositional phrases with no nominal equivalents (e.g. *a tree by a stream* ≠ **a stream tree*), and the acceptability of the premodifier increases if the more explicit postmodified structure has been used in the preceding co-text (Quirk et al. 1985: §17.104). Premodification also "confers relative permanence" (Quirk et al. 1985: §17.105); prepositional phrases describing potentially temporary states, for example *in the corner* in *the man in the corner*, therefore do not readily turn into premodifying nouns (?*the corner man*). As regards genitives vs. premodifying proper nouns, these constructions are equivalent mainly when the proper noun has an identifying function (as in *the Yorkshire moors*, as opposed to the classifying function in *a Yorkshire terrier*) and the noun phrase is definite; moreover, the two constructions need not have the same meaning in those contexts where both are possible (Breban et al. 2019: 798–9). Biber et al. (2016: 363–5) examined the extent to which genitives, nominal premodifiers, and prepositional phrases with *of* were interchangeable in texts from the eighteenth, nineteenth, and twentieth centuries. They found that interchangeability varied with time and genre and that premodifying nouns were in general exchangeable less frequently with genitives than with *of*-phrases.

As the examples above demonstrate, the amount of work involved in a variationist approach aiming at comprehensive coverage would be insurmountable; and as Biber et al. (2016) show, an incomplete analysis may obscure important correspondences. Against this background, I opted for a text-linguistic analysis of nominal premodifiers in the present chapter. The data sets will thus be analysed mainly in terms of normalized frequencies in Section 7.3.1 (though I will consider proportions of occurrence within the nominal-premodifier paradigm in Section 7.3.2). This choice makes claims about densification somewhat less certain, as it cannot be ascertained that an increase in the frequency of premodifying nouns is matched by a decrease in that of lengthier options. However, as the use of merely two words (e.g. *telegraph cables*) is a maximally concise way to express the intended meaning, an increase in nominal premodification can be taken as a strong indication that densification took place.

7.3 Results

7.3.1 Frequencies

Based on their syntactic and semantic characteristics, the relevant tokens were divided into four categories. The category that will receive the most attention is that exemplified in (7.1)–(7.5) and (7.7) above: a premodifying common noun in the common case that modifies another common noun.⁵ The following types of premodifier were also retrieved and given separate codes in the database: genitives, as in (7.8), temporal nouns (mainly names of weekdays and months, as well as *tomorrow* and *yesterday*), as in (7.9), and other proper nouns, as in (7.10).

(7.8) The occupants of *a **colliers'** train*, on reaching their destination, threatened the fresh driver with violence if he drove them again, alleging he nearly drove the train off the line three times. (CNNE: 1875–1895, LL0016)

(7.9) I shall go out of town on ***Thursday*** *morning*, and return on ***Tuesday*** *evening*; we shall go to Guildford and walk round the neighbourhood; letters will be forwarded. (CONCE: Letters, 1870–1900, Butler, Samuel [1], p. 218)

(7.10) Of the former there were present between 300 and 400, and *the **Bradford** men* numbered about 600. (CNNE: 1875–1895, LM0017)

Only genitive nouns that occurred in the premodifier slot, as in (7.8), rather than the determiner slot were included in the counts.⁶ As Rosenbach (2019: 784–5) notes, they can also sometimes be variant expressions (e.g. the British/American pair *driving licence* vs. *driver's license* in Present-Day English), which makes it important to compare their frequency development. Premodifying proper nouns like *Bradford* in (7.10) take part in the general LModE increase in the incidence of nominal premodifiers (Breban and Kolkmann 2019: 749) and thus contribute to densification. However, the status of temporal nouns like *Thursday* in (7.9) as modifiers is less clear-cut compared with other proper nouns (Breban and De Smet 2019: 881), which justifies separating this category; as will be shown below, they are also distributed differently in texts.

---

⁵ All tokens included in the counts in Sections 7.3.1–7.3.2 share the characteristic that the premodified word is a common noun. Nominal premodifiers within complex proper nouns (as indicated mainly by capitalization), for example *Abbey* in *The Rev. S. E. Pennefather . . . has had the Abbey Field flooded* (CNNE: 1875–95, BDP0003), were not included in the counts, but were retrieved and given a separate code in the database. This procedure was adopted because capitalization practices may have changed over time and affected classification; for instance, if the same token had instead read *the Abbey field*, it would have been classified as a proper noun premodifying a common noun and included in the counts. It was therefore important to be able to check whether any apparent increases in nominal premodification may actually be a manifestation of shifts in capitalization practice. However, there were no signs of this in the data: for both CNNE and CONCE, the frequency of nominal premodification within complex proper nouns in fact increased over time and thus paralleled the increase in nominal premodification of common nouns.

⁶ As noted by Rosenbach (2019: 784–5), the distinction between determiner and modifier is not always easy to make for genitives. In (7.8), a modifier interpretation is the only possible one, as *a* and *colliers'* would have to agree in number if they formed a determiner; but *the butcher's knife* could be interpreted either as *[[the butcher's] knife]* 'the knife that belongs to the butcher' or as *[[the] [butcher's] knife]* 'the knife of the type that a butcher uses'. In practice, however, the co-text was sufficient to disambiguate the tokens.

7.3 Results

Table 7.1 *Common nouns in CNNE premodified by common, genitive, temporal, and proper nouns by period (raw frequencies)*

Period	Common	Genitive	Temporal	Proper
1	580	33	158	221
2	1,108	41	165	437
Total	1,688	74	323	658

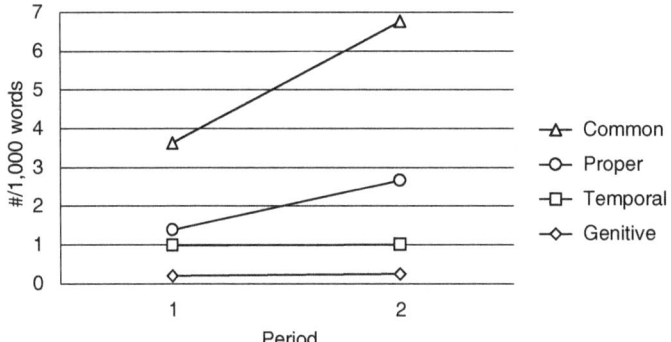

Figure 7.1 Common nouns in CNNE premodified by common, genitive, temporal, and proper nouns (frequencies per 1,000 words)

The distribution of common nouns, genitive nouns, temporal nouns, and proper nouns as premodifiers in CNNE is given in Table 7.1; Figure 7.1 presents the corresponding normalized frequencies. As Figure 7.1 demonstrates, the smaller groups comprising temporal and genitive nouns display no change over time. In contrast, common and proper nouns almost double in frequency during the period covered by CNNE (the increase is 86 per cent for common and 93 per cent for proper nouns). Overall, there are strong indications that densification is taking place in CNNE with regard to premodifying nouns.

Some differences among newspapers with regard to the frequency of common nouns as premodifiers are worth examining from a densification perspective. As mentioned in Section 7.1, the trend towards economy in writing is often considered to come at the cost of explicitness (Biber and Clark 2002: 63), which has consequences for the reader-friendliness of the text. The implicitness of the relation between premodifying and premodified nouns means that structures with nominal premodifiers may require specialized knowledge – linguistic and/or extralinguistic – for successful interpretation. We might therefore expect papers aimed at a readership with comparatively little schooling to feature fewer premodifying nouns than other papers. In CNNE, the *Poor Man's Guardian* is the clearest candidate in this regard, and the hypothesis is supported by the data: this paper has the lowest normalized frequency of common nouns as premodifiers (1.8 tokens per 1,000 words). It is noteworthy that, although most readers of the *Poor Man's Guardian* came from the working classes, and although an aim of the paper was to promote working-class consciousness and solidarity (Williams 2010: 88), the paper itself was largely a middle-class endeavour (Claridge 2017: 139–40). In other words, not only may its journalists and editors have assumed that readers would have little specialized knowledge about politics, economics, and so on compared with other papers' target audiences; they could also count on less *shared* knowledge, as the paper and its readers were separated by a class divide. As will be demonstrated in Section 8.3.2, the *Poor Man's Guardian* is also the paper with the lowest frequency of participle clauses, another feature that makes language more concise but also potentially less explicit.

In some articles in the *Poor Man's Guardian*, it is possible to identify loci of variation where nominal premodifiers could have been, but were not, used. Consider (7.11):

> (7.11) We dislike going over the old ground so often, but seeing that the ministerial organ (the Globe) has now come round to the Ballot, seeing it also advocated by the Chronicle, and being convinced, that to enact it in the present state of the suffrage would be the deadliest blow that could be struck at the hopes and interests of the working classes, we must crave our readers' indulgence for once more calling their attention to the subject. (CNNE: 1830–50, PG0004)

From a purely grammatical perspective (i.e. without considering idiomaticity or minor differences in meaning), nominal premodifiers could replace several other, longer structures in (7.11), for example *working-class hopes and interests* vs. *the hopes and interests of the working classes*, *the present suffrage state* vs. *the present state of the suffrage*, and *reader indulgence* for *our readers' indulgence*. However, in many extracts, it is difficult to identify specific noun phrases where such replacement operations can easily be carried out. This is hardly surprising: it is unlikely that editors and journalists at the *Poor Man's Guardian* made a conscious effort to avoid particular linguistic features, such as premodifying nouns. Rather, they are likely to have had a holistic sense of the style they were aiming at considering their intended readership and to have made more or less subconscious linguistic choices accordingly. In many cases, using a premodifying noun instead of the structure actually chosen might have required more extensive changes to sentence structures than a mere exchange of noun phrases. This relative dearth of clearly exchangeable linguistic forms to express the same meaning (as opposed to, say, different phonemes that can be used in the pronunciation of the same word) points to a further problem in analysing syntax from a strictly variationist perspective (see Section 4.4.1).

At the opposite end of the spectrum are the *Liverpool Mercury* samples from period 2, with 10.2 tokens per 1,000 words. One text about Liverpool's water supply, exemplified in (7.12), is remarkable in this respect.

(7.12) The effect of constructing this embankment was to dam back the river so as, without any further enclosure than *the natural **valley** sides*, to form a lake some 4 3/4 miles long, with *a **water** area at the surface of about 1115 acres*. *The **surface** area of Bala Lake*, it may be mentioned, is 1100 acres. (CNNE: 1875–95, LIM0002)

The last two tokens in (7.12) illustrate a pattern mentioned in Section 7.2: a compressed form like *surface area* is more likely to occur after the relevant concept has been introduced using a longer unit, here *water area at the surface* (cf. Quirk et al. 1985: §17.104).

The sharp increase in the frequency of proper nouns as premodifiers tallies with the results reported on in Breban and De Smet (2019).[7] Premodification by proper nouns is interesting from a linguistic perspective, as a modifier like *London* in *the London marathon* potentially "restrict[s] the denotation of the noun phrase to a particular referent"; but unlike other identifying elements, which typically occur near the beginning of the noun phrase, proper-noun modifiers are placed near the head (Breban and Kolkmann 2019: 750; see also Rosenbach 2010: 162–3). In charting the development of premodifying proper nouns through the history of English, Breban and De Smet (2019: 893) consider, among other things, the semantic fields to which the proper nouns belong; I shall return to that topic in Section 7.3.2.

The figures for premodification by common, genitive, temporal, and proper nouns by genre and period in CONCE are given in Table 7.2. Genitive and temporal premodification is rare in most genres in CONCE; the only period/genre samples where either category has a normalized frequency of > 0.5 per 1,000 words are temporal nouns in Letters, period 3 (0.80) and Trials, period 1 (1.48). The high frequency in Trials, period 1 is

---

[7] Selection criteria differ somewhat between the studies: Breban and De Smet (2019) include members of my Temporal group as well as complex proper nouns (e.g. *Easter Monday*) in their figures.

Table 7.2 *Common nouns in the S-coefficient subcorpus premodified by common, genitive, temporal, and proper nouns by genre and period (raw frequencies)*

Genre	Period	Common	Genitive	Temporal	Proper
Debates	1	26	1	0	3
	3	84	1	0	23
	Total	110	2	0	26
Drama	1	63	2	1	12
	3	102	1	10	17
	Total	165	3	11	29
Fiction	1	112	5	0	12
	3	102	9	12	19
	Total	214	14	12	31
History	1	37	1	0	6
	3	58	3	2	23
	Total	95	4	2	29
Letters	1	129	6	18	55
	3	145	2	30	58
	Total	274	8	48	113
Science	1	110	0	0	2
	3	105	1	0	12
	Total	215	1	0	14
Trials	1	213	3	92	23
	3	163	5	16	39
	Total	376	8	108	62

mainly due to an outlier: the samples from the trial of Charles Angus contain sixty-one of the ninety-two relevant temporal nouns. A large number of tokens occur in questions from lawyers concerning what happened on specific days, which was of considerable importance to the trial, as in (7.13).

(7.13) [$Q.$] Now you noticed her dress on *the **Friday** morning?* – [$A.$] Yes, sir.
[$Q.$] Was that the same she had on, on *the **Thursday** night?*
(CONCE: Trials, 1800–30, Angus, p. 66)

As will be shown below, topic is a strong conditioning factor on the distribution of linguistic features in Trials as well as Debates. Of course, the subject matter treated affects linguistic choices in any genre, but speech-based, dialogic genres are likely to be more influenced in this regard than many other genres, as dialogue can be expected to promote the recurrence of previously used linguistic forms in subsequent turns.

The high frequency of temporal premodification in private letters from period 3, in contrast, is not related to any particular file. Instead, the greater tendency to use such temporal references in period 3 may be due in part to the introduction of the Penny Post in 1840. As discussed in Section 2.3.3, this reform resulted in a drastic increase in correspondence; letters were thus sent more frequently in period 3 than in period 1. Consider (7.14):

(7.14) On ***Thursday*** *afternoon* I went over the factory here with Miss Downward. I had no idea it was so large or so important – it sends thread and twine to every part of the world, & you can't buy any of it in Shrewsbury. It was rather nice to see all my factory girls at their work, & gave one a homelike feeling with them.
On ***Monday*** *night* I have to play at a little concert & reading of Mrs. Bentley's here, for the school and clothing club, – ...
(CONCE: Letters, 1870–1900, Butler, May, p. 96)

Temporal references of the kind exemplified in (7.14) would be easier to process if intervals between letters were comparatively short. Long intervals would have made such references impractical, as the reader would need to look at the date of the letter to be certain which Thursday and Monday were intended.

Since the only categories in which high frequencies of nominal premodifiers were noted in several period/genre samples were common and proper nouns, I will restrict the discussion of normalized frequencies to these two categories. Figure 7.2 presents the developments for common nouns as premodifiers. All genres except Trials, where a decrease of 29 per cent takes place, display increasing frequencies of premodifying common nouns; increases are by between 19 per cent (Science) and 222 per cent (Debates). In CONCE as a whole, there is an increase of 24 per cent, from 2.5 to 3.1 occurrences per 1,000 words. Overall, the frequencies in CONCE are far below those attested in CNNE, especially at the end of the 1800s. Even though scientific writing lagged behind news reportage with regard to the frequency of premodifying nouns until the early twentieth century in Biber and Gray's (2011: 231) and Gray and Biber's (2018: 135) analyses, the large difference between these two genres in my results (5.2 vs. 3.1 tokens per 1,000 words for the genre totals,

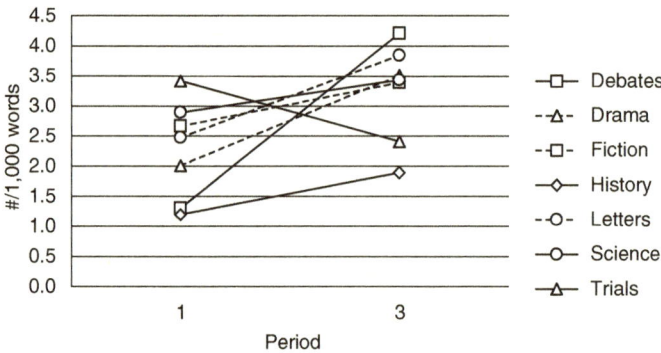

Figure 7.2 Common nouns in the S-coefficient subcorpus premodified by common nouns by period and genre (frequencies per 1,000 words)

which, however, do not cover exactly the same time spans) is somewhat unexpected. Biber and Clark (2002: 52–4) showed that news reports stand out from all the other genres analysed with a far higher frequency of noun–noun sequences in the nineteenth century, but this difference is due to a large extent to the prevalence of titles in news texts; as titles are not included in the results presented in this section, that feature does not explain the discrepancy.[8]

The co-occurrence of an increase in Debates and a decrease in Trials is unexpected, considering that both genres represent speech taken down. However, the subject matter treated in the debates and trials sampled is an important factor. As will be shown in Section 7.3.2, one topic of the late-nineteenth-century debates – the right to vote – contributes strongly to the high frequency in period 3 by favouring one particular semantic relation between modifier and head. As regards Trials, three corpus texts display high frequencies: the trial of Jonathan Martin (period 1, 4.6 tokens per 1,000 words), the Maybrick case (period 3, 4.3), and the trial of Charles Angus (period 1, 3.9), which, as shown above, also has a large number of temporal premodifiers. The subjects taken up in these trials favour recurring noun–noun combinations; for instance, in the Martin trial, five combinations occur five times or more: *lunatic asylum(s)* (12 ×), *prayer book(s)* (6 ×), *class leader(s)* (5 ×), *coal cart(s)* (5 ×), and *rope ladder* (5 ×). Similar tendencies are present in the two other trials, for example *castor oil*

---

[8] Biber and Clark (2002), Biber and Gray (2011), and Gray and Biber (2018) used different selectional criteria compared with the present study; all premodifying nouns (and titles) or even all noun–noun sequences were included in their studies, which decreases the comparability of the findings.

in the Angus trial (10 ×) and *meat juice* in the Maybrick case (11 ×). Trials may thus not be an ideal genre for tracing the integration of nominal premodification into English syntax, as noun phrases referring to topical entities are likely to be repeated in lawyers' questions and, to a lesser extent, in witnesses' answers.[9]

The other genres in CONCE display more homogeneous developments, with increases of between 19 and 74 per cent. Previous research might lead us to expect that Science would take the lead in this development, given the increased specialization and informational load of scientific texts during the LModE period (see, for instance, Biber and Gray 2012). However, although Science does have the highest overall frequency of premodifying nouns in CONCE (3.1 tokens per 1,000 words), it changes less than other genres. Moreover, History, which, like Science, contains written expository texts, displays the lowest frequency of all genres in CONCE (1.5), despite an increase of 59 per cent. These somewhat unexpected findings raise the question of whether idiolectal and/or text-specific tendencies might be at work in the material.

Science is a very heterogeneous genre, especially in period 3. Lockyer's *Chemistry of the Sun* (1887) has a frequency of 6.6 tokens per 1,000 words, which is close to the CNNE mean for the period 1875–95 (6.8). Lockyer uses recurring patterns of premodifying nouns to identify different vapours and spectral lines (see also Section 7.3.2), as in (7.15):

> (7.15) Next I found that of *the many **iron** lines observed by Ångström*, only a very few were indicated in the spectrum of the chromosphere when ***iron** vapour* was injected into it from below. (CONCE: Science, 1870–1900, Lockyer, p. 148)

However, Lockyer does not employ this strategy exclusively: phrases such as *the line of sodium* and *one of the lines due to hydrogen* also occur, which shows that several options were available for use in academic texts in his idiolect. In contrast, Bateson's *Materials for the Study of Variation* (1894) has the second lowest frequency of all CONCE texts from period 3 (0.8). As will be shown in Section 8.3.2, Bateson's text conversely has the highest frequency of participle clauses, the other feature indicative of densification treated in this study. There are thus differences among authors with regard to both the overall tendency towards condensed expression and the strategies employed to achieve this condensation. This diversity is not

---

[9] Smitterberg (2006: 258) reached a similar result regarding partitive constructions in Trials: *glass* was found to be the commonest partitive noun in the genre, owing largely to the recurrence of the partitive construction *glass of water*.

surprising, as it is fully possible for an idiolect to be progressive in one respect but conservative or neutral in another (cf. Nevalainen and Raumolin-Brunberg 2017: 210).

History also features increased diversity among the texts over time. While all texts have low frequencies in period 1, one text from period 3 – Gardiner's *History of England* – stands out, with the lowest frequency of premodifying common nouns in CONCE (0.5 tokens per 1,000 words). Manual examination of the text indicates that Gardiner used *of*-phrases where premodifying nouns would also have been possible, for example *a wall of mountains* (p. III.264), *the field of battle* (p. III.265), *the united inheritance of the family* (p. III.266), and *the Spaniard of the sixteenth century* (p. III.268). While none of these phrases is remarkable in itself, Gardiner's text comes across as linguistically conservative overall owing to the cumulative effect of such repeated choices. Although the other History texts display higher frequencies, the overall impression is that this genre seems not to have been affected by a tendency towards increased economy in the nineteenth century; as we shall see in Chapter 8, the same is true with regard to participle clauses. Biber and Gray (2011: 230–2) note that the increase in the frequency of premodifying nouns has been more pronounced in science research articles than in academic writing in general; the significant difference between History and Science found in this study underscores the heterogeneity of academic writing in this regard.

Drama, Fiction, and Letters might be expected to be less affected than other genres by densification during this period. Drama and Fiction have mainly entertainment purposes and undergo little change in overall informational load over time. Previous work (Biber and Gray 2011, 2012) indicates that Drama does not change between the eighteenth and twentieth centuries with regard to the frequency of premodifying nouns; there is an increase for Fiction, but it appears to take place mainly between the nineteenth and twentieth centuries. In Letters, the introduction of the Penny Post in 1840 might, if anything, have led to less pressure on writers to economize on words, as the price of postage was reduced (and costs transferred to the sender). Biber et al. (2016: 372–3) found only modest increases in personal letters before the twentieth century.

Somewhat surprisingly, the frequency of premodifying common nouns rises in all three genres (by 74 per cent in Drama, 27 per cent in Fiction, and 55 per cent in Letters), which may indicate that the increase in nominal premodification during the 1800s is more general than has sometimes been assumed. That hypothesis is strengthened by considering the distribution

Table 7.3 *Common nouns in the Letters genre in the S-coefficient subcorpus premodified by common nouns by period and letter writer (raw frequencies, word counts, and frequencies per 1,000 words)*

Period	Letter writer	Raw freq.	Word count	Norm. freq.
1	Jane Austen	23	10,321	2.23
	William Blake	17	8,101	2.10
	Sara Hutchinson	63	19,987	3.15
	Robert Southey	26	13,755	1.89
3	May Butler	43	8,385	5.13
	Samuel Butler	35	11,520	3.04
	Mary Sibylla Holland	59	12,686	4.65
	Thomas Huxley	8	5,137	1.56

in Letters from a gender perspective. As shown in Table 7.3, women letter writers consistently have higher frequencies of premodifying common nouns per 1,000 words than their male counterparts. Eight texts are too few to form the basis for any firm conclusions, but this gender difference may indicate that the rise of premodifying common nouns did not take place only in genres where economy was a concern (with a later spread of the feature to other genres). Women are typically ahead of men in linguistic change from below (Labov 2001: 292), and that pattern has been shown to occur in CONCE (see, for instance, Geisler 2003: 104–5; Smitterberg 2005: 78–87; Kytö and Smitterberg 2006: 222). If, as indicated by these gender differences, some of the increase in the frequency of premodifying common nouns is due to change from below, the CNNE and CONCE data may indicate that two simultaneous, and possibly mutually reinforcing, processes are at work:

1. A general shift towards more nouns in the premodifier slot, which proceeds along the usual lines of change from below, affecting speech-related writing and being more advanced on average in women's idiolects.
2. An additional increase in the use of this pattern in some genres characterized by an informational purpose, space limitations that promote an economical style, and/or increasingly specialized audiences (Gray and Biber 2018: 124).

The first process would underlie most of the frequency increase in non-expository genres as well as women's more advanced usage in Letters;

the second would be the main reason for the high frequencies and dramatic increase in CNNE as well as the comparatively high frequencies in Science. History texts, which are neither speech-related nor subject to space limitations in the nineteenth century (see Section 8.3.2), do not fully take part in either type of change. In some speech-based genres, including Debates and Trials, subject matter is likely to have an overriding influence on the incidence of premodifying nouns. More extensive studies of differences among genres, speaker groups, and idiolects need to be undertaken to test this hypothesis, but it would tally with Leech et al.'s (2009) suggestion that other genres were catching up with news and science texts with regard to nominal premodification in the late twentieth century. Texts from these other genres may increasingly contain premodifying nouns as they gradually go through process (1), with possible influence from process (2) as well; news and science, which manifested earlier increases as these genres underwent both process (1) and process (2), gradually neared a "saturation point" where "rising information density no longer pays its way" (Leech et al. 2009: 218–19).

Figure 7.3 presents the results for proper nouns premodifying common nouns. The expository genres all exhibit sharp increases, which may, however, be due mostly to the very low frequency of proper nouns as premodifiers in period 1 (eleven tokens in all three genres taken together). The dramatic increase in Debates (665 per cent) is, again, topic-related: debates on franchise reform in period 3 lead to recurring patterns such as *London boroughs* and *County Council elections*. Science displays almost as sharp an increase (646 per cent). In this genre, one significant factor behind

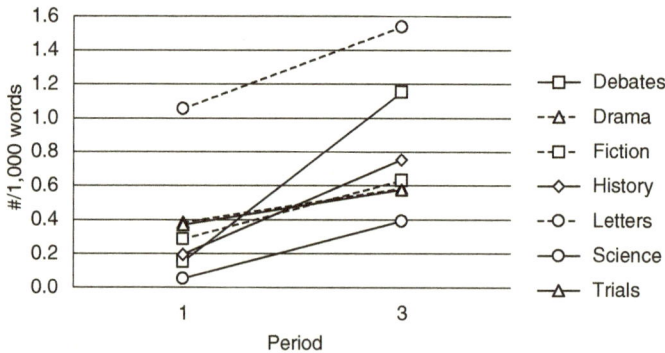

Figure 7.3 Common nouns in the S-coefficient subcorpus premodified by proper nouns by period and genre (frequencies per 1,000 words)

the increase is the plethora of objects and scientific concepts named after the people who discovered or invented them, as in (7.16):[10]

(7.16) It happened, however, that in *the **Geissler** tubes employed when the molecules of the gas were most agitated so as to give the phenomena of great pressure*, the current might be held to give us the highest temperature. (CONCE: Science, 1870–1900, Lockyer, p. 128)

In History, finally, place names like *Delhi* in *the Delhi road* predominate in the samples from period 3.

Three of the non-expository genres – Drama, Fiction, and Trials – behave similarly with regard to premodification by proper nouns: frequencies range between 0.3 and 0.4 in period 1 and between 0.5 and 0.6 in period 3, resulting in increases of between 52 and 121 per cent. Place names predominate among the premodifiers, though nouns such as *Priory* and *Deanery* also occur, and especially in one trial, which centres on a case of disputed identity, the name *Tichborne* is frequent (e.g. *the Tichborne family*). The dominance of place names also holds for Letters, though with far higher frequencies overall. As was the case with premodification by common nouns, women letter writers were more likely to use premodifying proper nouns (1.5 tokens per 1,000 words on average compared with 0.9 for men). Sara Hutchinson (1.9 tokens per 1,000 words) stands out as an early adopter of the pattern in period 1, with modern-looking combinations such as *the Rydal Mount party* and *the Borodale scheme*.

7.3.2 Semantic Analyses

As discussed in Section 7.1, the semantic relation between a nominal premodifier and the modified noun is not made explicit, yet the structure "can represent a bewildering array of meaning relationships" (Biber and Clark 2002: 63). Biber and Gray (2011: 238–40) argue that this array expanded during LModE, paralleling the increased use of the construction. For Present-Day English, Biber et al. (1999: §8.3) identify fifteen such relations, but they also demonstrate that some tokens belong to multiple categories and that there are tokens whose relation does not match any one of the fifteen well. However, there is, to my knowledge, no quantitative

---

[10] See Rosenbach (2019: 784) for a discussion of these modifiers, which have been described as having a "commemorative" relation to their head nouns, and of their relation to onomastic genitives like *Planck's constant*.

analysis of the developments that may have taken place in LModE and of genre differences in this regard. In the present section, I will attempt to fill this gap, focussing on tokens where the premodifier is a common noun. I then examine the referents of proper nouns as premodifiers, as there are indications in previous work that there has been an increase in animate referents of these proper nouns over time.

Based on previous work (Biber et al. 1999; Biber and Clark 2002; Biber and Gray 2011) as well as my own data-driven analysis of the tokens, a total of nineteen relations between premodifying common noun and head were identified (though some relations were very rare). Each token was classified with regard to what relation seemed to be the most important one; tokens where it was difficult to decide what relationship was primary were left unclassified.[11] In describing the relations, I will use the labels *M* and *H* to stand for '(pre)modifying common noun' and 'head noun', respectively.[12] The numbered list below presents definitions and examples of the relations, in alphabetical order according to their labels.

1. ABOUT. H is about or concerns M (*parish business*); M is a type of an (inanimate) H (*bridge company*; cf. KIND for animate Hs); M is the topic or a prominent feature of H (*domino party*).
2. AS. M and H are in a subject–subject complement or subject complement–subject relationship (*lady superintendent*); M is a hyponym of H (*elm tree*); H represents M (*the F line*) or a general category of which M is one example (*the farming sort*).
3. AT. M measures H (*4lb. loaves*); this relation also includes less exact measurements (*a folio Shakespeare*).
4. BASE. H is based on M directly (*mob force*) or indirectly (*household suffrage* 'right to vote consequent on being a householder'); M is an instrument used by H (*a framework knitter*).
5. DURING. H takes place during or at M (*winter months*).
6. EXT(ENDED MEANING). The relation between M and H is indirect; for instance, it may be based on perceived similarity (*corkscrew*

---

[11] A total of sixty-one tokens (roughly 2 per cent of the data) resisted classification because the relation was either unique to that token or impossible to determine (see Biber and Gray 2016: 225–6 for similar problems of interpretation in Present-Day English).

[12] In the few cases where a noun phrase included more than one premodifying noun, a nominal premodifier may relate primarily to different linguistic units semantically. For instance, in *army hospital men* (CNNE: 1875–95, RW0017), *army* relates to *hospital* and *army hospital* relates to *men*; in *deputy town clerk* (CNNE: 1875–95, RW0017), *town* relates to *clerk* and *deputy* relates to *town clerk*; and in *infant Factory worker* (CNNE: 1830–50, NS0010), either both *infant* and *factory* relate to *worker* or *factory* relates to *worker* and *infant* to *factory worker*. The labels *M* and *H* are intended to cover all such constituents as well.

staircase) or it may indirectly imply one of the other relations (*health resort* 'place that people resort to for health purposes').
7. FOR. H is used for or by M or is intended for M (*police station*); H facilitates M (*walking stick*); M is the purpose of H (*market place*); M receives H (*family dinner*).
8. FROM. H is from M (*country people*); M is the source of H (*milk fat*).
9. GEN(ITIVE). M's relation with H is semantically similar to that between the head and (i) a genitive determiner (*family name*) or (ii) an *of*-phrase corresponding in sense to a genitive determiner (*book price*; *parish officer*).
10. KIND. M describes a specialization of an (animate) H (*telegraph staff*).
11. LOC(ATION). H is located at/in M (*mountain caves*); H takes place in/at M (*street riot*).
12. OBJ(ECT) 1. M is the direct object of the process described by H (*silk manufacture* 'place where people manufacture silk').
13. OBJ(ECT) 2. M is the direct object of the process whose agent is H (*steel manufacturer*; *science student*).
14. OF. H consists of M, literally (*iron wheels*) or metaphorically (*iron pride*).
15. PART(ITIVE) 1. H is part of M (*chancel wall*).
16. PART(ITIVE) 2. M is part of H (*marrow bones*); H features/contains M (*hooping Cough*).
17. RANK. M describes the status of H, explicitly (*deputy mayor*) or implicitly (*favourite maxim*).
18. SUBJ(ECT) 1. M is the subject of the – typically intransitive – process described by H (*pauper emigration*).
19. SUBJ(ECT) 2. H is the subject of the process described by M (*choke fumes*; *parting words*).

While this set of categories, several of which were taken from or inspired by previous work, covered almost all tokens in the analysis, other data may require additional categories. In addition, a number of tokens permit several classifications; for instance, *ankle bones* can be seen as 'bones of the ankle' (GEN), 'bones that are located in the ankle' (LOC), or 'bones that are part of the ankle' (PART 1). (Nor is there of course any guarantee that these categories match those made in nineteenth-century language users' idiolects, or that all idiolects feature the same categories.) I focussed on making the classification internally consistent while basing decisions regarding which relation was primary on careful reading of the co-text. When one of the categories based on syntactic clause elements – AS, OBJ 1,

OBJ 2, SUBJ 1, and SUBJ 2 – was a possible reading, precedence was typically given to that category over one established on purely semantic grounds; for instance, *science student* was categorized as OBJ 2 rather than KIND.

Owing to the large number of categories required to capture the variation in the data, raw frequencies are low for several relations. I will therefore focus on (i) diachronic differences in CNNE and CONCE and (ii) genre variation within CONCE. The period differences in CNNE and CONCE are presented in Tables 7.4 and 7.5. For each corpus/period sample, raw frequencies, normalized frequencies, and the percentage each category makes up in relation to all classified tokens in the period sample are specified. Note that, owing to low expected frequencies in several cells, the period differences in the tables do not bear testing for statistical significance.

In CNNE, the normalized frequencies of all categories except FROM are higher in period 2. The three commonest relations – FOR, LOC, and OF – account for over 40 per cent of all premodification; they all roughly double in frequency between the periods. The categories that exhibit the biggest increases percentage-wise – SUBJ 2 (which does not occur in period 1), SUBJ 1 (225 per cent), RANK (219 per cent), DURING (193 per cent), and PART 1 (168 per cent) – are all quite rare in the data, accounting for 8 per cent of all tokens taken together. There is thus no particular semantic relation that in itself underlies the rapid frequency increase seen in CNNE. Rather, newspaper writers appear to have adapted the construction with common nouns as premodifiers to the needs of the text and of their target audience in order to achieve an appropriate compromise between economy and clarity.

CONCE as a whole displays slightly more varied developments, as shown in Table 7.5. While most semantic relations increase in frequency, AT, OBJ 2, SUBJ 1, and SUBJ 2 (and, marginally, FOR and RANK) become rarer. However, period fluctuations may be due to the content of individual texts, and raw frequencies are so low that no certain conclusions can be drawn based on these decreases. As in CNNE, the three most frequent relations are FOR, OF, and LOC, which account for 40 per cent of tokens; these three relations are clearly well established in LModE in general. Four semantic relations more than double in frequency: OBJ 1 (148 per cent; however, raw frequencies are low for this category), GEN (133 per cent), AS (107 per cent), and KIND (105 per cent). As will be shown below, several of these developments are associated with particular genres.

Given that common nouns are far more frequent as premodifiers in CNNE than in CONCE, comparing the percentages accounted for by the

Table 7.4 Semantic relations between premodifying common nouns and heads in CNNE by period (raw frequencies, normalized frequencies, and percentages)

Relation	Period 1			Period 2			Total		
	#	Norm.	%	#	Norm	%	#	Norm.	%
About	40	0.25	6.98	86	0.53	7.84	126	0.39	7.54
As	54	0.34	9.42	61	0.37	5.56	115	0.36	6.89
At	36	0.23	6.28	44	0.27	4.01	80	0.25	4.79
Base	34	0.21	5.93	71	0.43	6.47	105	0.32	6.29
During	12	0.08	2.09	36	0.22	3.28	48	0.15	2.87
Ext	24	0.15	4.19	35	0.21	3.19	59	0.18	3.53
For	112	0.70	19.55	233	1.42	21.24	345	1.07	20.66
From	6	0.04	1.05	6	0.04	0.55	12	0.04	0.72
Gen	47	0.29	8.20	75	0.46	6.84	122	0.38	7.31
Kind	20	0.13	3.49	48	0.29	4.38	68	0.21	4.07
Loc	60	0.38	10.47	118	0.72	10.76	178	0.55	10.66
Obj 1	21	0.13	3.66	35	0.21	3.19	56	0.17	3.35
Obj 2	21	0.13	3.66	40	0.24	3.65	61	0.19	3.65
Of	51	0.32	8.90	111	0.68	10.12	162	0.50	9.70
Part 1	4	0.03	0.70	11	0.07	1.00	15	0.05	0.90
Part 2	14	0.09	2.44	28	0.17	2.55	42	0.13	2.51
Rank	11	0.07	1.92	36	0.22	3.28	47	0.15	2.81
Subj 1	6	0.04	1.05	20	0.12	1.82	26	0.08	1.56
Subj 2	0	0.00	0.00	3	0.02	0.27	3	0.01	0.18
Total	573	3.58		1,097	6.70		1,670	5.16	

Table 7.5 Semantic relations between premodifying common nouns and heads in the S-coefficient subcorpus by period (raw frequencies, normalized frequencies, and percentages)

Relation	Period 1 #	Period 1 Norm.	Period 1 %	Period 3 #	Period 3 Norm	Period 3 %	Total #	Total Norm.	Total %
About	33	0.12	5.04	37	0.15	4.93	70	0.13	4.98
As	44	0.16	6.72	81	0.33	10.79	125	0.24	8.89
At	15	0.05	2.29	9	0.04	1.20	24	0.05	1.71
Base	48	0.17	7.33	63	0.26	8.39	111	0.21	7.89
During	25	0.09	3.82	30	0.12	3.99	55	0.11	3.91
Ext	21	0.08	3.21	37	0.15	4.93	58	0.11	4.13
For	127	0.46	19.39	112	0.46	14.91	239	0.46	17.00
From	25	0.09	3.82	27	0.11	3.60	52	0.10	3.70
Gen	28	0.10	4.27	58	0.24	7.72	86	0.16	6.12
Kind	17	0.06	2.60	31	0.13	4.13	48	0.09	3.41
Loc	68	0.25	10.38	65	0.26	8.66	133	0.25	9.46
Obj 1	10	0.04	1.53	22	0.09	2.93	32	0.06	2.28
Obj 2	14	0.05	2.14	6	0.02	0.80	20	0.04	1.42
Of	102	0.37	15.57	95	0.39	12.65	197	0.38	14.01
Part 1	9	0.03	1.37	13	0.05	1.73	22	0.04	1.56
Part 2	34	0.12	5.19	40	0.16	5.33	74	0.14	5.26
Rank	19	0.07	2.90	16	0.07	2.13	35	0.07	2.49
Subj 1	10	0.04	1.53	6	0.02	0.80	16	0.03	1.14
Subj 2	6	0.02	0.92	3	0.01	0.40	9	0.02	0.64
Total	655	2.37		751	3.06		1,406	2.69	

different relations in the two corpora may shed light on the changes that have taken place in newspaper English: if newspaper language is at a more advanced stage than other genres regarding the use of common nouns as premodifiers, the relations that "lag behind" in CONCE may be those where developments in news texts occurred. Although differences are fairly small overall, the four relations that stand out are FOR, AT, ABOUT, and OBJ 2, with differences of 3.7, 3.1, 2.6, and 2.2 percentage points, respectively. The differences regarding OBJ 2 and AT are arguably genre-related. Reports of newsworthy events typically include the occupation of the people involved, with OBJ 2 tokens such as *pattern maker* and *toll collectors*; statements of the monetary value (e.g. *the fourpenny stamp*) and scale (e.g. *an 8in. pump*) of objects that are described in articles also characterize many texts. The FOR and ABOUT relations are of more interest in that some tokens from these groups place considerable demands on readers (see also the discussion of genre differences below); consider (7.17) for FOR and (7.18) for ABOUT:

(7.17) Mr. C. T. LOWE, of the Queen's Westminster Rifle Volunteers, in a letter to the St. James's Gazette, declares that *the **service** ammunition* was found to be very erratic in the shooting at Wimbledon for the QUEEN'S Prize. (CNNE: 1875–95, DN0018)

(7.18) The Irish landlords – to go no further back than the time when they threw out the Compensation for Disturbance Bill – have ever rejected the proposals made by those who desired to effect a settlement of *the **land** question* on other grounds than the ruin of an entire class. (CNNE: 1875–95, PMG0008)

Noun phrases such as these may seem straightforward, but they require a great deal of the reader. The sense 'employed, or suitable for use, on active service', which is required to process *service ammunition* in (7.17) successfully, is quite opaque and specialized. It also appears to have been a recent introduction into English: the earliest example of *service* in this sense in the *OED*, s.v. *service* (n.¹), is from 1776. *The land question* in (7.18) is easy to process on the surface – 'the question that concerns land' – but that definition in itself is so empty that readers need to make use of their extralinguistic knowledge of Ireland in order to connect the noun phrase to its intended referent. The relative prominence in CNNE of semantic relations that require a great deal of readers forms a partial parallel to the quantitative prevalence of nominal premodifiers in newspaper writing.

As regards genre differences within CONCE, raw frequencies are low in many cases, so I will restrict the discussion to the most robust tendencies in the data. An overall trend in the data is that FOR relations account for the largest number of tokens in the non-expository genres (Drama, Fiction, Letters, and Trials), as was also the case for CNNE, while other relations predominate in the expository genres Debates, History, and Science. I will therefore discuss these two groups of genres separately.

In Drama, FOR accounts for 22 per cent of tokens, but they differ from many examples from CNNE (see 7.17) in that establishing the connection between M and H typically requires little specialized linguistic or extralinguistic knowledge; examples include *shavin' water* and *coal cellar*. Fiction displays a high proportion of both FOR and OF relations (19 per cent each). OF relations typically specify the main constituent of concrete heads, as in (7.19):

> (7.19) Selina wears her Sunday clothes, the last fashionable thing in *black **silk** jackets*, a good deal of hay-coloured horsehair at the back of her head, and a Parisian bonnet at half a guinea from the Brompton-road. (CONCE: Fiction, 1870–1900, Braddon, p. III.102)

Mary Braddon's novel *Hostages to Fortune*, exemplified in (7.19), accounts for 51 per cent of all OF relations in Fiction, and her text also features the highest frequency of premodification by common nouns in the genre (5.1 tokens per 1,000 words). If Braddon's idiolect is comparatively advanced in this regard, it may be that common-noun premodification in fiction texts increased partly through a rising use of OF relations between modifiers and heads. In Letters, LOC relations account for the second largest proportion of tokens (14 per cent, vs. 17 per cent for FOR relations). The thirty-nine tokens are quite heterogeneous, with tokens that concern, for instance, accommodation (*a bedroom life*) and even the body (*a little stomach derangement*). The Trials genre is quite similar to Fiction in that the two biggest categories are FOR (24 per cent) and OF (15 per cent) relations. However, as mentioned in Section 7.3.1, the distribution of relations in Trials texts may depend more on subject matter than on genre; for instance, in the trial of Jonathan Martin (period 1), there is a great deal of interest in a *rope ladder* (5 ×) used to leave York Minster after the building had been set on fire, which increases the share of OF relations.

Among the expository genres, the Debates genre features a large proportion of BASE relations (37 per cent). Thirty-seven of the forty instances are from period 3, and BASE tokens thus contribute to the high frequency of premodification by common nouns in that period (see Section 7.3.1). The distribution is due to the main subject debated in the samples – the basis for suffrage – rather than the genre itself, however. Consider (7.20):

(7.20) But as it became easy and cheap to travel *the non-resident **freehold** voters* assumed a much greater importance, and it became worth while to acquire ***freehold** qualifications* in counties for the express purpose of giving votes. (CONCE: Debates, 1870–1900, pp. IV.1,183–4)

To Members of Parliament, the sense of *freehold voter* and of similar noun phrases in which the modifier is the basis for the right to vote expressed by the head would have been obvious;[13] economy could be achieved with no loss of clarity. History is instead characterized by a large proportion of OF tokens (22 per cent), all except one of which are from period 3; this period difference is largely responsible for the increase in premodification by common nouns in History over time. Most of these noun phrases refer to concrete objects, as in Fiction, but especially in Spencer Walpole's *History of England*, there are also military units, for example *cavalry regiment*.[14] In Science, BASE (19 per cent), OF (18 per cent), and As (17 per cent) predominate, and two texts account for the bulk of tokens. Most BASE tokens are from Ricardo's text on political economy and taxation and feature *market* 'based on the market' as a premodifier (e.g. *the market wages of labour*). OF relations are also frequent in Ricardo's text, but Lockyer's *Chemistry of the Sun* has an even higher normalized frequency of OF as well as As relations. In the chemistry text, OF tokens typically concern what different gases (*sodium vapour*) or objects used in experiments (*a long india-rubber tube*) consist of.

The analysis of CNNE and CONCE does not provide clear evidence of a qualitative increase in the range of semantic modifier–head relations, as hypothesized by Biber and Gray (2016: 178–9). Several of the "additional meaning relationships commonly expressed by NN sequences in the late twentieth century" listed in Biber and Gray (2016) were attested in the first half of the nineteenth century in my analysis, for example "an inanimate entity (N2) that regulates or administers N1" and "a text (N2) about the topic identified in N1" (e.g. *prison law, revolution settlement*, or *ghost stories*, all classified as ABOUT in this study), though criteria for inclusion may of course

---

[13] Since the fifteenth century, owners of freehold property of an annual rent value of at least 40s. had been given a county vote.
[14] *Cavalry regiment* illustrates the element of subjectivity inherent in the categorization: it may also be thought of as a unit with a cavalry-related purpose (FOR) or as a unit consisting of soldiers who specialize in cavalry duty (KIND); since even specialized military units like cavalry regiments typically contain soldiers from other fields as well, PART 2 is also a possible classification. (Even concrete objects rarely consist only of one element; for instance, a *silver spoon* is often made of an alloy like sterling silver, which contains 92.5 per cent silver by weight.) An OF relation is necessarily an idealization of the real-world situation, but this does not make the category invalid; what matters is how most language users are likely to have perceived the relation (see Comrie 1976: 41–4 and Smitterberg 2005: 165 for a related discussion concerning non-durative situation types). The OF relation was considered the most prominent semantic connection between *cavalry* and *regiment*.

differ between our studies. This is not to say that there has been no semantic expansion – it would be odd if the increase in tokens were not accompanied by an extension of the range of types – but such an expansion must perhaps be identified in an even more fine-grained analysis with additional semantic features.

What is clear from the analyses is that different genres favour specific types of relation between premodifier and head. Some genre patterns are noteworthy. First, popular genres – including CNNE – favour FOR relations, which may require more or less interpretive effort, while other relations predominate in specialist or expository texts. Secondly, the three genres in CONCE that were found to be the most narrative in Geisler's (2002) factor-score analysis of CONCE – Fiction, History, and Trials – all favour OF relations, as do many texts in CNNE, where news reports can also be expected to include narrativity. A tentative connection between narrativity and OF relations can thus be established.

I now turn to the semantic analysis of premodifying proper nouns. Here the research question concerns whether the increase in their frequency (see Section 7.3.1) is paralleled by an expansion in productivity whereby animate referents become increasingly available in this position over time, as suggested by Rosenbach's (2007: 166) results. My analysis focusses on CNNE, as the 304 tokens in the 7 different genres of CONCE are too few to allow safe conclusions.[15] The premodifying proper nouns were divided into six categories, which are listed, defined, and exemplified below, using the labels *M* and *H* in the same way as for semantic relations between common nouns as premodifiers and heads above.[16]

---

[15] Breban and De Smet (2019) carry out a more detailed analysis, where the semantic status of the head noun and the status of the entire noun phrase as onomastic or non-onomastic, that is, whether it is "a name in its own right" (Breban and De Smet 2019: 891), are taken into account. With only 658 tokens, the CNNE data do not allow for the level of detail of their analysis. Instead, I focus on the status of the premodifier and on narrower periods (Breban and De Smet contrast Old, Middle, Late Modern, and Present-Day English); it is hoped that this complementary perspective will shed light on short-term developments. Although in this analysis I focus on the referent of the premodifier rather than the relation between premodifier and head, several premodifier categories correspond closely to semantic relations.

[16] As noted by Breban and De Smet (2019: 883), some proper nouns can be seen as designating several categories; for instance, *Queen Victoria* in *the Queen Victoria public-house* (CNNE: 1830–1850, RW0005) might be taken to refer to a name, a collective (the establishment), or a location. Such tokens were coded as locations unless there was clear evidence that another category's semantics were in focus (cf. Breban et al. 2019: 822). However, such potentially ambiguous contexts are worthy of study based on a bigger corpus, as they may constitute bridging contexts that facilitate the transition from Place to Collective readings.

1. PLACE. M specifies the location of H (*the Carnarvonshire shore*).
2. TIME. M specifies when H takes place or obtains (*the Kirkwall Lammas market*).
3. GOAL. M identifies the purpose or goal of H (*the Recreation Ground movement*).
4. NAME. M identifies an example or hyponym of the inanimate category specified by H (*the City of Edinburgh steam-vessel*; *Champion potatoes*).
5. COLLECTIVE. M identifies a collective – a board, committee, government body, company, or similar – that the animate H is associated with (*The Central News correspondent*).
6. INDIVIDUAL. M identifies a particular animate entity associated with H (*the Griffiths case*).

Because the frequency of premodification by proper nouns increases drastically over time, it is necessary to consider both proportions and normalized frequencies of the six semantic categories. Table 7.6 presents raw frequencies and percentages (eight tokens that resisted classification are excluded). Semantic broadening is clearly present in the newspaper data. The two most animate categories, COLLECTIVE and INDIVIDUAL, increase by 7.3 and 1.7 percentage points, respectively, while the proportions accounted for by the PLACE and NAME categories go down. GOAL and TIME remain marginal categories throughout.[17] Owing to low expected frequencies of those categories, the differences in Table 7.6 do not bear testing for statistical significance. However, if PLACE, TIME, GOAL, and NAME are conflated into one single INANIMATE category, the differences can be tested, and the results are significant (d.f. = 2; χ^2 = 6.96; p = 0.031). While this type of conflation is somewhat artificial, it does support the hypothesis concerning an increased proportion of premodifiers with animate referents.

Normalized frequencies by period of the four categories with total raw frequencies of > 10 are given in Figure 7.4. Table 7.6 and Figure 7.4 paint different pictures with regard especially to the PLACE category. While the share of all proper-noun premodification it accounts for decreases (Table 7.6), its frequency still rises by 80 per cent (Figure 7.4). This is considerably less than the COLLECTIVE (200 per cent) and INDIVIDUAL

---

[17] As discussed in Section 7.3.1, most premodifiers with a temporal function and potential proper-name status, for example *Sunday morning*, were grouped together in a Temporal category that was kept separate from the proper nouns included in this analysis. As shown in Figure 7.1, this category remains stable over time.

Table 7.6 Common nouns in CNNE premodified by proper nouns by semantic field and period (raw frequencies and percentages)

Period	Place		Time		Goal		Name		Collective		Individual		Total
	#	%	#	%	#	%	#	%	#	%	#	%	
1	163	74.1	2	0.9	4	1.8	17	7.7	28	12.7	6	2.7	220
2	301	70.0	4	0.9	5	1.2	15	3.5	86	20.0	19	4.4	430
Total	464	71.4	6	0.9	9	1.4	32	4.9	114	17.5	25	3.8	650

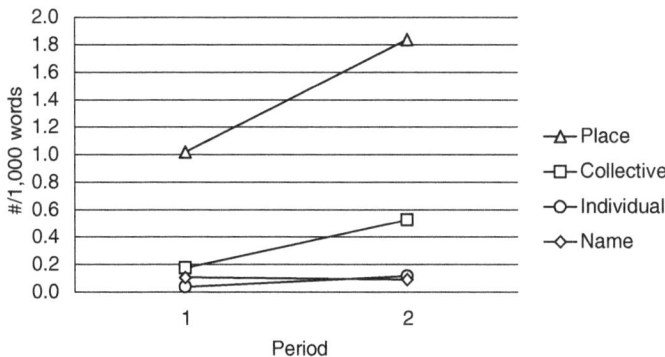

Figure 7.4 Common nouns in CNNE premodified by proper nouns by semantic field and period (frequencies per 1,000 words)

(209 per cent) categories, but still a very noticeable increase. The shift in the distribution of semantic categories thus needs to be considered against the background of a very clear frequency increase for the pattern as a whole.

7.4 Discussion

With regard to densification, the results presented in this chapter broadly tally with what previous research has found for nineteenth-century English. There is clear evidence that newspaper English underwent densification, with high and increasing frequencies of nominal premodifiers. The genres in CONCE display far lower frequencies and/or smaller increases by comparison. The idea that newspapers would be at the forefront of this change, while scientific writing lagged behind into the twentieth century, matches results from studies that cover longer time periods, though it is remarkable that such pronounced increases in CNNE are visible over the span of considerably less than a century. The pressure to communicate increasing amounts of information while constrained by space limitations clearly had linguistic repercussions in newspaper articles. The fact that newspapers aimed at working-class readers seemed not to take part in the change in the period 1830–50 indicates that journalists' and editors' hypotheses about the papers' target audiences may counteract tendencies towards densification.

However, as results for Drama and Letters show, densification may not be the only factor behind the change. These genres have traditionally not been associated with densification, and Drama does not take part in the trend towards more premodifying nouns discussed in Biber and Gray (2011: 230–2); yet Drama in CONCE exhibits clear increases in frequency. Private letters also display an increase, and women are ahead of men as regards premodification by both common and proper nouns. This gender difference implies that, in private letters, the increase in nominal premodification is mainly a change from below and may not be a response to pressure to economize on words. We might thus be looking at two mutually reinforcing tendencies in LModE: an increased availability of nouns as premodifiers in general and increased pressure to make use of this resource for densification purposes in newspapers and, to a lesser extent, scientific prose. In this regard, it is noteworthy that History and Science, the two written expository genres in CONCE, behave very differently: History has the lowest and Science the highest frequency of common nouns as premodifiers in the corpus. As will be shown in Chapter 8, a similar difference holds for participle clauses. Gray and Biber (2018: 135) demonstrate that related differences between areas of scholarship still persist today, and Biber and Gray (2016: 23–5) suggest that there has been less development in humanities texts than in scientific texts with regard to features such as clausal embedding and premodifying nouns. The extracts from Science and History examined here thus reveal genre differences that would remain in place over the next 100 years.

Gray and Biber (2018: 124) argue that features that indicate densification such as premodifying nouns can proliferate in genres provided that (i) writers have sufficient time when producing and editing their texts, (ii) texts presuppose specialist knowledge that is shared between writers and readers, and/or (iii) the purpose of the text is informational (often resulting in a need for conciseness). If we compare CNNE, Science, and History from these perspectives, it appears that (iii) and, to a somewhat lesser extent, (ii) are the most important factors for nineteenth-century English (see Biber and Gray 2012: 326; 2016: 145). Newspaper writers' need to be economical with word counts appears to be what caused them to use more nominal premodification than what was attested in any other genre, despite the relative lack of shared specialized knowledge; it also appears that this need became more pronounced across the nineteenth century. In contrast, newspapers were produced with less time for writing and editing than either of the two written expository genres in CONCE. As Gray and Biber (2018: 133) report greater tendencies towards densification for scientific writing than for newspapers between 1750 and 1990, it appears that the relative importance of these factors may have shifted over time. Results presented in Biber and Clark (2002: 52) as well as Gray and Biber (2018: 135) also indicate that academic writing may have lagged behind news into the early twentieth century (although findings in Biber and Gray 2013: 108 indicate more similar frequencies in the two genres before the 1900s).

The combination of a relatively concise stylistic ideal and shared specialized knowledge contributed to a fairly high frequency of nominal premodifiers in Science as well, though there were no large changes over time. The History texts, in contrast, appear to have been produced without pressing constraints on space (see Section 8.3.2 for further discussion). Also, although the audience of a science text was more multidisciplinary in the 1800s than today (Biber and Gray 2016: 56, 158), history writing was in all likelihood read by a lay audience to a greater extent than texts in the natural sciences. Indeed, even in recent English, history texts tend to focus on more familiar topics and include larger passages devoted to description and argumentation, making the overall purpose less information-centred compared with science writing (Biber and Gray 2013: 102). Consequently, writers in this genre could count on less specialist knowledge that was shared with their target group (much as the – largely middle-class – writers for newspapers such as the *Poor Man's Guardian* could not count on specialist knowledge that was shared with their readers). The two subgenres of an umbrella "academic writing" genre – Science and History – are in fact more distinct linguistically than either of them is from any other genre in CONCE on this parameter. As shown by Biber and Gray (2016: 113), similar differences are found in Present-Day English, where nominal premodifiers are more than three times more common in the sciences than in the humanities. However, while Biber and Gray's (2016) nineteenth-century humanities texts actually had more premodifying nouns than science texts did, the relationship was reversed in the present study, something which appears to match the overall trends between 1800 and 2000 more closely.[18]

The above analysis starts out from a functional perspective; it is assumed that different genre-specific pressures acted on writers of texts. Such a perspective doubtless has great explanatory power. But it is worth

---

[18] Biber and Gray's (2016) results appear to concern all nouns that premodify other nouns, thus conflating several of the categories kept distinct in this study and potentially also including other categories. This difference may also explain the higher frequencies found by Biber and Gray.

pointing out that, as discussed in Chapter 3, idiolects may undergo change for other reasons as well. Even if it had been functionally motivated to use premodifying nouns as often in Science as in CNNE, newspaper writing may have featured higher frequencies of the feature for social reasons. If, say, nominal premodification became associated with newspaper language and was seized on by journalists whom their peers wished to emulate, densification could be a result of social as well as functional pressure. Purely functional explanations, while very valuable, do not tell the whole story, because they do not take into account the full range of influences on the language users whose idiolects are undergoing change. While it is likely that social pressures of this type, which would have caused a linguistic feature to spread through a community of journalists primarily via weak network ties, are less influential on written language than on face-to-face spoken communication, they should not be disregarded.

The semantic analyses of (i) premodification relations between common nouns and (ii) the reference of premodifying proper nouns shed light on the process by which nominal premodifiers were gradually integrated into English syntax. Proper nouns as premodifiers in CNNE became less restricted to inanimate referents over time, which tallies with previous research. The semantic relations between common nouns as premodifiers and their heads exhibited less clear quantitative trends, though a close examination of individual tokens indicated that some of the relations which accounted for a greater proportion of tokens in CNNE than in CONCE also established more abstract, indirect connections between modifier and head. From this perspective, the higher incidence figures for the syntactic pattern in CNNE were matched by more implicitness in the semantic relations established. Topic and genre constraints also influenced the distribution of semantic relations; for instance, non-expository and narrative writing favoured FOR and OF relations, respectively, and certain topics in Debates and Trials promoted a high frequency of particular relations through recurring premodifier–head combinations.

Future work on the linguistic status of noun–noun sequences may contribute further insights into the use of nominal premodifiers in LModE. As mentioned in Section 7.2, nominal premodification as defined in this study to some extent straddles the boundary between lexis and syntax: some of the noun–noun sequences can arguably be interpreted as (lexical) compounds rather than (syntactic) combinations of premodifier and head. I followed recent corpus-based work in using orthographical separation of the nouns as an indication that they were considered separate lexemes by contemporary language users. However, applying criteria that

7.4 Discussion

can separate compounds from syntactic structures (see Huddleston and Pullum 2002: §5.14.4 and Sanchez-Stockhammer 2018: 23–60 for discussion) to LModE data to see whether there are diachronic shifts in the proportions of noun–noun compounds and premodifier–head combinations would be a valuable extension of work in the field.[19] Beal (2004: 14, 21–9) demonstrates that the nineteenth century featured a great deal of lexical innovation, partly in response to external developments such as colonialization and the industrial and scientific revolutions, and it is reasonable to assume that one aspect of this innovation would be an increase in noun–noun compounds. If so, a proportion of the noun + noun tokens in this chapter may be lexical units rather than syntactic alternatives to longer forms of expression, such as prepositional phrases. The two processes – lexical innovation and syntactic productivity – may also have facilitated each other, as they result in similar or identical surface structures; propagation-dependent innovation may have caused language users to use one feature more because they were exposed to the other one.

---

[19] I am grateful to Sarah Schwarz for this suggestion. Huddleston and Pullum (2002: §5.14.4) argue that a syntactic test – the ability of the nouns to "enter separately into relations of coordination and modification" – is what best separates compounds from modifier + head combinations; they are critical of using stress as a criterion, for instance.

CHAPTER 8

Densification II: Participle Clauses as Postmodifiers in Noun Phrases

8.1 Introduction

The present chapter is concerned with participle clauses that function as postmodifiers in noun phrases: present-participle clauses, as in (8.1), and past-participle clauses, as in (8.2). (In numbered corpus examples in this chapter, italics are used to highlight the relevant noun phrase, in which the relevant postmodifier is rendered in boldface.) A participle clause with this function often expresses a meaning that is similar to what can be expressed by a finite adnominal relative clause (Biber et al. 1999: §8.8; Huddleston and Pullum 2002: §14.9), which is the most common type of clausal postmodifier in Present-Day English (Biber et al. 1999: §8.6.1). However, participle clauses are less explicit (Jucker 1992: 68), as they lack a relative marker, a finite verb, and possibly other features of the corresponding relative clause. The correspondence is illustrated in (8.1') and (8.2'):

(8.1) *The air **passing the windways*** was proved to be ample, but alleged to be ineffectually distributed to the working places. (CNNE: 1875–95, BDP0002)

(8.1') *The air **that /was passing/passed/is passing/passes/ the windways*** was proved to be ample, . . .

(8.2) EARLY one July morning we – that is, the writer and two brothers – embarked at the fish market of a northern seaport on board the steam trawler Frank Buckland, *a fine, powerful iron vessel **specially built for the purpose***, and representing (her owner told us) upwards of £5,000. (CNNE: 1875–95, PMG0004)

(8.2') . . . the steam trawler Frank Buckland, *a fine, powerful iron vessel **that /was/has been/ specially built for the purpose***, . . .

As seen in (8.1–2), present-participle clauses typically correspond to active relative clauses, and past-participle clauses to passive relative clauses. (In

8.1 Introduction

the interest of brevity, I will use the term *relative clause* to stand for 'finite, adnominal relative clause' in this chapter. Similarly, *participle clause* stands for 'participle clause functioning as a noun-phrase postmodifier' henceforth.)

It is this semantic similarity to relative clauses that makes participle clauses interesting to discuss from the perspective of densification. Participle clauses are shorter than relative clauses: as has already been mentioned and as shown in (8.1–2), linguistic material that would be present in the corresponding relative clause is absent from the participle clause. If participle clauses increase in frequency over time at the expense of relative clauses, this development may thus indicate densification: the same meaning is expressed using less linguistic material. In Biber and Clark's (2002: 63) "cline of compression" in the noun phrase, relative clauses are at the "expanded" endpoint, and non-finite clauses represent the first step towards the opposite, "compressed" end. This association with densification is strengthened by considering the genre distribution of participle clauses in Present-Day English. Compared with relative clauses, participle clauses (especially past-participle clauses) are more frequent in news texts and in academic prose than in fiction and conversation (Biber et al. 1999: §8.6.1), which is the genre pattern that would be expected from a feature that contributes to densification. Participle clauses are in fact the only clause type that is (i) more frequent in academic prose than in either fiction or newspapers and (ii) more frequent in the sciences than in the humanities in Present-Day English (Biber and Gray 2016: 106–7, 115).

There is somewhat conflicting evidence from previous research regarding the frequency development of participle clauses in LModE. Biber and Clark's (2002: 58–61) results indicate that the frequency of participle clauses was fairly stable between the seventeenth and twentieth centuries, though a slight increase is noticeable for present-participle clauses in Fiction. Biber and Gray (2012: 323) found that present-participle clauses decreased in frequency between 1800 and 2000, while past-participle clauses became more frequent in fiction and academic prose (but not in newspaper language).[1] In Hundt et al.'s (2012a: 231) analysis of scientific prose, both clause types increased in frequency in British English between the eighteenth and twentieth centuries, with the exception of present-participle clauses from the 1800s to the 1900s. Biber and Gray (2016: 142), who examine

---

[1] Biber and Gray's (2012) results for newspapers are based entirely on the *New York Times*; as will be shown in Section 8.3, there is a great deal of linguistic diversity among newspapers, so it is not certain that their results are generalizable to the genre as a whole.

fiction, news reportage, and science prose, report decreases in all genres for present-participle clauses between 1750 and 1990, while the incidence of past-participle clauses remained stable. Participle clauses displayed stability or slight decreases in frequency in Gray and Biber's (2018: 132) study.

In contrast, most studies indicate that relative clauses either remained fairly stable (Biber and Clark 2002: 57–60) or declined in frequency to a greater or lesser extent between the eighteenth and twentieth centuries (Biber and Gray 2011: 228–9, 2012: 323, 2016: 149–50; Hundt et al. 2012a: 233). This decrease is largely due to an increased dispreference for *wh*-clauses, while *that*-clauses remain stable and even increase in frequency in newspaper language; owing to this increase, newspaper language displays stable frequencies of relative clauses overall (Biber and Gray 2016: 142–3; Gray and Biber 2018: 132). Against this background, more research into the frequency development and genre distribution of relative and participle clauses in LModE, and into the relationship between the results of the analysis and densification, is clearly warranted.

An increase in the incidence of participle clauses need not in itself indicate densification, since densification implies a variationist perspective on linguistic variation (see Section 4.3.2). If the relative proportions of participle clauses and their wordier relative-clause near-equivalents remain unchanged, there is no evidence that language users chose shorter expressions at the expense of longer ones even if participle clauses became more frequent; conversely, even if the frequency of participle clauses was stable, results may still indicate densification if the frequency of relative clauses decreased. It is thus necessary to chart the frequency development of four constructions: active relative clauses vs. present-participle clauses; passive relative clauses vs. past-participle clauses.[2] In addition, only those tokens of these four constructions that are in fact interchangeable should be included in such a frequency comparison. As will be shown in Section 8.2, the latter criterion is not easy to meet. For this reason, I will analyse participle clauses from both variationist and text-linguistic perspectives: the subsets of the four constructions listed above that are deemed interchangeable will be compared with one another in a variationist analysis (Section 8.3.1), but the entire set of participle-clause tokens will also be analysed from a text-linguistic angle (Section 8.3.2). In the concluding section of the chapter

---

[2] As noted by de Haan (1989: 72–3), there are rare exceptions where a past-participle clause can have non-passive meaning. Two such tokens were attested and excluded from the counts, as they are instead in variation with relative clauses with active perfect verb phrases, for example *a man (who has) just come from India* (see Quirk et al. 1985: §17.29).

(Section 8.4), I will discuss the relative merits of the two perspectives against the background of the results reached.

The third type of non-finite clause that can postmodify noun-phrase heads, namely the *to*-infinitive clause, as in (8.3), will not be included in the study.

(8.3)   ... ; but we affirm that men have *duties* **to perform** as well as *rights* **to maintain**; ... (CNNE: 1830–50, RW0009)

Like participle clauses, *to*-infinitive clauses can be roughly equivalent to relative clauses. However, for three reasons, this clause type was excluded from investigation. First, many *to*-infinitive clauses do not fill the same functions as participle clauses. Most notably, the corresponding relative clause often includes a modal auxiliary (Kjellmer 1975; Quirk et al. 1985: §17.32; Geisler 1995: 74–7); for instance, the first noun phrase with a *to*-infinitive clause in (8.3) might correspond to *duties (that/which) they should/must perform*. Secondly, *to*-infinitive clauses can correspond to relative clauses with non-subject gaps (Quirk et al. 1985: §17.30); both clauses in (8.3) correspond to relative clauses with direct-object gaps. In contrast, participle clauses can correspond only to relative clauses with subject gaps (Quirk et al. 1985: §§17.28–9), where a relative marker is obligatory in Standard English.[3] Consequently, restricting the scope to participle clauses made it possible to avoid the difficult task of retrieving relative clauses with zero relative markers for comparison. Finally, *to*-infinitive clauses differ from participle clauses in that they are proportionally more frequent in conversation than in writing in Present-Day English (Biber et al. 1999: §8.6.1). This distribution makes it unlikely that they would be involved in densification, which tends to affect written before spoken genres (Leech et al. 2009: 234–5).

8.2 Method

Relative clauses with subject gaps and present-participle clauses contain specific linguistic forms that can be retrieved using a concordancer (*who*, *which*, *that*, and **ing*, including spelling variants). However, going through the resulting concordances to exclude false positives would be

---

[3] Technically, an active relative clause with an object gap, which may lack an overt relative marker, can roughly correspond in meaning to a past-participle clause, for example *the man Ø the police arrested yesterday* ≈ *the man arrested by the police yesterday*. However, such changes in informational focus were considered to result in non-equivalence of meaning, and only relative clauses with subject gaps were retrieved.

very time-consuming considering the frequency of forms like *that* in English; moreover, as there is no way to retrieve English past participles lexically, past-participle clauses could not be retrieved in such a fashion. Consequently, I decided to base retrieval on tagged versions of CNNE and CONCE. As regards CONCE, I used the S-coefficient subcorpus (Smitterberg 2005: 52–3, 271–5), since cases where the tagger could not decide between a past-tense and a past-participle reading of a verb form have been manually disambiguated in this corpus. This refinement drastically improved precision in the semi-automatic retrieval of past-participle clauses from the corpus files.

Potential relative clauses were retrieved differently in the two corpora used. For CNNE, I searched for (i) words tagged as nouns and (ii) selected pronouns[4] followed by *who*, *which*, or *that* within a window of four words. No tagging restrictions were imposed on the retrieval of *who*, *which*, or *that*, as especially the last item was sometimes mistagged. The tagger used for CONCE included a tag that reliably identified relative pronouns, which meant that retrieval here was more straightforward: all tokens of *which*, *who*, or *that* that had the relative-pronoun tag either as the only tag or as one of several possible tags were retrieved.

The next step was to exclude groups of tokens that could not be replaced by participle clauses. These were (i) false positives, that is, non-relative clauses (including the relative-like clause in *it*-cleft constructions), (ii) relative clauses with non-subject gaps, (iii) sentential relative clauses, and (iv) relative clauses with embedded material (e.g. comment clauses) that could not easily be transferred to a corresponding participle clause. However, further examination of the data revealed that many of the remaining relative clauses nevertheless lacked a participle-clause equivalent and needed to be excluded. This exclusion process was partly data-driven, as some new categories of non-equivalent relative tokens were discovered during classification. My approach here was to start out from each retrieved relative clause and compare it with the nearest equivalent participle clause. That participle clause was then back-translated into a relative clause. If the original and back-translated relative clauses were not the same, the token was excluded from the counts. While this method involves a degree of subjectivity, it enabled me to set up a number of categories where relative

---

[4] The forms retrieved were *everybody, everyone, everything, somebody, someone, something, anybody, anyone, anything, nobody, one, no-one, none, nothing, those, all, some, many, half, both, more, any, that, other*, and *others*. The same set was used for retrieval of relative and participle clauses in all searches. The restriction on pronoun retrieval was based on Biber et al.'s (1999: §8.1.2) analysis of what pronouns take postmodification in Present-Day English.

clauses could be excluded from the counts based on common denominators. I account for the most important categories below.

Perfect, modal, and tense marking in relative clauses normally cannot be transferred to participle clauses (Harwood 2018: 428; see Quirk et al. 1985: §17.28 for rare exceptions with indefinite noun phrases); in addition, progressive marking is available only in past-participle clauses (Quirk et al. 1985: §§17.28–9). This lack of formal marking in participle clauses frequently meant that the closest participle-clause equivalent to a given relative clause suggested a different meaning than that expressed by the relative clause: the participle clause would not imply perfect, modal, or progressive meaning that was explicitly marked in the relative clause, or would imply another tense than that of the relative clause.[5] Such tokens were excluded from the counts. I discuss three corpus examples below to illustrate the decisions involved.

With regard to perfect marking, active relative clauses with perfect auxiliaries like (8.4) typically lose their perfective semantics when they are turned into present-participle clauses, as in (8.4'):

(8.4) ... and I have reason to believe that his academical discourse will startle that venerable body, still imbued with a classical horror of innovation and of *the modern schools of thought* **which have nolens volens modified the ideals of modern literature**. (CNNE: 1875–95, DN0012)

(8.4') ... of *the modern schools of thought* nolens volens **modifying the ideals of modern literature**.

Since a reader would be more likely to expand the verb phrase in (8.4') to a present progressive (... *which are nolens volens modifying* ...) than to a present perfect, (8.4) was excluded.[6] Past-participle clauses, in contrast, can correspond to relative clauses with perfect marking (de Haan 1989: 63–4, 73), as in (8.5):

(8.5) Adverting to *the laudable endeavours* **that have been made in the instruction of the poor**, he expressed his surprise that the middling and richer classes should still trudge on the old and worn-out road, ... (CNNE: 1830–50, EX0001)

---

[5] Hudson (1973) demonstrates that the implied tense form of the participle clause is not necessarily identical with that of the matrix clause; for instance, in *Books published before the nineteenth century are very expensive to buy*, the participle clause has past-time reference, the present-tense main verb notwithstanding. Hudson uses sentences such as these to argue for a deep-structure distinction between participle and relative clauses from a generative perspective.

[6] Another possible interpretation of (8.4') would be as a gerund clause rather than a participle clause; if the participle-clause equivalent displayed such ambiguity, the original relative clause was excluded from the counts.

(8.5') Adverting to *the laudable endeavours* **made in the instruction of the poor**, he ...

As perfective semantics appear to be understood in (8.5'), (8.5) was kept in the database.[7] In most relative clauses with modal auxiliaries, the modal contributed meaning that was not inferrable from the corresponding participle clause; for instance, in (8.6'), *influencing* would be likely to be interpreted as corresponding to 'which influence' or 'which are influencing' rather than the *which may influence* of (8.6).

(8.6) ... and *the causes* **which may influence the market price of bills, or the rate of exchange**, is no consideration of his. (CONCE: Science, 1800–30, Ricardo, p. 165)

(8.6') ... and *the causes* **influencing the market price of bills, or the rate of exchange**, ...

Such tokens with modal auxiliaries were excluded from the counts.[8]

Finally, one category that arose during the examination of the tokens concerns active relative clauses with BE as main verb, such as (8.7):

(8.7) Do you know that *persons* **who are in the habit of taking arsenic** suffer in leaving it off? (CONCE: Trials, 1870–1900, Maybrick, p. 229)

(8.7') ... that *persons* **being in the habit of taking arsenic** ...?

These relative tokens generally lack clear participle-clause equivalents (Quirk et al. 1985: §15.61); a more natural equivalent to (8.7) would be a prepositional phrase (... *persons in the habit of taking arsenic* ...). Including tokens like (8.7) would thus involve a different set of variants in the analysis.[9] Tokens like (8.7) were therefore excluded. The only exception to the practice concerned relative clauses in which BE was followed by a past participle, such as (8.8).

---

[7] The participle clause in (8.5') is arguably still ambiguous regarding tense, that is, *made* may correspond to either *that had been made* or *that have been made*. This ambiguity was considered unimportant enough for (8.5) to be included, but the need for such decisions underscores the difficulty – and potential subjectivity – of the classification process.

[8] One exception in this regard concerns a small number of relative clauses whose modal auxiliaries express more or less pure future meaning that was deemed inferrable from the co-text. For instance, in *before I actually consent to take the irrevocable step that will place me on the pinnacle of my fondest hopes* (CONCE: Drama, 1870–1900, Gilbert, p. 8), *before I ... consent* makes it clear that the step has not been taken even without future marking in the postmodifier. Such tokens could thus be kept in the data set.

[9] If the relative clause is non-restrictive, a potentially equivalent construction with *being* would in many cases be interpreted as part of a nonfinite adverbial clause expressing reason (Quirk et al. 1985: §§15.60nb, 15.61) and not as a participle clause. As will be shown below, the non-restrictive paradigm was excluded from the counts on the grounds of ambiguity between adnominal and adverbial readings.

(8.8) I have also heard a good story of *a boy **who was asked by an examiner, 'What are the postulates?'*** ... (CONCE: Letters, 1870–1900, Butler, Samuel [1], p. 217)

In such tokens, the past participle can be either verbal, like *asked* in (8.8), in which case there is a past-participle-clause equivalent, or adjectival, in which case BE is the main verb and the token belongs to the same syntactic category as (8.7). In theory, it would have been possible to examine tokens with BE + past participle manually and exclude those where the participle was likely to be adjectival with the aid of, for instance, Quirk et al.'s (1985: §§3.74–8) passive gradient. However, not all of Quirk et al.'s criteria are applicable to non-finite structures, which would have made it difficult to apply the same gradient to potential past-participle clauses. Both verbal and adjectival past participles were therefore included in the counts as regards relative as well as participle clauses, as long as the participle was a possible verb form.

Participle clauses present a retrieval problem as they do not contain relative markers that can be searched for. Hundt et al. (2012a: 230) even suggest that "participle clauses are virtually impossible to extract from a tagged-only corpus" and instead opt for retrieval based on parsed material. However, the risk of parsing error complicates this choice. Hundt et al. (2012a: 227) provide data on the precision of their automated retrieval of participle clauses, which ranges between 78 and 89 per cent, but I was unable to find corresponding information on recall. However, parser recall for relative clauses with *that*, a *wh*-word, or zero as relative marker was between 40 and 50 per cent after parser adaptation (Hundt et al. 2012a: 216), which was deemed too low for the purposes of the present study. For this reason, I instead based retrieval on tagged corpus texts combined with manual post-processing, the extra work involved in achieving high recall and precision notwithstanding. A number of trial searches were carried out and compared with manual identification of participle clauses in individual corpus texts until recall was sufficiently high. As the taggers had difficulty assigning participles to the correct syntactic category in some contexts, a fairly wide selection of tags was retrieved.

For participle clauses in CNNE, words that (i) had been tagged as singular nouns, plural nouns, or proper nouns or (ii) belonged to a preselected set of pronouns (see note 4) were retrieved if they were followed by the following tags at a distance of no more than ten words:

- For present-participle clauses: a word ending in *-ing* tagged as a present participle, a premodifying adjective, a singular noun, or a premodifying noun.
- For past-participle clauses: a word tagged as a past participle, a past-tense verb, an adjective heading a noun phrase, or a postmodifying adjective.

In the S-coefficient subcorpus, the tag for *-ing* forms proved very reliable, and all forms the tagger considered ambiguous between past-tense and past-participle readings had been manually disambiguated (see Section 4.5.1); thus only *-ing*-form and past-participle tags needed to be taken into account. In other respects, the same searches were carried out as for CNNE.

Virtually all participle clauses had possible relative-clause equivalents. The main difficulty in deciding what participle clauses to include in the variationist analysis – a difficulty that also affected counts for relative clauses – instead concerned ambiguity, which has long been a problem for variationist analyses in general (see, for instance, Tagliamonte 2012: 238–9). In this case study, the non-restrictive paradigm proved problematic from this perspective. As Quirk et al. (1985: §17.34) note, it is very often difficult to distinguish non-restrictive adnominal participle clauses (which would be relevant tokens) from adverbial participle clauses (which do not have relative-clause equivalents and should be excluded).[10] Consider (8.9):

(8.9) The flames, **fanned by the breeze**, were 10 ft. high. (CNNE: 1875–95, MG0012)

(8.9') The flames, **which were fanned by the breeze**, were 10 ft. high.

(8.9") Fanned by the breeze, *the flames* were 10 ft. high.

Example (8.9) might be read as corresponding either to a non-restrictive relative clause (8.9') or, as is evident from the fact that it can be moved, to an adverbial clause (8.9"). Because non-restrictive participle clauses like (8.9) thus have a different range of interpretation compared with relative clauses, I excluded the non-restrictive paradigm from the variationist comparison of relative and participle clauses (Section 8.3.1). Non-restrictive tokens were included in the text-linguistic analysis of participle clauses, as adnominal postmodification remains one possible function of

---

[10] Visser (1963–73: §§1,044, 1,062, 1,140–1, 1,147) classifies restrictive and non-restrictive participle clauses as *post-nominal attributive adjuncts* and *related free adjuncts*, respectively, though his categories include a wider range of structures than those studied here. In Visser's (1963–73: §1,147) framework, non-restrictive past-participle clauses appear to be given primarily adverbial interpretations.

such clauses, but I will present separate counts for restrictive and non-restrictive participle clauses in Section 8.3.2. As will be shown in that section, the textual functions of restrictive and non-restrictive participle clauses also differ.

A few tokens, for example (8.10), were ambiguous between a participle-clause reading and an augmented-absolute reading in which an absolute construction would have been introduced ("augmented") by a preposition, typically *with* (see van de Pool 2016: 22–4, 239–316 for an in-depth discussion of augmented absolutes).

(8.10) The representative of the Upper House, who did not take spirits and water, sat calmly dignified in his arm-chair by the fireplace, and in front of him, on the other side, sat his wife, with *black thread mittens drawn tightly over her little hands and thin arms*, bolt upright, and conscious of her rank. (CONCE: Fiction, 1870–1900, Besant, p. I.82)

Drawn . . . arms in (8.10) can be expanded into a relative clause (. . . *mittens that/which were/had been drawn* . . .), which makes it a potentially valid token. However, I follow van de Pool (2016: 23) in considering structures like (8.10) as absolute constructions even when they are augmented by a preposition;[11] they were thus not included in the counts.

To ensure that the semi-automated retrieval based on tagged texts had resulted in sufficient recall, two texts from the S-coefficient subcorpus and four texts from CNNE were randomly selected and examined manually. Relative clauses had the highest recall figures (100 per cent in CONCE; 94 per cent in CNNE), followed by present-participle clauses (93 per cent for both corpora) and past-participle clauses (84 and 87 per cent, respectively). This stratification in recall, which should be borne in mind when results are interpreted, is most likely due to differences among the features and between the taggers. Relative clauses have an overt relative marker, and the tagger used for CONCE was very accurate in identifying tokens where *who*, *which*, and *that* may be relative markers; the lower recall figure for CNNE is due to the context requirement that a noun should occur to the left of the relative marker, which was necessary as the tagger used for CNNE did not identify relative pronouns as a separate subcategory. Present-participle clauses also have a ubiquitous marker – the form in *-ing* – but required a noun in the preceding co-text for both corpora, which explains the similarity in recall between (i) present-participle clauses in

---

[11] Although Quirk et al. (1985) classify such clauses as supplementive rather than absolute, they note (§15.60na) that clauses introduced by *with(out)* "often convey little more than a vague notion of accompanying circumstance".

both corpora and (ii) relative clauses in CNNE. In past-participle clauses, in contrast, there is no common formal denominator, as past participles can take different forms, many of which are identical to past-tense forms. The slightly better recall figure for CNNE is most likely due to both past-tense and past-participle tags being retrieved for this corpus; in CONCE, ambiguous tags had been corrected, but the few cases where the tagger erroneously assigned an unambiguous past-tense tag to a past participle would not have been retrieved. On the whole, however, these recall figures were deemed acceptable.

A brief word on the subdivision of relative and participle clauses into restrictive and non-restrictive tokens is in order. This distinction has been the subject of a great deal of debate in the scholarly literature; for instance, scholars have suggested that restrictiveness is better seen as a continuum, that binary categorization is insufficient (see, for instance, Rydén 1984), or that relative clauses should be subdivided using different categories (see Huddleston and Pullum 2002: §12.4 for an example of the last strategy). Denison and Hundt (2013) propose a four-way distinction in which a relative clause can be restrictive, aspective (where the relative clause is part of the intonation contour of its matrix clause and where the information in the relative clause is essential to the discourse although the antecedent has already been clearly identified), non-restrictive, or continuative (a subcategory of non-restrictive clauses where the clause is added at what could have been the end of the sentence); however, they also allow for underdetermined (e.g. "restrictive/aspective") and ambiguous tokens. They go through several criteria for restrictiveness in order to classify their data and demonstrate that their typology may help to decrease the number of indeterminate tokens.

Denison and Hundt's (2013) typology and discussion were very helpful when I classified the CNNE and CONCE data. However, as the present study does not focus wholly on the issue of restrictiveness, time limitations precluded adopting as careful a coding scheme as the one they suggest. Instead, I followed Hundt et al. (2012a) in maintaining a binary distinction between restrictive and non-restrictive clauses for relative as well as participle clauses.

My classification focussed on two of the features mentioned by Denison and Hundt (2013: 141): whether the clause (i) restricted the set of entities denoted by the head and (ii) was essential for full understanding of the matrix clause. If the answer to (i) and (ii) was "yes", the clause was coded as restrictive; if the answer was "no", it was coded as non-restrictive. If both restrictive and non-restrictive readings seemed possible, I examined the co-text further to see which reading was more probable. This examination included considering the occurrence of punctuation around the postmodifier and (for relative clauses) the choice of relative marker.

Using punctuation as a criterion is not generally a reliable method when applied to historical texts, but texts do move closer to present-day norms when we approach the twentieth century. In Montgomery's (1989) analysis of an early-nineteenth-century version of the New Testament, 72.2 per cent of restrictive relative clauses but only 6.6 per cent of non-restrictive clauses lacked punctuation (Montgomery 1989: 134). Denison and Hundt (2013: 149) found punctuation "to be somewhat more consistent than [they] had expected" in their Modern English data set; in their analysis of nineteenth-century Science texts from A Representative Corpus of Historical English Registers (ARCHER), only 5.1 per cent of clearly non-restrictive clauses lacked punctuation, and a mere 4.8 per cent of clearly restrictive clauses were preceded by a punctuation mark. Against the background of those results, it was deemed possible to use the presence or absence of punctuation before the postmodifier as a partial indication of restrictiveness in the classification of nineteenth-century data. Similarly, although the relative marker *that* is not wholly limited to restrictive clauses, Hundt et al. (2012a: 224) show that, in British nineteenth-century scientific writing, *that* was very rare in non-restrictive relative clauses (1 token out of 54). The occurrence of *that* was thus taken as an indication that the token was restrictive in cases of doubt. In the few cases where doubt remained after close scrutiny, the token was classified as non-restrictive in order to maintain high precision in the variationist analysis, which included only restrictive environments.

8.3 Results

8.3.1 Variationist Analyses

In CNNE, the relevant participle and relative clauses pattern as shown in Tables 8.1 and 8.2.

Table 8.1 *Restrictive present-participle clauses and restrictive active relative clauses in CNNE by period*

Period	Participle		Relative		Total
	#	%	#	%	
1	138	32.3	289	67.7	427
2	229	44.8	282	55.2	511
Total	367	39.1	571	60.9	938

Table 8.2 *Restrictive past-participle clauses and restrictive passive relative clauses in CNNE by period*

Period	Participle		Relative		Total
	#	%	#	%	
1	478	84.8	86	15.2	564
2	618	84.7	112	15.3	730
Total	1,096	84.7	198	15.3	1,294

As these tables show, the variationist perspective yields different results depending on which paradigm is considered. There is a clear tendency towards densification as regards present-participle clauses (Table 8.1), which account for less than a third of tokens in the first period but for almost 45 per cent in the late nineteenth century, a difference that is statistically significant (d.f. = 1; χ^2 = 15.25; $p < 0.001$). In contrast, there is virtually no change in the proportions of past-participle clauses and passive relative clauses. Despite a clear increase in the frequency of past-participle clauses (see Section 8.3.2 for frequency counts), the proportions of the two clause types remain virtually identical across time, because a similar increase is attested for passive relative clauses.

The figures for the S-coefficient subcorpus of CONCE paint a different picture. Table 8.3 presents results for present-participle clauses vs. active relative clauses. There are few clear increases in the proportion of present-participle clauses. Debates, Drama, Letters, and Trials display indications of changes in the other direction, but as none of the differences is statistically significant (in Drama, the difference does not bear testing owing to low expected frequencies), the situation is perhaps best considered stable, as is the case for Fiction. Science displays a difference approaching significance (d.f. = 1; χ^2 = 1.99; $p = 0.158$) in the direction of densification; this is of some interest, as Leech et al. (2009: 218) and Biber and Gray (2012: 316) suggest that academic Late Modern English was susceptible to pressure in the direction of economy of expression. Surprisingly, however, the only significant change among the genres in CONCE is in the opposite direction: present-participle clauses become significantly less likely to occur in place of active relative clauses in History (d.f. = 1; χ^2 = 14.35; $p < 0.001$). I shall return to possible reasons

Table 8.3 Restrictive present-participle clauses and active relative clauses in the S-coefficient subcorpus by period and genre

Genre	Period 1				Period 3				Total			
	Participle		Relative		Participle		Relative		Participle		Relative	
	#	%	#	%	#	%	#	%	#	%	#	%
Debates	19	34.5	36	65.5	22	25.0	66	75.0	41	28.7	102	71.3
Drama	5	12.8	34	87.2	3	8.3	33	91.7	8	10.7	67	89.3
Fiction	10	13.2	66	86.8	11	15.5	60	84.5	21	14.3	126	85.7
History	18	24.0	57	76.0	8	6.0	126	94.0	26	12.4	183	87.6
Letters	23	28.4	58	71.6	14	23.3	46	76.7	37	26.2	104	73.8
Science	42	32.6	87	67.4	58	40.8	84	59.2	100	36.9	171	63.1
Trials	40	42.1	55	57.9	31	38.8	49	61.3	71	40.6	104	59.4
Total	157	28.5	393	71.5	147	24.1	464	75.9	304	26.2	857	73.8

for this discrepancy between History and Science, which was also commented on in Chapter 7, in Section 8.3.2.

The results for past-participle clauses vs. passive relative clauses are given in Table 8.4. The period differences for Debates, Fiction, Science, and Trials in Table 8.4 do not reach significance, and the results for Drama cannot be tested for significance owing to the complete absence of restrictive passive relative clauses in this genre. The Letters genre changes significantly towards a higher proportion of past-participle clauses (d.f. = 1; χ^2 = 4.91; p = 0.027), though the raw frequencies indicate that this shift may be due mainly to the avoidance of passive relative clauses. History, again, stands out by changing significantly towards extended use of relative clauses compared with participle clauses (d.f. = 1; χ^2 = 7.90; p = 0.005), that is, the opposite trend from what would be expected in densification.

The variationist analyses of the restrictive paradigm reveal that the distribution of relative and participle clauses is clearly affected by voice. Active relative clauses always outnumber present-participle clauses; past-participle clauses are consistently more frequent than passive relative clauses. In other words, in the restricted environments where the two constructions can be considered exchangeable, the unmarked choices appear to be (i) active relative clauses and (ii) past-participle clauses (cf. Biber et al. 1999: §8.8.1.1).

To sum up the findings so far, there are three genres that display change in the material examined: news texts increasingly favour present-participle clauses over active relative clauses; the Letters genre contains more past-participle clauses compared with passive relative clauses across time; and in History, participle clauses become a less popular choice regardless of the voice of the corresponding relative clause. The results support the indication in Chapter 7 that academic writing does not behave uniformly with regard to densification in nineteenth-century English: while Science is stable with some possible tendency towards densification, History changes away from the trend towards densification found for science prose in previous research (e.g. Biber and Gray 2012: 323).

8.3.2 *Text-Linguistic Analyses*

In this section, I will look at participle clauses – non-restrictive as well as restrictive – in more detail from the perspective of normalized frequencies. Where relevant, relative clauses will also be considered. In addition,

Table 8.4 *Restrictive past-participle clauses and passive relative clauses in the S-coefficient subcorpus by period and genre*

Genre	Period 1				Period 3				Total			
	Participle		Relative		Participle		Relative		Participle		Relative	
	#	%	#	%	#	%	#	%	#	%	#	%
Debates	55	76.4	17	23.6	40	63.5	23	36.5	95	70.4	40	29.6
Drama	11		–		16		–		27		–	
Fiction	36	78.3	10	21.7	22	78.6	6	21.4	58	78.4	16	21.6
History	46	79.3	12	20.7	36	55.4	29	44.6	82	66.7	41	33.3
Letters	21	58.3	15	41.7	22	84.6	4	15.4	43	69.4	19	30.6
Science	123	73.7	44	26.3	104	73.2	38	26.8	227	73.5	82	26.5
Trials	46	68.7	21	31.3	49	59.8	33	40.2	95	63.8	54	36.2
Total	338	74.0	119	26.0	289	68.5	133	31.5	627	71.3	252	28.7

Table 8.5 *Restrictive and non-restrictive participle clauses in CNNE by period*

Period	Present-participle clauses			Past-participle clauses		
	Rest.	Non-rest.	Total	Rest.	Non-rest.	Total
1	138	179	317	478	176	654
2	229	147	376	618	161	779
Total	367	326	693	1,096	337	1,433

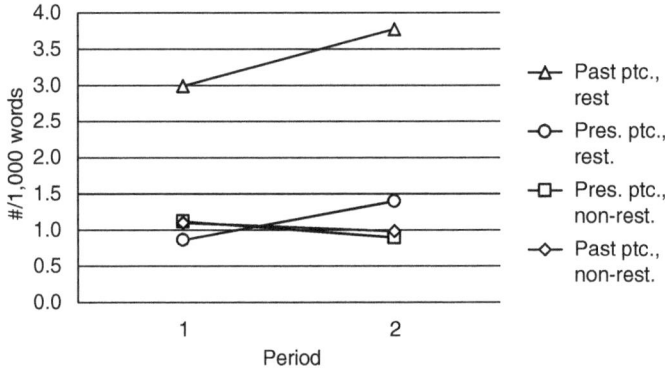

Figure 8.1 Participle clauses in CNNE by period (frequencies per 1,000 words)

newspaper-specific tendencies in CNNE as well as text-specific and/or idiolectal preferences in the S-coefficient subcorpus will be discussed.

Table 8.5 and Figure 8.1 present the results for CNNE. As Figure 8.1 shows, with a frequency between 3.0 and 3.8 tokens per 1,000 words, restrictive past-participle clauses stand out from the other clause types, which cluster in the 0.9–1.4 range. In terms of change over time, it is the restrictive clause types that become more entrenched in newspaper language: present-participle clauses (which, as shown in Section 8.3.1, also became more likely to be employed instead of active relative clauses) increase by 62 per cent and past-participle clauses by 26 per cent. The non-restrictive clause types display comparatively low and decreasing frequencies (though, as will be seen below, they are nevertheless more frequent in newspaper language than in most other genres). My discussion of CNNE here will focus on the restrictive paradigm, which appears to be more open to change; I will comment on non-restrictive participle clauses in CNNE further below, when I account for the patterns in CONCE.

The frequency developments indicate that, consciously or subconsciously, newspaper writers expected their readers to be able to process increasingly compressed information over the nineteenth century. Newspapers that appear to be spearheading this development towards the condensed mode of expression permitted by restrictive participle clauses include *Lloyd's*, the *Manchester Guardian*, and *The Times*, all of which feature a total frequency of restrictive participle clauses of between 6.4 and 6.9 tokens per 1,000 words in period 2. By way of comparison, the highest score for any paper in period 1 is 5.5 (the *Manchester Guardian*, which may thus have been an early adopter of this style). Example (8.11) is a case in point:

(8.11) In some recent contracts for vessels to be constructed of open-hearth steel, the material has been purchased as low as £10 10s. per ton, which is less than *half the lowest price* **paid for steel plates only ten or twelve years ago**. Manufacturers have, moreover, applied their energies to the production of *a metal* **specially adapted to shipbuilding** – *a metal so mild as to bend rather than break in case of a severe strain, and yet* **possessing a higher tensile strength than wrought iron**. (CNNE: 1875–95, TT0017)

Several noun phrases in (8.11) place considerable demands on the reader in terms of length as well as syntactic complexity; for instance, the entire passage *the production . . . wrought iron* in fact consists only of noun-phrase material complementing the preposition *to*. In contrast, there are only three finite clauses in (8.11). Such complexity presupposes a target group whose members are well acquainted with a written mode of presentation.

This suggested association between assumed readership and restrictive participle clauses is supported by evidence from the other end of the frequency range. The paper with the lowest frequency of restrictive (as well as non-restrictive) participle clauses (2.0 tokens per 1,000 words) is the *Poor Man's Guardian*, most of whose readers came from the working classes, and which argued for an extension of the suffrage and for the right of members of the working class to the products of their labour (Hollis 1970: 106; see also Chapter 7). A short extract from the *Poor Man's*

Guardian (8.12), in which another paper – the *Weekly Dispatch* – is criticized, looks dramatically different from (8.11):

(8.12) Open your eyes, we beseech you, and read this paper as it ought to be read; examine its opinions thoroughly and deliberately; and you will be ashamed of having so long subscribed to your own unworthiness and degradation; you give it all its power, and that power you will find invariably employed against yourselves; nor be deceived by an occasional observation in favour of a poor soldier, or its advocacy of somewhat greater comforts for your oppressed classes; these things are but intended to make you contented with an unnatural condition of servitude and dependence, and at most are but a mere fraction of your positive rights; the merest compassion would give you these things, while JUSTICE owes you a thousand times as much. (CNNE: 1830–50, PG0006)

While (8.12) may seem to feature a highly complex sentence structure – the entire extract is one single orthographic sentence – this impression is largely an effect of punctuation practice that has little effect on readers' processing cost: semicolons are used to separate main clauses that would typically be placed in separate sentences today. Structurally, (8.12) relies on finite clauses (13 ×) to a far greater extent than (8.11). The remarkable difference in the linguistic choices made by writers for *The Times* in period 2 and the *Poor Man's Guardian* in period 1 clearly indicates that newspaper writers and editors adapted their language to their preconceptions about their intended target groups, an impression that is further strengthened by the finding that the *Poor Man's Guardian* also displayed the lowest frequency of nominal premodifiers of all papers in CNNE (see Chapter 7).[12] Moreover, the newspaper with the second lowest overall frequency of participle clauses, the Chartist *Northern Star* (2.9), was also a voice of working-class discontent. Unlike the *Poor Man's Guardian*, the *Northern Star* was stamped, which put its price beyond the means of many workers. However, it was designed to be read aloud (Brown 1985: 50–1), which made it possible for one copy of the paper to be shared among a large group of people; this type of audience design is also likely to have constrained the use of heavy and complex noun-phrase structures.

---

[12] As discussed in Chapter 7, the *Poor Man's Guardian* was run mainly by members of the middle classes (Claridge 2017: 140), and this socio-economic distance from the intended readership is visible in (8.12). As Claridge (2017: 142–7) notes, the paper typically separates itself (*we*) from its readers (*you*) rather than uniting the two groups in an inclusive *we*; the readers' task is to be instructed by the paper. The linguistic adaptation implied in the difference between (8.11) and (8.12) was thus not mirrored by sociocultural identification with its readers on the part of the publishers of the *Poor Man's Guardian*.

The genres in CONCE pattern very differently with respect to the four types of participle clause. Table 8.6 presents raw frequencies, while Figures 8.2–5 chart the development of normalized frequencies with one figure per clause type, beginning with restrictive present-participle clauses in Figure 8.2. (Note that Figures 8.2–5 do not have the same frequency scale on the value axis.)

My discussion focusses on History and Science, as these genres display the clearest trends in diachrony. The variationist analysis in Section 8.3.1

Table 8.6 *Restrictive and non-restrictive participle clauses in the S-coefficient subcorpus by genre and period*

Genre	Period	Present-participle clauses			Past-participle clauses		
		Rest.	Non-rest.	Total	Rest.	Non-rest.	Total
Debates	1	19	10	29	55	7	62
	3	22	4	26	40	3	43
	Total	41	14	55	95	10	105
Drama	1	5	4	9	11	5	16
	3	3	1	4	16	1	17
	Total	8	5	13	27	6	33
Fiction	1	10	32	42	36	39	75
	3	11	27	38	22	24	46
	Total	21	59	80	58	63	121
History	1	18	15	33	46	26	72
	3	8	14	22	36	8	44
	Total	26	29	55	82	34	116
Letters	1	23	11	34	21	7	28
	3	14	6	20	22	8	30
	Total	37	17	54	43	15	58
Science	1	42	22	64	123	27	150
	3	58	8	66	104	6	110
	Total	100	30	130	227	33	260
Trials	1	40	1	41	46	5	51
	3	31	8	39	49	4	53
	Total	71	9	80	95	9	104

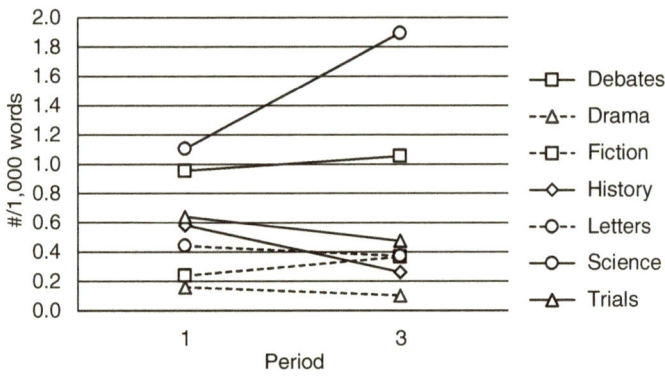

Figure 8.2 Restrictive present-participle clauses by genre and period in the S-coefficient subcorpus (frequencies per 1,000 words)

indicated that Science, though mainly stable, may have tended towards densification over time, whereas History was moving in the opposite direction. The normalized frequencies given in Figure 8.2 largely support this result: the frequency in History decreases by 55 per cent, while restrictive present-participle clauses become 72 per cent more common in Science between the periods investigated. These developments in opposite directions in two written expository genres are remarkable. Science even exhibits higher normalized frequencies than CNNE (cf. Figure 8.1). The dramatic increase between periods 1 and 3 is due mainly to one text, Bateson's *Materials for the Study of Variation*, with a frequency of no less than 3.4 tokens per 1,000 words. The increase may thus be due in part to idiolectal preferences, which makes it interesting to see whether Bateson might be innovative in his use of restrictive present-participle clauses. The commonest verb used by Bateson in such clauses is STAND (8 ×), which is often used to describe the position of teeth, as in (8.13):

(8.13) Of the cases of numerical Variation in teeth the larger number concern the presence or absence of *teeth* **standing at the ends of Series**. (CONCE: Science, 1870–1900, Bateson, p. 269)

Although, like other stance verbs, STAND can express dynamic as well as stative meanings (Quirk et al. 1985: §4.32), the sense in (8.13) and similar tokens appears stative: the discussion concerns the permanent position of teeth in the series to which they belong. Biber et al. (1999: §8.8.1.1) note that many verbs in present-participle clauses have stative senses in

Present-Day English. Bateson's frequent use of stative senses of STAND in these clauses seems modern in this regard.

The decrease in the frequency of restrictive present-participle clauses in History partly supports the hypothesis that relative clauses may have been increasingly used in place of participle clauses in this genre: the two highest frequencies of active restrictive relative clauses in the S-coefficient subcorpus are from History, period 3. However, idiolectal preferences are also noticeable: the text with the second-highest frequency of restrictive active relative clauses (4.5), Walpole's *History of England from the Conclusion of the Great War in 1815*, also has a near-average frequency of present-participle clauses (0.5), and these types of postmodifier frequently co-occur in the same passage, as in (8.14):

(8.14) The man, however, **who authorises**, not the adviser **who suggests a policy**, should have the credit **attaching to it**. (CONCE: History, 1870–1900, Walpole, p. VI.314)

Walpole thus appears to have had a preference for clausal postmodification in general.

The normalized frequencies of restrictive past-participle clauses are given in Figure 8.3. The figure reveals that the three expository genres have higher frequencies of restrictive past-participle clauses, which indicates that these clauses are associated with a high informational load. The non-expository genres, in contrast, converge on a low frequency of this clause type (0.6–0.7 tokens per 1,000 words) in period 3. As shown in Section 8.3.1, the Letters genre appears to change in the direction of

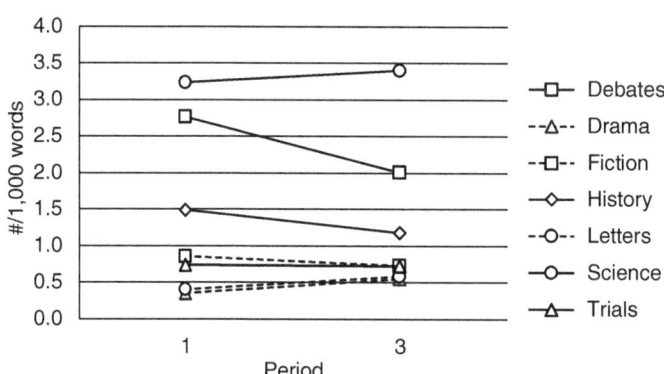

Figure 8.3 Restrictive past-participle clauses by genre and period in the S-coefficient subcorpus (frequencies per 1,000 words)

densification concerning restrictive past-participle clauses. However, Figure 8.3 reveals that the frequency of these clauses is quite stable in Letters; the change discussed in Section 8.3.1 is mainly due to the increased avoidance of passive relative clauses in Letters, period 3.

Debates and History exhibit decreasing frequencies of restrictive past-participle clauses, which tallies with results presented in Section 8.3.1. In Debates, it is possible that the shift from indirect to direct speech between periods 1 and 3 affects the results. Examples like (8.15) demonstrate that some passages from Debates, period 1 are characterized by a mixture of features that might be associated with spoken language, such as a high density of clauses, and features that would be rare in present-day speech, like two nested participle clauses (*that [contained in the book [alluded to]]*).

> (8.15) The Chancellor of the Exchequer, thought bringing forward one of the cases would answer every purpose. If there were a distinction of cases he could bring forward two. It would be better than encumbering the House with the whole. He was anxious the calumnies should be met and refuted, but wished the noble lord would seek better information than *that **contained in the book alluded to***. (CONCE: Debates, 1800–30, p. XV.479)

Although this hypothesis must remain speculative, it is possible that some formulations like the participle clauses in (8.15) were not original to the speech events, and that such interference decreased with the shift to direct speech that took place between the periods.

As regards History, there are no specific texts that stand out from the others in terms of frequency; instead, the genre as a whole appears to have developed towards relying more on relative than on participle clauses. It is possible that the difference between History and Science is due in part to different publication norms in the two fields. Nineteenth-century history writing was dominated by book-length publications (the oldest English-language history journal, the *English Historical Review*, was first published in 1886). In addition, as discussed in Section 7.4, books on history arguably had a wider readership than research in the natural and social sciences in the 1800s. Historians may have felt less pressure to densify their writing if they (i) worked in a field where books were the norm and (ii) had a partly non-specialist audience for those books. In the natural sciences, in contrast, periodicals had been an alternative form of publication since 1665, when the *Philosophical Transactions of the Royal Society* was first published;

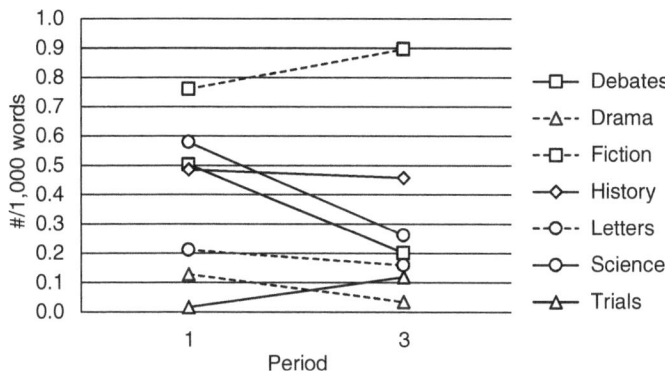

Figure 8.4 Non-restrictive present-participle clauses by genre and period in the S-coefficient subcorpus (frequencies per 1,000 words)

although the Science texts in CONCE were taken from monographs, the existence of an established, shorter medium of publication in the natural sciences may possibly have favoured economy of expression in general as part of a developing genre norm. As mentioned in Section 7.4, such genre norms may also have developed for social reasons instead of – or in addition to – functional pressures.

Science is the only genre in CONCE that displays frequencies close to those attested for newspaper language (cf. Figure 8.1). The two genres singled out by Biber and Gray (2012: 316) as being sensitive to pressure to economize on words owing to an increased informational load are thus also those that stand out in terms of high frequencies of restrictive past-participle clauses. However, in neither genre do these high frequencies – which also display moderate increases over time, by 5 per cent (Science) and 26 per cent (CNNE) respectively – appear to correlate with a replacement of passive relative clauses by past-participle clauses. There thus seems to be no straightforward substitutional relationship between the two structures.

I now turn to non-restrictive present-participle clauses. Normalized frequencies, which are considerably lower than for the restrictive paradigm, are given in Figure 8.4. As shown in Table 8.6, raw frequencies are too low to allow definite conclusions regarding diachronic trends in several cases (notably Drama and Trials), but by period 3 most genres in CONCE are characterized by low normalized frequencies, with the exception of Fiction and – to a lesser extent – History. Apart from Trials, Fiction is the most narrative genre in CONCE, and History changes in the direction of narrativity over time in Geisler's (2002: 258–62) factor-score analysis; this connection with narrative concerns may help to explain the distribution. Non-restrictive present-participle clauses often contribute to characterization by commenting either on a person (real or fictional) or on their speech or actions, as in (8.16–17):

(8.16) Even *Wheeler*, **distrusting his own men**, decided on asking him to take charge, with his armed retinue, of the treasury. (CONCE: History, 1870–1900, Walpole, p. VI.305)

(8.17) "Oh – ho – I like that!" said *Troy*, **recovering himself**. (CONCE: Fiction, 1870–1900, Hardy, p. II.122)

The increase attested for Fiction is supported by Grund's (2020) investigation of speech descriptors. Grund (2020: 305) found that participle constructions as speech descriptors appeared to become drastically more common than previously in the period 1850–1920 (though, as Grund notes, this increase may be due to an outlier in that period). The increase between the periods is not limited to individual Fiction texts in the CONCE data. In contrast, the comparatively high frequency in History, period 3 is mainly due to Walpole's text; as that text also featured high frequencies of other clausal postmodifiers, idiolectal preferences may be at work here.

As mentioned in Section 8.2, most non-restrictive participle clauses, including those in (8.16) and (8.17), are ambiguous between adnominal ('who distrusted his own men'; 'who recovered himself') and adverbial (e.g. 'because he distrusted his own men'; 'as he recovered himself') readings. This very ambiguity may be the reason for an author's choice to employ them, but it may also help to explain why Trials displays low frequencies of this construction despite being the most narrative genre in CONCE in Geisler's (2002) analysis. Ambiguity is not typically promoted in trials, where cross-examinations often focus on disambiguation and clarification. In addition, the fact that Trials are speech-based texts may constrain the occurrence of participle clauses; as Biber et al. (1999: §8.6.1) show, present-day conversation employs few non-finite postmodifiers in general.

The suggested connection with narrativity leaves the high frequencies of non-restrictive present-participle clauses in the Debates and Science samples from period 1 to be accounted for. As regards Science, this is entirely due to one text: Lyell's *Principles of Geology*. In this text, the use of such clauses in combination with descriptive adjectives seems to impart a narrative flavour that would be uncharacteristic of a present-day text in the natural sciences to sentences like (8.18):

(8.18) Not far from Soriano, which was levelled to the ground by the great shock of February the 5th, *a small valley*, **containing a beautiful olive-grove**, *called Fra Ramondo*, underwent a most extraordinary revolution. (Science, 1800–30, Lyell, p. 425)

Lyell may thus be conservative in his use of narrative features in a natural-sciences text. In Debates from period 1, although raw frequencies are too low to be wholly reliable (10 ×), non-restrictive present-participle clauses are frequently used to comment on the contents of a speech, Act of Parliament, question, document, etc., as in (8.19).

(8.19) Sir J. Nichols, **alluding to the pamphlet that had been mentioned**, said it contained gross and palpable misstatements. (CONCE: Debates, 1800–30, p. XV.476)

The use of such clauses seems to be connected with the shift of speech representation in Debates from indirect to direct speech mentioned above. In the absence of actual recordings, we cannot be certain about the origin of participle clauses like the one in (8.19), but it seems unlikely that Sir J. Nichols would have included it in his original speech event; instead, it looks as if it was inserted at a later stage. Such creation of a narratorial presence in Debates, period 1 would tally with the third-person mode in which the speeches were represented (see also the discussion of 8.15 above).

As shown in Figure 8.1, the frequency of non-restrictive present-participle clauses in CNNE goes down slightly across time and is roughly the same as that in Fiction towards the end of the century. As illustrated in (8.20), there may be a link between non-restrictive present-participle clauses and narrative concerns in the news texts as well.

(8.20) In the higher order, again, is produced a body of *men, rapacious, naturally unscrupulous as to the means of obtaining power, unwilling, or* **thinking it degrading, to live by their own labour**, *assuming to themselves the rank of an aristocracy without any of the external graces and refinements which sometimes varnish privilege in the eyes of the unprivileged*, and **looking to the offices of government as their natural inheritance**. (CNNE: 1830–50, DN0008)

Several non-restrictive present-participle clauses in CNNE, such as those in (8.20), insert narratorial, potentially subjective interpretations of places, people, documents, and so on into the texts.

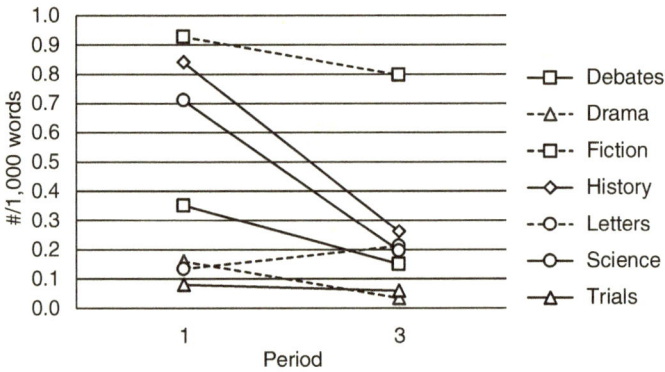

Figure 8.5 Non-restrictive past-participle clauses by genre and period in the S-coefficient subcorpus (frequencies per 1,000 words)

In sum, non-restrictive present-participle clauses appear to be connected to narrativity rather than densification. The decrease in their frequency attested in several genres should thus not be interpreted as evidence against densification in the data.

Finally, the results for non-restrictive past-participle clauses are given in Figure 8.5. In all non-expository genres except Fiction, to which I will return below, raw frequencies are so low that the only safe conclusion to be drawn is that, outside fiction, non-restrictive past-participle clauses are rare in non-expository writing. The expository genres exhibit parallel developments in that frequencies decrease by between 57 (Debates) and 72 per cent (Science). Moreover, in History and Science, the decreases would have been even more pronounced if it had not been for one outlier each in period 3 with relatively high frequencies: Lockyer's *Chemistry of the Sun* and Walpole's *History of England* (which, again, stands out in its preference for clausal postmodification). Especially in History, the decrease seems to be linked to a decrease in partly subjective commentary, as illustrated in (8.21):

(8.21) On the return of Herod, *his sister Salome,* **wounded at the haughtiness with which she had ever been treated by the proud Asmonean princess**, endeavoured to poison his mind with suspicions of his wife, whom she accused of too intimate correspondence with Joseph the governor. (CONCE: History, 1800–30, Milman, p. II.102)

In period 1, several non-restrictive past-participle clauses, for example (8.21), are used to comment on historical people's characteristics in a way that is largely absent from the samples from period 3.

Taken together, these developments leave Fiction and newspaper language as the only genres in which this clause type is reasonably frequent in the late 1800s (between 0.8 and 1.0 tokens per 1,000 words), despite minor decreases in frequency (by 14 and 11 per cent, respectively). In Fiction, the continued use of non-restrictive past-participle clauses indicates a connection between non-restrictive participle clauses and narrativity in general; as shown in (8.22), these clauses frequently present narrators' interpretations of characters' behaviour or utterances, much like the non-restrictive present-participle clause in (8.17).

(8.22) "No, miss. I don't – I know it is not true!" said Liddy, **frightened at Bathsheba's unwonted vehemence**. (CONCE: Fiction, 1870–1900, Hardy, p. I.330)

In contrast, the commonest function of non-restrictive past-participle clauses in CNNE is to provide background detail. One of the most frequent verbs is ACCOMPANY (15 ×), as in (8.23):

(8.23) *Mr. Valentine, an Inspector of the K Division of police,* **accompanied by Mr. Belson, a surgeon, in High-street, who was the parish doctor of St. John, Wapping, before the introduction of the New Poor Law, and is now one of the medical officers of the Stepney Union**, related to Mr. Broderip, at the Thames office, London, on Tuesday last, a case of severe distress which had come under their notice. (CNNE: 1830–50, NS0001)

In tokens like (8.23), the past-participle clause appears to fulfil a backgrounding function: Mr. Valentine's company is relegated to secondary status in terms of information structure.

8.4 Discussion

The analysis undertaken in this chapter has revealed that participle clauses as noun-phrase postmodifiers are a more multifaceted phenomenon than can be captured by simple proportion or frequency counts for all types taken together. Detailed examination of individual tokens from several genres is necessary if we wish to combine frequency data with information on the functions of the feature(s) examined.

If variationist and text-linguistic analyses are combined, there is support for the hypothesis that densification is taking place in some genres. From a variationist perspective, restrictive present-participle clauses become significantly more frequent compared with active restrictive relative clauses in CNNE. In Letters, restrictive past-participle clauses become significantly more common in relation to passive restrictive relative clauses. However, the findings for Letters are of doubtful validity as far as densification is concerned, as they seem mainly to be due to increased avoidance of passive relative clauses.

In addition, text-linguistic analyses revealed that the frequency of restrictive past-participle clauses increased by 26 per cent in CNNE, and that of restrictive present-participle clauses rose by 72 per cent in Science. As these diachronic increases take place in genres where previous research would predict that densification may be taking place, they should be taken into consideration even if they were not matched by statistically significant shifts from relative towards participle clauses. Taking such developments into account is especially important if the relationship between two constructions alone does not fully capture the choices actually made by nineteenth-century writers.

Outside the restrictive paradigm, participle clauses were considered only from a text-linguistic perspective, as the frequent ambiguity between adnominal and adverbial readings of non-restrictive participle clauses made a variationist approach unfeasible. The only genre that combines robust raw frequencies with an attested increase in frequency is Fiction, where non-restrictive present-participle clauses become 18 per cent more frequent over time. Fiction and newspaper language are the only genres that exhibit high frequencies of non-restrictive participle clauses at the end of the 1800s. Most non-restrictive participle clauses in these text categories are linked to narrative descriptions of characters and/or their utterances, but non-restrictive past-participle clauses in CNNE rather tend to achieve backgrounding and/or condensation of information, two functions that may of course be linked: non-finite structures are not only shorter but also more likely to be backgrounding compared with finite ones (Wårvik 1990: 533). But in general it is the restrictive participle clauses that appear to be primarily involved in densification.

Against this background, a question of general importance concerns whether participle clauses should be examined from a variationist or a text-linguistic perspective. The concept of densification presupposes the existence of interchangeable linguistic units with different sizes but roughly the same semantic content, which is also a requirement for applying a variationist framework. However, circumscribing the envelope of variation becomes problematic for relative and participle clauses. On the one hand, not all tokens of these constructions are interchangeable; as was demonstrated in Section 8.2, far from all relative clauses can be replaced

8.4 Discussion

with participle clauses. Moreover, many non-restrictive participle clauses are inherently ambiguous between adnominal and adverbial readings, and they are roughly equivalent to relative clauses only in their adnominal reading. In the absence of information on what the speaker or writer meant by each example, such ambiguous tokens can be argued to be simultaneously inside and outside the envelope of variation – perhaps a linguistic equivalent of Schrödinger's cat.

On the other hand, the variant field can arguably also be extended to include additional linguistic features. Kretzschmar (2015b: 24–8, 180) argues that the number of variants in a variant field is often underestimated by researchers. I discussed relative clauses with BE as main verb being problematic in Section 8.2; I opted for excluding these tokens, but if they had been included, some constructions with prepositional phrases would also have had to be included in the variant field; see (8.7). For yet other tokens, for example the non-restrictive (8.24), constructions with postposed adjectives are also potential variants given the possible paraphrase in (8.24'):

(8.24)   Yet this was denied to be a service, where the enemy fled with so much loss, that the roads were covered with his magazines, exploded; his mules, and beasts of burden, houghed or slaughtered; his carriages broken to pieces, and *his men,* **who were unable to follow his army,** *left to be cruelly massacred by an enraged and justly exasperated peasantry.* (CONCE: Debates, 1800–30, pp. XV.449–50)

(8.24') ... and *his men, unable to follow his army, left to be cruelly massacred by* ....

As will be discussed below, Sag (1997: 471) includes such structures in the category of reduced relative clauses.

A similar problem arises with many relative tokens with HAVE as main verb. Even if the relative clause is restrictive, so that there is no adverbial–adnominal ambiguity in the corresponding participle clause, the variant field is often difficult to pin down. Consider (8.25) and its two paraphrases (8.25') and (8.25"):

(8.25)   I know *many men among my own friends* **who have four or five votes for different constituencies.** (CONCE: Debates, 1870–1900, p. IV.1,184)

(8.25') I know *many men among my own friends* ***having four or five votes for different constituencies.***

(8.25") I know *many men among my own friends with four or five votes for different constituencies.*

A prepositional phrase introduced by *with*, as in (8.25"), often seems highly idiomatic and roughly semantically equivalent to a relative clause with HAVE (see also Quirk et al. 1985: §17.37; Biber et al. 1999: §8.9). As participle clauses with main-verb HAVE on the pattern of (8.25') occurred with some frequency in the material, relative clauses like (8.25) were included in the counts in the present study, but it should be noted that the envelope of variation is arguably incomplete for these tokens, as tokens of *with* that were potentially equivalent to relative and participle clauses were not examined.

The idiolectal perspective adds a further level of difficulty. Can it be assumed, for example, that all speakers considered non-restrictive participle clauses ambiguous between adverbial and adnominal readings to the same extent? The decision to exclude these clauses from the variationist study was based on the hypothesis that they were ambiguous to all language users; but that is a hypothesis only.

Within sociolinguistics, researchers sometimes relax the criterion of semantic equivalence somewhat, and labels such as *weak complementarity* and *structural equivalence* have been suggested instead (Tagliamonte 2012: 16–17). In such approaches, criteria such as whether two or more features are used in identical linguistic environments and whether their proportions of occurrence appear to correlate with an extralinguistic factor are important in order to establish a type of variant field. Restrictive relative and participle clauses do occur in the same linguistic environments, and their proportions of occurrence vary with genre. It may thus be possible to consider them variants in this slightly weaker sense of the term. However, the problem with other linguistic features being potential variants in some environments would still need to be addressed, and this problem is likely to increase in importance the more relaxed the notion of equivalence becomes.

Insights from several fields of linguistics have a bearing on this discussion. Participle clauses are sometimes called *reduced relative clauses* by scholars, which implies functional equivalence. Sag (1997) includes participle clauses – as well as prepositional and adjective phrases that can be expanded into relative clauses (e.g. *the people in Rome* from something like *the people who live/are in Rome*) – in this category, and also explicitly refers to his notion of a reduced relative clause as a "type of relative clause" (Sag 1997: 471).[13] The term *reduced relative (clause)* is also used by Harwood

---

[13] Quirk et al. (1985: §§7.21, 17.56) also argue that postposed adjectives can typically be seen as reduced relative clauses.

(2018) and in many studies of language processing, for example Spivey-Knowlton et al. (1993), Juffs (1998), Rah and Adone (2010), and Yang and Shih (2013). These studies often focus on how native speakers and/or learners process sentences such as *The horse raced past the barn fell*, where *raced* is likely to be interpreted as the main-clause verb phrase until *fell* is encountered. However, the three major grammars of Present-Day English adopt a more neutral terminology. Quirk et al. (1985: §§17.28–9) and Biber et al. (1999: §8.8.1) both use the term *participle clauses*, though they note that these clauses often correspond to or have paraphrases with relative clauses. Huddleston and Pullum (2002: §14.9) refer to them as *participials* and explicitly reject a relative-clause analysis "since there is no possibility of them containing a relative phrase".

A number of studies of the relative paradigm have identified differences between relative and participle clauses. Hundt et al. (2012b: 5–6) exclude participle clauses from their retrieval of relatives in historical material. The reasons for their choice include the difficulty of deciding which structures (e.g. postmodifying prepositional phrases and postpositive adjectives) can be expanded into relative clauses, the fact that not all present participles in present-participle clauses correspond to a progressive in a relative clause (e.g. *a syrup resembling Molasses* ≈ *a syrup which resembles Molasses*), and the ambiguity between adverbial and adnominal functions of non-restrictive participle clauses (see also Section 8.2).

In what they call a meaning-through-syntax view of language comprehension, McKoon and Ratcliff's (2003: 493) approach is that a passive relative clause and a past-participle clause "are assumed, until it has been shown otherwise, to have different meanings".[14] Past-participle clauses are argued to allow "only verbs that provide a template structure in which causality resides in some entity other than the one that is the head of the reduced relative" (McKoon and Ratcliff 2003: 496); in contrast, situations where the antecedent engages in the activity, which is thus seen as having an internal cause, or where there is a change of state of the antecedent owing to an internal cause, are argued not to allow past-participle clauses (McKoon and Ratcliff 2003: 497). The authors support this argument with, among other things, corpus studies, an acceptability test, and an

---

[14] Somewhat surprisingly, McKoon and Ratcliff (2003) nevertheless refer to participle clauses as *reduced relatives*. While their argument covers restrictive clauses only, their general principle that "a difference in syntactic structure is likely to correspond to a difference in meaning" (McKoon and Ratcliff 2003: 493) implies that there should be a semantic difference in the non-restrictive paradigm as well. The fact that non-restrictive participle clauses often exhibit semantic ambiguity with adverbial clauses (see Section 8.2) adds a further layer of complexity to the issue.

experiment where subjects were asked to rate pairs of sentences with passive relative clauses and their corresponding past-participle clauses according to how well written they were. They demonstrate that the occurrence restriction is not as pronounced for passive relative clauses (McKoon and Ratcliff 2003: 509). According to McKoon and Ratcliff (2003: 502–4), their results indicate that past-participle clauses are not simply abbreviated versions of passive relative clauses: a noun phrase with a past-participle clause introduces one single entity into the discourse, while a noun phrase with a passive relative clause introduces both an entity (the noun phrase minus the relative clause) and information about that entity (the relative clause); the linguistic and extralinguistic environment may make one of these constructions more suitable than the other.[15]

My tentative conclusion is that the text-linguistic analysis in Section 8.3.2 is the safer option at present, considering (i) the difficulty of establishing a variant field that combines high recall and high precision, (ii) the different functions of the types of participle clause investigated, and (iii) the arguments in previous research against seeing participle clauses as straightforward, reduced versions of relative clauses. However, when we know more about the exact relationship – semantic and structural – between participle clauses and other linguistic features, a variationist perspective may be feasible. Moreover, even at the present stage, variationist analyses may provide valuable complementary evidence; for instance, the assumption that the increase in restrictive present-participle clauses in CNNE is connected to densification is certainly strengthened by the statistically significant shift in relation to active restrictive relative clauses. Moreover, the differences that have been established between relative and participle clauses in previous research do not in themselves constitute evidence against these two constructions being variants; for instance, the genitive and the *of*-construction are often treated as variants in some environments, although they differ syntactically in several respects.

As regards other important findings in the chapter, the investigation has highlighted the importance of considering the four types of participle clause separately, as they fulfil partly different functions. The relative rarity of the non-restrictive clause types by the end of the 1800s might have led to their narrative and backgrounding functions being obscured by the distribution and functions of their

---

[15] McKoon and Ratcliff's (2003) study stimulated a debate on the meaning-through-syntax model; see McRae et al. (2005a), McKoon and Ratcliff (2005), and McRae et al. (2005b).

more frequent restrictive counterparts if separate analyses had not been carried out.

The pronounced differences between Science and History (see also Chapter 7) are also worthy of note. Especially when it comes to restrictive participle clauses, which are most indicative of densification, History and Science display very different trajectories. Although it is well known that academic writing is a heterogeneous genre in Present-Day English (see, for instance, Gray and Biber 2018: 135), such pronounced differentiation between two written expository genres was unexpected. The discrepancy is probably due to a combination of factors, including a more narrative focus in History writing and a more noticeable trend towards economy in the natural and/or social sciences. Biber and Gray (2016: 112) demonstrate that the frequency of participle clauses varies in present-day academic English as well: the sciences favour especially present-participle clauses to a greater extent than do the humanities.

Finally, the idiolectal perspective has been of some importance. In particular, idiolects that appeared conservative were identified in academic writing. The unexpectedly high frequency of non-restrictive present-participle clauses in Science, period 1 was shown to be due to an outlier text containing several narrative features that were becoming uncharacteristic of scientific writing at the time. Similarly, a conservative outlier in History, period 3, featured an unexpectedly high frequency of non-restrictive past-participle clauses, used as a vehicle for partly subjective characterization.

In CNNE, important insights were gained by comparing individual newspapers. Many articles in the *Poor Man's Guardian* were written with very little participle-clause postmodification, which can arguably be explained with reference to the target group of the newspaper. This hypothesis was further strengthened by the finding that the *Northern Star*, another paper with a largely working-class readership, also disfavoured participle clauses. Moreover, the *Poor Man's Guardian* was the paper with the lowest frequency of nominal premodifiers (see Chapter 7), the other feature indicating densification that has been studied in this book. The linguistic make-up of nineteenth-century newspapers aimed at the working classes is clearly a topic that deserves further study.

More work on participle clauses is needed to establish a valid envelope of variation. Further linguistic and extralinguistic factors that affect the distribution of relative and participle clauses should also be examined. To take one example, I included both affirmative and negated clauses in the analyses in this chapter, because negated participle clauses like *not admitting of delay* in *Yesterday were admitted at the General Infirmary 26 In and 54 Out-Patients, 9 of the former and 14 of the latter being cases not admitting of delay* (CNNE: 1830–50, LM0002) do occur in the material. However, the presence of negation appears to make participle clauses a less likely variant, and this hypothesis and others could be tested in studies based on larger data sets. Finally, within historical pragmatics, qualitative form-to-function analyses of what purposes different types of participle clauses serve in texts would fill an important gap in research and increase our understanding of what choices language users make when using this clause type. Nevertheless, I hope to have shown that the study of participle clauses can shed light on several important topics in diachronic linguistics, including densification, variationist vs. text-linguistic frequency measures, genre differentiation, and the importance of considering particular publications, idiolects, and linguistic environments.

CHAPTER 9

Concluding Discussion

In this book, I have attempted to reach three goals, outlined in Chapter 1. In this concluding chapter, I will revisit these aims and account for how they were addressed in Sections 9.1–9.3, before ending the book with some brief remarks in Section 9.4. As full references to previous work have been given in Chapters 1–8, I provide fewer references in this concluding discussion.

9.1 The Stability Paradox

The first aim of the study was to critically examine the claim that LModE displays relatively little language change and/or comparatively few changes to the structure of the language. I showed in Chapter 2 that there is an apparent mismatch between sociocultural and linguistic change between 1700 and 1900. A large number of changes to LModE society promoted the weakening of existing strong network ties as well as the establishment of new weak ties. Such developments can be expected to correlate with widespread language change, yet LModE appears to feature little structural change compared with previous periods. This results in what I referred to as the stability paradox.

In Chapter 3, which was devoted to resolving the stability paradox, I argued that the true locus of language – and of language change – is a language user's idiolect. Communal languages such as English are abstractions from shared properties of a large number of idiolects. Owing to widespread convergence resulting from interaction between speakers, idiolects identified as belonging to the same language share a large number of properties. Languages can thus often be studied and described as if they were entities with an independent existence, but it is important not to confuse the idiolectal level with the language level when we attempt to quantify linguistic change. Since the idiolect is the true locus of change, a valid measure of change should start out from the number of idiolects that have gone through changes, not from changes perceived in the (structure of the) communal language.

The fact that the idiolect is the most natural unit of language change does not invalidate analyses such as those by Nevalainen et al. (2020b), who attempt to correlate communal-language change – as evidenced in the Helsinki Corpus – with extralinguistic events during the Middle English period. However, such correlations must take a large number of other factors into account, some of which are at best partly known to us. These factors include the degree of similarity of the idiolects that belonged to speakers who were in contact with one another and the representativity of the texts that have survived and can be examined. Nevalainen et al. (2020b) focus on Middle English; in LModE, where most weak ties were established between speakers with fairly similar idiolects, where most features that spread between idiolects were already attested in the language, and where most texts that have typically been subjected to analysis feature influence from the written standard, a similar method is likely to significantly underestimate the amount of idiolectal change that took place.

Idiolectal change can be divided into a small number of types. Independent innovation happens when a language user's idiolect undergoes a change to which the speaker has not been exposed. Propagation takes place when a language user's idiolect is altered through the incorporation of a change to which the speaker has been exposed in the output of one or several other users. A change in a communal language like LModE is the result of propagation across a large number of idiolects. Most innovations are never propagated and thus die out. However, a change is more likely to be propagated if it (i) is compatible with the structure of potential recipient idiolects and (ii) occurs in the output of language users to whom other people wish to accommodate; social factors are thus important in propagation.

Propagation typically involves propagation-dependent innovation as well, owing to imperfect replication in propagation. When a change is being propagated through a community, speakers have to make interpretations based on incomplete evidence – that is, the linguistic output that they have access to containing the change – in order to adopt that change. They are thus likely to incorporate similar, but not identical, changes into their idiolects based on this output, because they analyse the output somewhat differently and because they are not exposed to exactly the same output. When, as the next step, they produce language based on their changed idiolects, propagation is coupled with propagation-dependent innovation, as their output reflects a slightly different change compared with the output which they were exposed to and which triggered the change. However, such propagation-dependent innovation is unlikely to lead to the emergence of wholly new structural features in idiolects, as the relevant speakers were attempting to replicate changes that were already present in other idiolects. (One apparent exception to this rule concerns cases of language contact: if partly or wholly bilingual language users introduce a feature into one of their idiolects through propagation from another idiolect, the new feature constitutes structural change in the recipient idiolect even though its origin is intra-speaker propagation from an idiolect mapped onto another communal language. The amount of propagation-dependent innovation is likely to be considerable in such cases, as the feature is adjusted to a recipient idiolect that may differ greatly from the source idiolect.) Since propagation-dependent innovation occurs as a consequence of propagation, it is influenced by extralinguistic as well as linguistic factors.

In contrast, independent innovation – that is, innovation that is *not* a result of imperfect replication in propagation – is likely to be constrained mainly by linguistic factors. Such independent innovation may be categorical, that is, involve the appearance of new features of linguistic structure, but can also consist in, for instance, new uses of an existing feature. While the exact reasons why a speaker produces an independent innovation are unknown, speakers are more likely to produce categorical innovations that are compatible with patterns in their current idiolect and/or general linguistic principles. In contrast, there is no social reason for speakers to produce such independent innovations, as there are no other speakers they could be accommodating to by producing a new feature.

The reason why the distinction between independent innovation and propagation (which is typically accompanied by propagation-dependent innovation) is important is that they have different relations to sociocultural phenomena such as social networks. Independent innovation, which is an important source of categorical change, is not affected by social factors. There is thus no reason to expect the increasingly weak network ties that characterize LModE society to correlate with the appearance of new structural features in LModE idiolects (and, by extension through propagation, in LModE). Rather, what we should expect is the propagation of existing features between idiolects, together with propagation-dependent innovation. Two important ways in which speakers' idiolects changed through propagation between 1700 and 1900 concerned the replacement of rural with urban dialects and the adoption of Standard English patterns (at least in writing), and both of these developments involved the spread of features that were already present in the communal language. The stability paradox is thus a result of considering the communal language rather than the idiolect as the unit truly undergoing change.

Processes such as colloquialization and densification are also examples of the changes that can be expected. Some language users begin to employ syntactic options that are already available in their idiolects more frequently and with fewer constraints than previously in certain written genres. This extension of use may happen as a result of propagation-dependent innovation, if the language users "overshoot the mark" when trying to accommodate to written output containing the features in question; in particular, densification may also involve independent innovation if the users spontaneously begin to extend the use of the features in response to, for instance, functional pressure to economize on words. However, these processes do not change the apparent structure of the communal language, the large number of idiolects affected notwithstanding.

One of the remaining questions is why LModE as a communal language appears to feature less categorical innovation than previous periods. If there is no correlation between independent innovation and network ties, it could be expected that the amount of innovation should be similar in LModE and in previous stages of the history of English. While this is an area where more research is needed, I provided some suggestions in Chapter 3. First, during a period when a great deal of propagation is taking place, speakers may reach a "saturation point" regarding how much change they can incorporate into their idiolects, and independent innovations, which are likely to be used by fewer people on average, may then be at a disadvantage; that is, they occur but are very rarely successful. The emergence of Standard English during the LModE period is likely to have further constrained the amount of successful innovation. Although it is an open question whether and to what extent prescriptive pressure can cause language change, most LModE texts that have been the subject of linguistic research were arguably affected by standard norms. In addition, large segments of LModE society – the middle, and especially the lower-middle classes – presumably wished to identify with Standard English, and they would thus have been open to influence in the direction of standardized language regardless of prescriptive pressure. Finally, LModE is a period during which many language users were forced to command an increasingly wide range of usage, owing to factors such as more widespread access to literacy and the increasing specialization of some written genres. At the same time, processes such as democratization and popularization were contributing to altering the norms for some written texts in the direction of orality. The resulting broadening and diversification of many language users' idiolects may have constrained the amount of innovation that was likely to be successful at this time.

In sum, the resolution of the stability paradox makes LModE seem less exceptional as a period in the history of English. The connection between social-network structure and language change, the uniformitarian principle, and so on are all applicable to LModE once specific characteristics of the period 1700–1900 are taken into account. It is hoped that this book has contributed to placing research on LModE on a sounder theoretical footing.

9.2 The Corpus-Based Study of (Late Modern English) Grammar

Against the background of the discussion summarized in Section 9.1, the inclusion of four corpus-linguistic case studies in this book may seem an odd choice. Corpora are often sampled with the aim of representing a language variety, a domain of usage, or the like, rather than idiolects; idiolectal influence on the overall results may in fact be seen as a potential problem. However, provided that researchers are explicit about what results based on corpora can and cannot tell us, there are several reasons why corpus linguistics is a suitable method for studying changes in grammar. In other words, while idiolects are the true locus of language change, they are not necessarily the ideal level for the *study* of language change. This discrepancy is due to the limitations of linguistic data, some of which apply to linguistics in general (e.g. the lack of direct access to language users' idiolects) and some of which are particular to historical linguistics (e.g. the patchy survival of historical texts and the absence of spoken data).

First, the available evidence indicates that there is a great deal of convergence among idiolects as regards what independent innovations are likely to occur, what changes are likely to be propagated, and what propagation-dependent innovations are likely to take place. This convergence enables powerful generalizations to be made in terms of how a change is likely to have proceeded through groups of idiolects. To some extent, a trade-off in terms of granularity vs. generalization is involved here: using a typical corpus, we lose the chance to fully describe how particular idiolects went through a change; but instead, common patterns in data from several language users can indicate properties of the change that are shared by groups of speakers of the communal language. Considering extralinguistic categories shared by corpus texts, for example the gender or socio-economic status of language users or the genre provenance of texts, also enables us to say more about the granularity and generalizability of our account of language change.

In addition, although corpora are seldom compiled to represent idiolects, valuable knowledge can be gleaned from considering idiolectal variation within a corpus (provided that the identity of the speakers sampled can be ascertained). For instance, several language users whose output is untypical with regard to a change may also share other linguistic characteristics, and such shared features may help us to form hypotheses about factors that promoted or constrained the change in question. Idiolectal tendencies should be recognized and considered a potential window on the process of change, not removed from the analysis as unrepresentative outliers.

The suitability of corpus linguistics for the study of language change notwithstanding, it is also important to acknowledge what corpora most likely cannot tell us about past language-states. To begin with, the evidence of change we can see in corpora is basically limited to propagation and propagation-dependent innovation; independent innovations are unlikely to be recorded in corpus texts (see also Milroy and Milroy 1985: 370). This limitation is especially important as regards changes that can be hypothesized to have originated in speech. (In this regard, colloquialization, which concerns the spread of oral features into writing, and densification, which comprises changes assumed to have originated in informational writing, are ideally suited for corpus-based investigation.) Secondly, corpora cannot ultimately tell us much about the amount of change that characterizes a particular period. If it is accepted that idiolects are the true locus of change, an estimation of the scope of change during a given period on the basis of corpus findings is vulnerable to multiple sources of error. In particular, for such estimations to be valid, we need extensive knowledge about (i) idiolects that have not been preserved in texts and (ii) the extent to which changes led to the adoption of linguistic features that were already in evidence. Finally, as is well known, we should avoid unwarranted generalization of the results based on a corpus to categories of speakers and texts not included in that corpus; for instance, case studies such as those in Chapters 5–8 cannot tell us much about grammar patterns in pauper letters or in official correspondence, as those speakers and texts are not represented in CONCE or CNNE. Both the speakers whose idiolects are sampled and the parts of their idiolects that are sampled (e.g. genres) are of crucial significance when the scope of generalization is decided on.

In order to quantify variation and change over time, a choice must often be made between two ways of measuring the frequency of a linguistic feature: the variationist perspective, in which this frequency is related to the frequency of one or several other features; and the text-linguistic perspective, in which this frequency is related to a coefficient – in corpus linguistics, typically 1,000 or 1 million words – in order to make raw frequencies independent of text length. This choice may affect conclusions regarding whether or not change occurs in the texts examined.

In the present study, no real choice in this regard needed to be made for Chapter 6, on the functions of *and*. This is because this analysis starts out from a linguistic form – the co-ordinator itself – and looks at whether it operates on a phrasal, intermediate, or super-phrasal level; this direction of analysis is analogous to what has been called *form-to-function mapping* in historical pragmatics (see Jacobs and Jucker 1995). Chapters 5, 7, and 8, in contrast, presented a choice between variationist and text-linguistic strategies. In Chapters 5 and 8, mixed approaches were opted for. For parts of the analyses, I attempted to limit the scope of the investigation to contexts where language users could be expected to have made a choice between two roughly equivalent variants (in Chapter 5, uncontracted vs. *not*-contracted forms; in Chapter 8, restrictive active relative clauses vs. restrictive present-participle clauses and restrictive passive relative clauses vs. restrictive past-participle clauses). The findings from these variationist approaches were complemented with insights from text-linguistic analyses. For Chapter 7, in contrast, no variationist set-up was attempted: the analysis was text-linguistic only, since a large number of forms can potentially fill the same function as premodifying nouns and since the forms that constitute variants can often be identified only on a token-by-token basis.

The present study has shown that a corpus-linguistic framework can greatly increase our knowledge of syntactic change in LModE even within the overall framework of an idiolect-centred theory of language change. The combination of careful generalizations based on corpus evidence and close analyses of the output of individual idiolects offers linguists an excellent opportunity to access the language of past language users. As regards the choice between variationist and text-linguistic quantification, several difficulties of circumscribing the envelope of variation in studies of historical syntax have been made apparent. The number of potential variants that can be identified frequently varies depending on how strictly the criterion of sameness of meaning is adhered to and how much difference in surface structure between variants is allowed. Moreover, token-specific features may make one or several variants unlikely or unavailable in individual cases. A tentative recommendation that emerges from the relevant case studies is to complement any variationist analysis of historical syntax with a text-linguistic perspective unless it can be considered certain that the envelope of variation has been successfully identified (as was broadly the case in Chapter 5). Researchers need to be explicit about the limitations of their approaches in terms of what variants are considered (i) grammatically possible and (ii) semantically equivalent. (A further complication is that assumptions of equivalence and of grammaticality are typically based on the communal language; but there are likely to be interidiolectal differences on both parameters.)

9.3 Colloquialization and Densification in Nineteenth-Century English

The third aim of this book was to examine the occurrence of colloquialization and densification in LModE through four case studies. For both types of change, the inclusion of two features that could be hypothesized to display different developments proved to be of considerable importance.

As regards colloquialization, *not*-contraction and co-ordination by *and* displayed very different genre patterns, though both features indicated that colloquialization was taking place in parts of the nineteenth-century material. As an explicitly proscribed feature, *not*-contraction did not occur in the expository genres in CONCE and was very rare in CNNE. Instead, Drama and Fiction were the genres where *not*-contractions could make inroads into written nineteenth-century English (the Letters genre was not included, and Trials displayed stability at a low level of frequency). The stigmatization of *not*-contraction was also borne out by the tendencies for women to use *not*-contraction less than men, with Jane Austen and Mary Shelley standing out as conservative authors. An analysis of word order in questions indicated that the *would not she* pattern in *would not she miss her little moonbeam?* might have been used – increasingly in Trials, but less and less in Drama and Fiction – as a more acceptable way of rendering spoken *not*-contractions in writing. A multifactorial analysis of the data confirmed the importance of the genre parameter in colloquialization and also demonstrated that several linguistic parameters, including clause type and operator, influenced contraction ratios; also, the propagation of *not*-contraction as a colloquial feature appears first to have taken off in the present tense and the imperative, while the past tense exhibited low but increasing proportions across the 1800s. Overall, colloquialization through propagation of *not*-contraction was primarily a feature of speech-purposed (and, to a lesser extent, speech-based) dialogue in the nineteenth century.

In contrast, the co-ordinator *and* with both phrases and larger units as conjoins was an unmarked feature of any type of speech or writing throughout the nineteenth century. Super-phrasal co-ordination, which characterizes speech, is thus a less apparent indicator of orality, and its genre distribution differs considerably from that of *not*-contraction. Most genres displayed stability on the parameter of phrasal vs. intermediate vs. super-phrasal co-ordination. However, as shown in Smitterberg (2014), there was significant change in the direction of orality in CNNE; super-phrasal co-ordination was an oral feature that could be safely employed in newspaper English. In CONCE, similar changes were attested in Debates and in men's private letters. Women's letters developed in the opposite direction, but a close reading of letters by selected letter writers revealed that this unexpected finding was largely due to a shift in discourse organization. Three women letter writers from period 1 – Mary Wordsworth, Sara Hutchinson, and Mary Shelley – favoured a division of letters into units separated by dashes and syndetic co-ordination rather than into Standard English sentences. As the syntactic sentence became more prominent as a written discourse unit in women's letters from period 3, the frequency of *and* as a super-phrasal co-ordinator decreased. Finally, sentence-initial *and*, which was a proscribed feature, was used and became more frequent primarily in Drama and Trials, where the feature both indicated colloquialization and functioned as a device for linking two utterances occurring before and after an extralinguistic event (in Drama) or two questions by a lawyer separated by a witness's answer (in Trials).

The two features indicating densification were also hypothesized to display partly different developments. The increasing use of premodifying nouns over the past few centuries is a well-known feature of LModE syntax. As expected, the newspaper texts in CNNE displayed clear indications of densification in the form of frequency increases regarding common as well as proper nouns as premodifiers. The genre pattern in CONCE was somewhat less orderly, however, and the fact that women's private letters contained higher frequencies than letters by men led me to hypothesize that not all of the increase in nominal premodification was due to densification: we may also be witnessing a change from below towards higher frequencies of this feature, which co-occurs with a trend towards increased information density in some expository texts. An analysis of the semantic relationship between the premodifying and premodified nouns evinced a good deal of diachronic continuity in relationships between common nouns, though there were indications that somewhat more demanding combinations were used in news texts towards the end of the century. The analysis of proper nouns as premodifiers in CNNE, in contrast, revealed a clear tendency towards semantic broadening of the referent of the premodifying noun, whereby animate premodifiers became less marked over time.

Participle clauses as postmodifiers in noun phrases are a less clear-cut feature of densification, for two reasons: previous research does not point to a clear increase in their frequency during the LModE period; and although participle clauses are more condensed than their most obvious alternative (the finite relative clause), they remain clausal units, and densification has primarily resulted in phrasal rather than clausal complexity. The results were also less conclusive than for nominal premodifiers. Restrictive present-participle clauses clearly increased in frequency in Science – and in CNNE, where they appeared to be used in place of their closest relative-clause equivalents to a significant extent. CNNE also displayed an increase in the frequency of restrictive past-participle clauses, though here restrictive passive relative clauses also became more common, resulting in no significant shift in their proportions; conversely, private letters did display a significant shift in the direction of densification on this parameter, but this development seemed more likely to be due to avoidance of passive relative clauses. Conversely, History texts developed in the opposite direction: restrictive participle clauses became less frequent in relation to relative clauses. The occurrence of non-restrictive participle clauses did not appear to be connected to densification; instead, such clauses fulfilled narrative and/or backgrounding functions in texts.

The four case studies indicate that both colloquialization and densification were underway in nineteenth-century English, though neither process was as pervasive as in the following century. Pressures towards popularization and economy interacted with other societal and functional factors to contest and renegotiate genre norms. An increasing number of language users responded to these developments by adjusting their idiolects with regard to the linguistic and extralinguistic contexts in which the features were used, resulting in shifts in the frequencies with which they occurred. In doing so, language users not only propagated the changes but also innovated and thus took colloquialization and densification further. On a lower level of granularity, the results of these processes are observable as differences between period and genre samples in corpora.

The results point to a number of desiderata for studies of colloquialization and densification in LModE, in addition to the more general points discussed in Sections 9.1 and 9.2. First, both considering several linguistic features that may indicate colloquialization or densification and considering several genres is important; for instance, *not*-contraction, super-phrasal co-ordination, and sentence-initial *and* all patterned differently across the genre parameter. There are several other features than those treated in Chapters 5–8 that would be valuable indicators of colloquialization or densification. To take one example, appositive noun phrases are an important sign of densification and increase greatly in frequency between the eighteenth and twentieth centuries (Biber and Gray 2011: 229, 234; see also, for instance, Rydén 1975 and Jucker 1992: 207–50 for name apposition in twentieth-century newspaper language). This increase is also mirrored within the nineteenth century for CNNE and CONCE. Appositions captured by the retrieval of nominal premodifiers became considerably more frequent over the 1800s in both corpora (in CNNE, 107 × in period 1 and 206 × in period 3, corresponding to 0.7 and 1.3 tokens per 1,000 words; in CONCE, 119 × in period 1 and 164 × in period 3, corresponding to 0.4 and 0.7 tokens per 1,000 words). Apposition clearly deserves more attention from a diachronic perspective.

Secondly, although the genre concept remains indispensable for work in these fields, genres are not linguistically homogeneous categories, and may in themselves subsume orderly heterogeneity. The remarkably different behaviour of History and Science with respect to densification is a case in point: if CONCE had subsumed these genres under a larger umbrella genre of Academic Writing, important differences would have been obscured.

Finally, quantitative analyses of corpus findings, which form the backbone of the linguistic evidence in the case studies in Chapters 5–8, should always be complemented with close readings of passages from key texts, which is crucial in terms of reaching safe conclusions regarding not just the *how*, but also the *why* of the propagation of a change. Outliers may be important in this regard. In the present study, for instance, careful examination of passages from individual letters and newspapers revealed valuable indications of why women's letters and articles from the *Poor Man's Guardian* did not take part in specific processes of colloquialization and densification, respectively.

9.4 Concluding Remarks

Like many studies before it, this book has shown that LModE is a many-faceted field of research. The interplay of a large number of extralinguistic parameters, including gender, class, access to education, and occupational specialization, contributed to increasing the amount of linguistic variation *among* genres – and consequently *within* idiolects – between 1700 and 1900. This book is a contribution to exploring this shifting textual landscape. I have attempted to set up a model for how language change takes place which is based on the individual speaker's idiolect and which is compatible with the available evidence on the relative prevalence of weak network ties in the LModE period. Furthermore, I have tried to show how this model can be reconciled with corpus-linguistic method and have aimed to illustrate this in case studies that also contribute to our knowledge of colloquialization and densification. It is hoped that, taken together, these different aspects of the book have added to our understanding of language change, LModE syntax, colloquialization, and densification.

Appendix

This Appendix contains tables indicating non-significant period differences which were not included in Chapter 6.

Table A.1 *Co-ordination by period in Drama (periods 1 and 3)*

	Phrasal		Intermediate		Super-phrasal		
Period	#	%	#	%	#	%	Total
1	110	31.7	28	8.1	209	60.2	347
3	147	38.9	33	8.7	198	52.4	378
Total	257	35.4	61	8.4	407	56.1	725

(d.f. = 2; χ^2 = 4.72; p = 0.095)

Table A.2 *Co-ordination by period in Fiction (periods 1 and 3)*

	Phrasal		Intermediate		Super-phrasal		
Period	#	%	#	%	#	%	Total
1	169	43.8	25	6.5	192	49.7	386
3	168	43.9	27	7.0	188	49.1	383
Total	337	43.8	52	6.8	380	49.4	769

(d.f. = 2; χ^2 = 0.110; p = 0.946)

Table A.3 *Co-ordination by period in History (periods 1 and 3)*

	Phrasal		Intermediate		Super-phrasal		
Period	#	%	#	%	#	%	Total
1	203	51.4	16	4.1	176	44.6	395
3	194	49.1	12	3.0	189	47.8	395
Total	397	50.3	28	3.5	365	46.2	790

(d.f. = 2; χ^2 = 1.24; p = 0.538)

Table A.4 *Co-ordination by period in Science (periods 1 and 3)*

	Phrasal		Intermediate		Super-phrasal		
Period	#	%	#	%	#	%	Total
1	193	51.6	25	6.7	156	41.7	374
3	205	53.5	12	3.1	166	43.3	383
Total	398	52.6	37	4.9	322	42.5	757

(d.f. = 2; χ^2 = 5.13; p = 0.077)

Table A.5 *Co-ordination by period in Trials (periods 1 and 3)*

	Phrasal		Intermediate		Super-phrasal		
Period	#	%	#	%	#	%	Total
1	123	32.2	32	8.4	227	59.4	382
3	130	34.3	26	6.9	223	58.8	379
Total	253	33.2	58	7.6	450	59.1	761

(d.f. = 2; χ^2 = 0.838; p = 0.658)

References

Aarts, Bas, López-Couso, María José, and Méndez-Naya, Belén. 2012. "Late Modern English: Syntax". In Bergs, Alexander, and Brinton, Laurel J. (eds.), *English Historical Linguistics: An International Handbook*. Vol. 1. Berlin and Boston: Mouton de Gruyter, 869–87.

Aitchison, Jean. 2001. *Language Change: Progress or Decay?* 3rd ed. Cambridge: Cambridge University Press.

Altick, Richard D. 1957. *The English Common Reader: A Social History of the Mass Reading Public 1800–1900*. Chicago and London: The University of Chicago Press.

Anderwald, Lieselotte. 2002. *Negation in Non-Standard British English: Gaps, Regularizations and Asymmetries*. London and New York: Routledge.

Anderwald, Lieselotte. 2014a. "'Pained the Eye and Stunned the Ear': Language Ideology and the Progressive Passive in the Nineteenth Century". In Pfenninger, Simone E., Timofeeva, Olga, Gardner, Anne-Christine, Honkapohja, Alpo, Hundt, Marianne, and Schreier, Daniel (eds.), *Contact, Variation, and Change in the History of English*. Amsterdam and Philadelphia: John Benjamins, 113–36.

Anderwald, Lieselotte. 2014b. "The Decline of the BE-Perfect, Linguistic Relativity, and Grammar Writing in the Nineteenth Century". In Hundt, Marianne (ed.), *Late Modern English Syntax*. Cambridge: Cambridge University Press, 13–37.

Anderwald, Lieselotte. 2016. *Language between Description and Prescription: Verbs and Verb Categories in Nineteenth-Century Grammars of English*. Oxford: Oxford University Press.

ARCHER = A Representative Corpus of Historical English Registers. 1990– 1993/2002/2007/2010/2013/2016. Originally compiled under the supervision of Douglas Biber and Edward Finegan at Northern Arizona University and University of Southern California; modified and expanded by subsequent members of a consortium of universities. Current member universities are Bamberg, Freiburg, Heidelberg, Helsinki, Lancaster, Leicester, Manchester, Michigan, Northern Arizona, Santiago de Compostela, Southern California, Trier, Uppsala, Zurich.

Asquith, Ivon. 1978. "The Structure, Ownership and Control of the Press, 1780–1855". In Boyce, George, Curran, James, and Wingate, Pauline (eds.), *Newspaper*

History: From the Seventeenth Century to the Present Day. London: Constable, 98–116.
Atkinson, Dwight. 1999. *Scientific Discourse in Sociohistorical Context: The Philosophical Transactions of the Royal Society of London, 1675–1975*. Mahwah, NJ: Lawrence Erlbaum Associates.
Auer, Anita. 2012. "Late Modern English: Standardization". In Bergs, Alexander, and Brinton, Laurel J. (eds.), *English Historical Linguistics: An International Handbook*. Vol. 1. Berlin and Boston: Mouton de Gruyter, 939–52.
Auer, Anita. 2014. "Nineteenth-Century English: Norms and Usage". In Rutten, Gijsbert, Vosters, Rik, and Vandenbussche, Wim (eds.), *Norms and Usage in Language History, 1600–1900: A Sociolinguistic and Comparative Perspective*. Amsterdam and Philadelphia: John Benjamins, 151–69.
Auer, Anita, and González-Díaz, Victorina. 2005. "Eighteenth-Century Prescriptivism in English: A Re-evaluation of Its Effects on Actual Language Use". *Multilingua* 24(4), 317–41.
Auer, Anita, and Laitinen, Mikko. 2014. "Letters of Artisans and the Labouring Poor (England, c. 1750–1835): Approaching Linguistic Diversity in Late Modern English". In Pfenninger, Simone E., Timofeeva, Olga, Gardner, Anne-Christine, Honkapohja, Alpo, Hundt, Marianne, and Schreier, Daniel (eds.), *Contact, Variation, and Change in the History of English*. Amsterdam and Philadelphia: John Benjamins, 187–211.
Auer, Anita, Schreier, Daniel, and Watts, Richard J. (eds.). 2015. *Letter Writing and Language Change*. Cambridge: Cambridge University Press.
Austin, Frances O. 1985. "Relative *Which* in Late 18th Century Usage: The Clift Family Correspondence". In Eaton, Roger, Fischer, Olga, Koopman, Willem, and van der Leek, Frederike (eds.), *Papers from the 4th International Conference on English Historical Linguistics: Amsterdam, 10–13 April, 1985*. Amsterdam and Philadelphia: John Benjamins, 15–29.
Bailey, Richard W. 1996. *Nineteenth-Century English*. Ann Arbor: The University of Michigan Press.
Bailey, Richard W. 2010. "Variation and Change in Eighteenth-Century English". In Hickey, Raymond (ed.), *Eighteenth-Century English: Ideology and Change*. Cambridge: Cambridge University Press, 182–99.
Ball, C. N. 1994. "Automated Text Analysis: Cautionary Tales". *Literary and Linguistic Computing* 9(4), 295–302.
Ball, Catherine N. 1996. "A Diachronic Study of Relative Markers in Spoken and Written English". *Language Variation and Change* 8(2), 227–58.
Barnard, John (ed.). 2014. *John Keats: Selected Letters*. London: Penguin.
Barth, Danielle, and Kapatsinski, Vsevolod. 2017. "A Multimodel Inference Approach to Categorical Variant Choice: Construction, Priming and Frequency Effects on the Choice between Full and Contracted Forms of *Am, Are* and *Is*". *Corpus Linguistics and Linguistic Theory* 13(2), 203–60.

Beal, Joan. 1993. "The Grammar of Tyneside and Northumbrian English". In Milroy, James, and Milroy, Lesley (eds.), *Real English: The Grammar of English Dialects in the British Isles*. Harlow: Longman, 187–213.
Beal, Joan C. 2004. *English in Modern Times: 1700–1945*. London: Arnold.
Beal, Joan C. 2010a. *An Introduction to Regional Englishes: Dialect Variation in England*. Edinburgh: Edinburgh University Press.
Beal, Joan C. 2010b. "Prescriptivism and the Suppression of Variation". In Hickey, Raymond (ed.), *Eighteenth-Century English: Ideology and Change*. Cambridge: Cambridge University Press, 21–37.
Beal, Joan C., Fitzmaurice, Susan, and Hodson, Jane (eds.). 2012. *Selected Papers from the Fourth International Conference on Late Modern English*. Special issue of *English Language and Linguistics* 16(2).
Beckner, Clay, Blythe, Richard, Bybee, Joan, Christiansen, Morten H., Croft, William, Ellis, Nick C., Holland, John, Ke, Jinyun, Larsen-Freeman, Diane, and Schoenemann, Tom (The "Five Graces Group"). 2009. "Language Is a Complex Adaptive System: Position Paper". *Language Learning* 59 (Suppl. 1), 1–26.
Bergs, Alexander. 2005. *Social Networks and Historical Sociolinguistics: Studies in Morphosyntactic Variation in the Paston Letters (1421–1503)*. Berlin and New York: Mouton de Gruyter.
Berridge, Virginia. 1978. "Popular Sunday Papers and Mid-Victorian Society". In Boyce, George, Curran, James, and Wingate, Pauline (eds.), *Newspaper History: From the Seventeenth Century to the Present Day*. London: Constable, 247–64.
Biber, Douglas. 1988. *Variation across Speech and Writing*. Cambridge: Cambridge University Press.
Biber, Douglas. 1993. "Representativeness in Corpus Design". *Literary and Linguistic Computing* 8(4), 243–57.
Biber, Douglas. 2003. "Variation among University Spoken and Written Registers: A New Multi-Dimensional Analysis". In Leistyna, Pepi, and Meyer, Charles F. (eds.), *Corpus Analysis: Language Structure and Language Use*. Amsterdam and New York: Rodopi, 47–70.
Biber, Douglas. 2012. "Register as a Predictor of Linguistic Variation". *Corpus Linguistics and Linguistic Theory* 8(1), 9–37.
Biber, Douglas, and Clark, Victoria. 2002. "Historical Shifts in Modification Patterns with Complex Noun Phrase Structures: How Long Can You Go without a Verb?" In Fanego, Teresa, López-Couso, María José, and Pérez-Guerra, Javier (eds.), *English Historical Syntax and Morphology: Selected Papers from 11 ICEHL, Santiago de Compostela, 7–11 September 2000*. Vol. 1. Amsterdam and Philadelphia: John Benjamins, 43–66.
Biber, Douglas, with Egbert, Jesse, Gray, Bethany, Oppliger, Rahel, and Szmrecsanyi, Benedikt. 2016. "Variationist versus Text-Linguistic Approaches to Grammatical Change in English: Nominal Modifiers of Head Nouns". In Kytö, Merja, and Pahta, Päivi (eds.), *The Cambridge*

Handbook of English Historical Linguistics. Cambridge: Cambridge University Press, 351–75.

Biber, Douglas, and Finegan, Edward. 1997. "Diachronic Relations among Speech-Based and Written Registers in English". In Nevalainen, Terttu, and Kahlas-Tarkka, Leena (eds.), *To Explain the Present: Studies in the Changing English Language in Honour of Matti Rissanen.* Helsinki: Société Néophilologique, 253–75.

Biber, Douglas, and Gray, Bethany. 2011. "Grammatical Change in the Noun Phrase: The Influence of Written Language Use". *English Language and Linguistics* 15(2), 223–50.

Biber, Douglas, and Gray, Bethany. 2012. "The Competing Demands of Popularization vs. Economy: Written Language in the Age of Mass Literacy". In Nevalainen, Terttu, and Traugott, Elizabeth Closs (eds.), *The Oxford Handbook of the History of English.* Oxford and New York: Oxford University Press, 314–28.

Biber, Douglas, and Gray, Bethany. 2013. "Nominalizing the Verb Phrase in Academic Science Writing". In Aarts, Bas, Close, Joanne, Leech, Geoffrey, and Wallis, Sean (eds.), *The Verb Phrase in English: Investigating Recent Language Change with Corpora.* Cambridge: Cambridge University Press, 99–132.

Biber, Douglas, and Gray, Bethany. 2016. *Grammatical Complexity in Academic English: Linguistic Change in Writing.* Cambridge: Cambridge University Press.

Biber, Douglas, Johansson, Stig, Leech, Geoffrey, Conrad, Susan, and Finegan, Edward. 1999. *Longman Grammar of Spoken and Written English.* Harlow: Pearson.

Biber, Douglas, and Reppen, Randi. 2015. "Introduction". In Biber, Douglas, and Reppen, Randi (eds.), *The Cambridge Handbook of English Corpus Linguistics.* Cambridge: Cambridge University Press, 1–8.

Bickerton, Derek. 2014. "The Myth of Creole 'Exceptionalism'". In Åfarli, Tor A., and Mæhlum, Brit (eds.), *The Sociolinguistics of Grammar.* Amsterdam and Philadelphia: John Benjamins, 191–201.

Blythe, Richard A., and Croft, William. 2012. "S-Curves and the Mechanisms of Propagation in Language Change". *Language* 88(2), 269–304.

Bös, Birte. 2015. "From 1760 to 1960: Diversification and Popularization". In Facchinetti, Roberta, Brownlees, Nicholas, Bös, Birte, and Fries, Udo, *News as Changing Texts: Corpora, Methodologies and Analysis.* 2nd ed. Newcastle: Cambridge Scholars Publishing, 91–143.

Boyce, George. 1978. "The Fourth Estate: The Reappraisal of a Concept". In Boyce, George, Curran, James, and Wingate, Pauline (eds.), *Newspaper History: From the Seventeenth Century to the Present Day.* London: Constable, 19–40.

Brainerd, Barron. 1989 [1993]. "The Contractions of *Not*: A Historical Note". *Journal of English Linguistics* 22(2), 176–96.

Breban, Tine, and De Smet, Hendrik. 2019. "How Do Grammatical Patterns Emerge? The Origins and Development of the English Proper Noun Modifier Construction". *English Language and Linguistics* 23(4), 879–99.
Breban, Tine, and Kolkmann, Julia (eds.). 2019. "Special Issue: Different Perspectives on Proper Noun Modifiers". *English Language and Linguistics* 23(4), 749–58.
Breban, Tine, Kolkmann, Julia, and Payne, John. 2019. "The Impact of Semantic Relations on Grammatical Alternation: An Experimental Study of Proper Name Modifiers and Determiner Genitives". *English Language and Linguistics* 23(4), 797–826.
Brewer, Charlotte. 2007. "Reporting Eighteenth-Century Vocabulary in the *OED*". In Considine, John, and Iamartino, Giovanni (eds.), *Words and Dictionaries from the British Isles in Historical Perspective*. Newcastle: Cambridge Scholars Publishing, 109–35.
Brown, Lucy. 1985. *Victorian News and Newspapers*. Oxford: Clarendon Press.
Butterfield, Jeremy (ed.). 2015. *Fowler's Dictionary of Modern English Usage*. 4th ed. Oxford: Oxford University Press.
Bybee, Joan. 2015. *Language Change*. Cambridge: Cambridge University Press.
Bybee, Joan, and Thompson, Sandra. 2000. "Three Frequency Effects in Syntax". In Juge, Matthew L., and Moxley, Jeri L. (eds.), *Proceedings of the Twenty-Third Annual Meeting of the Berkeley Linguistics Society: General Session and Parasession on Pragmatics and Grammatical Structure*. Berkeley: Berkeley Linguistics Society, 378–88.
Calvo Cortés, Nuria. 2020. "Women Writers in the 18th Century: The Semantics of Motion in Their Choice of Perfect Auxiliaries". In Kytö, Merja, and Smitterberg, Erik (eds.), *Late Modern English: Novel Encounters*. Amsterdam and Philadelphia: John Benjamins, 203–18.
Castillo González, María del Pilar. 2007. Uncontracted Negatives and Negative Contractions in Contemporary English: A Corpus-Based Study. (PhD thesis, University of Santiago de Compostela, unpublished.)
CED = A Corpus of English Dialogues 1560–1760. 2006. Compiled by Kytö, Merja, and Culpeper, Jonathan.
Chambers, J. K. 1995. *Sociolinguistic Theory: Linguistic Variation and Its Social Significance*. Oxford and Cambridge: Blackwell.
Chambers, J. K., and Trudgill, Peter. 1998. *Dialectology*. 2nd ed. Cambridge: Cambridge University Press.
The Chicago Manual of Style Online. 2017. 17th ed. Chicago: University of Chicago Press.
Claridge, Claudia. 2000. *Multi-Word Verbs in Early Modern English: A Corpus-Based Study*. Amsterdam and Atlanta: Rodopi.
Claridge, Claudia. 2012. "Linguistic Levels: Styles, Registers, Genres, Text Types". In Bergs, Alexander, and Brinton, Laurel J. (eds.), *English Historical Linguistics: An International Handbook*. Vol. 1. Berlin and Boston: Mouton de Gruyter, 237–53.

Claridge, Claudia. 2017. "The *Poor Man's Guardian*: The Linguistic Construction of Social Groups and Their Relations". In Palander-Collin, Minna, Ratia, Maura, and Taavitsainen, Irma (eds.), *Diachronic Developments in English News Discourse*. Amsterdam and Philadelphia: John Benjamins, 137–55.
Clark, John W. 1975. *The Language and Style of Anthony Trollope*. London: André Deutsch.
Clarke, Bob. 2004. *From Grub Street to Fleet Street: An Illustrated History of English Newspapers to 1899*. Aldershot: Ashgate.
CLMETEV = The Corpus of Late Modern English Texts (Extended Version). 2006. Compiled by De Smet, Hendrik.
CNNE = The Corpus of Nineteenth-Century Newspaper English (n.d.). Compiled by Smitterberg, Erik.
COHA = The Corpus of Historical American English: 400 Million Words, 1810–2009. 2010–. Compiled by Davies, Mark.
Comrie, Bernard. 1976. *Aspect: An Introduction to the Study of Verbal Aspect and Related Problems*. Cambridge: Cambridge University Press.
Conboy, Martin. 2010. *The Language of Newspapers: Socio-Historical Perspectives*. London and New York: Continuum.
Conboy, Martin. 2017. "British Popular Newspaper Traditions: From the Nineteenth Century to the First Tabloid". In Palander-Collin, Minna, Ratia, Maura, and Taavitsainen, Irma (eds.), *Diachronic Developments in English News Discourse*. Amsterdam and Philadelphia: John Benjamins, 119–36.
CONCE = A Corpus of Nineteenth-Century English (n.d.). Compiled by Kytö, Merja, and Rudanko, Juhani.
Conde-Silvestre, Juan Camilo. 2012. "The Role of Social Networks and Mobility in Diachronic Sociolinguistics". In Hernández-Campoy, Juan Manuel, and Conde-Silvestre, Juan Camilo (eds.), *The Handbook of Historical Sociolinguistics*. Chichester: John Wiley & Sons, 332–52.
Cotter, Colleen. 2003. "Prescription and Practice: Motivations behind Change in News Discourse". *Journal of Historical Pragmatics* 4(1), 45–74.
Cournane, Ailís. 2017. "In Defence of the Child Innovator". In Mathieu, Éric, and Truswell, Robert (eds.), *Micro-Change and Macro-Change in Diachronic Syntax*. Oxford: Oxford University Press, 10–24.
Croft, William. 2000. *Explaining Language Change: An Evolutionary Approach*. Harlow: Pearson.
Culpeper, Jonathan, and Kytö, Merja. 2010. *Early Modern English Dialogues: Spoken Interaction as Writing*. Cambridge: Cambridge University Press.
Curran, James. 1978. "The Press as an Agency of Social Control: An Historical Perspective". In Boyce, George, Curran, James, and Wingate, Pauline (eds.), *Newspaper History: From the Seventeenth Century to the Present Day*. London: Constable, 51–75.
Curzan, Anne. 2014. *Fixing English: Prescriptivism and Language History*. Cambridge: Cambridge University Press.

Cuyckens, Hubert, D'hoedt, Frauke, and Szmrecsanyi, Benedikt. 2014. "Variability in Verb Complementation in Late Modern English: Finite vs. Non-finite Patterns". In Hundt, Marianne (ed.), *Late Modern English Syntax*. Cambridge: Cambridge University Press, 182–203.
Davies, Mark. 2012. "Some Methodological Issues Related to Corpus-Based Investigations of Recent Syntactic Changes in English". In Nevalainen, Terttu, and Traugott, Elizabeth Closs (eds.), *The Oxford Handbook of the History of English*. Oxford and New York: Oxford University Press, 157–74.
de Haan, Pieter. 1989. *Postmodifying Clauses in the English Noun Phrase: A Corpus-Based Study*. Amsterdam and Atlanta: Rodopi.
Dekeyser, Xavier. 1975. *Number and Case Relations in 19th Century British English: A Comparative Study of Grammar and Usage*. Antwerp and Amsterdam: Uitgeverij De Nederlandsche Boekhandel.
Denison, David. 1998. "Syntax". In Romaine, Suzanne (ed.), *The Cambridge History of the English Language. Vol. IV: 1776–1997*. Cambridge: Cambridge University Press, 92–329.
Denison, David. 1999. "Slow, Slow, Quick, Quick, Slow: The Dance of Language Change?" In Bringas López, Ana, González Álvarez, Dolores, Pérez Guerra, Javier, Rama Martínez, Esperanza, and Varela Bravo, Eduardo (eds.), *"Woonderous Ænglissce"*: SELIM *Studies in Medieval English Language*. Vigo: Servicio de Publicacións da Universidade de Vigo, 51–64.
Denison, David. 2003. "Log(ist)ic and Simplistic S-curves". In Hickey, Raymond (ed.), *Motives for Language Change*. Cambridge: Cambridge University Press, 54–70.
Denison, David, and Hundt, Marianne. 2013. "Defining Relatives". *Journal of English Linguistics* 41(2), 135–67.
De Smet, Hendrik. 2009. "Analysing Reanalysis". *Lingua* 119, 1,728–55.
De Smet, Hendrik. 2016. "How Gradual Change Progresses: The Interaction between Convention and Innovation". *Language Variation and Change* 28(1), 83–102.
Devitt, Amy J. 1989. *Standardizing Written English: Diffusion in the Case of Scotland 1520–1659*. Cambridge: Cambridge University Press.
de Vries, Jan. 1984. *European Urbanization 1500–1800*. London: Methuen.
Dixon, R. M. W. 1997. *The Rise and Fall of Languages*. Cambridge: Cambridge University Press.
Dollinger, Stefan. 2008. *New-Dialect Formation in Canada: Evidence from the English Modal Auxiliaries*. Amsterdam and Philadelphia: John Benjamins.
Dorgeloh, Heidrun. 2004. "Conjunction in Sentence and Discourse: Sentence-Initial *and* and Discourse Structure". *Journal of Pragmatics* 36(10), 1,761–79.
Dossena, Marina. 2012. "Late Modern English: Semantics and Lexicon". In Bergs, Alexander, and Brinton, Laurel J. (eds.), *English Historical Linguistics: An International Handbook*. Vol. 1. Berlin and Boston: Mouton de Gruyter, 887–900.

Dossena, Marina (ed.). 2015. *Transatlantic Perspectives on Late Modern English*. Amsterdam and Philadelphia: John Benjamins.
Dossena, Marina, and Jones, Charles (eds.). 2003. *Insights into Late Modern English*. Bern: Peter Lang.
Dossena, Marina, and Tieken-Boon van Ostade, Ingrid (eds.). 2008. *Studies in Late Modern English Correspondence: Methodology and Data*. Bern: Peter Lang.
Durrell, Martin. 2015. "'Representativeness', 'Bad Data', and Legitimate Expectations: What Can an Electronic Historical Corpus Tell Us That We Didn't Actually Know Already (and How)?" In Gippert, Jost, and Gehrke, Ralf (eds.), *Historical Corpora: Challenges and Perspectives*. Tübingen: Narr, 13–33.
Enrique-Arias, Andrés. 2018. "Some Methodological Issues in the Corpus-Based Study of Morphosyntactic Variation: The Case of Old Spanish Possessives". In Whitt, Richard J. (ed.), *Diachronic Corpora, Genre, and Language Change*. Amsterdam and Philadelphia: John Benjamins, 261–79.
Evans, Mel. 2013. *The Language of Queen Elizabeth I: A Sociolinguistic Perspective on Royal Style and Identity*. Chichester: Wiley-Blackwell.
Fairclough, Norman. 1992. *Discourse and Social Change*. Cambridge: Polity Press.
Fairman, Tony. 2006. "Words in English Record Office Documents of the Early 1800s". In Kytö, Merja, Rydén, Mats, and Smitterberg, Erik (eds.), *Nineteenth-Century English: Stability and Change*. Cambridge: Cambridge University Press, 56–88.
Fanego, Teresa. 2007. "Drift and the Development of Sentential Complements in British and American English from 1700 to the Present Day". In Pérez-Guerra, Javier, González-Álvarez, Dolores, Bueno-Alonso, Jorge L., and Rama-Martínez, Esperanza (eds.), *"Of Varying Language and Opposing Creed": New Insights into Late Modern English*. Bern: Peter Lang, 161–235.
Fanego, Teresa. 2010. "Variation in Sentential Complements in Eighteenth- and Nineteenth-Century English: A Processing-Based Explanation". In Hickey, Raymond (ed.), *Eighteenth-Century English: Ideology and Change*. Cambridge: Cambridge University Press, 200–20.
Farrelly, Michael, and Seoane, Elena. 2012. "Democratization". In Nevalainen, Terttu, and Traugott, Elizabeth Closs (eds.), *The Oxford Handbook of the History of English*. Oxford and New York: Oxford University Press, 392–401.
Filppula, Markku, Klemola, Juhani, and Paulasto, Heli. 2008. *English and Celtic in Contact*. New York and London: Routledge.
Finkenstaedt, Thomas, Leisi, Ernst, and Wolff, Dieter. 1970. *A Chronological English Dictionary: Listing 80,000 Words in Order of Their Earliest Known Occurrence*. Heidelberg: Winter.
Fischer, Olga. 2016. "Morphosyntactic Change". In Kytö, Merja, and Pahta, Päivi (eds.), *The Cambridge Handbook of English Historical Linguistics*. Cambridge: Cambridge University Press, 237–55.

Fleisher, Nicholas. 2006. "The Origin of Passive *Get*". *English Language and Linguistics* 10(2), 225–52.
Fries, Udo. 2012. "English and the Media: Newspapers". In Bergs, Alexander, and Brinton, Laurel J. (eds.), *English Historical Linguistics: An International Handbook*. Vol. 1. Berlin and Boston: Mouton de Gruyter, 1,063–75.
Fries, Udo. 2015. "Newspapers from 1665 to 1765". In Facchinetti, Roberta, Brownlees, Nicholas, Bös, Birte, and Fries, Udo, *News as Changing Texts: Corpora, Methodologies and Analysis*. 2nd ed. Newcastle upon Tyne: Cambridge Scholars Publishing, 49–89.
Fritz, Clemens W. A. 2007. *From English in Australia to Australian English: 1788–1900*. Frankfurt am Main: Peter Lang.
Geisler, Christer. 1995. *Relative Infinitives in English*. Uppsala: Acta Universitatis Upsaliensis.
Geisler, Christer. 2002. "Investigating Register Variation in Nineteenth-Century English: A Multi-Dimensional Comparison". In Reppen, Randi, Fitzmaurice, Susan M., and Biber, Douglas (eds.), *Using Corpora to Explore Linguistic Variation*. Amsterdam and Philadelphia: John Benjamins, 249–71.
Geisler, Christer. 2003. "Gender-Based Variation in Nineteenth-Century English Letter Writing". In Leistyna, Pepi, and Meyer, Charles F. (eds.), *Corpus Analysis: Language Structure and Language Use*. Amsterdam and New York: Rodopi, 87–106.
Görlach, Manfred. 1999. *English in Nineteenth-Century England: An Introduction*. Cambridge: Cambridge University Press.
Görlach, Manfred. 2001. *Eighteenth-Century English*. Heidelberg: Winter.
Görlach, Manfred. 2004. *Text Types and the History of English*. Berlin and New York: Mouton de Gruyter.
Gray, Bethany, and Biber, Douglas. 2018. "Academic Writing as a Locus of Grammatical Change: The Development of Phrasal Complexity Features". In Whitt, Richard J. (ed.), *Diachronic Corpora, Genre, and Language Change*. Amsterdam and Philadelphia: John Benjamins, 117–46.
Gries, Stefan T. 2005. "Null-Hypothesis Significance Testing of Word Frequencies: A Follow-Up on Kilgarriff". *Corpus Linguistics and Linguistic Theory* 1(2), 277–94.
Gries, Stefan T., and Hilpert, Martin. 2010. "Modeling Diachronic Change in the Third Person Singular: A Multifactorial, Verb- and Author-Specific Exploratory Approach". *English Language and Linguistics* 14(3), 293–320.
Grieve, Jack. 2011. "A Regional Analysis of Contraction Rate in Written Standard American English". *International Journal of Corpus Linguistics* 16(4), 514–46.
Grund, Peter J. 2020. "What It Means to Describe Speech: Pragmatic Variation and Change in Speech Descriptors in Late Modern English". In Kytö, Merja, and Smitterberg, Erik (eds.), *Late Modern English: Novel Encounters*. Amsterdam and Philadelphia: John Benjamins, 295–314.
Grund, Peter J., and Smitterberg, Erik. 2014. "Conjuncts in Nineteenth-Century English: Diachronic Development and Genre Diversity". *English Language and Linguistics* 18(1), 157–81.

Grund, Peter J., and Walker, Terry. 2006. "The Subjunctive in Adverbial Clauses in Nineteenth-Century English". In Kytö, Merja, Rydén, Mats, and Smitterberg, Erik (eds.), *Nineteenth-Century English: Stability and Change*. Cambridge: Cambridge University Press, 89–109.
Günther, Christine. 2019. "A Difficult to Explain Phenomenon: Increasing Complexity in the Prenominal Position". *English Language and Linguistics* 23(3), 645–70.
Harrison, Dick. 2018. *Englands historia. Del II: Från 1600 till idag*. Lund: Historiska media.
Harvie, Christopher. 1992. "Revolution and the Rule of Law (1789–1851)". In Morgan, Kenneth O. (ed.), *The Oxford Illustrated History of Britain*. Oxford: Oxford University Press, 419–62.
Harwood, William. 2018. "Reduced Relatives and Extended Phases: A Phase-Based Analysis of the Inflectional Restrictions on English Reduced Relative Clauses". *Studia Linguistica* 72(2), 428–71.
Haselow, Alexander. 2015. "Speech-Like Syntax in Written Texts: Changing Syntactic Conventions in News Discourse". In Bös, Birte, and Kornexl, Lucia (eds.), *Changing Genre Conventions in Historical English News Discourse*. Amsterdam and Philadelphia: John Benjamins, 191–221.
Haugland, Kari E. 1995. "Is't Allow'd or Ain't It? On Contraction in Early Grammars and Spelling Books". *Studia Neophilologica* 67(2), 165–84.
Helsinki Corpus = The Helsinki Corpus of English Texts. 1991. Department of Modern Languages, University of Helsinki. Compiled by Rissanen, Matti (Project leader), Kytö, Merja (Project secretary), Kahlas-Tarkka, Leena and Kilpiö, Matti (Old English), Nevanlinna, Saara and Taavitsainen, Irma (Middle English), and Nevalainen, Terttu and Raumolin-Brunberg, Helena (Early Modern English).
Hickey, Raymond. 2003. "How Do Dialects Get the Features They Have? On the Process of New Dialect Formation". In Hickey, Raymond (ed.), *Motives for Language Change*. Cambridge: Cambridge University Press, 213–39.
Hickey, Raymond (ed.). 2004a. *Legacies of Colonial English: Studies in Transported Dialects*. Cambridge: Cambridge University Press.
Hickey, Raymond. 2004b. "Appendix 2: Timeline for Varieties of English". In Hickey, Raymond (ed.), *Legacies of Colonial English: Studies in Transported Dialects*. Cambridge: Cambridge University Press, 621–26.
Hickey, Raymond (ed.). 2010a. *Eighteenth-Century English: Ideology and Change*. Cambridge: Cambridge University Press.
Hickey, Raymond. 2010b. "Preface". In Hickey, Raymond (ed.), *Eighteenth-Century English: Ideology and Change*. Cambridge: Cambridge University Press, xvii–xviii.
Hickey, Raymond. 2010c. "Attitudes and Concerns in Eighteenth-Century English". In Hickey, Raymond (ed.), *Eighteenth-Century English: Ideology and Change*. Cambridge: Cambridge University Press, 1–20.
Hickey, Raymond. 2010d. "English in Eighteenth-Century Ireland". In Hickey, Raymond (ed.), *Eighteenth-Century English: Ideology and Change*. Cambridge: Cambridge University Press, 235–68.

Hickey, Raymond. 2012. "Standard English and Standards of English". In Hickey, Raymond (ed.), *Standards of English: Codified Varieties around the World*. Cambridge: Cambridge University Press, 1–33.

Hickey, Raymond. 2020. "The Interplay of Internal and External Factors in Varieties of English". In Kytö, Merja, and Smitterberg, Erik (eds.), *Late Modern English: Novel Encounters*. Amsterdam and Philadelphia: John Benjamins, 43–64.

Hilpert, Martin. 2020. "The Great Temptation: What Diachronic Corpora Do and Do Not Reveal about Social Change". In Rautionaho, Paula, Nurmi, Arja, and Klemola, Juhani (eds.), *Corpora and the Changing Society: Studies in the Evolution of English*. Amsterdam and Philadelphia: John Benjamins, 3–27.

Hilpert, Martin, and Correia Saavedra, David. 2016. "The Unidirectionality of Semantic Changes in Grammaticalization: An Experimental Approach to the Asymmetric Priming Hypothesis". *English Language and Linguistics* 22(3), 357–80.

Hilpert, Martin, and Mair, Christian. 2015. "Grammatical Change". In Biber, Douglas, and Reppen, Randi (eds.), *The Cambridge Handbook of English Corpus Linguistics*. Cambridge: Cambridge University Press, 180–200.

Hoffmann, Sebastian. 2004. "Using the *OED* Quotations Database as a Corpus – a Linguistic Appraisal". *ICAME Journal* 28, 17–30.

Hollis, Patricia. 1970. *The Pauper Press: A Study in Working-Class Radicalism of the 1830s*. Oxford: Oxford University Press.

Huddleston, Rodney, and Pullum, Geoffrey K. 2002. *The Cambridge Grammar of the English Language*. Cambridge: Cambridge University Press.

Hudson, R. A. 1973. "Tense and Time Reference in Reduced Relative Clauses". *Linguistic Inquiry* 4(2), 251–6.

Hundt, Marianne. 2001. "What Corpora Tell Us about the Grammaticalisation of Voice in *Get*-Constructions". *Studies in Language* 25(1), 49–88.

Hundt, Marianne. 2004. "Animacy, Agentivity, and the Spread of the Progressive in Modern English". *English Language and Linguistics* 8(1), 47–69.

Hundt, Marianne. 2009. "*Colonial Lag, Colonial Innovation* or Simply *Language Change?*" In Rohdenburg, Günter, and Schlüter, Julia (eds.), *One Language, Two Grammars? Differences between British and American English*. Cambridge: Cambridge University Press, 13–37.

Hundt, Marianne, Denison, David, and Schneider, Gerold. 2012a. "Relative Complexity in Scientific Discourse". *English Language and Linguistics* 16(2), 209–40.

Hundt, Marianne, Denison, David, and Schneider, Gerold. 2012b. "Retrieving Relatives from Historical Data". *Literary and Linguistic Computing* 27(1), 3–16.

Hundt, Marianne, and Leech, Geoffrey. 2012. "'Small Is Beautiful': On the Value of Standard Reference Corpora for Observing Recent Grammatical Change". In Nevalainen, Terttu, and Traugott, Elizabeth Closs (eds.), *The*

Oxford Handbook of the History of English. Oxford and New York: Oxford University Press, 175–88.
Hundt, Marianne, and Mair, Christian. 1999. "'Agile' and 'Uptight' Genres: The Corpus-Based Approach to Language Change in Progress". *International Journal of Corpus Linguistics* 4(2), 221–42.
Jacobs, Andreas, and Jucker, Andreas H. 1995. "The Historical Perspective in Pragmatics". In Jucker, Andreas H. (ed.), *Historical Pragmatics: Pragmatic Developments in the History of English*. Amsterdam and Philadelphia: John Benjamins, 3–33.
Johansson, Christine. 2006. "Relativizers in Nineteenth-Century English". In Kytö, Merja, Rydén, Mats, and Smitterberg, Erik (eds.), *Nineteenth-Century English: Stability and Change*. Cambridge: Cambridge University Press, 136–82.
Johnson, Samuel. 1755. *A Dictionary of the English Language*. London.
Johnstone, Barbara. 1996. *The Linguistic Individual: Self-Expression in Language and Linguistics*. New York and Oxford: Oxford University Press.
Jones, Charles. 2012. "Late Modern English: Phonology". In Bergs, Alexander, and Brinton, Laurel J. (eds.), *English Historical Linguistics: An International Handbook*. Vol. 1. Berlin and Boston: Mouton de Gruyter, 827–42.
Joseph, Brian D. 1992. "Diachronic Explanation: Putting Speakers Back into the Picture". In Davis, Garry W., and Iverson, Gregory K. (eds.), *Explanation in Historical Linguistics*. Amsterdam and Philadelphia: John Benjamins, 123–44.
Joyce, Patrick. 1991. "The People's English: Language and Class in England c.1840–1920". In Burke, Peter, and Porter, Roy (eds.), *Language, Self, and Society: A Social History of Language*. Cambridge: Polity Press, 154–90.
Jucker, Andreas H. 1992. *Social Stylistics: Syntactic Variation in British Newspapers*. Berlin and New York: Mouton de Gruyter.
Juffs, Alan. 1998. "Main Verb versus Reduced Relative Clause Ambiguity Resolution in L2 Sentence Processing". *Language Learning* 48(1), 107–47.
Keizer, Evelien. 2007. *The English Noun Phrase: The Nature of Linguistic Categorization*. Cambridge: Cambridge University Press.
Keller, Rudi. 1994 [1990]. *On Language Change: The Invisible Hand in Language*. Translated by Brigitte Nerlich. London: Routledge.
Kilgarriff, Adam. 2005. "Language Is Never, Ever, Ever, Random". *Corpus Linguistics and Linguistic Theory* 1(2), 263–76.
Kjellmer, Göran. 1975. "Are Relative Infinitives Modal?" *Studia Neophilologica* 47(2), 323–32.
Kjellmer, Göran. 1998. "On Contraction in Modern English". *Studia Neophilologica* 69(2), 155–86.
Kjellmer, Göran. 2009. "The Revived Subjunctive". In Rohdenburg, Günter, and Schlüter, Julia (eds.), *One Language, Two Grammars? Differences between British and American English*. Cambridge: Cambridge University Press, 246–56.
Knowles, Gerry. 1997. *A Cultural History of the English Language*. London and New York: Arnold.

Koplenig, Alexander. 2019. "Against Statistical Significance Testing in Corpus Linguistics". *Corpus Linguistics and Linguistic Theory* 15(2), 321–46.
Kranich, Svenja. 2010. *The Progressive in Modern English: A Corpus-Based Study of Grammaticalization and Related Changes*. Amsterdam and New York: Rodopi.
Kretzschmar, William A., Jr. 2009. *The Linguistics of Speech*. Cambridge: Cambridge University Press.
Kretzschmar, William A., Jr. 2015a. "Complex Systems in the History of American English". In Taavitsainen, Irma, Kytö, Merja, Claridge, Claudia, and Smith, Jeremy (eds.), *Developments in English: Expanding Electronic Evidence*. Cambridge: Cambridge University Press, 251–64.
Kretzschmar, William A., Jr. 2015b. *Language and Complex Systems*. Cambridge: Cambridge University Press.
Kroch, Anthony S. 1989. "Reflexes of Grammar in Patterns of Language Change". *Language Variation and Change* 1(3), 199–244.
Kytö, Merja. 1991. *Variation and Diachrony, with Early American English in Focus: Studies on CAN/MAY and SHALL/WILL*. Frankfurt am Main: Peter Lang.
Kytö, Merja. 1997. "*Be/Have* + Past Participle: The Choice of the Auxiliary with Intransitives from Late Middle to Modern English". In Rissanen, Matti, Kytö, Merja, and Heikkonen, Kirsi (eds.), *English in Transition: Corpus-Based Studies in Linguistic Variation and Genre Styles*. Berlin and New York: Mouton de Gruyter, 17–85.
Kytö, Merja, and Pahta, Päivi. 2012. "Evidence from Historical Corpora up to the Twentieth Century". In Nevalainen, Terttu, and Traugott, Elizabeth Closs (eds.), *The Oxford Handbook of the History of English*. Oxford and New York: Oxford University Press, 123–33.
Kytö, Merja, and Romaine, Suzanne. 2006. "Adjective Comparison in Nineteenth-Century English". In Kytö, Merja, Rydén, Mats, and Smitterberg, Erik (eds.), *Nineteenth-Century English: Stability and Change*. Cambridge: Cambridge University Press, 194–214.
Kytö, Merja, Rudanko, Juhani, and Smitterberg, Erik. 2000. "Building a Bridge between the Present and the Past: A Corpus of 19th-Century English". *ICAME Journal* 24, 85–97.
Kytö, Merja, Rydén, Mats, and Smitterberg, Erik (eds.). 2006a. *Nineteenth-Century English: Stability and Change*. Cambridge: Cambridge University Press.
Kytö, Merja, Rydén, Mats, and Smitterberg, Erik. 2006b. "Introduction: Exploring Nineteenth-Century English – Past and Present Perspectives". In Kytö, Merja, Rydén, Mats, and Smitterberg, Erik (eds.), *Nineteenth-Century English: Stability and Change*. Cambridge: Cambridge University Press, 1–16.
Kytö, Merja, and Smitterberg, Erik. 2006. "19th-Century English: An Age of Stability or a Period of Change?" In Facchinetti, Roberta, and Rissanen, Matti (eds.), *Corpus-Based Studies of Diachronic English*. Bern: Peter Lang, 199–230.

Kytö, Merja, and Smitterberg, Erik. 2019. "The Conjunction *and* in Phrasal and Clausal Structures in the *Old Bailey Corpus*". In Yáñez-Bouza, Nuria, Moore, Emma, van Bergen, Linda, and Hollmann, Willem B. (eds.), *Categories, Constructions, and Change in English Syntax*. Cambridge: Cambridge University Press, 234–50.

Kytö, Merja, and Smitterberg, Erik (eds.). 2020a. *Late Modern English: Novel Encounters*. Amsterdam and Philadelphia: John Benjamins.

Kytö, Merja, and Smitterberg, Erik. 2020b. "Introduction: Late Modern English Studies into the Twenty-First Century". In Kytö, Merja, and Smitterberg, Erik (eds.), *Late Modern English: Novel Encounters*. Amsterdam and Philadelphia: John Benjamins, 1–17.

Kytö, Merja, and Walker, Terry. 2003. "The Linguistic Study of Early Modern English Speech-Related Texts: How 'Bad' Can 'Bad' Data Be?" *Journal of English Linguistics* 31(3), 221–48.

Labov, William. 1972. "Some Principles of Linguistic Methodology". *Language in Society* 1(1), 97–120.

Labov, William. 1994. *Principles of Linguistic Change. Vol. 1: Internal Factors*. Malden and Oxford: Blackwell.

Labov, William. 2001. *Principles of Linguistic Change. Vol. 2: Social Factors*. Malden and Oxford: Blackwell.

Labov, William. 2007. "Transmission and Diffusion". *Language* 83(2), 344–87.

Labov, William. 2010. *Principles of Linguistic Change. Vol. 3: Cognitive and Cultural Factors*. Chichester: Wiley-Blackwell.

Lange, Claudia. 2012. "Standardization: Standards in the History of English". In Bergs, Alexander, and Brinton, Laurel J. (eds.), *English Historical Linguistics: An International Handbook*. Vol. 1. Berlin and Boston: Mouton de Gruyter, 994–1,006.

Langford, Paul. 1992. "The Eighteenth Century (1688–1789)". In Morgan, Kenneth O. (ed.), *The Oxford Illustrated History of Britain*. Oxford: Oxford University Press, 350–418.

Lass, Roger. 1980. *On Explaining Language Change*. Cambridge: Cambridge University Press.

Lass, Roger. 1997. *Historical Linguistics and Language Change*. Cambridge: Cambridge University Press.

Lass, Roger. 1999. "Phonology and Morphology". In Lass, Roger (ed.), *The Cambridge History of the English Language. Vol. III: 1476–1776*. Cambridge: Cambridge University Press, 56–186.

Lee, Alan J. 1976. *The Origins of the Popular Press in England: 1855–1914*. London: Croom Helm.

Lee, Alan. 1978. "The Structure, Ownership and Control of the Press, 1855–1914". In Boyce, George, Curran, James, and Wingate, Pauline (eds.), *Newspaper History: From the Seventeenth Century to the Present Day*. London: Constable, 117–29.

Leech, Geoffrey. 2004. "Recent Grammatical Change in English: Data, Description, Theory". In Aijmer, Karin, and Altenberg, Bengt (eds.), *Advances in Corpus Linguistics*. Amsterdam: Rodopi, 61–81.

Leech, Geoffrey. 2007. "New Resources, or Just Better Old Ones? The Holy Grail of Representativeness". In Hundt, Marianne, Nesselhauf, Nadja, and Biewer, Carolin (eds.), *Corpus Linguistics and the Web*. Amsterdam and New York: Rodopi, 133–49.

Leech, Geoffrey, Hundt, Marianne, Mair, Christian, and Smith, Nicholas. 2009. *Change in Contemporary English: A Grammatical Study*. Cambridge: Cambridge University Press.

Lehto, Anu. 2013. "Complexity and Genre Conventions: Text Structure and Coordination in Early Modern English Proclamations". In Jucker, Andreas H., Landert, Daniela, Seiler, Annina, and Studer-Joho, Nicole (eds.), *Meaning in the History of English: Words and Texts in Context*. Amsterdam and Philadelphia: John Benjamins, 233–56.

Leonard, Sterling Andrus. 1929. *The Doctrine of Correctness in English Usage: 1700–1800*. Madison: University of Wisconsin.

Levshina, Natalia. 2015. *How to Do Linguistics with R: Data Exploration and Statistical Analysis*. Amsterdam and Philadelphia: John Benjamins.

Lewis, Diana M. 2012. "Late Modern English: Pragmatics and Discourse". In Bergs, Alexander, and Brinton, Laurel J. (eds.), *English Historical Linguistics: An International Handbook*. Vol. 1. Berlin and Boston: Mouton de Gruyter, 901–15.

Liddle, Dallas. 1999. "Who Invented the 'Leading Article'? Reconstructing the History and Prehistory of a Victorian Newspaper Genre". *Media History* 5(1), 5–18.

Lightfoot, David. 2003. "Grammaticalisation: Cause or Effect?" In Hickey, Raymond (ed.), *Motives for Language Change*. Cambridge: Cambridge University Press, 99–123.

Ljung, Magnus. 2000. "Newspaper Genres and Newspaper English". In Ungerer, Friedrich (ed.), *English Media Texts Past and Present: Language and Textual Structure*. Amsterdam and Philadelphia: John Benjamins, 131–49.

Longman = *Longman Dictionary of Contemporary English*. 2014. 6th ed. Harlow: Pearson.

López-Couso, María José. 2007. "Auxiliary and Negative Cliticisation in Late Modern English". In Pérez-Guerra, Javier, González-Álvarez, Dolores, Bueno-Alonso, Jorge L., and Rama-Martínez, Esperanza (eds.), *"Of Varying Language and Opposing Creed": New Insights into Late Modern English*. Bern: Peter Lang, 301–23.

López-Couso, María José. 2017. "Transferring Insights from Child Language Acquisition to Diachronic Change (and *Vice Versa*)". In Hundt, Marianne, Mollin, Sandra, and Pfenninger, Simone E. (eds.), *The Changing English Language: Psycholinguistic Perspectives*. Cambridge: Cambridge University Press, 332–47.

Lowth, Robert. 1762. *A Short Introduction to English Grammar: With Critical Notes*. London.

Lyne, Susanna. 2011. The Subject of the Verbal Gerund: A Study of Variation in English. (Doctoral thesis, Uppsala University, unpublished.)

MacKenzie, Laurel. 2013. "Variation in English Auxiliary Realization: A New Take on Contraction". *Language Variation and Change* 25, 17–41.
MacMahon, Michael K. C. 1998. "Phonology". In Romaine, Suzanne (ed.), *The Cambridge History of the English Language. Vol. IV: 1776–1997*. Cambridge: Cambridge University Press, 373–535.
Maguire, Warren, Clark, Lynn, and Watson, Kevin. 2013. "Introduction: What Are Mergers and Can They Be Reversed?"*English Language and Linguistics* 17(2), 229–39.
Mahlberg, Michaela. 2013. *Corpus Stylistics and Dickens's Fiction*. New York: Routledge.
Mair, Christian. 1997. "Parallel Corpora: A Real-Time Approach to the Study of Language Change in Progress". In Ljung, Magnus (ed.), *Corpus-Based Studies in English: Papers from the Seventeenth International Conference on English Language Research on Computerized Corpora (ICAME 17), Stockholm, May 15–19, 1996*. Amsterdam and Atlanta: Rodopi, 195–209.
Mair, Christian. 2006a. "Nonfinite Complement Clauses in the Nineteenth Century: The Case of *Remember*". In Kytö, Merja, Rydén, Mats, and Smitterberg, Erik (eds.), *Nineteenth-Century English: Stability and Change*. Cambridge: Cambridge University Press, 215–28.
Mair, Christian. 2006b. *Twentieth-Century English: History, Variation, and Standardization*. Cambridge: Cambridge University Press.
Mair, Christian, and Hundt, Marianne. 1995. "Why Is the Progressive Becoming More Frequent in English? A Corpus-Based Investigation of Language Change in Progress". *Zeitschrift für Anglistik und Amerikanistik* 43(2), 111–22.
Matheson, Donald. 2000. "The Birth of News Discourse: Changes in News Language in British Newspapers, 1880–1930". *Media, Culture & Society* 22, 557–73.
Mathieu, Éric, and Truswell, Robert. 2017. "Micro-Change and Macro-Change in Diachronic Syntax". In Mathieu, Éric, and Truswell, Robert (eds.), *Micro-Change and Macro-Change in Diachronic Syntax*. Oxford: Oxford University Press, 1–9.
Matthew, H. C. G. 1992. "The Liberal Age (1851–1914)". In Morgan, Kenneth O. (ed.), *The Oxford Illustrated History of Britain*. Oxford: Oxford University Press, 463–522.
Matthews, P. H. 2014. *The Concise Oxford Dictionary of Linguistics* (online). 3rd ed. Oxford: Oxford University Press.
Mazzon, Gabriella. 2004. *A History of English Negation*. Harlow: Pearson.
McCafferty, Kevin. 2014. "'[W]ell Are You Not Got Over Thinking about Going to Ireland Yet': The BE-Perfect in Eighteenth- and Nineteenth-Century Irish English". In Hundt, Marianne (ed.), *Late Modern English Syntax*. Cambridge: Cambridge University Press, 333–51.
McElhinny, Bonnie S. 1993. "Copula and Auxiliary Contraction in the Speech of White Americans". *American Speech* 68(4), 371–99.
McEnery, Tony, Xiao, Richard, and Tono, Yukio. 2006. *Corpus-Based Language Studies: An Advanced Resource Book*. Abingdon: Routledge.

McFadden, Thomas. 2017. "On the Disappearance of the BE Perfect in Late Modern English". *Acta Linguistica Hafniensia* 49(2), 159–75.
McKoon, Gail, and Ratcliff, Roger. 2003. "Meaning through Syntax: Language Comprehension and the Reduced Relative Clause Construction". *Psychological Review* 110(3), 490–525.
McKoon, Gail, and Ratcliff, Roger. 2005. "'Meaning through Syntax' in Sentence Production and Comprehension: Reply to McRae et al. (2005)". *Psychological Review* 112(4), 1,032–9.
McMahon, April M. S. 1994. *Understanding Language Change*. Cambridge: Cambridge University Press.
McRae, Ken, Hare, Mary, and Tanenhaus, Michael K. 2005a. "Meaning through Syntax Is Insufficient to Explain Comprehension of Sentences with Reduced Relative Clauses: Comment on McKoon and Ratcliff (2003)". *Psychological Review* 112 (4), 1,022–31.
McRae, Ken, Hare, Mary, and Tanenhaus, Michael K. 2005b. "Postscript: Rejoinder to McKoon and Ratcliff (2005)". *Psychological Review* 112(4), 1,031.
Milic, Louis T. 1977. "Tone in Steele's 'Tatler' ". In Bond, Donovan H., and McLeod, W. Reynolds (eds.), *Newsletters to Newspapers: Eighteenth-Century Journalism*. Morgantown: School of Journalism, West Virginia University, 33–45.
Millar, Neil. 2009. "Modal Verbs in TIME: Frequency Changes 1923–2006". *International Journal of Corpus Linguistics* 14(2), 191–220.
Milroy, James. 1992a. *Linguistic Variation and Change: On the Historical Sociolinguistics of English*. Oxford and Cambridge: Blackwell.
Milroy, James. 1992b. "A Social Model for the Interpretation of Language Change". In Rissanen, Matti, Ihalainen, Ossi, Nevalainen, Terttu, and Taavitsainen, Irma (eds.), *History of Englishes: New Methods and Interpretations in Historical Linguistics*. Berlin and New York: Mouton de Gruyter, 72–91.
Milroy, James. 1996. "Linguistic Ideology and the Anglo-Saxon Lineage of English". In Klemola, Juhani, Kytö, Merja, and Rissanen, Matti (eds.), *Speech Past and Present: Studies in English Dialectology in Memory of Ossi Ihalainen*. Frankfurt am Main: Peter Lang, 169–86.
Milroy, James. 1997. "Internal vs. External Motivations for Linguistic Change". *Multilingua* 16(4), 311–23.
Milroy, James. 1998. "Children Can't Speak or Write Properly Any More". In Bauer, Laurie, and Trudgill, Peter (eds.), *Language Myths*. London: Penguin, 58–65.
Milroy, James, and Milroy, Lesley. 1985. "Linguistic Change, Social Network and Speaker Innovation". *Journal of Linguistics* 21(2), 339–84.
Milroy, Lesley. 1987. *Language and Social Networks*. 2nd ed. Oxford and New York: Blackwell.
Milroy, Lesley. 2000. "Social Network Analysis and Language Change: Introduction". *European Journal of English Studies* 4(3), 217–23.
Mondorf, Britta. 2009. *More Support for More-Support: The Role of Processing Constraints on the Choice between Synthetic and Analytic Comparative Forms*. Amsterdam and Philadelphia: John Benjamins.

Mondorf, Britta. 2012. "Late Modern English: Morphology". In Bergs, Alexander, and Brinton, Laurel J. (eds.), *English Historical Linguistics: An International Handbook*. Vol. 1. Berlin and Boston: Mouton de Gruyter, 842–69.
Montgomery, Michael. 1989. "The Standardization of English Relative Clauses". In Trahern, Joseph B., Jr. (ed.), *Standardizing English: Essays in the History of Language Change in Honor of John Hurt Fisher*. Knoxville: The University of Tennessee Press, 113–38.
Moskowich, Isabel, and Crespo, Begoña (eds.). 2012. *Astronomy "Playne and Simple": The Writing of Science between 1700 and 1900. Including CD-ROM: A Corpus of English Texts on Astronomy (CETA)*. Amsterdam and Philadelphia: John Benjamins.
Moskowich, Isabel, Crespo, Begoña, Puente-Castelo, Luis, and Monaco, Leida Maria (eds.). 2019. *Writing History in Late Modern English: Explorations of the Coruña Corpus*. Amsterdam and Philadelphia: John Benjamins.
Mufwene, Salikoko S. 2008. *Language Evolution: Contact, Competition and Change*. London and New York: Continuum.
Mufwene, Salikoko S. 2014. "Language Ecology, Language Evolution, and the Actuation Question". In Åfarli, Tor A., and Mæhlum, Brit (eds.), *The Sociolinguistics of Grammar*. Amsterdam and Philadelphia: John Benjamins, 13–35.
Mugglestone, Lynda. 2003. *"Talking Proper": The Rise of Accent as Social Symbol*. 2nd ed. Oxford: Oxford University Press.
Mugglestone, Lynda. 2006. "English in the Nineteenth Century". In Mugglestone, Lynda (ed.), *The Oxford History of English*. Oxford: Oxford University Press, 274–304.
Nahkola, Kari, and Saanilahti, Marja. 2004. "Mapping Language Changes in Real Time: A Panel Study on Finnish". *Language Variation and Change* 16(2), 75–92.
Nevalainen, Terttu. 1999. "Early Modern English Lexis and Semantics". In Lass, Roger (ed.), *The Cambridge History of the English Language. Vol. III: 1476–1776*, 332–458.
Nevalainen, Terttu, Palander-Collin, Minna, and Säily, Tanja (eds.). 2018. *Patterns of Change in 18th-Century English: A Sociolinguistic Approach*. Amsterdam and Philadelphia: John Benjamins.
Nevalainen, Terttu, and Raumolin-Brunberg, Helena. 2017. *Historical Sociolinguistics: Language Change in Tudor and Stuart England*. 2nd ed. Abingdon and New York: Routledge.
Nevalainen, Terttu, Säily, Tanja, and Vartianen, Turo. 2020a. "Comparative Sociolinguistic Perspectives on the Rate of Linguistic Change". *Journal of Historical Sociolinguistics* 6(2), 1–15.
Nevalainen, Terttu, Säily, Tanja, Vartianen, Turo, Liimatta, Aatu, and Lijffijt, Jefrey. 2020b. "History of English as Punctuated Equilibria? A Meta-Analysis of the Rate of Linguistic Change in Middle English". *Journal of Historical Sociolinguistics* 6(2), 1–40.

Nevalainen, Terttu, and Tissari, Heli. 2010. "Contextualising Eighteenth-Century Politeness: Social Distinction and Metaphorical Levelling". In Hickey, Raymond (ed.), *Eighteenth-Century English: Ideology and Change*. Cambridge: Cambridge University Press, 133–58.

Newmeyer, Frederick J. 2014. "Syntactic Change: Between Universal Grammar and Fuzzy Grammar". In Åfarli, Tor A., and Mæhlum, Brit (eds.), *The Sociolinguistics of Grammar*. Amsterdam and Philadelphia: John Benjamins, 37–66.

OBC = *The Old Bailey Corpus: Spoken English in the 18th and 19th Centuries*. 2012. Compiled by Huber, Magnus, Nissel, Magnus, Maiwald, Patrick, and Widlitzki, Bianca.

OED = *Oxford English Dictionary Online*. www.oed.com.

Oldireva Gustafsson, Larisa. 2002. *Preterite and Past Participle Forms in English 1680–1790: Standardisation Processes in Public and Private Writing*. Uppsala: Acta Universitatis Upsaliensis.

Övergaard, Gerd. 1995. *The Mandative Subjunctive in American and British English in the 20th Century*. Uppsala: Acta Universitatis Upsaliensis.

Paul, Hermann. [1891] 1978. "On Sound Change". In Baldi, Philip, and Werth, Ronald N. (eds.), *Readings in Historical Phonology: Chapters in the Theory of Sound Change*. University Park and London: The Pennsylvania State University Press, 3–22. [Originally published in *Principles of the History of Language* (London, 1891), 36–64, translated by H. A. Strong from the 2nd ed. of *Prinzipien der Sprachgeschichte* (1886).]

Percy, Carol. 2002. "The Social Symbolism of Contractions and Colloquialisms in Contemporary Accounts of Dr Samuel Johnson: Bozzy, Piozzi, and the Authority of Intimacy". *Historical Sociolinguistics and Sociohistorical Linguistics* 2, n.p.

Percy, Carol. 2012. "Attitudes, Prescriptivism, and Standardization". In Nevalainen, Terttu, and Traugott, Elizabeth Closs (eds.), *The Oxford Handbook of the History of English*. Oxford and New York: Oxford University Press, 446–56.

Pérez-Guerra, Javier, González-Álvarez, Dolores, Bueno-Alonso, Jorge L., and Rama-Martínez, Esperanza (eds.). 2007. *"Of Varying Language and Opposing Creed": New Insights into Late Modern English*. Bern: Peter Lang.

Petré, Peter, and Van de Velde, Freek. 2018. "The Real-Time Dynamics of the Individual and the Community in Grammaticalization". *Language* 94(4), 867–901.

Phillipps, K. C. 1970. *Jane Austen's English*. London: André Deutsch.

Phillipps, K. C. 1978. *The Language of Thackeray*. London: André Deutsch.

Phillipps, K. C. 1984. *Language and Class in Victorian England*. Oxford and New York: Blackwell.

Pitman, Isaac. 1852. *A Manual of Phonography, or, Writing by Sound: A Natural Method of Writing by Signs That Represent Spoken Sounds; Adapted to the English Language as a Complete System of Phonetic Shorthand*. 9th ed. London: Fred Pitman.

Plonsky, Luke, and Oswald, Frederick L. 2017. "Multiple Regression as a Flexible Alternative to ANOVA in L2 Research". *Studies in Second Language Acquisition* 39, 579–92.

Porter, G. R. 1912. *The Progress of the Nation in Its Various Social and Economic Relations from the Beginning of the Nineteenth Century.* New ed. by F. W. Hirst. London: Methuen.

Potsma, Gertjan. 2017. "Modelling Transient States in Language Change". In Mathieu, Éric, and Truswell, Robert (eds.), *Micro-Change and Macro-Change in Diachronic Syntax.* Oxford: Oxford University Press, 75–93.

Pratt, Lynda, and Denison, David. 2000. "The Language of the Southey–Coleridge Circle". *Language Sciences* 22(3), 401–22.

Quirk, Randolph, Greenbaum, Sidney, Leech, Geoffrey, and Svartvik, Jan. 1985. *A Comprehensive Grammar of the English Language.* London and New York: Longman.

Rah, Anne, and Adone, Dany. 2010. "Processing of the Reduced Relative Clause versus Main Verb Ambiguity in L2 Learners at Different Proficiency Levels". *Studies in Second Language Acquisition* 32, 79–109.

Raumolin-Brunberg, Helena. 1988. "Variation and Historical Linguistics: A Survey of Methods and Concepts". *Neuphilologische Mitteilungen* 89(2), 136–54.

Raumolin-Brunberg, Helena. 1991. *The Noun Phrase in Early Sixteenth-Century English: A Study Based on Sir Thomas More's Writings.* Helsinki: Société Néophilologique.

Raumolin-Brunberg, Helena. 2005. "Language Change in Adulthood: Historical Letters as Evidence". *European Journal of English Studies* 9(1), 37–51.

Raumolin-Brunberg, Helena, and Nurmi, Arja. 2011. "Grammaticalization and Language Change in the Individual". In Narrog, Heiko, and Heine, Bernd (eds.), *The Oxford Handbook of Grammaticalization.* Oxford: Oxford University Press, 251–62.

Reuter, David. 2017. *Newspapers, Politics, and Canadian English: A Corpus-Based Analysis of Selected Linguistic Variables in Early Nineteenth-Century Ontario Newspapers.* Heidelberg: Winter.

Rissanen, Matti. 1975. "'Strange and Inkhorne Tearmes': Loan-Words as Style Markers in the Prose of Edward Hall, Thomas Elyot, Thomas More and Roger Ascham". In Ringbom, Håkan (ed.), *Style and Text: Studies Presented to Nils Erik Enkvist.* Stockholm: Skriptor, 250–62.

Rissanen, Matti. 1986. "Variation and the Study of English Historical Syntax". In Sankoff, David (ed.), *Diversity and Diachrony.* Amsterdam and Philadelphia: John Benjamins, 97–109.

Rissanen, Matti. 1994. "The Position of *Not* in Early Modern English Questions". In Kastovsky, Dieter (ed.), *Studies in Early Modern English.* Berlin and New York: Mouton de Gruyter, 339–48.

Rissanen, Matti. 1999a. "Syntax". In Lass, Roger (ed.), *The Cambridge History of the English Language. Vol. III: 1476–1776.* Cambridge: Cambridge University Press, 187–331.

Rissanen, Matti. 1999b. "*Isn't It?* Or *Is It Not?* On the Order of Postverbal Subject and Negative Particle in the History of English". In Tieken-Boon van Ostade, Ingrid, Tottie, Gunnel, and van der Wurff, Wim (eds.), *Negation in the History of English*. Berlin and New York: Mouton de Gruyter, 189–205.

Roberts, Gareth, and Sneller, Betsy. 2020. "Empirical Foundations for an Integrated Study of Language Evolution". *Language Dynamics and Change* 10(2), 188–229.

Rodríguez-Puente, Paula. 2019. *The English Phrasal Verb, 1650–Present: History, Stylistic Drifts, and Lexicalisation*. Cambridge: Cambridge University Press.

Rohdenburg, Günter. 2003. "Cognitive Complexity and *Horror Aequi* as Factors Determining the Use of Interrogative Clause Linkers in English". In Rohdenburg, Günter, and Mondorf, Britta (eds.), *Determinants of Grammatical Variation in English*. Berlin and New York: Mouton de Gruyter, 205–49.

Rohdenburg, Günter. 2006. "The Role of Functional Constraints in the Evolution of the English Complementation System". In Dalton-Puffer, Christiane, Kastovsky, Dieter, Ritt, Nikolaus, and Schendl, Herbert (eds.), *Syntax, Style and Grammatical Norms: English from 1500–2000*. Bern: Peter Lang, 143–66.

Rohdenburg, Günter. 2009. "Reflexive Structures". In Rohdenburg, Günter, and Schlüter, Julia (eds.), *One Language, Two Grammars? Differences between British and American English*. Cambridge: Cambridge University Press, 166–181.

Romaine, Suzanne. 1984. "On the Problem of Syntactic Variation and Pragmatic Meaning in Sociolinguistic Theory". *Folia Linguistica* 18, 409–37.

Romaine, Suzanne (ed.). 1998a. *The Cambridge History of the English Language. Vol. IV: 1776–1997*. Cambridge: Cambridge University Press.

Romaine, Suzanne. 1998b. "Introduction". In Romaine, Suzanne (ed.), *The Cambridge History of the English Language. Vol. IV: 1776–1997*. Cambridge: Cambridge University Press, 1–56.

Romaine, Suzanne. 1999. *Communicating Gender*. Mahwah: Lawrence Erlbaum.

Romaine, Suzanne. 2016. "The Variationist Approach". In Kytö, Merja, and Pahta, Päivi (eds.), *The Cambridge Handbook of English Historical Linguistics*. Cambridge: Cambridge University Press, 19–35.

Rosenbach, Anette. 2007. "Emerging Variation: Determiner Genitives and Noun Modifiers in English". *English Language and Linguistics* 11(1), 143–89.

Rosenbach, Anette. 2010. "How Synchronic Gradience Makes Sense in the Light of Language Change (and *Vice Versa*)". In Traugott, Elizabeth Closs, and Trousdale, Graeme (eds.), *Gradience, Gradualness and Grammaticalization*. Amsterdam and Philadelphia: John Benjamins, 149–79.

Rosenbach, Anette. 2019. "On the (Non-)Equivalence of Constructions with Determiner Genitives and Noun Modifiers in English". *English Language and Linguistics* 23(4), 759–96.

Rubenhold, Hallie. 2019. *The Five: The Untold Lives of the Women Killed by Jack the Ripper*. London: Transworld.

Rubery, Matthew. 2009. *The Novelty of Newspapers: Victorian Fiction after the Invention of the News.* Oxford: Oxford University Press.

Rudanko, Juhani. 2006. "Watching English Grammar Change: A Case Study on Complement Selection in British and American English". *English Language and Linguistics* 10(1), 31–48.

Rydén, Mats. 1975. "Noun-Name Collocations in British English Newspaper Language". *Studia Neophilologica* 47(1), 14–39.

Rydén, Mats. 1979. *An Introduction to the Historical Study of English Syntax.* Stockholm: Almqvist & Wiksell International.

Rydén, Mats. 1984. "När är en relativsats 'nödvändig'?" *Moderna språk* 78(1), 19–22.

Rydén, Mats, and Brorström, Sverker. 1987. *The Be/Have Variation with Intransitives in English: With Special Reference to the Late Modern Period.* Stockholm: Almqvist & Wiksell International.

Sag, Ivan A. 1997. "English Relative Clause Constructions". *Journal of Linguistics* 33(2), 431–83.

Sairio, Anni. 2009. *Language and Letters of the Bluestocking Network: Sociolinguistic Issues in Eighteenth-Century Epistolary English.* Helsinki: Société Néophilologique.

Salmon, Vivian. 1999. "Orthography and Punctuation". In Lass, Roger (ed.), *The Cambridge History of the English Language. Vol. III: 1476–1776.* Cambridge: Cambridge University Press, 13–55.

Sanchez-Stockhammer, Christina. 2018. *English Compounds and Their Spelling.* Cambridge: Cambridge University Press.

Sankoff, Gillian. 2013. "Longitudinal Studies". In Bayley, Robert, Cameron, Richard, and Lucas, Ceil (eds.), *The Oxford Handbook of Sociolinguistics.* Oxford: Oxford University Press, 261–79.

Saussure, Ferdinand de. [1916] 1986. *Course in General Linguistics.* Trans. by Roy Harris. La Salle: Open Court.

Schalck, Harry. 1988. "Fleet Street in the 1880s: The New Journalism". In Wiener, Joel H. (ed.), *Papers for the Millions: The New Journalism in Britain, 1850s to 1914.* New York, Westport, and London: Greenwood, 73–87.

Schiffrin, Deborah. 1987. *Discourse Markers.* Cambridge: Cambridge University Press.

Schlüter, Julia. 2009. "The Conditional Subjunctive". In Rohdenburg, Günter, and Schlüter, Julia (eds.), *One Language, Two Grammars? Differences between British and American English.* Cambridge: Cambridge University Press, 277–305.

Schneider, Kristina. 2002. *The Development of Popular Journalism in England from 1700 to the Present: Corpus Compilation and Selective Stylistic Analysis.* (PhD dissertation, University of Rostock, unpublished.)

Schwarz, Sarah. 2017. "'Like Getting Nibbled to Death by a Duck': Grammaticalization of the GET-Passive in the TIME Magazine Corpus". *English World-Wide* 38(3), 305–35.

Schwarz, Sarah. 2018. *Passive Voices: BE-, GET- and Prepositional Passives in Recent American English.* (PhD dissertation, Uppsala University.)

Schwarz, Sarah. 2019. "Signs of Grammaticalization: Tracking the GET-Passive through COHA". In Claridge, Claudia, and Bös, Birte (eds.), *Developments in English Historical Morpho-Syntax*. Amsterdam and Philadelphia: John Benjamins, 199–221.
Seoane, Elena, and Loureiro-Porto, Lucía. 2005. "On the Colloquialization of Scientific British and American English". *ESP across Cultures* 2, 106–18.
Siemund, Rainer. 1995. "'For Who the Bell Tolls' – or Why Corpus Linguistics Should Carry the Bell in the Study of Language Change in Present-Day English". *Arbeiten aus Anglistik und Amerikanistik* 20(2), 351–77.
Smakman, Dick, and Nekesa Barasa, Sandra. 2017. "Defining 'Standard': Towards a Cross-Cultural Definition of the Language Norm". In Tieken-Boon van Ostade, Ingrid, and Percy, Carol (eds.), *Prescription and Tradition in Language: Establishing Standards across Time and Space*. Bristol and Blue Ridge Summit, PA: Multilingual Matters, 23–38.
Smith, Anthony. 1978. "The Long Road to Objectivity and Back Again: The Kinds of Truth We Get in Journalism". In Boyce, George, Curran, James, and Wingate, Pauline (eds.), *Newspaper History: From the Seventeenth Century to the Present Day*. London: Constable, 153–71.
Smith, Jeremy J. 2007. *Sound Change and the History of English*. Oxford: Oxford University Press.
Smith, Jeremy. 2015. "Introduction to Part IV". In Taavitsainen, Irma, Kytö, Merja, Claridge, Claudia, and Smith, Jeremy (eds.), *Developments in English: Expanding Electronic Evidence*. Cambridge: Cambridge University Press, 197–9.
Smith, Nicholas, and Rayson, Paul. 2007. "Recent Change and Variation in the British English Use of the Progressive Passive". *ICAME Journal* 31, 129–59.
Smitterberg, Erik. 2005. *The Progressive in 19th-Century English: A Process of Integration*. Amsterdam and New York: Rodopi.
Smitterberg, Erik. 2006. "Partitive Constructions in Nineteenth-Century English". In Kytö, Merja, Rydén, Mats, and Smitterberg, Erik (eds.), *Nineteenth-Century English: Stability and Change*. Cambridge: Cambridge University Press, 242–71.
Smitterberg, Erik. 2008. "The Progressive and Phrasal Verbs: Evidence of Colloquialization in Nineteenth-Century English?" In Nevalainen, Terttu, Taavitsainen, Irma, Pahta, Päivi, and Korhonen, Minna (eds.), *The Dynamics of Linguistic Variation: Corpus Evidence on English Past and Present*. Amsterdam and Philadelphia: John Benjamins, 269–89.
Smitterberg, Erik. 2009. "Multal Adverbs in Nineteenth-Century English". *Studia Neophilologica* 81(2), 121–44.
Smitterberg, Erik. 2012a. "Late Modern English: Sociolinguistics". In Bergs, Alexander, and Brinton, Laurel J. (eds.), *English Historical Linguistics: An International Handbook*. Vol. 1. Berlin and Boston: Mouton de Gruyter, 952–65.

Smitterberg, Erik. 2012b. "Colloquialization and NOT-Contraction in Nineteenth-Century English". In Markus, Manfred, Iyeiri, Yoko, Heuberger, Reinhard, and Chamson, Emil (eds.), *Middle and Modern English Corpus Linguistics: A Multi-Dimensional Approach*. Amsterdam and Philadelphia: John Benjamins, 191–206.

Smitterberg, Erik. 2014. "Syntactic Stability and Change in Nineteenth-Century Newspaper Language". In Hundt, Marianne (ed.), *Late Modern English Syntax*. Cambridge: Cambridge University Press, 311–29.

Spivey-Knowlton, Michael J., Trueswell, John C., and Tanenhaus, Michael K. 1993. "Context Effects in Syntactic Ambiguity Resolution: Discourse and Semantic Influences in Parsing Reduced Relative Clauses". *Canadian Journal of Experimental Psychology* 47(2), 276–309.

Straaijer, Robin. 2018. "The Usage Guide: Evolution of a Genre". In Tieken-Boon van Ostade, Ingrid (ed.), *English Usage Guides: History, Advice, Attitudes*. Oxford: Oxford University Press, 11–30.

Strang, Barbara M. H. 1970. *A History of English*. London: Methuen.

Ström Herold, Jenny, and Levin, Magnus. 2019. "*The Obama Presidency*, *the Macintosh Keyboard* and *the Norway Fiasco*: English Proper Noun Modifiers and Their German and Swedish Correspondences". *English Language and Linguistics* 23(4), 827–54.

Sundby, Bertil, Bjørge, Anne Kari, and Haugland, Kari E. 1991. *A Dictionary of English Normative Grammar 1700–1800*. Amsterdam and Philadelphia: John Benjamins.

Swales, John M. 1990. *Genre Analysis: English in Academic and Research Settings*. Cambridge: Cambridge University Press.

Sweetser, Eve. 1990. *From Etymology to Pragmatics: Metaphorical and Cultural Aspects of Semantic Structure*. Cambridge: Cambridge University Press.

Szmrecsanyi, Benedikt, Biber, Douglas, Egbert, Jesse, and Franco, Karlien. 2016. "Toward More Accountability: Modeling Ternary Genitive Variation in Late Modern English". *Language Variation and Change* 28(1), 1–29.

Taavitsainen, Irma, and Hiltunen, Turo (eds.). 2019. *Late Modern English Medical Texts: Writing Medicine in the Eighteenth Century*. Amsterdam and Philadelphia: John Benjamins.

Taavitsainen, Irma, and Jucker, Andreas H. 2010. "Expressive Speech Acts and Politeness in Eighteenth-Century English". In Hickey, Raymond (ed.), *Eighteenth-Century English: Ideology and Change*. Cambridge: Cambridge University Press, 159–181.

Tagliamonte, Sali A. 2012. *Variationist Sociolinguistics: Change, Observation, Interpretation*. Chichester: John Wiley & Sons.

Tagliamonte, Sali, and Smith, Jennifer. 2002. "'Either It Isn't or It's Not': NEG/AUX Contraction in British Dialects". *English World-Wide* 23(2), 251–81.

Thim, Stefan. 2012. *Phrasal Verbs: The English Verb–Particle Construction and Its History*. Berlin and Boston: Mouton de Gruyter.

Thoms, Gary, Adger, David, Heycock, Caroline, and Smith, Jennifer. 2019. "Syntactic Variation and Auxiliary Contraction: The Surprising Case of Scots". *Language* 95(3), 421–55.

Tieken-Boon van Ostade, Ingrid. 1987. *The Auxiliary Do in Eighteenth-Century English: A Sociohistorical-Linguistic Approach*. Dordrecht and Providence, RI: Foris.
Tieken-Boon van Ostade, Ingrid. 2009. *An Introduction to Late Modern English*. Edinburgh: Edinburgh University Press.
Tieken-Boon van Ostade, Ingrid. 2011. *The Bishop's Grammar: Robert Lowth and the Rise of Prescriptivism*. Oxford: Oxford University Press.
Tieken-Boon van Ostade, Ingrid. 2012. "The Codification of English in England". In Hickey, Raymond (ed.), *Standards of English: Codified Varieties around the World*. Cambridge: Cambridge University Press, 34–54.
Tieken-Boon van Ostade, Ingrid. 2014a. *In Search of Jane Austen: The Language of the Letters*. Oxford: Oxford University Press.
Tieken-Boon van Ostade, Ingrid. 2014b. "Eighteenth-Century English Normative Grammars and Their Readers". In Rutten, Gijsbert, Vosters, Rik, and Vandenbussche, Wim (eds.), *Norms and Usage in Language History, 1600–1900: A Sociolinguistic and Comparative Perspective*. Amsterdam and Philadelphia: John Benjamins, 129–50.
Tieken-Boon van Ostade, Ingrid. 2020. *Describing Prescriptivism: Usage Guides and Usage Problems in British and American English*. London and New York: Routledge.
Tieken-Boon van Ostade, Ingrid, and van der Wurff, Wim (eds.). 2009. *Current Issues in Late Modern English*. Bern: Peter Lang.
TIME = TIME Magazine Corpus: 100 Million Words, 1920s–2000s. 2007–. Compiled by Davies, Mark.
Tottie, Gunnel. 1991. *Negation in English Speech and Writing: A Study in Variation*. San Diego, CA: Academic Press.
Trask, R. L. 2010. *Why Do Languages Change?* Revised by Robert McColl Millar. Cambridge: Cambridge University Press.
Traugott, Elizabeth Closs. 2003. "From Subjectification to Intersubjectification". In Hickey, Raymond (ed.), *Motives for Language Change*. Cambridge: Cambridge University Press, 124–39.
Traugott, Elizabeth Closs. 2016. "Identifying Micro-Changes in a Particular Linguistic Change-Type: The Case of Subjectification". In Kytö, Merja, and Pahta, Päivi (eds.), *The Cambridge Handbook of English Historical Linguistics*. Cambridge: Cambridge University Press, 376–89.
Traugott, Elizabeth Closs, and Trousdale, Graeme. 2010. "Gradience, Gradualness and Grammaticalization: How Do They Intersect?" In Traugott, Elizabeth Closs, and Trousdale, Graeme (eds.), *Gradience, Gradualness and Grammaticalization*. Amsterdam and Philadelphia: John Benjamins, 19–44.
Traugott, Elizabeth Closs, and Trousdale, Graeme. 2013. *Constructionalization and Constructional Changes*. Oxford: Oxford University Press.
Tristram, Hildegard L. C. 2004. "Diglossia in Anglo-Saxon England, or What Was Spoken Old English Like?" *Studia Anglica Posnaniensia* 40, 87–110.

Trudgill, Peter. 2000. *Sociolinguistics: An Introduction to Language and Society*. 4th ed. London: Penguin.
Trudgill, Peter. 2010. *Investigations in Sociohistorical Linguistics: Stories of Colonisation and Contact*. Cambridge: Cambridge University Press.
Trudgill, Peter. 2020. "Sociolinguistic Typology and the Speed of Linguistic Change". *Journal of Historical Sociolinguistics* 6(2), 1–13.
Upton, Clive, Parry, David, and Widdowson, J. D. A. 1994. *Survey of English Dialects: The Dictionary and Grammar*. London and New York: Routledge.
van de Pool, Nikki. 2016. The Development of the Absolute Construction in English: Between Bird's Eye View and Magnifying Glass. (Doctoral thesis, KU Leuven, unpublished.)
Váradi, Tamás. 2001. "The Linguistic Relevance of Corpus Linguistics". In Rayson, Paul, Wilson, Andrew, McEnery, Tony, Hardie, Andrew, and Khoja, Shereen (eds.), *Proceedings of the Corpus Linguistics 2001 Conference, Lancaster University (UK), 29 March–2 April 2001*. Special issue of *UCREL Technical Papers* 13, 587–93.
Varantola, Krista. 1984. *On Noun Phrase Structures in Engineering English*. Turku: Turun Yliopisto.
Varela Pérez, José Ramón. 2013. "Operator and Negative Contraction in Spoken British English: A Change in Progress". In Aarts, Bas, Close, Joanne, Leech, Geoffrey, and Wallis, Sean (eds.), *The Verb Phrase in English: Investigating Recent Language Change with Corpora*. Cambridge: Cambridge University Press, 256–85.
Vartianen, Turo, Nevala, Minna, and Hintikka, Marianna. 2017. "Linguistic Representations of the Social Margins in Early and Late Modern English". *Journal of Historical Sociolinguistics* 3(2), 135–50.
Vincent, David. 1989. *Literacy and Popular Culture: England 1750–1914*. Cambridge: Cambridge University Press.
Visser, F. Th. 1963–73. *An Historical Syntax of the English Language*. 4 vols. Leiden: Brill.
Vosberg, Uwe. 2003. "Cognitive Complexity and the Establishment of *-ing* Constructions with Retrospective Verbs in Modern English". In Dossena, Marina, and Jones, Charles (eds.), *Insights into Late Modern English*. Bern: Peter Lang, 197–220.
Wagner, Susanne. 2012. "Late Modern English: Dialects". In Bergs, Alexander, and Brinton, Laurel J. (eds.), *English Historical Linguistics: An International Handbook*. Vol. 1. Berlin and Boston: Mouton de Gruyter, 915–38.
Walker, James A. 2005. "The *Ain't* Constraint: *Not*-Contraction in Early African American English". *Language Variation and Change* 17, 1–17.
Walker, James A. 2010. *Variation in Linguistic Systems*. New York and London: Routledge.
Walker, John. 1791. *A Critical Pronouncing Dictionary and Expositor of the English Language*. London.

Walker, Terry. 2007. Thou *and* You *in Early Modern English Dialogues: Trials, Depositions, and Drama Comedy*. Amsterdam and Philadelphia: John Benjamins.
Wang, Ying. 2017. "Lexical Bundles in News Discourse 1784–1983". In Palander-Collin, Minna, Ratia, Maura, and Taavitsainen, Irma (eds.), *Diachronic Developments in English News Discourse*. Amsterdam and Philadelphia: John Benjamins, 97–116.
Warner, Anthony R. 1997. "Extending the Paradigm: An Interpretation of the Historical Development of Auxiliary Sequences in English". *English Studies* 78(2), 162–89.
Wårvik, Brita. 1990. "On the History of Grounding Markers in English Narrative: Style or Typology?" In Andersen, Henning, and Koerner, Konrad (eds.), *Historical Linguistics 1987: Papers from the 8th International Conference on Historical Linguistics (8. ICHL)*. Amsterdam and Philadelphia: John Benjamins, 531–42.
Weiner, E. Judith, and Labov, William. 1983. "Constraints on the Agentless Passive". *Journal of Linguistics* 19, 29–58.
Weinreich, Uriel, Labov, William, and Herzog, Marvin I. 1968. "Empirical Foundations for a Theory of Language Change". In Lehmann, W. P., and Malkiel, Yakov (eds.), *Directions for Historical Linguistics: A Symposium*. Austin and London: University of Texas Press, 95–188.
Wells, J. C. 1982. *Accents of English. Vol. I: An Introduction*. Cambridge: Cambridge University Press.
Westergaard, Marit. 2017. "Gradience and Gradualness vs. Abruptness". In Ledgeway, Adam, and Roberts, Ian (eds.), *The Cambridge Handbook of Historical Syntax*. Cambridge: Cambridge University Press, 446–66.
Westergren Axelsson, Margareta. 1998. *Contraction in British Newspapers in the Late 20th Century*. Uppsala: Acta Universitatis Upsaliensis.
Westin, Ingrid. 2002. *Language Change in English Newspaper Editorials*. Amsterdam and New York: Rodopi.
Whitt, Richard J. 2018. "Using Diachronic Corpora to Understand the Connection between Genre and Language Change". In Whitt, Richard J. (ed.), *Diachronic Corpora, Genre, and Language Change*. Amsterdam and Philadelphia: John Benjamins, 1–15.
Whyte, Ian D. 2000. *Migration and Society in Britain: 1550–1830*. Houndmills: Macmillan.
Wiener, Joel H. 1988a. "Introduction". In Wiener, Joel H. (ed.), *Papers for the Millions: The New Journalism in Britain, 1850s to 1914*. New York, Westport, and London: Greenwood, xi–xix.
Wiener, Joel H. 1988b. "How New Was the New Journalism?" In Wiener, Joel H. (ed.), *Papers for the Millions: The New Journalism in Britain, 1850s to 1914*. New York, Westport, and London: Greenwood, 47–71.
Williams, Kevin. 2010. *Read All about It! A History of the British Newspaper*. Abingdon: Routledge.

Williams, Raymond. 1978. "The Press and Popular Culture: An Historical Perspective". In Boyce, George, Curran, James, and Wingate, Pauline (eds.), *Newspaper History: From the Seventeenth Century to the Present Day*. London: Constable, 41–50.

Willis, David. 2017. "Endogenous and Exogenous Theories of Syntactic Change". In Ledgeway, Adam, and Roberts, Ian (eds.), *The Cambridge Handbook of Historical Syntax*. Cambridge: Cambridge University Press, 491–514.

Xekalakis, Elefteria. 1999. Newspapers through the Times: Foreign Reports from the 18th to the 20th Centuries. (PhD dissertation, University of Zurich, unpublished.)

Yaeger-Dror, Malcah. 1997. "Contraction of Negatives as Evidence of Variance in Register-Specific Interactive Rules". *Language Variation and Change* 9, 1–36.

Yaeger-Dror, Malcah, Hall-Lew, Lauren, and Deckert, Sharon. 2002. "*It's Not* or *Isn't It?* Using Large Corpora to Determine the Influences on Contraction Strategies". *Language Variation and Change* 14, 79–118.

Yáñez-Bouza, Nuria. 2014. *Grammar, Rhetoric and Usage in English: Preposition Placement 1500–1900*. Cambridge: Cambridge University Press.

Yang, Charles D. 2000. "Internal and External Forces in Language Change". *Language Variation and Change* 12, 231–50.

Yang, Pi-Lan, and Shih, Su-Chin. 2013. "A Reading-Time Study of the Main Verb versus Reduced Relative Clause Ambiguity Resolution by English Learners in Taiwan". *Applied Psycholinguistics* 34(6), 1,109–33.

Zwicky, Arnold M., and Pullum, Geoffrey K. 1983. "Cliticization vs. Inflection: English *n't*". *Language* 59(3), 502–13.

Index

actuation problem, 49n5
adjective comparison, 34
African-American Vernacular English, 73, 159
ambiguity, 57, 101, 108, 178n9, 214n16, 228n7, 230–1, 232, 246, 250–1, 252, 253n14, 253
American English, 31, 32, 35, 44, 92, 179
analogy, 26, 51, 56n8, 59, 87
apposition, 191n3, 267
Arabic, 46
ARCHER, 233
attributive adjectives, 187, 190, 192, 230
Austen, Jane, 130, 137, 140–1, 264

Bateson, William, 201, 242
BATH/TRAP split, the, 27, 68
Besant, Walter, 137
borrowing, 55, 56
Braddon, Mary, 137, 212
Butler, Samuel, 175n8, 175

categorical change, 2, 4, 22, 42, 53, 54, 55, 61, 62, 64, 71, 257, 259–60
CED, 161
Celtic languages, 7, 72n17, 72, 73
change from above, 58n11, 59, 62, 64–70
change from below, 6, 17n4, 49, 59, 62–4, 88, 137, 203, 218, 265
CLMETEV, 106
CNNE, 9, 81, 82, 106–7, 115–25, 116n19, 129, 162, 163–4, 168–70, 179, 181, 185, 189, 191, 194n5, 195, 199, 201, 203, 204, 208, 213–14, 214n15, 217, 218, 220, 226, 229, 231, 233, 236–9, 240, 242, 245, 247, 249–50, 254, 255, 262, 264, 265–6, 267
codification, 37, 64, 66, 68n15, 68
COHA, 9, 106, 107n15, 158
communal languages, 2, 5, 38, 41, 42, 44–6, 47, 48, 53–4, 55, 64, 67n14, 67, 70, 71, 72–3, 77, 80, 83, 84, 87, 88, 90, 102n12, 125, 257–60, 261, 264
comparability, 80, 81, 106

complexity, 22, 35, 37, 55, 88, 90, 96, 152, 161, 164n4, 239, 266
Complexity Principle, the, 33
compounds, 190, 220, 221n19
CONCE, 9, 37, 81, 82, 106–15, 129, 130n3, 132, 136, 138, 143n9, 148n13, 152, 153, 156, 162, 163–4, 168, 169–70, 172, 174, 177, 179–80, 185, 203, 218, 226, 245, 262, 264, 265, 267
  S-coefficient subcorpus, the, 108, 189–90, 191n4, 191, 194n5, 197, 199, 201, 208–11, 213, 217, 219, 220, 226, 230, 231, 234, 241, 245, 265, 267
concord, 35
conjuncts, 103, 168
convergence, 45, 51, 60, 63, 73, 84, 86, 87–8, 89, 102n12, 125, 257, 261
Corpus of English Dialogues, the. *See* CED
Corpus of Historical American English, the. *See* COHA
Corpus of Late Modern English Texts, the. *See* CLMETEV
Corpus of Nineteenth-Century English, a. *See* CONCE
Corpus of Nineteenth-Century Newspaper English, the. *See* CNNE

Daily Mail, the, 121
Daily News, the, 120, 179
Daily Telegraph, the, 118
democratization, 16, 91–2, 260
determiners, 35, 192, 194n6, 207
Dickens, Charles, 137

economy, 36, 37, 88, 93, 96, 113, 195, 202, 203, 208, 213, 218, 234, 245, 255, 260, 266
editorials, 37, 92, 122–4
education, 8, 17, 19n6, 21, 25, 36, 46, 65, 66, 93, 268
E-language, 74, 105n13
envelope of variation, the, 99–101, 102, 104, 145, 250, 252, 255, 263

299

factor analysis, 112, 128, 161, 168, 171
factor-score analysis, 35, 108, 112, 114, 161, 214, 246
first-language acquisition, 74
form-to-function mapping, 168, 256, 263
French, 25n11, 25, 28, 55
futurity, expressions of, 31, 57, 73, 75, 101, 228n8

Gardiner, Samuel, 202
Gaskell, Elizabeth, 137
gender, 4, 19, 36, 66, 81, 84, 87, 88, 92, 99, 112, 137–8, 156, 158–9, 163, 177, 203, 218, 262, 268
genitive, the, 33, 35n19, 101, 187, 192–3, 194n6, 194, 195, 197, 205n10, 207, 254
genre, 6, 35, 37–8, 52, 53, 55, 79n1, 79–80, 81, 87–9, 97, 99, 104, 122, 143–5, 148, 150, 153, 157, 158, 169, 193, 197, 219–20, 262, 264–5, 266–7
genre diversity, 5, 54, 90, 95, 107, 126, 128, 129, 145, 156, 161, 169, 171, 185, 186, 188, 189, 208, 211, 218, 223, 256, 268
genre evolution, 81
genre norms, 4–5, 55, 76, 86, 90, 130n3, 141n7, 158, 159, 171, 176, 177, 182, 186, 245, 261, 266
genres
  academic writing, 22, 36–7, 92, 96–7, 98, 104, 124, 128, 161, 170, 179, 181, 187, 188, 202, 219, 223, 234, 236, 255, 267
  conversation, 19, 67, 79–80, 114, 128, 170, 177, 179, 181, 223, 225, 246
  drama, 80, 108n16, 108, 111, 127, 129, 130n3, 132–3, 137, 140, 143, 145, 150–2, 154, 156–8, 170, 171, 181–2, 183, 185, 186, 188, 202, 205, 212, 218, 234–6, 264, 265
  expository vs. non-expository, 111, 212, 243, 248
  fiction, 108n16, 108, 111, 112, 124, 129, 130n3, 132–3, 136–8, 140, 143, 144, 150–2, 153, 156–8, 170, 171, 179, 184n12, 184, 186, 188, 202, 205, 212, 214, 223, 234, 245, 249, 250, 264
  history writing, 37, 108, 111, 114, 115n18, 129, 170, 172, 178, 181, 201–2, 204, 205, 213, 214, 218–19, 234–6, 242–3, 244, 245, 248, 255, 266, 267
  letters, 13, 19–21, 26, 36n20, 36, 80, 81, 108–11, 112, 129, 130n3, 163, 169–71, 172, 173–7, 184, 185–6, 188, 199, 202, 203, 205, 212, 218, 234–6, 243, 250, 265–6, 267
  medical writing, 37, 188
  newspaper language, 6, 8, 37, 79n1, 88, 90n7, 91, 92, 93, 96, 97, 115–25, 128, 163, 178, 179, 187, 188, 199, 204, 211, 217, 218, 220, 223–4, 236, 238, 245, 249, 250, 265
  oral vs. literate, 31, 36, 90, 91, 111, 128, 161–2, 171, 186
  parliamentary debates, 108, 111, 114, 129, 170, 171, 172, 177, 183, 185, 199–200, 204, 212, 220, 234, 244, 247, 248, 265

proclamations, 161, 178
scientific writing, 34, 92, 93, 96, 108, 111, 114, 129, 169–70, 171, 178, 181, 188, 199, 201–2, 204, 213, 217–20, 223, 233, 234, 236, 242, 245, 246, 248, 250, 255, 266, 267
  speech-related vs. non-speech-related, 80
  trial proceedings, 80, 81, 104, 108, 111, 113, 129, 130n3, 132–3, 136, 137, 138, 141, 144, 150, 156, 157, 158, 164, 169, 172, 173, 181, 182, 183, 185, 186, 197, 199–201, 201n9, 204, 205, 212, 214, 220, 234, 246, 264, 265
GET-passive, the, 30, 55, 180n11
grammaticalization, 30, 60, 73, 75, 127, 128n1
Greek, 25, 55
Guardian, the, 92, 119, 239

/h/-dropping, 28, 155
Hardy, Thomas, 137, 156
Helsinki Corpus, the, 178, 258
Hook, Theodore Edward, 137, 152
Hutchinson, Sara, 174, 205, 265

Icelandic, 13–14
idiolects, 2, 4–5, 38, 43n1, 43–8, 46n4, 49n5, 50–1, 55, 58, 59, 60–2, 63, 67, 68, 69, 71, 78, 80, 83–9, 95, 102n12, 113, 115, 125, 171, 176, 186, 202, 203, 204, 207, 212, 242–3, 246, 252, 255, 256, 257, 259, 261, 262, 263, 268
  and language change, 1, 3, 42, 48–9, 49n5, 52–5, 62, 63, 64, 67, 69–73, 74–5, 76, 83, 85–6, 86n5, 87, 88, 89, 90, 96, 104, 220, 257–62, 263, 266, 268
I-language, 48, 74, 105
imperative, the, 146n12, 146–7, 150, 157, 264
industrialization, 14, 16–17, 62, 118, 221
informalization, 91–3
informational writing, 76, 88, 90, 91, 92, 96, 203, 262
-*ing* forms, 33, 191, 230
innovation, 2, 4, 12, 18, 29, 36, 41, 48, 50–4, 55–8, 58n11, 60–1, 74, 79, 86, 266
  independent, 42, 56, 58–62, 70–1, 73, 126, 258, 259–60, 261, 262
  propagation-dependent, 42, 51, 56–7, 59, 61–2, 63, 64, 70, 71–2, 73, 75, 89, 221, 258, 259–60, 261–2

Keats, John, 176
knock-out factors, 102

language contact, 71–2, 72n17, 73, 75, 259
Latin, 24, 25, 26, 55
levelling, 63–4
lexical innovation, 23–4, 26, 39, 55, 59, 221
linguistic areas, 56

literacy, 4, 8, 19, 20n6,7, 21, 37, 93, 260
Liverpool Mercury, the, 197
Lloyd's Weekly Newspaper, 120, 123, 239
Lockyer, J. Norman, 201, 213, 248
Longman, 190
Longman Dictionary of Contemporary English, the. See Longman
Lyell, Charles, 246

Manchester Guardian, the. See Guardian, the
mobility
  geographical, 14, 16, 62
  social, 14, 16, 17, 20, 62, 65, 66, 69
modal auxiliaries, 30, 31, 100, 134, 146n11, 225, 228n8, 228
multiple negation, 69, 143n8, 154

New Journalism, 120–2, 124
New York Times, the, 223n1
nominalization, 90n7, 95, 111, 114, 115
no-negation, 132, 142–5, 143n8,9, 145n10, 157, 158
non-prevocalic /r/, loss of, 27, 28, 87
North Germanic languages, 72n17, 72, 73
Northern Star, the, 117, 118, 119, 123, 240, 255

OBC, 106, 114, 158, 162
OED, 9n3, 23–6, 42, 190, 211
Old Bailey Corpus, the. See OBC
operator, 127, 128n1, 129n2, 130, 131n4, 133, 134n6, 136–7, 138, 139, 145, 146, 147, 155, 156, 157, 159, 264
operator contraction, 129n2, 129, 131–6, 138, 142, 143n8, 158, 159
optical character recognition, 8, 106, 116
outliers, 85, 86, 108, 152, 179, 198, 246, 248, 255, 262, 267
Oxford English Dictionary, the. See OED

Pall Mall Gazette, the, 120n23, 120
passive voice, 30, 91, 92, 100, 111, 112, 139, 180n11, 222, 224, 229, 234, 236, 244, 245, 250, 253, 263, 266
Penny Post, the, 20, 113, 177, 199, 202
perfect auxiliaries, 30, 55, 68, 224n2, 227
phrasal verbs, 30, 31n17, 90n7, 111–13, 114–15
Poor Man's Guardian, the, 37, 117, 123, 196–7, 219, 239, 240n12, 255, 267
popularization, 8, 20, 36, 37, 93, 95, 116, 124, 260, 266
population growth, 7, 15, 16
precision, 82, 99, 102, 226, 229, 233, 254
prepositional phrases, 6, 90n7, 98, 101, 165, 167n5, 167, 192, 221, 228, 251–2
prescriptivism, 5, 18, 28, 31n17, 31, 32, 34, 37, 68n15, 68, 78, 93, 95, 128, 153n15, 178, 179, 181, 185, 260

Press Association, the, 118, 125
progressive passive, the, 29n15, 29, 36, 51n6, 51, 55, 68
progressive, the, 29n15, 30, 51n6, 51, 54, 90n7, 90, 91, 103, 104, 111–13, 114–15, 115n18, 179, 227, 253
propagation, 6, 12, 39, 42, 45, 51n7, 51–3, 54–7, 58, 60n13, 60–2, 67, 70–5, 76, 79, 86, 87n5, 88, 89, 104, 258–60, 261, 262, 264, 266, 267

railways, 19, 119
reanalysis, 33, 35, 56n8, 56, 57n9
recall, 82–3, 99, 191n4, 191, 229, 231, 254
Received Pronunciation, 28–9, 39, 64, 65
Reform Acts, the, 14–15, 117
relative clauses, 6, 98, 188, 222–3, 224n2, 224–9, 225n3, 226n4, 227n5, 228n8, 230–6, 238, 243–5, 249–54, 255, 263, 266
relative markers, 34, 44, 69, 99n11, 225n3, 225, 229, 231, 232
representativeness. See representativity
representativity, 80–2, 106, 121, 123, 177, 258, 261
Reynolds's Weekly Newspaper, 120, 123
Ricardo, David, 213
Robertson, T.W., 152

S-curves, 22, 86n5, 86, 89
second-person pronouns, 33, 53, 146, 155
semantic equivalence, 90n7, 95n10, 95, 100, 102n12, 143, 144, 250, 252, 263
sentence length, 124
sentence type, 147, 150, 153
Shelley, Mary, 137, 174, 264–5
social networks, 1, 17n4, 18, 36, 54, 62, 83, 88, 259
  and language change, 2, 3, 12–14, 39–41, 261
  strong ties in, 12, 13n2, 13, 16, 40, 73
  weak ties in, 2, 3, 12, 13n2, 13–14, 15, 16, 18, 19, 20, 39–41, 42, 62, 63, 66, 70, 71, 220, 257, 258, 259, 268
socio-economic status, 4, 15, 17, 65, 81, 83–4, 87, 262, 268
  middle classes, the, 13, 17–18, 20, 27, 29, 41, 65–7, 94, 112, 117, 120, 124, 196, 219, 240n12, 260
  working classes, the, 16, 17n4, 18, 20n7, 20, 25, 27, 29, 36n20, 37, 66, 94n9, 94, 112, 117, 119–20, 124, 196, 217, 239–40, 255
specialization, 8, 96, 115, 196, 201, 203, 211, 260, 268
speech communities, 43, 45, 46, 52, 54, 58, 60, 64, 74, 75, 76, 84, 86, 87
speech representation, 111, 114, 173, 185, 244, 247

stability paradox, the, 2, 11, 39, 41, 42, 257, 260, 261
stamp duty, the, 82, 117–18
Standard English, 26, 29, 36n20, 53, 65, 67–8, 69, 73, 99n11, 134, 143n8, 153n14, 153, 156, 174, 176, 178, 179, 225, 259, 260, 265
standardization, 31n17, 46, 50, 64–70, 72n17, 75, 85, 260
subjunctive, the, 31, 69, 100, 154–5
suffrage, 14–15, 117, 200, 204, 212, 213, 239

tagging, 82, 106, 108, 143, 189, 226, 230, 231–2
Taxes on Knowledge, the, 116, 117
text-linguistic analysis, 7, 98, 102–5, 193, 224, 230, 236–50, 254, 256, 263–4
TIME Magazine Corpus, the, 128, 180n11
Times, The, 116, 119, 120, 239, 240
titles, 187, 189, 200n8, 200
to-infinitive clauses, 32, 225
Twopenny Trash, the, 117

unidirectionality, 59, 73, 116n19
uniformitarian principle, the, 2–3, 13n2, 40, 261
urbanization, 15–16, 41, 62–4

variable context, the. *See* envelope of variation, the
variables, 81, 100, 145, 146, 150, 152, 157
dependent, 99, 142
independent, 99, 148, 153
variationist analysis, 6, 96, 98–102, 103, 106, 130, 140, 142, 157, 191–3, 197, 224, 230, 233–6, 249–52, 254, 256, 263–4
verb complementation, 32–3

Walpole, Spencer, 181, 213, 243, 246, 248
Weekly Dispatch, the, 240
Wordsworth, Mary, 174, 265

yod-dropping, 28
Yonge, Charlotte, 137, 154, 155

Milton Keynes UK
Ingram Content Group UK Ltd.
UKHW042259040924
447435UK00030B/114